The Dialogue of

DEVDAS

The Dialogue of

DEVDAS

Bimal Roy's Immortal Classic

Based on the Bengali novella by Sarat Chandra Chattopadhyay

Dialogue: Rajinder Singh Bedi
Screenplay: Nabendu Ghosh
Lyrics: Sahir Ludhianvi

Original dialogue transcribed in Urdu & Roman scripts: Suhail Akhtar
Original dialogue transcribed in Hindi: Kamal Ahmad

Concept, introduction & translation: Nasreen Munni Kabir

OM
Om Books International

hyphen films

Published in 2012 by

OM
Om Books International

hyphen films

Corporate & Editorial Office
A-12, Sector 64, Noida 201 301, Uttar Pradesh, India
Phone: +91 120 477 4100
Email: editorial@ombooks.com
Website: www.ombooksinternational.com

Sales Office
4379/4B, Prakash House, Ansari Road, Darya Ganj, New Delhi 110 002, India
Phone: +91 11 2326 3363, 2326 5303 Fax: +91 11 2327 8091
Email: sales@ombooks.com
Website: www.ombooks.com

Editor: Dipa Chaudhuri
Introduction editors: Shameem Kabir & Dipa Chaudhuri
Design: Vijay Jani

ISBN: 978-93-80069-88-3

Printed in India by Gopsons Papers Ltd., Noida

CONTENTS

Bimal Roy's 1955 film Devdas, *starring Dilip Kumar in the lead role is based on Sarat Chandra Chattopadhyay's 1917 Bengali novella of the same name.*

The Elusive Devdas

Devdas is one of the best-known fictional characters in North India, and the eponymous novel by Sarat Chandra Chattopadhyay remains the only literary work to have been repeatedly adapted for the screen. These adaptations started from Naresh Mitra's 1928 silent film to Anurag Kashyap's *Dev D* in 2009. In a recent interview, when asked why he chose to make yet another version in an era that generally regards Devdas as a romantic weakling, Kashyap, who is regarded to be an edgy, in-vogue filmmaker, astutely said: "I was not making a film on the character of Devdas, but on Devdas the adjective."

"Devdas" is a 1917 Bengali novella that has been translated into several Indian languages, and also into English by Sreejata Guha (Penguin Books, 2002, India). Sarat Chandra's novel continues to have a huge following and reputation. The story, set in Bengal, centres on Devdas, the young son of Narain, a rich village landlord. Devdas has no friends except for Parvati whose love for him blinds her to his unruly behaviour. Unable to control Devdas's increasing defiance, Narain sends his son away to Calcutta where he is raised and educated. Some years later, the adult Devdas, now quiet and unassuming, returns to the village. He is silently overjoyed to see Parvati again and although they have never previously declared their love to one another, they secretly hope to be married. Devdas's father, however, refuses to entertain the thought, asserting that no son of his will marry into a family of lower-caste Brahmins who also happen to be his neighbours.

Late one night, Parvati comes to ask Devdas to marry her, but he does not have the courage to go against his parents' wishes. He hurries away to Calcutta while Parvati's father marries her off to a rich widower with grown children. Through Chunni Babu, a friend who shares his living quarters in Calcutta, Devdas meets Chandramukhi, a prostitute who instantly falls in love with him. But Devdas can never get over his love for Parvati and turns to drink. Years of alcohol abuse lead to failing health, and when Devdas knows his end is near, he fulfills his promise to Parvati that he will come to her before he dies. Before Parvati can rush to his side, Devdas breathes his last outside the imposing gates of her husband's mansion.

Sarat Chandra Chattopadhyay was said to have been reserved and private man. His stories of strong women and the complexities of family relations fascinated generations of readers. As his English translator Sreejata Guha comments: "...the novels of his peak period represented nothing less than a revolution in the way literature was being approached: these were books that were essentially not about ideas, events or even narrative cruxes; they

Publicity booklets of the 1936 version by P.C. Barua, starring K.L. Saigal and Jamuna.

Suchitra Sen and Dilip Kumar in the roles of Parvati and Devdas.

(Facing page) Vyjayanthimala as Chandramukhi. She won Filmfare's Best Supporting Actress Award in 1957 for her performance in the film.

With Pandit Nehru and the fine actress Nutan who starred in Bimal Roy's award-winning film Bandini *(1963).*

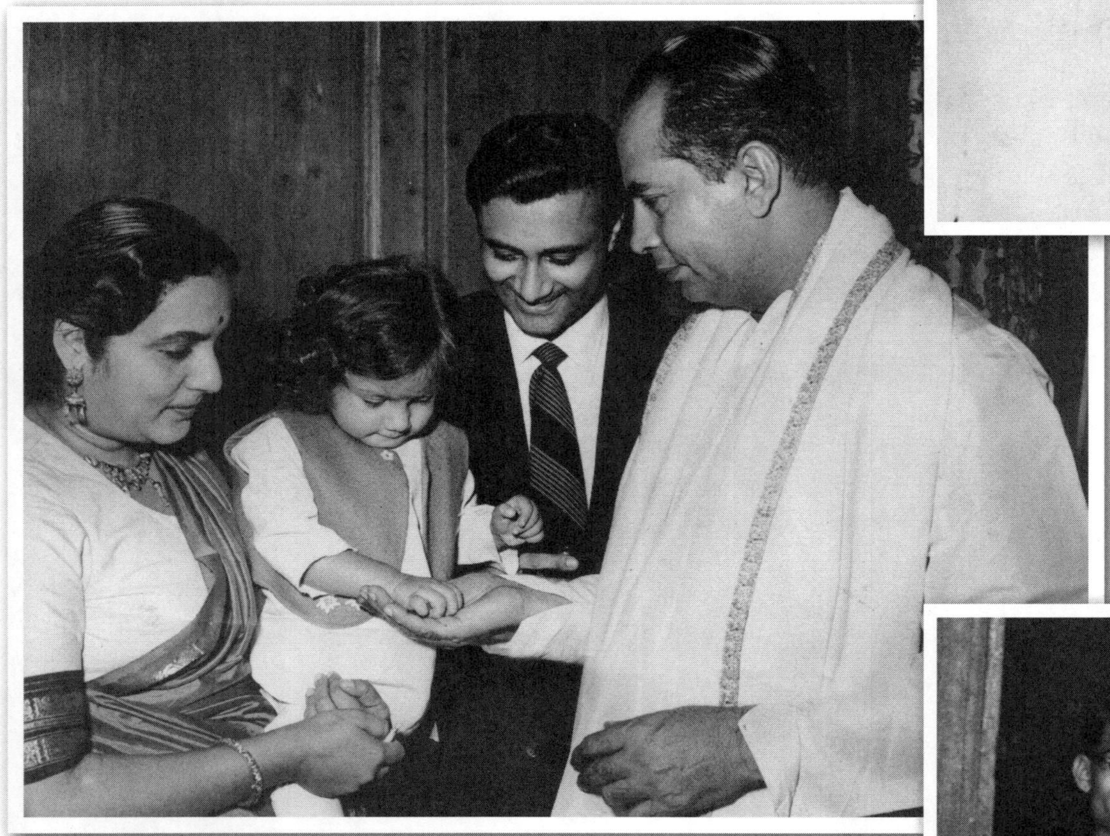

With his wife Manobina Roy, son Joy and Dev Anand at the Karlovy Vary Film Festival, 1956.

Bimal Roy (centre) with friends (unidentified) during his New Theatre days in Calcutta. 1940s.

were about people. Sarat Chandra was at the forefront of the movement of realistic fiction that would find many followers in the course of the twentieth century." (Guha, Introduction to the translation of "Devdas," *ibid.*)

For many years, P.C. Barua's Bengali *Devdas* (with Barua playing the lead), and his Hindi version with K.L. Saigal, Indian film's first real star, were hailed as the superior screen adaptations. Barua's films (the Hindi version was famously photographed by Bimal Roy when at New Theatres) became the benchmark against which the early remakes of *Devdas* were compared. But the leisurely pace and acting style of the 1930 films hold little interest for spectators today. Love for older films is fading fast and only some 1950s classics, made by a handful of acknowledged masters, hold any sway. Among the past directors whose work remains vivid in the minds of audiences is Bimal Roy, and it is his 1955 *Devdas* with its subtle screenplay and dialogue, fluid direction and sublime cast that is widely considered the most important film version of the Bengali novella.

Bimal Roy began his career as a cinematographer at New Theatres in Calcutta, but soon turned to direction. Audiences fell in love with his first film *Udayer Pathey* (1944), thanks to its fresh treatment and choice of subject. The great Ritwik Ghatak described the impact of *Udayer Pathey* and *Hamrahi* (the Hindi remake): "People for the first time saw in them their everyday life — this revolutionised the concept of film as a social document of contemporary reality." (Ghatak, *Filmfare*, 4 March, 1966.) It is interesting to note how closely Ghatak's comments on Bimal Roy's work mirrors the description of Sarat Chandra's novels.

In the early 1950s, following the decline of New Theatres, Bimal Roy moved from Calcutta to Bombay with his family and close colleagues. By 1952, he started "BR Productions," and produced the heartrending *Do Bigha Zameen* (1953).

Many prominent filmmakers of the time, previously employed by the great studios, knew that creative freedom was guaranteed only when they could finance their own films. Running a production company was therefore of primary importance, allowing many directors, film writers and lyricists to make films driven by their political and social beliefs rather than concerns for box-office success. This was a key factor as to why the fifties had so many socially relevant films.

With the acclaim that he rightfully deserved following the release of *Do Bigha Zameen*, Bimal Roy, who was about 44 years old at the time, embarked on retelling Sarat Chandra's "Devdas," the second film that he would produce under his banner.

To play Parvati, Bimal Roy chose Suchitra Sen, the highly adept and stunningly beautiful Bengali actress. Her impressive performance brings a dignified elegance and depth to the character. When it was decided that the prostitute Chandramukhi would also be a dancer, Bimal Roy cast Vyjayanthimala whose substantial acting abilities were equalled by her tremendous dancing skill. Her performance is mature and thoughtful and it is

Bengali cinema's most popular and wonderful actress Suchitra Sen in her first Hindi film Devdas.

Dilip Kumar won Filmfare's Best Actor Award in 1957 for his extraordinary performance as Devdas.

astonishing to think that Vyjayanthimala had only one film to her credit *(Nagin)* when she played Chandramukhi.

Rinki Bhattacharya recalls that her father had considered Guru Dutt for the role of Devdas. Bimal Roy's second daughter, Yashodhara remembered her father would privately call Guru Dutt "Devdas," as he believed Guru Dutt had a similar temperament to Sarat Chandra's hero. It is unknown whether Bimal Roy ever offered Guru Dutt the part, but his choice finally fell on Dilip Kumar. This was the first film they made together, and it is evident that no other actor in Indian cinema could have been the better choice.

To the psychological layering the role demanded, Dilip Kumar brings gravitas to the performance through his subtle expressions, muted voice and gentle demeanour. He is simply brilliant in the film and it is now impossible to distinguish between Dilip Kumar the person and Dilip Kumar as Devdas.

In a 1988 interview, this gifted actor spoke of his understanding of the role: "Devdas was all bound in tradition. He does not have the courage to rebel. He loves Parvati immensely and he punishes her and punishes himself. But he couldn't assert himself and do what would be considered quite simple by prevailing standards. But that was the time when no one would consider going against their elders. When it came to performance, the question in *Devdas* was quite often of trying not to do, rather than doing." (Kumar, interview by NMK, for the television series, *Movie Mahal*, Channel 4 TV, UK, 1988.)

Bimal Roy's impeccable casting also extended to his choice of actors who played the secondary characters, and these included the sparkling Motilal (Chunni Babu), Ram Kumar (young Devdas), Baby Naaz (young Paro), Kanhaiyalal (the exasperated teacher), Kammo (Parvati's friend and confidante Manorama) and Murad (Devdas's unrelenting father). Special mention must be made of the underrated Nazir Hussain, who gives a remarkable performance as Devdas's personal attendant, Dharamdas. Utterly loyal to his young master, Dharamdas (whose name means "devoted to duty") is the loving father that Devdas never had.

In addition to Bimal Roy's knack for casting, he put together a formidably creative team consisting of Kamal Bose (photography), S.D. Burman (music), Sahir Ludhianvi (lyrics) and Hrishikesh Mukherjee (editing). Two major literary figures, Nabendu Ghosh and Rajinder Singh Bedi took on the task of adapting the screenplay and writing dialogue.

Expertly balanced, the screenplay closely follows Sarat Chandra's novella, but does not mechanically reproduce it scene by scene. The casting of older actors made a fundamental change from the original work — Devdas and Parvati are teenagers in Sarat Chandra's story, and their young age is critical to the understanding of their intense love — much in the way that youth is also central to the passion of Romeo and Juliet.

Other changes point to the need of making the story work beyond Bengal, for an all-India audience. Terms of address that would be acceptable in the cultural context of Bengal (in the book, Parvati calls Devdas "Dev-da," or elder brother, and Devdas calls Chandramukhi "bou," or wife) were dropped in the film, as these would have caused confusion among Hindi-speaking viewers.

The film's toning down of young Devdas's violent and aggressive behaviour towards Parvati is another departure from the book. But it is the meeting of Parvati and Chandramukhi that has been widely noticed. They never meet in Sarat Chandra's world, but in Bimal Roy's *Devdas*, they cross one another on the road to Talsonapur. The song "Manzil ki chaah mein," sung beautifully by Mohammed Rafi, underscores this chance encounter and though the two women do not speak, they exchange a long and meaningful look *(see screenshots and dialogue pp.184-6)*. The song works effectively as voice-over, describing what travellers seek and find on the road of life. Bimal Roy has given Indian cinema one of its most sublime scenes in these moments.

It is astonishing to have learned that the film was never shot on location in Bengal and instead was photographed in Mohan Studios in Andheri and in nearby Bombay suburbs, which then had sprawling expanses of undeveloped land. Yet nothing seems out of place thanks to Bimal Roy's great talent in visual detailing. His *Devdas* is replete with evocative images and subtle moods. The director's love of nature is ever-present — the changing seasons, the tall trees, the lotus blossoming on the pond, the sound of birdsong and the mango grove, all create a place of magic for young Devdas and Parvati. Inanimate objects also become symbols — because Narain is always seen smoking a hookah, when he passes away, his memory is evoked through the object now standing unlit in a corner of the verandah where Devdas and his brother Dwijodas sit in mourning.

Volumes have been written on various aspects of the *Devdas* phenomenon. The added interest in the *Devdas* films remade over the years is partly because they point to changing attitudes towards parental pressure, romantic love, social and caste differences and personal ambition. The idea of this publication, however, aimed at current and future lovers of cinema and language, is to preserve in book form a marvellous screenplay and superb dialogue.

The true power of the film's text comes from Bimal Roy's and his writers' love of the understatement. They have at all times avoided artificial situations and heavy-handed drama. Poignant scenes that could so easily have turned to sentiment and syrup are measured and discreet. In the moment when Parvati, full of anticipation, meets the adult Devdas for the first time — this scene coincides with the entrance of Dilip Kumar, the star-hero, which is always a terrifically important moment in Hindi films and given to exaggerated theatrics — Bedi provides simple dialogue that counters the emotionally charged situation. All that Devdas says

On set with the sophisticated and excellent Motilal who won Filmfare's Best Supporting Actor Award in 1957 for his role as Chunni Babu.

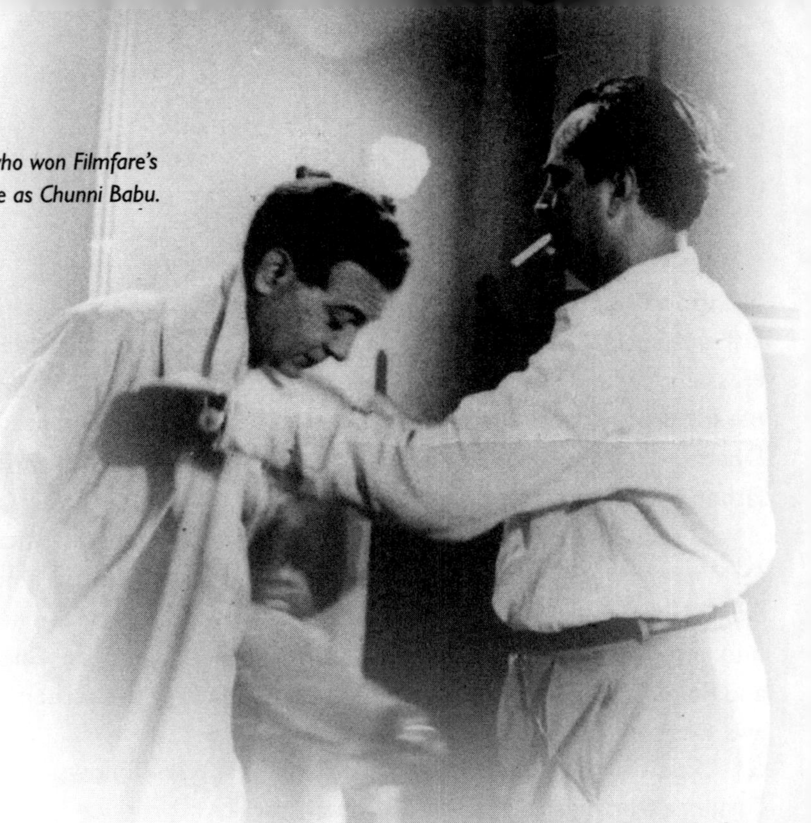

to Parvati is: "Tum, kya ho raha hai? Kitni badi ho gayi ho tum" (It's you? What's going on? How you've grown. *[p. 54]*), and saying a few more words of little significance, Devas leaves as abruptly as he came.

Dilip Kumar's refined Urdu diction and great skill in dialogue delivery have helped enormously in rendering the natural beauty of Rajinder Singh Bedi's words. Motilal who plays the mysterious Chunni Babu is also brilliant when it comes to delivering dialogue. Instead of falling into the trap of a long back story explaining that Chunni Babu is also suffering from having lost the love of his life, one sentence, spoken with the subtle irony that Motilal excelled at, says it all: "Oho! Tabb toh Devdas bhi humaara hi bhai hai" (I see! So Devdas and I are one of a kind. *[p. 130]*).

Besides having a prolific screenwriting career, including writing nine screenplays for Bimal Roy, in 1989, Nabendu Ghosh also directed *Trishagni*, an award-winning film. This celebrated author of Bengali literature passed away in 2007, at the age of 91. Writer of twenty novels and fourteen collections of short stories, his daughter, the journalist Ratnottama Sengupta, quotes A.K. Bandyopadhyay describing her father's literary work as having "…a deep empathy for human emotions, mysterious layers of meanings that add to the depth of the spoken word, subtle symbolism, descriptions of unbearable life, at the same time limitless flight in the open sky of imagination." (Sengupta, "Nabendu Ghosh," a monograph published on Ghosh's 90th birthday, March 2007.)

Working alongside Ghosh, the popular progressive Urdu writer Rajinder Singh Bedi had a distinguished literary career that spanned fifty years. Author of seventy short stories and many novels, he won the Sahitya Akademi Award in 1965 for his most famous work, "Ek Chadar Maili Si." In addition, Bedi also briefly turned to film direction in the 1970s.

Suchitra Sen retired from films in 1978. She will always be remembered for her moving and radiant performance as Parvati.

Credited for using *khari boli* (the common man's prose) over the dominant poetic style of Urdu literature of the time, Bedi, like many 1950s' writers and poets, was drawn to the cinema to earn a living. His first film, *Badi Bahen* (1949), was directed by D.D. Kashyap, and by the time he came to work on *Devdas*, Bedi had written dialogue for a number of well-loved films, including Sohrab Modi's 1954 *Mirza Ghalib.*

Interviewed in March 1982 by the American scholar Leslie Flemming, Bedi commented he had indeed studied Sarat Chandra's book and added that some of his dialogue lines were direct translations of the novel. Bedi also spoke of his preference for the more realistic Russian cinema over Hollywood. His wonderful choice of words shows his leanings towards a natural and realistic language over the melodramatic tone prevalent in much of Indian popular cinema of the time. Hindi cinema lost a great talent when this gifted Urdu writer died in 1984 at the age of 69.

The collaboration between Bimal Roy, Nabendu Ghosh and Rajinder Singh Bedi shows their vision of the story is so perfectly in line with the spirit of the book. The screenplay's beauty also lies in how successfully it contrasts the daring and innocence of childhood with the disappointment and disenchantment of adult life.

Devdas's story unfolds in a series of meetings and partings, meandering journeys and recurring events whose significance changes with passing time. Childhood scenes are repeated in adulthood, stressing the cyclic character of life. The film is full of wonderful examples of the revisiting of scenes.

Hearing the sound of a mango bounce off the tin roof, young Parvati (Baby Naaz) runs down the stairs onto the path outside her house knowing that Devdas (Ram Kumar) will be waiting there for her *(p. 28)*. The same situation returns when Parvati and Devdas are adults *(p. 58)*. The sound of the fruit hits the tin roof, Parvati once again runs down the stairs onto the path outside her house to see Devdas waiting there. The transition between

A celebrated and prolific Bengali author, Nabendu Ghosh also wrote dozens of screenplays for Hindi cinema. Calcutta, 1950s.

Photographed with Rajinder Singh Bedi in the 1950s. The highly prominent Urdu writer, Bedi won Filmfare's Best Dialogue Award for Madhumati *in 1959.*

Publicity still. Nazir Hussain, Ram Kumar and Baby Naaz are brilliantly cast as Dharamdas, young Devdas and Paro.

childhood and adulthood is thus illustrated, but the scene also suggests the change in their relationship — from friendship to romantic love.

Not only do identical situations return, but also different characters speak the same lines in different contexts. When Devdas scars Parvati's forehead in anger, she asks him (now a famous film quote): "Ye tumne kya kiya, Devdas?" (What have you done, Devdas? *[p. 98]*). This question comes from an earlier moment in which Devdas's conscience admonishes him for having written to Parvati to falsely say that it had never crossed his mind that he had ever loved her *(p. 84)*.

At the end of the story when Devdas lies in the throes of death outside the gates of Parvati's mansion, she stirs from her sleep believing she has heard Devdas whisper: "Paro, main aa gaya hoon" (Paro, I have come. *[p. 242]*). This line too comes from a critical scene in which Devdas rushes to the village and meets Parvati at the edge of the pond in the hope she will forgive him for having denied his love for her. *[p. 92]*). These same words become Devdas's dying utterances. Perhaps their re-use suggests the pond edge encounter was a crucial turning point. If Devdas had managed to persuade Parvati to forgive him and she had agreed, their lives would have changed forever. Instead false vanity comes in the way, the moment passes and they part *(pp. 92-98)*.

Despite the fact that Devdas and Parvati are drawn further and further apart, Bimal Roy shows them increasingly linked in spirit. He creates another gloriously evocative scene through a series of dissolves connecting Devdas sitting forlornly by the pond and Parvati, in Manekpur, reading her friend Manorama's letter that speaks of the sadness engulfing Devdas *(p. 178)*. This time it is Devdas's song "Mitwa," sung sublimely by Talat Mahmood that joins them despite the physical distance separating them. The lyrics of Sahir's "Mitwa" expresses Devdas's anguish, and in the next scene, Parvati, intuitively knowing of his despair, rushes back to Talsonapur to see him, but Devdas has fled again to Calcutta.

Dilip Kumar once commented about the risk of having Devdas sing at all, considering that the songs in Bimal Roy's film would invariably have been compared to the songs made famous by K.L. Saigal when he played the role in 1936. To avoid comparisons, "Mitwa" is the only song that Devdas sings, and this too has the mood of a lament. It would have been completely acceptable to have Parvati sing in the film, given that unhappy heroines, especially in the 1950s, nearly always sang melancholic songs — but Bimal Roy avoids the predictable and Parvati, as an adult, does not sing. Instead, wandering Vaishnava singers voice her feelings, thereby maintaining the sense of realism that so strongly characterises Bimal Roy's work.

Further stressing the symbiosis between Devdas and Parvati, Bimal Roy crosscuts scenes that take place at the same time, but have dramatically different outcomes for both lovers. As Parvati is made to sit in her bridal palanquin in Talsonapur, Devdas alights from a horse carriage to enter a Calcutta brothel where he meets Chandramukhi *(p. 108)*. Devdas later makes reference to the irony when he says: "Vo shaadi ke raaste pe chal di aur main barbaadi ke raaste pe" (She took the road to a married life and I, the road to my doom. *[p. 142]*).

Bimal Roy uses the crosscutting technique once again when, alone one night in a train compartment, the ailing Devdas coughs blood. At the same moment, Parvati slips and falls in her home in Manekpur. The scar that Devdas gave her on their fateful meeting at the pond edge when they had a last chance of being together, starts to bleed.

The screenplay provides many reasons why Devdas behaves the way he does and these point to his childhood. A rebellious boy, Devdas disobeys his family and in response to his defiance, his father, Narain, scolds and beats him. When Narain believes he can no longer control his son whom he describes as having crossed all limits *(p. 36)*, he sends the boy away to Calcutta. Even his doting mother can do nothing to stop Devdas's departure.

Like the elusive nightingale he tries to catch for Parvati, Devdas once departed from home can never settle again, nor find inner peace. The extraordinary poet-lyricist Sahir Ludhianvi expresses this idea in the song line: "Chhodi jo ek daali ik baar wahaan kab laut ke aana hai" (Never alighting on the same branch again when you fly away. *[pp. 30-6]*). The end of the song corresponds to the end of Devdas's idyllic childhood. The next scene has his father swiftly dispatching him to the city.

Parvati's grief at Devdas's departure is given fatalistic meaning, as though this were her lot. Her sorrow is expressed through the Vaishnavas's song and her emotions are compared to those of Radha who pines for the absent Krishna *(pp. 42-4)*. But Devdas's sudden removal from home, and more importantly, his separation from Parvati is a kind of exile for him. It is essentially punishment for having a strong mind and independent character.

In the Dilip Kumar interview earlier referred to, he speaks of Devdas as "punishing himself and punishing Parvati," and perhaps the fear of punishment explains the way Devdas develops from boy to man.

When we see Devdas again, years later, he is entirely changed, not only in age, but also in temperament. Unlike the defiant boy who left the village, the older Devdas is fearful and passive. This complete change in character is unexplained in the narrative. We are left to infer that because of his father's punishing behaviour, Devdas has internalised the fear of ostracism that his father instills in him. In the context of the period, a so-called dishonourable marriage could lead to disastrous social consequences, and Devdas is not radical enough to defy such conventions. In the scenes in which he tries to persuade his brother and father to consent to his marriage to Parvati, all we hear is their angry refusal *(p. 74)*. This is an example of the writers' excellent detailing of Devdas's psychology — because he has no dialogue of protest in these scenes, it supports the fact that Devdas has no voice when confronting authority.

What the first exile from home does is to set a pattern for Devdas, who later finds refuge in flight. His alcohol addiction is another symptom of his desire to escape reality, and helps him to cloak his inability to fight for his share of happiness. His inebriated state also allows him to speak his mind. Many famous lines of the film have come from his conversations with Chandramukhi, including "Kaun kam-bakht hai jo bardaasht karne ke liye peeta hai? Main toh peeta hoon ki bas saans le sakoon" (What unlucky fool drinks to tolerate? I drink so that I may breathe. *[p. 140]*).

After his father Narain has died, Devdas, no longer fearing punishment, playfully and for the only time, asks Parvati to run away with him *(p. 160)*. His playfulness is contrasted with the courage with which, earlier in the story, Parvati comes to him in the middle of the night, wanting him to marry her. A step considered audacious for a woman of the time — an unmarried girl entering the bedroom of a man so late at night would have been an inadmissible act and subject to slander and shame. Bimal Roy recognised that audiences in the 1950s would not accept Parvati's boldness, so in a preceding scene, unnoticed by many who have written on this crucial moment, we see Parvati in broad daylight attempting to call out to Devdas who is at some distance away near the pond *(p. 60)*. When an inquisitive villager asks Parvati why she is there, she becomes nervous and hurriedly makes her way

Bimal Roy during a visit to Moscow in 1954.

home. This does not take away from the fact that Parvati shows her strength of character in coming to Devdas on that fateful night — in fact she is always shown as stronger and more determined than Devdas.

Despite the passing years, Devdas's love for Parvati, so closely tied to his idyllic childhood, to a time that he can never retrieve, does not weaken. The feelings he later develops for Chandramukhi are of a more mature nature. Surprisingly, Devdas even tells Chandramukhhi that he loves her *(p. 206)*. He speaks of how close Parvati and Chandramukhi are in nature *(p. 210)* and soon they merge as one person in his mind.

Although their lives could not be more different, the two women revere Devdas almost as a god and gradually they begin to follow a similar spiritual path — removing themselves from the material world, they dress plainly and live austere lives. In many scenes, they even talk in a similar way. Parvati and Chandramukhi on different occasions ask Devdas to promise he will stop drinking. Though Devdas does not promise to give up alcohol, he assures Parvati that he will come to her before he dies *(p. 164)*, and consoles Chandramukhi by saying that if there is life after death he will not stay apart from her *(p. 216)*.

Finding no purpose in life, Devdas restlessly journeys from village to city, city to village, from Parvati to Chandramukhi. The journey becomes life's purpose, and finally, when he falls critically ill, he embarks on a long aimless train journey, telling Dharamdas that he seeks no destination and only desires to run away from himself *(p. 220)*.

When he realises he hasn't long to live, he decides to go to Parvati. The speeding train that he has travelled on for countless days and nights is sharply contrasted by the agonisingly slow bullock cart that takes him on his final journey to Parvati and to his death. He asks the cart driver poignantly: "Arey bhai, ye raasta kya kabhi khatm nahin hoga?" (Brother, will this road never end? *[p. 240]*).

Given Indian cinema's fondness for remakes, it is to be expected that *Devdas* will be made again in the years to come. Themes in *Devdas* have already been reworked into a number of films. The Devdas character has become synonymous with the idea of a flawed tragic hero — a troubled man fraught with repressed desires and complexities who perishes for the sake of his love. Devdas, Parvati and Chandramukhi are now in fact archetypes of Indian cinema and have been cloned in many subsequent films.

Bimal Roy's *Devdas* has also directly influenced Guru Dutt, to the extent that in *Pyaasa* (1957), he has used a line spoken by Parvati on the night she believes she hears knocking at her door and Devdas is lying outside her gates.In a similar scene, just before *Pyaasa*'s hero, Vijay, comes to Gulaab to ask her to come away with him, she wakes from her sleep, somehow sensing that Vijay is there. Gulaab's question is the same as Parvati's: "Kisi ne mujhe pukaara" (Someone has called me. *[p. 244]*).

In another *Devdas* scene in which we see Parvati overwhelmed with happiness *(p.188)* on learning that Devdas is back in the village, S.D. Burman's background music is none other than the tune of "Aaj sajan mohe ang lagaa lo," the song that Burman later developed for *Pyaasa*.

Nine years after the release of *Devdas*, Bimal Roy died of lung cancer on 8 January, 1966. He spent his life serving cinema and elevating the standard of Indian films. His *Devdas* is an example of his great understanding and love of filmmaking. It is a rare film that has everything just right — the visual experience, the performance, the music, the photography, an atmosphere seeped in quiet unease, and above all, a masterful screenplay and memorable dialogue with depth and meaning.

Reading Rajinder Singh Bedi's dialogue is a pleasure in itself and allows us to enter the interiority of its characters and discover the mind of Devdas. A deeper familiarity with the text will undoubtedly provide a fresh understanding of a first-rate film, and in addition give insight into the most melancholic character of Indian cinema.

Though loved by two exceptional women, Devdas cannot belong to anyone and perhaps that is the tragedy that makes him elusive and self-destructive. In one of his many train journeys *(p. 230)*, when Dharamdas tries desperately to persuade him to return home to those who love him, Devdas asks:

Kaun hai mera is duniya mein?
Who do I have in this world to call my own?

Dharamdas:
Kya keh rahe ho, Deva? Tumhaara sab koi hai.
What are you saying, Deva? You have so many.

Devdas:
Haan. Mera sab koi hai. Main hi kisi ka nahin.
Yes. I have many. But I belong to no one.

I am indebted to Bimal Roy's family for all the help and support that they have extended in making this book possible. Special thanks to Suhail Akhtar, Kamal Ahmad, Dipa Chaudhuri, my sister Shameem Kabir and designer Vijay Jani for their meticulous efforts in the book's production. For their encouragement and assistance, many thanks to Dilp Kumar, Peter Chappell, John Minchinton, Ramachandra Guha, Iqbal and Saeeda Khan, Ajay Mago, Ila Bedi, Leslie Flemming, Frances Pritchett, Ratnottama Sengupta, Ratna Menon, Anju Rodrigues, Nuna Sandy and Behroze Gandhy.

This book is dedicated to the memory of Manobina Roy.

Nasreen Munni Kabir
London, February 2012

The Dialogue of

DEVDAS

Bimal Roy's Immortal Classic

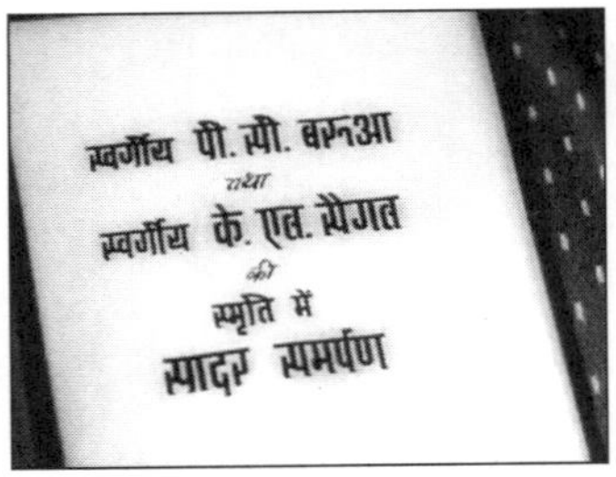

Fade in. Bimal Roy's insignia, "Bimal Roy Productions," is superimposed on a shot of the Rajabai Clock Tower located in the Fort campus of the University of Bombay. Fade out.

Fade in. A shot of the Devdas *Hindi book cover with the author's name, Saratchandra Chatterji (also known as Chattopadhyay), and a drawing of the central character Devdas, modelled on Dilip Kumar. The cast and crew titles appear in Hindi on the turning book pages. The music underscoring the credits is a medley of folk tunes and marriage songs. Dramatic musical phrases are followed by instrumental versions of the songs featured in the film. The last credit reads: "Dedicated to the memory of P.C. Barua and K.L. Saigal."*

Over a shot of the first page of the book, a narrator reads the first lines of the novel.

Narrator *(voice-over):*
One day, on a hot and sultry afternoon in April…

Ek din, Vaisaakh ki dopaher mein dhoop ka antt na tha aur garmi ki bhi hadd nahin thi…

Dissolve from the book page to a crane shot of a tree. The camera moves from the treetop to the ground, revealing a small village school with a thatched roof in the background.

Bholu *(off-screen):*
Six ones are six. Six twos are twelve.

Ek chhakke chhakka. Do chhakke baarah.

Children *(in unison off-screen):*
Six ones are six. Six twos are twelve.

Ek chhakke chhakka. Do chhakke baarah.

Bholu *(off-screen):*
Six ones are six. Six twos are twelve.

Ek chhakke chhakka. Do chhakke baarah.

दृश्य आरम्भ होता है। मुंबई विश्व-विद्यालय के फ़ोर्ट कैम्पस में लगे राजाबाई घंटाघर के एक शॉट पर "बिमल राय प्रोडक्शनस" सुपर इम्पोज़ होता है। फ़ेड आउट।

फ़ेड इन। देवदास हिन्दी उपन्यास के आवरण पृष्ठ का एक शॉट जिस पर उसके लेखक का नाम, शरत चंद्र चटर्जी और देवदास पात्र का हस्तचित्र जो दिलीप कुमार पर आधारित है, दर्शाया गया है। पुस्तक के पलटते हुए पन्नों पर कलाकारों एवं कर्मीदल के नाम हिन्दी में प्रकट होते हैं। पृष्ठभूमि में लोकधुन और विवाह गीत का संगीत चल रहा है। साथ में चित्रपट के गीतों का वाद्य संगीत भी बज रहा है। यह फ़िल्म पी.सी. बरुआ और के.एल. सैगल की याद में समर्पित की गई है।

पुस्तक का पहला पन्ना सामने आता है। कथा वाचक की आवाज़ सुनाई देती है।

कथा वाचक *(वॉइस-ओवर):*
एक दिन, वैशाख की दोपहर में धूप का अंत न था और गरमी की भी हद नहीं थी।

पुस्तक के पन्ने से डिज़ॉल्व करते हुए एक पेड़ का क्रेन शॉट। कैमरा ऊपर से नीचे आता है और हम पृष्ठभूमि में गाँव की पाठशाला देखते हैं।

भोलू *(ऑफ़-स्क्रीन):*
एक छक्के छक्का। दो छक्के बारह।

बच्चे *(ऑफ़-स्क्रीन, सामूहिक):*
एक छक्के छक्का। दो छक्के बारह।

भोलू *(ऑफ़-स्क्रीन):*
एक छक्के छक्का। दो छक्के बारह।

فیڈ اِن۔ ممبئی یونیورسٹی کے فورٹ کیمپس میں استادہ راجابائی کلاک ٹاور کے شاٹ پر 'بمل رائے پروڈکشنز' کے الفاظ نظر آتے ہیں۔ فیڈ آؤٹ۔

فیڈ اِن۔ 'دیوداس' ناول کے سرورق پر اُس کے مصنف، شرتچند راچٹرجی کا نام اور دیوداس کا ایک تصویری خاکہ نظر آتا ہے جو دلیپ کمار ہے۔ کتاب کے پلٹتے ہوئے اوراق پر فلم کے کرداروں اور دیگر متعلقین کے نام ہندی میں نظر آتے ہیں۔ اِس دوران گونجنے والی موسیقی میں شادی بیاہ اور دیہاتی انداز پایا جاتا ہے۔ فلم میں استعمال کئے گئے گیتوں کے مختلف موسیقی کے حصوں کا استعمال بھی کیا گیا ہے۔ یہ فلم پی سی بروا اور کے ایل سیگل کی یاد میں معنون کی گئی ہے۔

کتاب کا پہلا ورق سامنے آتا ہے۔ داستان گو کی آواز سنائی دیتی ہے۔

وائس اوور:
ایک دن، ویساکھ کی دوپہر میں دھوپ کا انت نہ تھا اور گرمی کی بھی حد نہیں تھی۔

کتاب کے ورق سے ڈزالو کرتے ہوئے ایک درخت کا کرین شاٹ۔ کیمرہ اوپر سے نیچے آتا ہے اور پس منظر میں اسکول دکھائی دیتا ہے۔

بھولو (آف اسکرین):
ایک چھکے چھکّا۔ دو چھکے بارہ۔

بچے (ایک ساتھ، آف اسکرین):
ایک چھکے چھکّا۔ دو چھکے بارہ۔

بھولو (آف اسکرین):
ایک چھکے چھکّا۔ دو چھکے بارہ۔

Dissolve to a classroom full of young girls and boys. Young Devdas who looks about fifteen is standing next to Parvati, affectionately called "Paro" by all. She is wearing a saree and appears to be about thirteen years old.

Children *(in unison):*
Six ones are six. Six twos are twelve.

Ek chhakke chhakka. Do chhakke baarah.

Bholu *(actor Mohan Choti):*
Six threes are eighteen. Six fours are twenty-four.

Teen chhakke atharah. Chaar chhakke chaubees.

Children *(in unison):*
Six threes are eighteen. Six fours are twenty-four.

Teen chhakke atharah. Chaar chhakke chaubees.

Bholu *(on a shot of the teacher who is nodding off):*
Six three are eighteen. Six fours are twenty-four.

Teen chhakke atharah. Chaar chhakke chaubees.

Children *(in unison):*
Six threes are eighteen. Six fours are twenty-four.

Teen chhakke atharah. Chaar chhakke chaubees.

Young Devdas *(actor Ram Kumar):*
Paro, Ram babu's garden is full of mangoes.

Paro, Ramu babu ke baagh mein aam hain.

Young Parvati *(actress Baby Naaz):*
That's why I've brought salt.

Isi liye namak laayi thi.

Young Devdas *(loudly):*
Good for you!

Shaabaash!

Devdas's cry wakes the teacher. The other children continue learning the times table.

Children *(in unison):*
Six threes are eighteen. Six fours are twenty-four.

Teen chhakke atharah. Chaar chhakke chaubees.

Bholu:
Six fives are thirty. Six sixes are thirty-six.

Paanch chhakke tees. Chhakkam chhakka chhattees.

दृश्य एक कक्षा में डिज़ॉल्व होता है जो लड़कों और लड़कियों से भरा है। बाल देवदास, आयु लगभग पंद्रह वर्ष, पार्वती के निकट खड़ा है। लगभग तेरह वर्षीय पार्वती को ''पारो'' भी बुलाते हैं। उसने साड़ी पहन रखी है।

बच्चे *(सामूहिक):*
एक छक्के छक्का। दो छक्के बारह।

भोलू *(अभिनेता मोहन चोटी):*
तीन छक्के अठारह। चार छक्के चौबीस।

बच्चे *(सामूहिक):*
तीन छक्के अठारह। चार छक्के चौबीस।

भोलू *(ऊँघते हुए अध्यापक का एक शॉट):*
तीन छक्के अठारह। चार छक्के चौबीस।

बच्चे *(सामूहिक):*
तीन छक्के अठारह। चार छक्के चौबीस।

बाल देवदास *(अभिनेता राम कुमार):*
पारो, राम बाबू के बाग़ में आम हैं।

बालिका पार्वती *(अभिनेत्री बेबी नाज़):*
इसीलिए नमक लाई थी।

बाल देवदास *(ज़ोर से):*
शाबाश!

देवदास की आवाज़ से अध्यापक की आँख खुल जाती है। बच्चे पहाड़ा याद करते रहते हैं।

बच्चे *(सामूहिक):*
तीन छक्के अठारह। चार छक्के चौबीस।

भोलू:
पाँच छक्के तीस। छक्कम छक्का छत्तीस।

ڈزالو۔لڑکے اورلڑکیوں سے بھری ہوئی کلاس کا منظر۔پندرا سال کی عمر کے آس پاس دیوداس، پاروتی کے برابر کھڑا ہوا ہے جسے پارو کہتے ہیں۔تقریباً تیرا سالہ پاروتی نے بنگالی طرز کی ساڑی باندھ رکھی ہے۔

بچے (ایک ساتھ):
ایک چھکے چھکّا۔دو چھکے بارہ۔

بھولو (اداکار، موہن چوٹی):
تین چھکے اٹھارا۔چار چھکے چوبیس۔

بچے (ایک ساتھ):
تین چھکے اٹھارا۔چار چھکے چوبیس۔

بھولو (اونگھتے ہوئے اُستاد کے شاٹ پر):
تین چھکے اٹھارا۔چار چھکے چوبیس۔

بچے (ایک ساتھ):
تین چھکے اٹھارا۔چار چھکے چوبیس۔

کمسن دیوداس (اداکار، رام کمار):
پارو، رام بابو کے باغ میں آم ہیں۔

کمسن پاروتی (اداکارہ، بے بی ناز):
اِسی لیے نمک لائی تھی۔

کمسن دیوداس (بلند آواز میں):
شاباش!

دیوداس کی آواز سے اونگھتا ہوا ٹیچر جاگ جاتا ہے۔بچے پہاڑہ پڑھنے میں مشغول رہتے ہیں۔

بچے (ایک ساتھ):
تین چھکے اٹھارا۔چار چھکے چوبیس۔

بھولو:
پانچ چھکے تیس۔چھکم چھکّا چھتیس۔

Children *(in unison):*
Six fives are thirty. Six sixes are thirty-six.

Paanch chhakke tees. Chhakkam chhakka chhattees.

Bholu:
Six fives are thirty. Six sixes are thirty-six.

Paanch chhakke tees. Chhakkam chhakka chhattees.

Children *(in unison):*
Six fives are thirty. Six sixes are thirty-six.

Paanch chhakke tees. Chhakkam chhakka chhattees.

The school bell rings and the children charge out of the classroom.

Bholu:
Teacher, Deva is running away.

Panditji, Deva bhaaga.

The teacher stops Devdas and Parvati as they try to leave.

Teacher *(actor Kanhaiyalal):*
Devdas, where do you think you're going? You rascal, come here. There's no sign of you once you disappear. You may be the landlord's son, but that's at home.
(changing his tone and softening)
Your father has said that all the children could go, but not you. Bholu!

Ae Devdas, kahaan ja raha hai? O re badmaash, chal idhar. Ek baar jaata hai toh phir aane ka naam hi nahin leta. Zamindar ka beta hoga toh ghar mein.

Zamindar saaheb ka hi hukm hai ki sab ko chhutti hogi, tujhe nahin. Bholu!

Bholu:
Yes?

Ji?

Teacher:
Call yourself a class monitor, do you?

Tu kya khaak-dhool ka monitor hai?

Bholu:
Yes.

Ji.

Teacher:
Bholu, listen very carefully. He runs and you'll pay for it. Do you understand?

Kaan khol kar sunn le, bhaagega ye, pitega tu. Samjha?

Bholu:
Yes.

Ji.

बच्चे *(सामूहिक):*
पाँच छक्के तीस। छक्कम छक्का छत्तीस।

भोलू:
पाँच छक्के तीस। छक्कम छक्का छत्तीस।

बच्चे *(सामूहिक):*
पाँच छक्के तीस। छक्कम छक्का छत्तीस।

पाठशाला की घंटी बजते ही बच्चे तुरंत कक्षा के बाहर भागते हैं।

भोलू:
पंडितजी, देवा भागा।

बाहर जाते हुए देवदास और पार्वती को अध्यापक रोकता है।

पंडितजी *(अभिनेता कन्हैयालाल):*
ए देवदास, कहाँ जा रहा है? ओ रे बदमाश, चल इधर। एक बार जाता है तो फिर आने का नाम ही नहीं लेता। ज़मींदार का बेटा होगा तो घर में।
(स्वर बदल कर नरम आवाज़ में)
ज़मींदार साहिब का ही हुक्म है कि सबको छुट्टी होगी, तुझे नहीं। भोलू!

भोलू:
जी?

पंडितजी:
तू क्या ख़ाक-धूल का मॉनिटर है?

भोलू:
जी।

पंडितजी:
कान खोल कर सुन ले, भागेगा यह, पिटेगा तू। समझा?

भोलू:
जी।

بچے (ایک ساتھ):
پانچ چھکے تیس۔ چھکم چھکّا چھتیس۔

بھولو:
پانچ چھکے تیس۔ چھکم چھکّا چھتیس۔

بچے (ایک ساتھ):
پانچ چھکے تیس۔ چھکم چھکّا چھتیس۔

اسکول کی گھنٹی بجتی ہے اور بچے فوراً کلاس سے باہر کی طرف لپکتے ہیں۔

بھولو:
پنڈت جی، دیوا بھاگا۔

ٹیچر دیوداس اور پاروتی کو روک لیتا ہے۔

پنڈت جی (اداکار، کنہیالال):
اے دیوداس، کہاں جا رہا ہے؟ او رے بدمعاش۔ چل اِدھر۔ ایک بار جاتا ہے تو پھر آنے کا نام ہی نہیں لیتا۔ زمیندار کا بیٹا ہوگا تو گھر میں۔
(نرم لہجے میں)
زمیندار صاحب کا ہی حکم ہے کہ سب کو چھٹی ہوگی، تجھے نہیں۔

بھولو:
جی؟

پنڈت جی:
تُو کیا خاک دھول کا مانیٹر ہے۔

بھولو:
جی؟

پنڈت جی:
کان کھول کر سن لے۔ بھاگے گا یہ، پٹے گا تُو۔ سمجھا؟

بھولو:
جی۔

 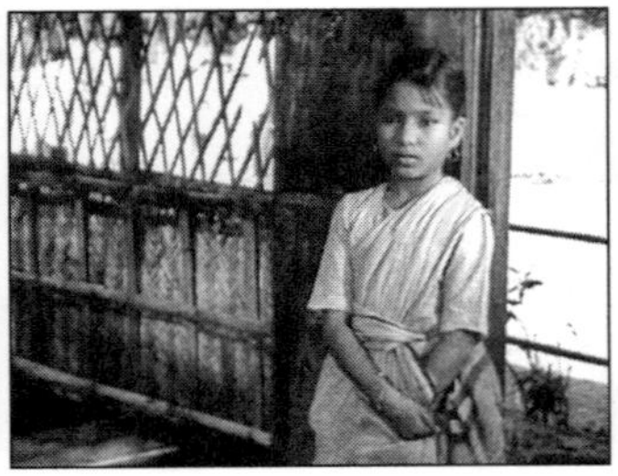   

Teacher:
Get him to do some sums.

De. Isay hisaab lagaane ko de.

Bholu:
Here. Add these up.

Le, ye hisaab laga.

Teacher *(to Devdas, as the teacher sits at his table again):*
Sit over there.

Ja, baith udhar.

Devdas sits on a classroom bench and does his sums. When Parvati sees Devdas working, she sits down and reads. The sound of children playing outside distracts Devdas. Parvati notices that the teacher has fallen asleep again. She draws a caricature of him on her slate and shows it to Devdas.

Young Parvati:
Devdas.

Devdas.

Her laughter startles Bholu. Devdas goes over to him.

Young Devdas *(to Bholu):*
I can't do it.

Mujh se hisaab nahin hota.

Bholu:
Show me the slate. If a ton of oil costs fourteen rupees, nine annas and three paise...

Silet dekhoon. Ek mann tel ka daam chauda rupay nau aane teen paayi ho...

Young Devdas *(pushing Bholu into a mound of lime powder):*
...so here.

...toh ye.

Parvati laughs and claps. The teacher wakes up with a start.

पंडितजीः
दे, इसे हिसाब लगाने को दे।

भोलूः
ले, यह हिसाब लगा।

पंडितजीः *(कुर्सी पर बैठते हुए देवदास से)*
जा, बैठ उधर।

देवदास कक्षा की बेंच पर बैठ कर हिसाब करने लगता है। देवदास को पढ़ते देख पार्वती भी बैठ कर पढ़ने लगती है। देवदास के कान बाहर खेलते बच्चों की आवाज़ पर लगे हुए हैं। पार्वती देखती है, अध्यापक फिर से ऊँघने लगा है। वह स्लेट पर अध्यापक का व्यंग्यचित्र बनाती है और देवदास को दिखाती है।

बालिका पार्वतीः
देवदास।

उनकी हँसी की आवाज़ से भोलू चौंकता है। देवदास उसके निकट जाता है।

बाल देवदास *(भोलू से):*
मुझसे हिसाब नहीं होता।

भोलूः
स्लेट देखूँ। एक मन तेल का दाम चौदह रुपए नौ आने तीन पाई हो...

बाल देवदास *(भोलू को चूने के ढेर में धक्का देते हुए):*
...तो यह।

पार्वती हँसती है और ताली बजाती है। अध्यापक चौंक कर जागता है।

پنڈت جی:
دے۔ اِسے حساب لگانے کو دے۔

بھولو:
لے۔ یہ حساب لگا۔

پنڈت جی (میز پر بیٹھتے ہوئے اُستاد، دیوداس سے):
جا۔ بیٹھ اُدھر۔

دیوداس بنچ پر بیٹھ کر سوال حل کرنے لگتا ہے۔ دیوداس کو کام کرتا دیکھ کر پاروتی بھی بیٹھ کر کچھ پڑھنے لگتی ہے۔ دیوداس کے کان باہر کھیلتے ہوئے بچوں کی آواز پر لگے ہوئے ہیں۔ پاروتی دیکھتی ہے کہ ٹیچر دوبارہ اونگھنے لگا ہے۔ پاروتی اُن کا سلیٹ پر خاکہ بنا کر دیوداس کو دکھاتی ہے۔

کمسن پاروتی:
دیوداس۔

پاروتی کی ہنسی کی آواز سے بھولو چونک جاتا ہے۔ دیوداس اُس کی طرف جاتا ہے۔

کمسن دیوداس (بھولو سے):
مجھ سے حساب نہیں ہوتا۔

بھولو:
سلیٹ دیکھوں۔ ایک من تیل کا دام چودا روپے نو آنے تین پائی ہوں تو۔۔۔

کمسن دیوداس (بھولو کو چونے کے ڈھیر پر دھکا دیتے ہوئے):
تو یہ۔۔۔

قہقہہ لگا کر پاروتی تالی بجاتی ہے۔ اونگھتا ہوا ٹیچر جاگ جاتا ہے۔

Teacher: What happened? Where's Deva?	Kya hua? Deva kahaan hai?
Young Parvati *(gleefully):* Teacher!	Panditji!
Bholu is covered with lime powder. Devdas runs away from the classroom. When he is chased by a band of boys, he pelts stones at them. A boy is hit on the forehead.	
Children *(repeating many times):* Catch him!	Pakdo, pakdo!
Cut. The classroom. Bholu struggles to his feet. The teacher is furious. Parvati is laughing.	
Teacher: I bought lime powder for my house because it was cheap and you're spoiling it?	Makaan banwaane ke liye sasta dekh ke khareeda aur tu isay barbaad kar raha hai?
Bholu: What did I do? I was just sitting quietly. It was Deva who pushed me and ran off.	Maine kya kiya? Main toh baitha tha. Deva mujhe dhakel kar bhaag gaya.
Teacher: So he pushed you and ran? You're such a strong boy, couldn't you have stopped him?	Dhakel kar bhaag gaya? Aur itne mushtande usay pakad bhi nahin sakay?
(to Parvati) Why are you giggling? Where's Deva?	Eh, tu kya khi-khi-khi kar rahi hai? Deva kahaan gaya?
Group of boys *(re-entering the classroom):* Deva ran so fast, we couldn't catch him.	Kitna tez bhaagta hai. Panditji, Deva pakda nahin gaya.

पंडितजीः
क्या हुआ? देवा कहाँ है?

बालिका पार्वती *(खिलखिलाते हुए):*
पंडितजी!

भोलू सर से पैर तक चूने से सना हुआ है। देवदास कक्षा से भागता है। छात्रों का समूह उसका पीछा करता है तो वह उन्हें पत्थर मारने लगता है। एक लड़के के माथे पर चोट लगती है।

बच्चे *(बार-बार):*
पकड़ो, पकड़ो।

कट। कक्षा। भोलू संभल कर खड़ा होता है। अध्यापक क्रोधित है। पार्वती हँस रही है।

पंडितजीः
मकान बनवाने के लिए सस्ता देख के ख़रीदा और तू इसे बरबाद कर रहा है?

भोलूः
मैंने क्या किया? मैं तो बैठा था। देवा मुझे धकेल कर भाग गया।

पंडितजीः
धकेल के भाग गया? और इतने मुशटंडे उसे पकड़ भी नहीं सके?
(पार्वती से)
ए, तू क्या खी-खी-खी कर रही है? देवा कहाँ गया?

छात्रों का समूह *(कक्षा में फिर से प्रवेश करता है):*
कितना तेज़ भागता है। पंडितजी, देवा पकड़ा नहीं गया।

پنڈت جی:
کیاہوا؟ دیوا کہاں ہے؟

کمسن پاروتی (کھلکھلاتے ہوئے):
پنڈت جی۔

سر سے پیر تک چونے میں بھولو رنگا ہوا ہے۔ دیوداس کلاس سے نکل کر باہر کی طرف بھاگتا ہے۔ پیچھے آنے والے بچوں پر دیوداس پتھر پھینکنے لگتا ہے۔ ایک لڑکے کی پیشانی پر پتھر لگتا ہے۔

بچے (دوہراتے ہوئے):
پکڑو۔ پکڑو۔

کٹ۔ کلاس روم۔ بھولو سنبھل کر کھڑا ہوتا ہے۔ ٹیچر نہایت غصے میں ہے۔ پاروتی ہنس رہی ہے۔

پنڈت جی:
مکان بنوانے کے لیے سستا دیکھ کے خریدا اور تُو اِسے برباد کر رہا ہے؟

بھولو:
میں نے کیا کیا؟ میں تو بیٹھا تھا۔ دیوا مجھے دھکیل کے بھاگ گیا۔

پنڈت جی:
دھکیل کے بھاگ گیا؟ اور اتنے مشٹنڈے اُسے پکڑ بھی نہیں سکے؟
(پاروتی سے)
اے۔ تُو کیا کھی کھی کھی کر رہی ہے؟ دیوا کہاں گیا؟

لڑکے (کلاس میں داخل ہوتے ہوئے):
کتنا تیز بھاگتا ہے، پنڈت جی، دیوا پکڑا نہیں گیا۔

Teacher:
Why not?

Kyun?

First pupil:
He started throwing stones at us.

Usnay patthar maarna shuru kar diya.

Second pupil:
He hit me with a stone. Right here.

Mujhe bhi patthar maara hai. Yahaan.

Teacher:
What?

Ein?

The second boy touches his injured head and wails.

Second pupil:
Blood!

Khoon!

Teacher:
So he hurt your head, did he? Let's go and see the landlord. Let him see what his son is up to. Now Devdas can't come back to school.
(to Bholu)
Come on, Bholu. Oh, what's this? Stealing lime powder?

Arey patthar maar ke sar phod diya? Chalo, sab mil ke chalte hain zamindar ki haveli mein. Dikhaate hain aaj unhen apne poot ki kartoot. Devdas aaj se paathshaala mein nahin aayega.
Chal, Bholu. Arey ye kya? Ye mann-bhar choona jeb mein bhar ke le ja raha hai.

Bholu *(sobbing):*
What have I done?

Maine kya kiya?

Teacher:
Put back that lime powder!
(Bholu empties the lime powder from his pocket)
You've ruined it all. Don't wipe it off your face. Let the landlord see the state you're in. Come on. Let's go.

Chal nikaal, nikaal. Rakh udhar.

Satyanaash kar ke rakh diya sab. Arey moonh se nahin pochhna, zamindar saaheb ko dikhaana hai abhi. Haan, chalo, chalo.

The teacher, Bholu and the boys leave the classroom. Parvati turns to her young friend Manorama whom she calls "Mano didi."

Young Parvati:
Mano didi, won't they let Devdas come back to school?

Mano didi, kya sachi Devdas ko paathshaala mein nahin aane denge?

पंडितजी:
क्यों?

पहला छात्र:
उसने पत्थर मारना शुरू कर दिया।

दूसरा छात्र:
मुझे भी पत्थर मारा है। यहाँ।

पंडितजी:
ऐं?

दूसरा छात्र अपने सर को छूता है और रोने लगता है।

दूसरा छात्र:
ख़ून!

पंडितजी:
अरे पत्थर मार के सर फोड़ दिया? चलो, सब मिलके चलते हैं ज़मींदार की हवेली में। दिखाते हैं आज उन्हें अपने पूत की करतूत। देवदास आज से पाठशाला में नहीं आएगा।
(भोलू से)
चल, भोलू। अरे यह क्या? यह मन-भर चूना जेब में भरके ले जा रहा है।

भोलू *(सिसकते हुए):*
मैंने क्या किया?

पंडितजी:
चल निकाल, निकाल। रख उधर।
(भोलू अपनी जेब से चूना निकालता है)
सत्यानाश करके रख दिया सब। अरे मुँह से नहीं पोंछना, ज़मींदार साहिब को दिखाना है अभी। हाँ, चलो, चलो।

अध्यापक, भोलू और सभी छात्र कक्षा से बाहर जाते हैं। पार्वती अपनी सहेली मनोरमा की ओर मुड़ती है, जिसे वह 'मनो दीदी' कहती है।

बालिका पार्वती:
मनो दीदी, क्या सच्ची देवदास को पाठशाला में नहीं आने देंगे?

پنڈت جی:
کیوں؟

ایک لڑکا:
اُس نے پتھر مارنا شروع کر دیا۔

دوسرا لڑکا:
مجھے بھی پتھر مارا ہے۔ یہاں۔

پنڈت جی:
ایں؟

دوسرا لڑکا اپنا سر پکڑ کر چیختا ہے۔

دوسرا لڑکا:
خون!

پنڈت جی:
ارے پتھر مار کر سر پھوڑ دیا؟ چلو۔ سب مل کے چلتے ہیں زمیندار کی حویلی میں۔ دکھاتے ہیں آج اُنھیں اپنے پوت کی کرتوت۔ دیوداس آج سے پاٹھ شالا میں نہیں آئے گا۔
(بھولو سے)
چل، بھولو۔ ارے یہ کیا؟ یہ من بھر چونا جیب میں بھر کے لے جا رہا ہے۔

بھولو (آہ وزاری کرتے ہوئے):
میں نے کیا کیا؟

پنڈت جی:
چل نکال، نکال۔ رکھ اِدھر۔
(بھولو اپنی جیب سے چونا نکالتا ہے)
ستیاناس کر کے رکھ دیا سب۔ ارے منہ سے نہیں پونچھنا، زمیندار صاحب کو دکھانا ہے ابھی۔ ہاں، چلو، چلو۔

ٹیچر، بھولو اور دوسرے بچے کلاس سے باہر جاتے ہیں۔ پاروتی مڑ کر اپنی دوست منورما سے کہتی ہے جسے وہ منو دیدی کہہ کر پکارتی ہے۔

کمسن پاروتی:
منو دیدی، کیا سچی دیوداس کو پاٹھ شالا میں آنے نہیں دیں گے؟

Young Manorama *(actress Baby Chand):*
Who knows? That silly teacher. If I had my way, I would not come back either. Let's go.

Kya pata? Ye mua pandit…mera toh aap hi aane ko ji nahin chaahta. Chal.

Dissolve from the classroom to a close-up of Devdas's father. He is smoking a hookah in his grand house. He is the rich and powerful landlord called Narain.

Teacher:
You tell me, sir, what can I do?

Ab aap hi hukum karein, zamindar saaheb, main kya karoon?

Narain *(actor Murad):*
This is terrible. My son? If the sheep dog starts devouring the sheep, who will protect them? Where is he?

Ye toh badi mushkil huwi. Mera ladka? Jab baad hi khet ko khaane lagay toh rakhwaali kaun karega? Gaya kahaan vo?

Teacher:
How do I know, sir? This is what he did to the boys who tried to catch him. Where is Devdas?

Main kya jaanun, zamindar saaheb? Jo ladke pakadne gaye, unki ye gati bani. Arey vo kahaan gaya?

(the teacher pulls the injured boy forward)
Come here. Look at the state he's in.

Idhar aa. Ye, iski haalat dekhiye.

Narain:
Dwijo!

Dwijo!

Devdas's elder brother, Dwijodas, a man in his late twenties, enters the room.

Dwijodas *(actor Iftekhar):*
Yes, father?

Ji, pitaji?

बालिका मनोरमा *(अभिनेत्री बेबी चाँद):*
क्या पता? यह मुआ पंडित...मेरा तो आप ही आने को जी नहीं चाहता। चल।

कक्षा से दृश्य बदलता है। अब हम देवदास के पिता, नारायण, के क्लोज़-अप पर आते हैं जो अपनी भव्य हवेली में बैठा हुक्क़ा पी रहा है। वह एक बहुत बड़ा ज़मींदार है।

पंडितजी:
अब आप ही हुक्म करें, ज़मींदार साहिब, मैं क्या करूँ?

नारायण *(अभिनेता मुराद):*
यह तो बड़ी मुश्किल हुई। मेरा लड़का? जब बाड़ ही खेत को खाने लगे तो रखवाली कौन करेगा? गया कहाँ वह?

पंडितजी:
मैं क्या जानूँ, ज़मींदार साहिब? जो लड़के पकड़ने गए, उनकी यह गति बनी। अरे वह कहाँ गया?
(घायल लड़के को आगे करते हुए)
इधर आ। यह, इसकी हालत देखिए।

नारायण:
द्विजो!

देवदास का बड़ा भाई, द्विजोदास, आयु लगभग पच्चीस वर्ष, कमरे में प्रवेश करता है।

द्विजोदास *(अभिनेता इफ़्तिख़ार):*
जी, पिताजी?

کمسن منورما (اداکارہ، بے بی چاند):
کیا پتا؟ یہ موا پنڈت ۔۔۔میرا تو آپ ہی آنے کو جی نہیں چاہتا۔چل۔

کلاس روم سے منظر بدل کر دیوداس کے والد کا پُرشکوہ گھر نظر آتا ہے جہاں وہ حقہ پی رہا ہے۔وہ ایک بہت بڑا زمین دار ہے جس کا نام نارائن ہے۔

پنڈت جی:
اب آپ ہی حکم کریں، زمیندار صاحب، میں کیا کروں؟

نارائن (اداکار، مراد):
یہ تو بڑی مشکل ہوئی۔میرا لڑکا؟ جب باڑ ہی کھیت کو کھانے لگے تو رکھوالی کون کرے گا؟ گیا کہاں وہ؟

پنڈت جی:
میں کیا جانوں، زمیندار صاحب؟ جو لڑکے پکڑنے گئے اُن کی یہ گت بنی۔ارے وہ کہاں گیا؟
(زخمی لڑکے کو آگے لاتے ہوئے)
اِدھر آ۔یہ، اِس کی حالت دیکھیے۔

نارائن:
دویجو!

دیوداس کا بڑا بھائی، دویجوداس جس کی عمر لگ بھگ پچیس سال ہوگی، کمرے میں داخل ہوتا ہے۔

دویجوداس (اداکار، افتخار):
جی، پتا جی؟

Narain:
Find Deva wherever he is and bring him to me.
(to the teacher)
Don't worry, teacher. Everyone is equal in my eyes. Deva may be a landlord's son, but he won't be spared.

Jahaan bhi Deva mile, usay pakad ke la.

Aap chinta na kijiye, Panditji. Dharam-kaante ka ek hi tol. Zamindar ka beta honay ke kaaran Deva ka paksh na hoga.

Teacher *(to the group of boys):*
Come on. Let's go.

Aao. Chalo, aao.

The teacher and boys leave the landlord's house. Bholu bows respectfully to Narain. Cut. The next scene. On a tree-lined village path, Devdas's attendant, Dharamdas, meets Parvati.

Dharamdas *(actor Nazir Hussain):*
Paro? You're back alone from school? Where is Deva?

Kyun, Paro? Aaj tu akeli laut rahi hai, Deva kahaan hai?

Young Parvati:
He ran away, Dharamda.

Vo toh bhaag gaye, Dharamda.

Dharamdas:
What do you mean? How could he have run away?

Kya bolti hai? Bhaag kaise gaya?

Young Parvati:
Who knows, Dharamda. He messed up the lime powder.
(laughs)
Did you see Bholu's face? He looks like a stork.

Kya pata hai, Dharamda. Ek-dam choone ke dher par chit-pat kar diya.
Bholu ki soorat dekhi hai? Poora bagla bana hua hai.

Dharamdas *(smiling):*
Will you stop laughing and tell me where Deva is?

Tu hanse hi jaayegi ya kuch kahegi bhi? Bata, bata, Deva kahaan hai?

Young Parvati:
How do I know?

Mujhe kya maaloom?

Dharamdas:
Of course you know. You know everything. Tell me. He must be hungry.

Tu jaanti hai. Tu sab jaanti hai. Bata, usay zaroor bhook lagi hogi.

नारायणः
जहाँ भी देवा मिले, उसे पकड़ के ला।
(अध्यापक से)
आप चिंता न कीजिए, पंडितजी। धरम-काँटे का एक ही तोल। ज़मींदार का बेटा होने के कारण देवा का पक्ष न होगा।

نارائن:
جہاں بھی دیوا ملے، اُسے پکڑ کے لا۔
(پنڈت سے)
آپ چنتا نہ کیجیے، پنڈت جی۔ دھرم کانٹے کا ایک ہی تول۔ زمیندار کا بیٹا ہونے کے کارن دیوا کا پکش نہ ہوگا۔

पंडितजी *(छात्रों से):*
आओ। चलो, आओ।

پنڈت جی (لڑکوں سے):
آؤ۔ چلو، آؤ۔

अध्यापक तथा छात्र ज़मींदार के घर से जाते हैं। भोलू आदर से ज़मींदार को प्रणाम करता है। कट। अगला दृश्य। पेड़ों से घिरे रास्ते पर धरमदास, देवदास का ख़ास सेवक, बालिका पार्वती से मिलता है।

ٹیچر اور بچے زمین دار کے گھر سے باہر نکلتے ہیں۔ بھولو جھک کر نارائن کو سلام کرتا ہے۔ کٹ۔ اگلا منظر۔ گاؤں کے درختوں سے گھرے ایک راستے پر دھرم داس، دیوداس کا خاص ملازم، پاروتی سے ملتا ہے۔

धरमदास *(अभिनेता नज़ीर हुसैन):*
क्यों, पारो? आज तू अकेली लौट रही है, देवा कहाँ है?

دھرم داس (نظیر حسین):
کیوں، پارو۔ آج تُو اکیلی لوٹ رہی ہے؟ دیوا کہاں ہے؟

बालिका पार्वतीः
वह तो भाग गए, धरमदा।

کمسن پاروتی:
وہ تو بھاگ گئے، دھرم دا۔

धरमदासः
क्या बोलती है? भाग कैसे गया?

دھرم داس:
کیا بولتی ہے؟ بھاگ کیسے گیا؟

बालिका पार्वतीः
क्या पता है, धरमदा। एकदम चूने के ढेर पर चित-पट कर दिया।
(हँसती है)
भोलू की सूरत देखी है? पूरा बगला बना हुआ है।

کمسن پاروتی:
کیا پتا ہے، دھرم دا۔ ایک دم چونے کے ڈھیر پر چت پٹ کر دیا۔
(ہنستے ہوئے)
بھولو کی صورت دیکھی ہے؟ پورا بگلا بنا ہوا ہے۔

धरमदास *(मुस्कुराते हुए):*
तू हँसे ही जाएगी या कुछ कहेगी भी? बता, बता, देवा कहाँ है?

دھرم داس (مسکراتے ہوئے):
تُو ہنسے ہی جائے گی یا کچھ کہے گی بھی؟ بتا۔ بتا دیوا کہاں ہے؟

बालिका पार्वतीः
मुझे क्या मालूम?

کمسن پاروتی:
مجھے کیا معلوم؟

धरमदासः
तू जानती है। तू सब जानती है। बता, उसे ज़रूर भूख लगी होगी।

دھرم داس:
تُو جانتی ہے۔ تُو سب جانتی ہے۔ بتا۔ اُسے ضرور بھوک لگی ہوگی۔

Young Parvati:
Yes, he must be. But I won't tell or else he will hit me. I'll take him something to eat.

Haan, bhook toh lagi hogi. Par main bataaungi nahin, vo mujhe maarenge. Main unhen khud hi ja ke khaana de aaungi.

Dharamdas:
Very well, you go. But make sure that he comes home before it gets dark.

Acha, acha, tu hi jaana. Par sunn, usay baaton mein bhula kar sandhiya se pehle-pehle ghar bhi le aana. Hein?

Young Parvati:
I'll bring him home. All right?

Acha baba, ghar bhi le aaungi. Bas?

Dissolve. Parvati returns back home. Her father Nilkanth is sitting on a bed.

Young Parvati *(giggling):*
Guess what happened at school today, father.

Jaante ho, pitaji, aaj paathshaala mein kya hua?

Nilkanth *(actor Shivraj):*
Have you gone crazy? What happened at school?

Arey baauli ho gayi hai? Kya hua paathshaala mein?

Young Parvati:
I'm hungry. Let me eat first.

Bhook lagi hai. Pehle kuch kha loon phir bataaungi.

Nilkanth:
Very well.

Acha, acha.

Reel Two

Parvati goes towards the kitchen and calls out to her mother. Her mother comes to the door.

Young Parvati:
Mother! I'm hungry. Give me something to eat.

Ma, ma. Ma, bhook lagi, kuch khaane ko do.

Parvati's mother *(unidentified actress):*
Just a minute.

Deti hoon.

Young Parvati:
Is that all? That won't fill me.

Bas, itne se? Itne se kya pait bharega?

बालिका पार्वती:
हाँ, भूख तो लगी होगी, पर मैं बताऊँगी नहीं, वह मुझे मारेंगे। मैं उन्हें ख़ुद ही जाके खाना दे आऊँगी।

धरमदास:
अच्छा, अच्छा, तू ही जाना, पर सुन, उसे बातों में भुला कर संध्या से पहले-पहले घर भी ले आना। हैं?

बालिका पार्वती:
अच्छा बाबा, घर भी ले आऊँगी। बस?

अगला दृश्य। पार्वती घर लौटती है। उसके पिता, नीलकंठ, बिस्तर पर बैठे हैं।

बालिका पार्वती *(खिलखिलाते हुए):*
जानते हो, पिताजी, आज पाठशाला में क्या हुआ?

नीलकंठ *(अभिनेता शिवराज):*
अरे बावली हो गई है? क्या हुआ पाठशाला में?

बालिका पार्वती:
भूख लगी है। पहले कुछ खा लूँ, फिर बताऊँगी।

नीलकंठ:
अच्छा, अच्छा।

रील दो

पार्वती अपनी माँ को पुकारते हुए रसोई की ओर जाती है। माँ द्वार पर आती है।

बालिका पार्वती:
माँ, माँ। माँ, भूख लगी, कुछ खाने को दो।

पार्वती की माँ *(कलाकार अज्ञात):*
देती हूँ।

बालिका पार्वती:
बस, इतने से? इतने से क्या पेट भरेगा?

کمسن پاروتی:
ہاں۔بھوک تو لگی ہوگی۔پر میں بتاؤنگی نہیں، وہ مجھے ماریں گے۔میں اُنھیں خود ہی جا کے کھانا دے آؤنگی۔

دھرم داس:
اچھا، اچھا۔تُو ہی جانا۔پر سن، اُسے باتوں میں بھلا کر سندھیا سے پہلے پہلے گھر بھی لے آنا۔ہَیں؟

کمسن پاروتی:
اچھا، بابا، گھر بھی لے آؤنگی، بس؟

اگلا منظر۔پاروتی گھر لوٹتی ہے۔اُس کے والد، نیل کنٹھ بستر پر بیٹھے ہوئے ہیں۔

کمسن پاروتی (کھلکھلاتے ہوئے):
جانتے ہو، پتا جی، آج پاٹھ شالا میں کیا ہوا؟

نیل کنٹھ (اداکار، شِوراج):
ارے باؤلی ہوگئی ہے؟ کیا ہوا پاٹھ شالا میں؟

کمسن پاروتی:
بھوک لگی ہے۔پہلے کچھ کھالوں پھر بتاؤنگی۔

نیل کنٹھ:
اچھا، اچھا۔

ریل دو

پاروتی باورچی خانے کے طرف جا کر ماں کو پکارتی ہے۔اُس کی ماں دروازے پر آتی ہے۔

کمسن پاروتی:
ماں، ماں۔ماں، بھوک لگی، کچھ کھانے کو دو۔

پاروتی کی ماں (اداکارہ، نامعلوم):
دیتی ہوں۔

کمسن پاروتی:
بس، اِتنے سے؟ اِتنے سے کیا پیٹ بھرے گا؟

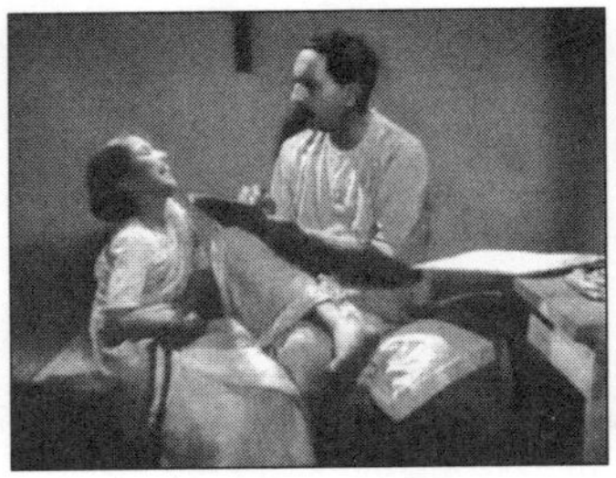    

Parvati's mother:
That's what you usually eat. Why do you want more today?

Hmm. Roz toh itne hi se pait bhar jaata tha, aaj kya baat ho gayi?

Grandmother *(unidentified actress, to Parvati's mother):*
Daughter-in-law, give her some more. That's nothing special, it's only puffed rice. Give some more to my little princess.

Arey de de na, bahu. Koi halwa-sandes thodi hai. Murmure hi toh hain. De de meri raani-bitya ko. De de.

Parvati's mother *(giving her daughter a handful more):*
Is that enough?

Bas?

Parvati leaves the house. Dissolve. Parvati runs into a mango grove with tall trees. She looks behind her to make sure that no one is following. She finds Devdas sitting on a tree branch. She climbs onto the branch and sits near him. He is smoking a small tobacco-filled chillum.

Young Devdas:
Who's there? Oh, Paro. Come and sit here.

Kaun? Oh Paro, aa baith.

Young Parvati:
Smoking tobacco again?

Phir tambaaku pi rahe ho na?

Young Devdas:
So what? All men smoke.

Toh kya hua? Mard log sabhi peete hain.

(he sees Parvati has brought some puffed rice)
You've brought me something to eat? Give it to me.

Oh. Khaane ko laayi hai? La de.

(they eat)
Listen, Paro. What did the teacher say?

Sunn, Paro. Panditji kya keh rahe thay?

Young Parvati:
He told your father everything.

Unhon ne sab baaten ja kar taayaji se keh di hain.

पार्वती की माँ:
हुँ। रोज़ तो इतने से पेट भर जाता था, आज क्या बात हो गई?

दादीमाँ *(कलाकर अज्ञात, पार्वती की माँ से):*
अरे दे दे ना, बहू। कोई हलवा-संदेश थोड़ी है। मुरमुरे ही तो हैं। दे दे मेरी रानी-बिटिया को। दे दे।

पार्वती की माँ *(थोड़ा और देते हुए):*
बस?

पार्वती घर से बाहर निकलती है। अगला दृश्य। वह एक कुँज में भागती हुई प्रवेश करती है। कुँज बड़े और घने पेड़ों से भरा है। वह पीछे मुड़ कर निश्चित करती है कि कोई उसका पीछा तो नहीं कर रहा है। देवदास उसे एक पेड़ की डाल पर बैठा दिखाई देता है। पार्वती भी पेड़ पर चढ़ कर उसके निकट बैठ जाती है। देवदास चिलम पी रहा है।

बाल देवदास:
कौन? ओह पारो, आ बैठ।

बालिका पार्वती:
फिर तंबाकू पी रहे हो ना?

बाल देवदास:
तो क्या हुआ? मर्द लोग सभी पीते हैं।
(पार्वती के हाथ में मुरमुरे देखकर)
ओह। खाने को लाई है? ला दे।
(दोनों खाते हैं)
सुन, पारो। पंडितजी क्या कह रहे थे?

बालिका पार्वती:
उन्होंने सब बातें जाकर तायाजी से कह दी हैं।

پاروتی کی ماں:
ہم۔ روز تو اِتنے ہی سے پیٹ بھر جاتا تھا؟ آج کیا بات ہوگئی؟

دادی (اداکارہ، نامعلوم، پاروتی کی ماں سے):
ارے دے دے نا، بہو۔ کوئی حلوا سندیس تھوڑی ہے؟ مرمرے ہی تو ہیں۔ دے دے میری رانی بٹیا کو۔ دے دے۔

پاروتی کی ماں (بچّی کو بڑھا کر اور دیتے ہوئے):
بس؟

پاروتی گھر سے نکلتی ہے۔ منظر بدلتا ہے۔ درختوں سے گھرے ایک کنج میں آتی ہے۔ وہ پلٹ کر دیکھتی ہے کہ کوئی پیچھے تو نہیں آ رہا ہے۔ دیوداس اُسے ایک درخت کی شاخ پر بیٹھا دکھائی دیتا ہے۔ درخت پر چڑھ کر وہ دیوداس کے قریب بیٹھ جاتی ہے۔ دیوداس بیٹھا چلم پی رہا ہے۔

کمسن دیوداس:
کون؟ اوہ پارو، آ بیٹھ۔

کمسن پاروتی:
پھر تمباکو پی رہے ہو، نا؟

کمسن دیوداس:
تو کیا ہوا؟ مرد لوگ سبھی پیتے ہیں۔
(پاروتی کے ہاتھ میں مُرمُرے دیکھ کر)
اوہ۔ کھانے کو لائی ہے؟ لا دے۔
(دونوں کھاتے ہیں)
سن، پارو۔ پنڈت جی کیا کہہ رہے تھے؟

کمسن پاروتی:
اُنھوں نے سب باتیں جا کر تایا جی سے کہہ دی ہیں۔

Young Devdas:
Everything? Then what happened?

Sab baaten babuji se keh dein? Phir kya hua?

Young Parvati:
They won't let you come back to school again.

Ab vo tumhen paathshaala mein nahin jaane denge.

Young Devdas:
Who cares if they don't! I don't want to study anyway. Give me a *sandesh*.

Na jaane den. Main padhna hi nahin chaahta. La, sandesh de.

Young Parvati:
Sandesh? I didn't bring any.

Sandesh? Vo toh main nahin laayi.

Young Devdas:
All right. Go and get me some water.

Acha toh ja paani la.

Young Parvati:
Where can I find any water here?

Paani yahaan kahaan milega?

Young Devdas:
No water, no *sandesh*. So why bother coming? Go and get me water. Go!

Paani nahin milega, sandesh nahin milega toh phir milega tera sar? Ja, ja ke paani la.

Young Parvati:
I won't go; I know you'll run away.

Main nahin jaaungi, mujhe maaloom hai, tum yahaan se bhaag jaaoge.

Young Devdas:
I won't run away. Now go.

Nahin bhaagunga, jaao keh raha hoon na.

Young Parvati:
I won't.

Main nahin jaaungi.

Young Devdas:
You won't go? I'm ordering you to go.

Nahin jaayegi? Ja main kehta hoon.

He slaps her across the face. She looks at him with tears in her eyes.

बाल देवदासः
सब बातें बाबूजी से कह दीं? फिर क्या हुआ?

बालिका पार्वतीः
अब वह तुम्हें पाठशाला में नहीं जाने देंगे।

बाल देवदासः
न जाने दें। मैं पढ़ना ही नहीं चाहता। ला, संदेश दे।

बालिका पार्वतीः
संदेश? वह तो मैं नहीं लाई।

बाल देवदासः
अच्छा तो जा पानी ला।

बालिका पार्वतीः
पानी यहाँ कहाँ मिलेगा?

बाल देवदासः
पानी नहीं मिलेगा, संदेश नहीं मिलेगा तो फिर मिलेगा तेरा सर? जा, जाके पानी ला।

बालिका पार्वतीः
मैं नहीं जाऊँगी, मुझे मालूम है, तुम यहाँ से भाग जाओगे।

बाल देवदासः
नहीं भागूँगा, जाओ कह रहा हूँ ना।

बालिका पार्वतीः
मैं नहीं जाऊँगी।

बाल देवदासः
नहीं जाएगी? जा मैं कहता हूँ।

वह उसे थप्पड़ मारता है। पार्वती की आँखों में आँसू आ जाते हैं।

کمسن دیوداس:
سب باتیں بابو جی سے کہہ دیں؟ پھر کیا ہوا؟

کمسن پاروتی:
اب وہ تمھیں پاٹھ شالا میں نہیں جانے دیں گے۔

کمسن دیوداس:
نہ جانے دیں۔ میں پڑھنا ہی نہیں چاہتا۔ لا، سندیش دے۔

کمسن پاروتی:
سندیش؟ وہ تو میں نہیں لائی۔

کمسن دیوداس:
اچھا تو جا پانی لا۔

کمسن پاروتی:
پانی یہاں کہاں ملے گا؟

کمسن دیوداس:
پانی نہیں ملے گا، سندیش نہیں ملے گا تو پھر ملے گا تیرا سر؟ جا، جاکے پانی لا۔

کمسن پاروتی:
میں نہیں جاؤں گی، مجھے معلوم ہے تم یہاں سے بھاگ جاؤ گے۔

کمسن دیوداس؛
نہیں بھاگوں گا، جاؤ کہہ رہا ہوں نا۔

کمسن پاروتی:
میں نہیں جاؤں گی۔

کمسن دیوداس:
نہیں جائے گی؟ جا میں کہتا ہوں۔

وہ اُسے تھپڑ مارتا ہے۔ آنکھوں میں آنسو لیے وہ اُسے دیکھ رہی ہے۔

   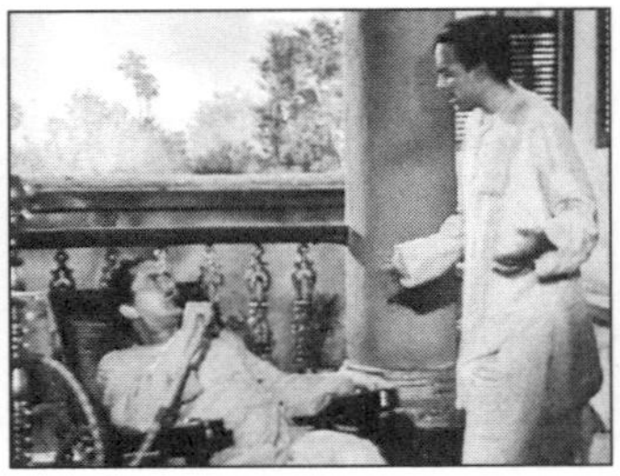 

Young Parvati: I'm going. I'll tell your father everything.	Main jaaungi. Sab ja ke taayaji se keh doongi.
Young Devdas *(calls after her):* Paro! Then go. Get lost!	Paro! O Paro, ja, dafa ho ja.
Cut. The next scene is at the landlord's house where Devdas's father is smoking a hookah on the verandah. The elder son enters.	
Dwijodas: Father, I've looked everywhere. He's nowhere to be found.	Pitaji, sab jagah dhoonda lekin Deva ka kahin pata nahin chala.
Narain: Where is he?	Kahaan gaya?
(to Parvati who has just arrived) Why are you crying?	Kyun beti, roti kyun hai?
Young Parvati *(sobbing):* Deva hit me.	Deva ne mujhe maara.
Narain: Where is that rascal?	Hai kahaan vo badmaash?
Young Parvati: In the garden. Did you know he hides there and smokes?	Bagheeche mein. Jaante hain, taayaji? Wahaan vo chhip-chhip ke tambaaku peete hain.
Narain *(furious):* Smokes? That's the limit. What a disaster. No more school or food for him. Dwijodas, go and drag him home by the ear. That wicked boy will give us a bad name.	Ain? Vo tambaaku bhi peene laga? Anarth ho gaya. Andher aa gaya. Aaj se is ladke ka school bandh, khaana bandh. Dwijodas, abhi ja aur jaise-taise usay kaan pakad ke la. Satyanaashi, ye kulkalank.

बालिका पार्वतीः
मैं जाऊँगी, सब जाके तायाजी से कह दूँगी।

बाल देवदास *(उसे पुकारता है):*
पारो! ओ पारो, जा, दफ़ा हो जा।

दृश्य समाप्त। अगला दृश्य ज़मींदार का घर - देवदास के पिता बरामदे में बैठे हुक्का पी रहे हैं। बड़ा बेटा प्रवेश करता है।

द्विजोदासः
पिताजी, सब जगह ढूँढ़ा लेकिन देवा का कहीं पता नहीं चला।

नारायणः
कहाँ गया?
(पार्वती से जो अभी आई है)
क्यों बेटी, रोती क्यों है?

बालिका पार्वती *(सिसकते हुए):*
देवा ने मुझे मारा।

नारायणः
है कहाँ वह बदमाश?

बालिका पार्वतीः
बग़ीचे में। जानते हैं, तायाजी? वहाँ वह छिप-छिपके तंबाकू पीते हैं।

नारायण *(गुस्से से):*
ऐं? वह तंबाकू भी पीने लगा? अनर्थ हो गया। अंधेर आ गया। आज से इस लड़के का स्कूल बंद, खाना बंद। द्विजोदास, अभी जा और जैसे–तैसे उसे कान पकड़के ला। सत्यानाशी, यह कुलकलंक।

کمسن پاروتی:
میں جاؤں گی۔ سب جا کے تایا جی سے کہہ دوں گی۔

کمسن دیوداس (پکارتے ہوئے):
پارو! او پارو، جا، دفع ہو جا۔

کٹ۔ اگلے منظر میں زمیندار، دیوداس کا باپ، اپنے گھر کے برآمدے میں حقہ پی رہا ہے۔ بڑا بیٹا داخل ہوتا ہے۔

دویجوداس:
پتا جی، سب جگہ ڈھونڈا لیکن دیوا کا کہیں پتا نہیں چلا۔

نارائن:
کہاں گیا؟
(آتی ہوئی پاروتی کو دیکھ کر)
کیوں بیٹی، روتی کیوں ہے؟

کمسن پاروتی (سسکتے ہوئے):
دیوا نے مجھے مارا۔

نارائن:
ہے کہاں وہ بدمعاش؟

کمسن پاروتی:
بغیچے میں۔ جانتے ہیں، تایا جی، وہاں وہ چھپ چھپ کر تمبا کو پیتے ہیں؟

نارائن (غصے سے):
ایں؟ وہ تمبا کو بھی پینے لگا؟ انرتھ ہو گیا۔ اندھیر آ گیا۔ آج سے اِس لڑکے کا اسکول بند، کھانا بند۔ دویجوداس، ابھی جا اور جیسے تیسے اُسے کان پکڑ کے لا۔ ستیاناسی، یہ کُل کلنک۔

Dissolve. Dwijodas looks for Devdas in the village. Devdas hears his brother coming and runs away. He bumps into a villager and upsets the basket the man is carrying on his head.

Dwijodas *(repeating many times as he chases Devdas):*
Catch him! — Pakdo, pakdo.

Dwijodas gives chase. With the help of a passer-by, his brother manages to catch Devdas.

Dissolve. Narain's house. Looking upset, Devdas's mother, Harimati Devi, and Dharamdas stand outside a door. We hear sounds of Devdas crying inside the room. His father is beating him.

Narain *(off-screen):*
So you ran away from school? — Paathshaala se bhaagta hai?
(to Devdas, also off-screen)
You hit your classmates, eh? You're useless. — Maara-maari karta hai? Naalaayeq.

Harimati Devi *(actress Pratima Devi):*
Stop! You've hit him enough. Stop. — Bas bas ji, bahot maar liya. Bas karo.
(Narain comes out of the room)
Dear God. Scold him, but don't beat him to death. — Haaye Ram, moonh se daant-dapat karte hain, maar hi toh nahin daalte?

Narain:
Step aside! It's your fault for spoiling him. No one had dare open this door. — Paray hato ji. Ye tumhaare hi chonchle hain jis ne usay bigaada hai. Khabardaar jo kisi ne darwaaza khola.
(closing the door behind him)
No food for him either. — Aaj isay khaana-waana kuch nahin milega.

As soon as Devdas's father has left, his mother opens the door and goes inside. She finds the young boy sitting on the bed, sobbing.

Harimati Devi:
Come, my son. Come and eat something. — Chal beta, chal ke khaana kha le.

Young Devdas:
No, I won't eat. — Nahin, main nahin khaaunga.

अगला दृश्य। गाँव के रास्ते पर बड़ा भाई द्विजोदास, देवदास को ढूँढ़ रहा है। देवदास उसे आता देख कर भागता है। वह एक गाँव वाले से टकराता है। उसके सर पर रखी टोकरी गिर जाती है।

द्विजोदास *(देवदास के पीछे आवाज़ देते हुए):*
पकड़ो, पकड़ो।

द्विजोदास उसका पीछा कर रहा है। एक राह चलते आदमी की सहायता से द्विजोदास देवदास को पकड़ लेता है।

अगला दृश्य। अप्रसन्न देवदास की माँ हरिमति देवी, धरमदास, कमरे के दरवाज़े के बाहर खड़े हैं। अंदर से देवदास के रोने की आवाज़ आ रही है। उसके पिता उसे पीट रहे हैं।

नारायण *(ऑफ़-स्क्रीन):*
पाठशाला से भागता है?
(देवदास से, ऑफ़-स्क्रीन)
मारा-मारी करता है? नालायक़।

हरिमति देवी *(अभिनेत्री प्रतिमा देवी):*
बस बस जी, बहुत मार लिया। बस करो।
(नारायण कमरे से बाहर आते हुए)
हाय राम, मुँह से डाँट-डपट करते हैं, मार ही तो नहीं डालते?

नारायणः
परे हटो जी। यह तुम्हारे ही चोंचले हैं जिसने उसे बिगाड़ा है। ख़बरदार जो किसी ने दरवाज़ा खोला।
(कमरे का दरवाज़ा बंद करते हुए)
आज इसे खाना-वाना कुछ नहीं मिलेगा।

देवदास के पिता के वहाँ से जाते ही, माँ द्वार खोल कर अंदर जाती है। देवदास बिस्तर पर बैठा रो रहा है।

हरिमति देवी:
चल बेटा, चलके खाना खा ले।

बाल देवदासः
नहीं, मैं नहीं खाऊँगा।

اگلا منظر۔ گاؤں کے راستے پر بڑا بھائی دوبجوداس، اُسے تلاش کررہا ہے۔ دیوداس اُس کی آہٹ پا کر بھاگ کھڑا ہوتا ہے۔ دوڑتے ہوئے وہ ایک دیہاتی سے ٹکراتا ہے اور اُس کے سر پر سے ٹوکری گر پڑتی ہے۔

دوبجوداس (دیوداس کے پیچھے آوازیں دیتے ہوئے):
پکڑو۔ پکڑو۔

دوبجوداس اُس کا تعاقب کر رہا ہے۔ پاس سے گزرتے ہوئے ایک شخص کی مدد سے وہ دیوداس کو پکڑ لیتا ہے۔

اگلا منظر۔ نارائن کا گھر۔ پریشان سے دیوداس کی ماں، ہری متی دیوی اور دھرم داس، کمرے کے دروازے کے باہر کھڑے ہیں۔ اندر سے دیوداس کے رونے کی آواز آ رہی ہے۔ اُس کے والد اُسے پیٹ رہا ہے۔

نارائن (آف اسکرین):
پاٹھ شالا سے بھاگتا ہے؟
(دیوداس سے، آف اسکرین)
مارا ماری کرتا ہے؟ نالائق۔

ہری متی دیوی (اداکارہ، پرتیما دیوی):
بس بس جی، بہت مارلیا۔ بس کرو۔
(نارائن کمرے سے باہر آتے ہوئے)
ہائے رام۔ منہ سے ڈانٹ ڈپٹ کرتے ہیں۔ مار ہی تو نہیں ڈالتے؟

نارائن:
پرے ہٹو جی۔ یہ تمہارے ہی چونچلے ہیں جس نے اُسے بگاڑا ہے۔ خبردار جو کسی نے دروازہ کھولا۔
(باہر سے دروازہ بند کرتے ہوئے)
آج اِسے کھانا وانا کچھ نہیں ملے گا۔

دیوداس کے باپ کے باہر جاتے ہی اُس کی ماں کمرے کے اندر جاتی ہے۔ دیوداس بستر پر بیٹھا سسکیاں لے رہا ہے۔

ماں:
چل، بیٹا۔ چل کے کھانا کھالے۔

کمسن دیوداس:
نہیں، میں نہیں کھاؤں گا۔

Harimati Devi:
Come, my prince.

Chal mera raja beta, chal.

Dissolve. Night scene. Looking upset, Parvati sits near a glass lantern. Her mother calls her from the other room.

Parvati's mother *(off-screen):*
Paro, the food is getting cold.

Paro, khaana thanda ho raha hai.

Young Parvati:
Mother, I won't eat today. My tummy hurts.

Ma, main aaj khaana nahin khaaungi. Mera pait dukhta hai.

A tracking shot to Parvati. Fade out.

Fade in. Day. Devdas skips merrily out of his grand mansion towards Parvati's house across the street. He climbs a mango tree and picks a fruit and throws it onto Parvati's roof. When she hears the sound of the mango bounce off the tin roof, Parvati knows Devdas is waiting for her. A crane shot. She runs out of her room onto the terrace and down the staircase that runs alongside the bungalow.

Young Devdas:
Come here, Paro.

Aa, idhar aa, Paro.

(she walks hesitantly towards him)
Why did you tell them I was smoking?

Tu ne tambaaku peene ki baat kyun keh di?

Young Parvati:
Why did you hit me?

Tumne mujhe maara kyun?

Young Devdas:
Why didn't you bring me water?

Tu paani kyun nahin laayi?

हरिमति देवी:
चल मेरा राजा बेटा। चल।

अगला दृश्य। रात। उदास पार्वती एक लालटेन के निकट बैठी है। उसकी माँ दूसरे कमरे से पुकारती है।

पार्वती की माँ: *(ऑफ़-स्क्रीन)*
पारो, खाना ठंडा हो रहा है।

बालिका पार्वती:
माँ, मैं आज खाना नहीं खाऊँगी। मेरा पेट दुखता है।

पार्वती पर एक ट्रैकिंग शॉट। फ़ेड आउट।

अगला दृश्य। दिन। देवदास उछलते-कूदते अपने बड़े घर से निकल कर पारो के घर की ओर जाता है, जो रास्ते के दूसरी ओर है। वह आम के पेड़ पर चढ़ता है और एक आम तोड़ कर पारो की छत पर फेंकता है। छत पर आम के गिरने की आवाज़ सुन कर पारो समझ जाती है कि देवदास उसकी प्रतीक्षा कर रहा है। क्रेन शॉट। वह भागती हुई अपने कमरे से निकलती है और तेज़ी से सीढ़ियाँ उतरते हुए भाग कर बाहर आती है।

बाल देवदास:
आ, इधर आ, पारो।
(वह हिचकिचाते हुए उसकी ओर बढ़ती है)
तूने तंबाकू पीने की बात क्यों कह दी?

बालिका पार्वती:
तुमने मुझे मारा क्यों?

बाल देवदास:
तू पानी क्यों नहीं लाई?

ہری متی دیوی:
چل میرا،راجا بیٹا۔چل۔

اگلا منظر۔رات۔اُداس سی پاروتی ایک لالٹین کے پاس بیٹھی ہوئی ہے۔اُس کی ماں دوسرے کمرے سے اُسے آواز دیتی ہے۔

پاروتی کی ماں(آف اسکرین):
پارو،کھانا ٹھنڈا ہو رہا ہے۔

کمسن پاروتی:
ماں، میں آج کھانا نہیں کھاؤں گی، میرا پیٹ دُکھتا ہے۔

پاروتی کا ٹریکنگ شاٹ۔فیڈ آؤٹ۔

اگلا منظر۔دن۔اُچھلتا کودتا دیوداس اپنے پُرشکوہ مکان سے نکل کر پاروتی کے گھر کی طرف جا رہا ہے جو راستے کے دوسری طرف ہے۔ایک آم توڑ کر وہ اُسے پاروتی کی چھت پر پھینکتا ہے۔چھت پر آم کے گرنے کی آواز سنائی دیتی ہے۔آواز سن کر پاروتی سمجھ جاتی ہے کہ دیوداس اُس کا انتظار کر رہا ہے۔کرین شاٹ۔دوڑتی ہوئی پاروتی اپنے کمرے سے نکل کر سیڑھیاں طے کر کے مکان سے باہر آ جاتی ہے۔

کمسن دیوداس:
آ،اِدھر آ،پارو۔
(وہ ہچکچاتے ہوئے اُس کے پاس آتی ہے)
تُو نے تمباکو پینے کی بات کیوں کہہ دی؟

کمسن پاروتی:
تم نے مجھے مارا کیوں؟

کمسن دیوداس:
تُو پانی کیوں نہیں لائی؟

Young Parvati:
Why did you shout at me?

Tum daant ke kyun bole?

Young Devdas *(coming near her):*
You're a fool. All right. Don't tell on me again.

Tu badi bewaqoof hai. Acha dekh phir kabhi matt kehna.

Young Parvati:
Don't hit me again.

Tum bhi matt mujhe maarna.

Young Devdas:
I won't hit you.

Nahin maarunga.

Young Parvati:
So, do you forgive me?

Toh phir tumne mujhe chhama kar diya?

Young Devdas:
Yes! Want it in writing? Listen, Paro. Let's go to Ram babu's garden. I saw a nightingale there. I'll catch it for you.

Haan baba kar diya. Aur kya hisaab likhwaana hai? Sunn, Paro, chal Ram babu ke baagh mein. Maine dekha hai wahaan bulbul ka bachcha hai, usay pakad ke tujhe doonga.

Young Parvati:
Let's go.

Chal.

Parvati is smiling again. They run into the depth of the mango grove where they see a nightingale (bulbul) perched on a branch. Before Devdas can climb the tree, he hands some coins to Parvati.

Young Devdas:
Paro, keep these three rupees.

Paro, ye teen rupay rakh, haan.

Asha Bhosle & Usha Mangeshkar sing for Devdas and Parvati.

Young Devdas:
O sweet bird, your home is far away

O albele panchhi tera door thikaana hai

Young Parvati:
Never alighting on the same branch again when you fly away

Chhodi jo daali ik baar wahaan kab laut ke aana hai

बालिका पार्वतीः
तुम डाँटके क्यों बोले?

کمسن پاروتی:
تم ڈانٹ کے کیوں بولے؟

बाल देवदास *(उसके पास आते हुए):*
तू बड़ी बेवकूफ़ है। अच्छा देख, फिर कभी मत कहना।

کمسن دیوداس *(اُس کے قریب آتے ہوئے):*
تُو بڑی بیوقوف ہے۔ اچھا دیکھ، پھر کبھی مت کہنا۔

बालिका पार्वतीः
तुम भी मत मुझे मारना।

کمسن پاروتی:
تم بھی مت مجھے مارنا۔

बाल देवदासः
नहीं मारूँगा।

کمسن دیوداس:
نہیں ماروں گا۔

बालिका पार्वतीः
तो फिर तुमने मुझे क्षमा कर दिया।

کمسن پاروتی:
تو پھر تم نے مجھے چھما کر دیا؟

बाल देवदासः
हाँ बाबा कर दिया। और क्या हिसाब लिखवाना है? सुन, पारो, चल राम बाबू के बाग़ में। मैंने देखा है वहाँ बुलबुल का बच्चा है, उसे पकड़के तुझे दूँगा।

کمسن دیوداس:
ہاں بابا کر دیا۔ کیا حساب لکھوانا ہے؟ سن، پارو۔ چل رام بابو کے باغ میں۔ میں نے دیکھا ہے، وہاں بلبل کا بچہ ہے، اُسے پکڑ کے تجھے دوں گا۔

बालिका पार्वतीः
चल।

کمسن پاروتی:
چل۔

पार्वती प्रसन्न है। दोनों भागते हुए आम के बाग़ में पहुँचते हैं। उन्हें पेड़ पर बैठी एक बुलबुल दिखाई देती है। पेड़ पर चढ़ने से पहले देवदास पार्वती को कुछ सिक्के देता है।

پاروتی خوش ہے۔ دوڑتے ہوئے دونوں آم کے باغ میں داخل ہوتے ہیں جہاں ایک درخت کی شاخ پر بیٹھی ہوئی بلبل دکھائی دیتی ہے۔ درخت پر چڑھنے سے پہلے دیوداس، پاروتی کو کچھ سکّے دیتا ہے۔

बाल देवदासः
पारो, यह तीन रुपए रख, हाँ।

کمسن دیوداس:
پارو، یہ تین روپے رکھ، ہاں۔

देवदास और पार्वती गाते हैं। स्वरः आशा भोंसले और ऊषा मंगेशकर।

آشا بھونسلے اور اوشا منگیشکر کی آواز میں دیوداس اور پاروتی۔

बाल देवदासः
ओ अलबेले पंछी तेरा दूर ठिकाना है

کمسن دیوداس:
او البیلے پنچھی تیرا دور ٹھکانا ہے

बालिका पार्वतीः
छोड़ी जो डाली इक बार वहाँ कब लौटके आना है

کمسن پاروتی:
چھوڑی جو ڈالی اک بار وہاں کب لوٹ کے آنا ہے

Young Devdas:
Sweet bird!

Panchhi!

Together:
O sweet bird, your home is far away
Never alighting on the same branch again when you fly away

O albele panchhi tera door thikaana hai
Chhodi jo daali ik baar wahaan kab laut ke aana hai

Young Parvati:
The blue sky is your swing…

Neel-gagan hai jhoola tera…

Young Devdas *(speaking):*
No, not swing, courtyard…

Arey arey jhoola nahin, aangan…

Young Parvati:
Oh! The blue sky is your courtyard, the rainbow is your lovely swing

O! Neel-gagan hai aangan tera dhanak hai tera jhoola

Young Devdas:
The rainbow is your lovely swing

Oho, dhanak hai tera jhoola

Young Parvati:
You glide joyfully on shimmering wings

Ujlay pankhon ki doli mein phirey tu phoola-phoola

Young Devdas:
Glide joyfully on shimmering wings

Doli mein phirey tu phoola-phoola

Young Parvati:
A graceful gait, shiny eyes, a picture of beauty

Chanchal chaal, nazar matwaali roop suhaana hai

Young Devdas:
Sweet bird!

Panchhi!

बाल देवदासः
पंछी!

साथः
ओ अलबेले पंछी तेरा दूर ठिकाना है
छोड़ी जो डाली इक बार वहाँ कब लौटके आना है

बालिका पार्वतीः
नील-गगन है झूला तेरा...

बाल देवदास *(बोलते हुए)*:
अरे अरे झूला नहीं, आँगन...

बालिका पार्वतीः
ओह! नील-गगन है आँगन तेरा धनक है तेरा झूला

बाल देवदासः
ओहो, धनक है तेरा झूला

बालिका पार्वतीः
उजले पंखों की डोली में फिरे तू फूला-फूला

बाल देवदासः
डोली में फिरे तू फूला-फूला

बालिका पार्वतीः
चंचल चाल, नज़र मतवाली, रूप सुहाना है

बाल देवदासः
पंछी!

کمسن دیوداس:
پنچھی!

پاروتی اور دیوداس:
او البیلے پنچھی تیرادور ٹھکانا ہے
چھوڑی جوڈالی اک بار وہاں کب لوٹ کے آنا ہے

کمسن پاروتی:
نیل گگن ہے جھولا تیرا۔۔۔

کمسن دیوداس (تحت میں):
ارے ارے جھولا نہیں، آنگن ۔۔۔

کمسن پاروتی:
اوہ! نیل گگن ہے آنگن تیرا دھنک ہے تیرا جھولا

کمسن دیوداس:
اوہو دھنک ہے تیرا جھولا

کمسن پاروتی:
اُجلے پنکھوں کی ڈولی میں پھرے تُو پھولا پھولا

کمسن دیوداس:
ڈولی میں پھرے تُو پھولا پھولا

کمسن پاروتی:
چنچل چال، نظر متوالی، روپ سہانا ہے

کمسن دیوداس:
پنچھی!

Together:
O sweet bird, your home is far away
Never alighting on the same branch again when you fly away

O albele panchhi tera door thikaana hai
Chhodi jo daali ik baar wahaan kab laut ke aana hai

Young Devdas:
Come down from the branch and hear our song

Is daali se neeche aa kar baat humaari sunn le

Young Parvati:
Sweet bird, come

Panchhi, aa

Young Devdas:
Our home is nearby, come with us and pick your seeds

Paas hi apna ghar hai chal kar daana-dunka chun le

Young Parvati:
Sweet bird, come

Panchhi, aa

Young Devdas:
You'll be our guest, we'll sing and laugh

Aaj tujhe mehmaan bana kar gaana-hasna hai

Young Parvati *(speaking):*
No! Laugh and sing

Nahin, nahin. Hasna-gaana hai

Young Devdas:
Sweet bird!

Panchhi!

Together:
O sweet bird, your home is far away
Never alighting on the same branch again when you fly away

O albele panchhi tera door thikaana hai
Chhodi jo daali ik baar wahaan kab laut ke aana hai

Young Devdas:
If you must depart, let us adorn you with flowers

Jaana hai toh aa hum tujhko phoolon sang saja den

Young Parvati:
Sweet bird, come

Panchhi, aa

Young Devdas:
Let us adorn your brow and tie bells to your feet

Maathe tilak laga den pairon mein jhaanjhan pehna den

Young Parvati:
Sweet bird, come

Panchhi, aa

साथः
ओ अलबेले पंछी तेरा दूर ठिकाना है
छोड़ी जो डाली इक बार वहाँ कब लौटके आना है

बाल देवदासः
इस डाली से नीचे आकर बात हमारी सुन ले

बालिका पार्वतीः
पंछी, आ

बाल देवदासः
पास ही अपना घर है चल कर दाना-दुनका चुन ले

बालिका पार्वतीः
पंछी, आ

बाल देवदासः
आज तुझे मेहमान बना कर गाना-हँसना है

बालिका पार्वती *(बोलते हुए):*
नहीं, नहीं। हँसना-गाना है

बाल देवदासः
पंछी!

साथः
ओ अलबेले पंछी तेरा दूर ठिकाना है
छोड़ी जो डाली इक बार वहाँ कब लौटके आना है

बाल देवदासः
जाना है तो आ हम तुझको फूलों संग सजा दें

बालिका पार्वतीः
पंछी, आ

बाल देवदासः
माथे तिलक लगा दें पैरों में झाँझन पहना दें

बालिका पार्वतीः
पंछी, आ

دیوداس اور پاروتی:
او البیلے پنچھی تیرا دور ٹھکانا ہے
چھوڑی جو ڈالی اک بار وہاں کب لوٹ کے آنا ہے

کمسن دیوداس:
اِس ڈالی سے نیچے آ کر بات ہماری سن لے

کمسن پاروتی:
پنچھی، آ

کمسن دیوداس:
پاس ہی اپنا گھر ہے چل کر دانہ دُنکا چن لے

کمسن پاروتی:
پنچھی، آ

کمسن دیوداس:
آج تجھے مہمان بنا کر گانا ہنسنا ہے

کمسن پاروتی (تحت میں):
نہیں، نہیں۔ ہنسنا گانا ہے

کمسن دیوداس:
پنچھی!

دیوداس اور پاروتی:
او البیلے پنچھی تیرا دور ٹھکانا ہے
چھوڑی جو ڈالی اک بار وہاں کب لوٹ کے آنا ہے

کمسن دیوداس:
جانا ہے تو آ ہم تجھ کو پھولوں سنگ سجا دیں

کمسن پاروتی:
پنچھی، آ

کمسن دیوداس:
ماتھے تلک لگا دیں، پیروں میں جھانجھن پہنا دیں

کمسن پاروتی:
پنچھی، آ

Young Devdas:
Then fly happily away wherever your fancy takes you

Phir tu khushi se jaana tujhko jahaan bhi jaana hai

Young Parvati:
Sweet bird!

Panchhi!

Together:
O sweet bird, your home is far away
Never alighting on the same branch again when you fly away
Sweet bird!
O sweet bird, your home is far away (3)

O albele panchhi tera door thikaana hai
Chhodi jo daali ik baar wahaan kab laut ke aana hai
Panchhi!
O albele panchhi tera door thikaana hai (3)

Devdas and Parvati skip away as the song ends. Fade out.

Reel Three

Dwijodas enters his father's sitting room. Narain is eating and his wife is sitting nearby.

Dwijodas:
Father, the fisherman Madhav came complaining. Devdas has torn his fishing net in the river. He's ruined it.

Pitaji, vo Madhav abhi rota-rota shikaayat le kar aaya hai. Machliyon ke liye jo jaal usne nadi mein lagaaya tha usay Devdas ne tod-phod kar barabar kar diya.

Narain *(to his wife)*:
Deva's pranks are just beyond the limit. I think we should send him to Calcutta to your brother Narendra.
(Parvati has just entered the house and overhears them)
If he stays here, he'll get utterly spoilt.

Deva ki sharaaraten ab hadd se ziyaada badhi ja rahi hain. Sochta hoon ki usay tumhaare bhai Narendra ke paas Kalkatte bhej doon.
Yahaan reh kar toh vo bilkul chaupat ho jaayega.

Harimati Devi:
He'll live in the city? At this young age?

Magar shaher aur is baali umar mein?

Dwijodas:
No, mother. Don't interfere. It's for his own good.

Nahin, ma, is maamaley mein rukaawat na daalo, ye sab usi ki bhalaayi ke liye toh hai.

Harimati Devi:
All right. Do what you think is best. I won't interfere.

Acha, jo tum log theek samjho vo karo. Main kisi baat mein dakhal nahin doongi.

बाल देवदासः
फिर तू खुशी से जाना तुझको जहाँ भी जाना है

बालिका पार्वतीः
पंछी!

साथः
ओ अलबेले पंछी तेरा दूर ठिकाना है
छोड़ी जो डाली इक बार वहाँ कब लौटके आना है
पंछी!
ओ अलबेले पंछी तेरा दूर ठिकाना है (३)

गाना समाप्त होते ही देवदास और पार्वती उछलते-कूदते एक ओर निकल जाते हैं। फ़ेड आउट।

रील तीन

द्विजोदास ज़मींदार की बैठक में प्रवेश करता है। नारायण कुछ खा रहा है, उसकी पत्नी भी पास में बैठी है।

द्विजोदासः
पिताजी, वह माधव अभी रोता-रोता शिकायत लेकर आया है। मछलियों के लिए जो जाल उसने नदी में लगाया था उसे देवदास ने तोड़-फोड़ कर बराबर कर दिया।

नारायण *(पत्नी से):*
देवा की शरारतें अब हद से ज़्यादा बढ़ी जा रही हैं। सोचता हूँ कि उसे तुम्हारे भाई नरेंद्र के पास कलकत्ते भेज दूँ।
(घर में प्रवेश करती हुई पार्वती उनकी बात सुन लेती है)
यहाँ रह कर तो वह बिल्कुल चौपट हो जाएगा।

हरिमति देवीः
मगर शहर और इस बाली उमर में?

द्विजोदासः
नहीं, माँ। इस मामले में रुकावट न डालो, यह सब उसी की भलाई के लिए तो है।

हरिमति देवीः
अच्छा, जो तुम लोग ठीक समझो वह करो। मैं किसी बात में दख़ल नहीं दूँगी।

کمسن دیوداس:
پھرتُو خوشی سے جانا تجھ کو جہاں بھی جانا ہے

کمسن پاروتی:
پنچھی!

دیوداس اور پاروتی:
او البیلے پنچھی تیرا دور ٹھکانا ہے
چھوڑی جو ڈالی اک بار وہاں کب لوٹ کے آنا ہے
پنچھی!
او البیلے پنچھی تیرا دور ٹھکانا ہے (۳)

گیت ختم ہوتے ہوتے پاروتی اور دیوداس اُچھلتے کودتے ایک طرف کو چلے جا رہے ہیں۔فیڈ آؤٹ۔

ریل تین

زمین دار کی بیٹھک میں دوبجوداس داخل ہوتا ہے۔نارائن کچھ کھا رہا ہے اور اُس کی بیوی پاس میں بیٹھی ہوئی ہے۔

دوبجوداس:
پتا جی، وہ مادھوابھی روتا روتا شکایت لے کر آیا ہے۔مچھلیوں کے لیے جو جال اُس نے ندی میں لگایا تھا اُسے دیوداس نے توڑ پھوڑ کر برابر کر دیا۔

نارائن (بیوی سے):
دیوا کی شرارتیں اب حد سے زیادہ بڑھی جا رہی ہیں۔سوچتا ہوں کہ اُسے تمہارے بھائی نریندر کے پاس کلکتے بھیج دوں۔
(پاروتی گھر میں داخل ہوتے ہوئے اُن کی باتیں سن لیتی ہے)
یہاں رہ کر تو وہ بالکل چوپٹ ہو جائے گا۔

ہری متی دیوی:
مگر شہر اور اِس بالی عمر میں؟

دوبجوداس:
نہیں، ماں، اِس معاملے میں رکاوٹ نہ ڈالو، یہ سب اُسی کی بھلائی کے لیے تو ہے۔

ہری متی دیوی:
اچھا، جو تم لوگ ٹھیک سمجھو وہ کرو۔میں کسی بات میں دخل نہیں دوں گی۔

   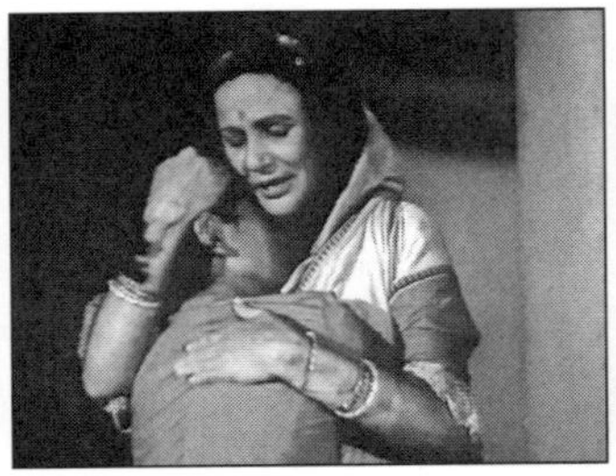 

Dissolve. Devdas is crying.

Young Devdas:
I won't go.

Nahin jaaunga.

Harimati Devi:
No, son. No crying.

Chhi, beta, rote nahin.

Young Devdas:
No, mother, I don't want to go to Calcutta.

Nahin, ma, main Kalkatta nahin jaaunga.

Harimati Devi:
It does not make me happy to see you go, son. We're sending you away so that you will study well. Come now, my child.

Tumhen bhej kar humen koi sukh nahin mil raha hai, beta. Lekin tum achi tarah padh-likh kar badho, isi liye bhejna pad raha hai. Chal, chal mera bachcha. Chal.

Devdas's mother tries to console the distraught Devdas. He is made to sit in the horse carriage waiting to take him to Calcutta.

Harimati Devi:
Sit in the carriage, son.

Ja, beta, gaadi mein baitho. Ja.

Dharamdas:
You shouldn't leave home with tears in your eyes. I am going with you. We'll be back in the holidays.

Jaate samay rote nahin, bhayya. Main bhi toh tumhaare saath hoon aur phir chhutti milegi, laut aayenge. Hein?

Young Devdas:
No, Dharamda, I don't want to go to Calcutta.

Nahin, Dharamda, main Kalkatta nahin jaaunga.

Dwijodas *(sternly):*
Of course you'll go. Come on.

Jaayega kaise nahin? Chal baith, chal.

(to the coach driver as he sits in the carriage)
Coachman, let's go.

Kochwaan, gaadi chalaao.

अगला दृश्य। देवदास रो रहा है।

बाल देवदासः
नहीं जाऊँगा।

हरिमति देवी:
छी: बेटा, रोते नहीं।

बाल देवदासः
नहीं, माँ, मैं कलकत्ता नहीं जाऊँगा।

हरिमति देवी:
तुम्हें भेज कर हमें कोई सुख नहीं मिल रहा है, बेटा। लेकिन तुम अच्छी तरह पढ़-लिख कर बढ़ो, इसीलिए भेजना पड़ रहा है। चल, चल मेरा बच्चा। चल।

ग़मगीन देवदास को माँ दिलासा देती है। उसे वहाँ खड़ी घोड़ागाड़ी में बिठा कर कलकत्ते ले जाने वाले हैं।

हरिमति देवी:
जा, बेटा, गाड़ी में बैठो। जा।

धरमदासः
जाते समय रोते नहीं, भैया। मैं भी तो तुम्हारे साथ हूँ और फिर छुट्टी मिलेगी, लौट आएँगे। हैं?

बाल देवदासः
नहीं, धरमदा, मैं कलकत्ता नहीं जाऊँगा।

द्विजोदास *(सख़्ती से):*
जाएगा कैसे नहीं? चल बैठ, चल।
(सवार होते हुए कोचवान से)
कोचवान, गाड़ी चलाओ।

اگلا منظر۔ دیوداس رو رہا ہے۔

کمسن دیوداس:
نہیں جاؤں گا۔

ہری متی دیوی:
چھی، بیٹا۔ روتے نہیں۔

کمسن دیوداس:
نہیں، ماں۔ میں کلکتہ نہیں جاؤں گا۔

ہری متی دیوی:
تمھیں بھیج کر ہمیں کوئی سکھ نہیں مل رہا ہے، بیٹا۔ لیکن تم اچھی طرح پڑھ لکھ کر بڑھو، اِسی لیے بھیجنا پڑ رہا ہے۔ چل۔ چل میرا بچہ۔ چل۔

غمگین دیوداس کی ماں اُسے منانے کی کوشش کر رہی ہے۔ دیوداس کو گھوڑا گاڑی میں بٹھا کر کلکتہ لے جانے والے ہیں۔

ہری متی دیوی:
جا، بیٹا۔ گاڑی میں بیٹھو، جا۔

دھرم داس:
جاتے سمے روتے نہیں، بھیا۔ میں بھی تو تمہارے ساتھ ہوں۔ اور پھر چھٹی ملے گی، لوٹ آئیں گے۔ ہیں؟

کمسن دیوداس:
نہیں، دھرم دا۔ میں کلکتہ نہیں جاؤں گا۔

دوبجوداس (سختی سے):
جائے گا کیسے نہیں؟ چل بیٹھ۔ چل۔
(سوار ہوتے ہوئے کوچوان سے)
کوچوان، گاڑی چلاؤ۔

Devdas's mother whispers his name under her breath as the coachman leaves with Devdas, Dwijodas and Dharamdas. Parvati is waiting near a tree on a village path. She sees Devdas in the carriage as it drives past. She calls out to him.

Young Parvati:
Devdas!

Devdas!

Young Devdas:
Paro, I'll be back as soon as the holidays start.

Paro, chhutti hote hi main waapas chala aaunga.

Devdas goes further and further away from Parvati. Cut to a tracking shot that pulls back from Parvati's forlorn face. She walks away. Fade out.

Fade in. Parvati sees two Vaishnava singers and their young child.

Young Parvati:
Vaishnavi, do you know any songs?

Eh, suno. Vaishnavi, tum gaana jaanti ho?

Female singer *(actress Dulaari):*
Of course we do, child.

Jaanti kyun nahin, beti?

Young Parvati:
Then sing.

Toh phir gaao na.

Male singer *(actor Nana Palsekar):*
We can't sing just like that. You must give us alms. Take us home. We'll sing there.

Gaana kya yunhi hota hai? Bhiksha deni hoti hai. Chalo tumhaare ghar chal ke gaayen.

Young Parvati:
No. Not there. Sing here.

Nahin nahin, wahaan nahin. Yahin gaao.

देवदास की माँ मन ही मन धीरे से उसे पुकारती है। कोचवान, द्विजोदास, धरमदास और देवदास को लेकर गाड़ी में रवाना होता है। गाँव के रास्ते पर पार्वती एक पेड़ के पास खड़ी है। देवदास को गाड़ी में जाते देख कर उसे पुकारती है।

बालिका पार्वतीः
देवदास!

बाल देवदासः
पारो, छुट्टी होते ही मैं वापस चला आऊँगा।

पार्वती से दूर जाता हुआ देवदास। कट। दुखी पार्वती का ट्रैकिंग शॉट जो पेड़ों के पास खड़ी देवदास को जाता देख रही है। पार्वती चली जाती है। फ़ेड आउट।

फ़ेड इन। पार्वती दो वैष्णव गानेवालों को देखती है। उनका छोटा बच्चा भी साथ में है।

बालिका पार्वतीः
ए, सुनो। वैष्णवी, तुम गाना जानती हो?

वैष्णवी *(अभिनेत्री दुलारी):*
जानती क्यों नहीं, बेटी?

बालिका पार्वतीः
तो फिर गाओ ना।

वैष्णव *(अभिनेता नाना पलसीकर):*
गाना क्या यूँ ही होता है? भिक्षा देनी होती है। चलो तुम्हारे घर चलके गाएँ।

बालिका पार्वतीः
नहीं नहीं, वहाँ नहीं। यहीं गाओ।

دھیرے سے دیوداس کی ماں اُسے پکار رہی ہے۔ کوچوان، دویجوداس اور دھرم داس کو دیوداس کے ساتھ لیے جا رہا ہے۔ گاؤں کے راستے میں، ایک درخت کے تنے سے لگی پاروتی کھڑی ہے۔ گھوڑا گاڑی میں جاتے ہوئے دیوداس کو دیکھ کر پاروتی اُسے آواز دیتی ہے۔

کمسن پاروتی:
دیوداس!

کمسن دیوداس:
پارو، چھٹی ہوتے ہی میں واپس چلا آؤں گا۔

پاروتی سے دور جاتا ہوا دیوداس۔ کٹ۔ پاروتی کے مایوس چہرے سے ہو کر دور جاتا ہوا ٹریکنگ شاٹ۔ پاروتی چلی جاتی ہے۔ فیڈ آؤٹ۔

فیڈ آؤٹ۔ پاروتی دیکھتی ہے کہ فقیرانہ طرز پر گیت گانے والے ویشنو سنگرز اور اُن کا چھوٹا سا بچہ چلے آ رہے ہیں۔

کمسن پاروتی:
اے، سنو۔ ویشنوی! تم گانا جانتی ہو؟

ویشنوی (اداکارہ، دلاری):
جانتی کیوں نہیں، بیٹی؟

کمسن پاروتی:
تو پھر گاؤ نا۔

ویشنو (اداکار، ناناپلسیکر):
گانا کیا یونہی ہوتا ہے؟ بھکشا دینی ہوتی ہے۔ چلو، تمہارے گھر چل کے گائیں۔

کمسن پاروتی:
نہیں، نہیں، وہاں نہیں۔ یہیں گاؤ۔

Female singer:
You'll have to give us money.

Paisa dena hoga.

Young Parvati:
Money? I don't have money. I have some rupees.

Paisa? Paisa toh nahin hai mere paas, rupay hain.

Male singer:
Rupees? Then come, child. We'll sing over there.

Rupay? Chalo, beta, udhar chal ke gaayen.

Geeta Dutt & Manna Dey sing.

Female singer:
Beloved Lord Krishna, appear before me (2)
Radha wanders alone and lost in Brij

Aan milo aan milo Shyam-saanwaare aan milo (2)
Brij mein akeli Radhe khoi-khoi phirey

Male singer:
Radha wanders lost, O Krishna, appear before me

O Radhe khoi-khoi phirey, o Kanha, aan milo

Together:
Beloved Lord Krishna, appear before me

Aan milo aan milo Shyam-saanwaare aan milo

Female singer:
Without You, the lanes of Brindavan are forlorn

Brindaban ki galiyan mein tum bin jiyaara na laage

Male singer:
So forlorn am I

O jiyaara na laage

Female singer:
My unfortunate eyes look for you

Nisdin tumhri baat nihaare biyaakul nain abhaage

Male singer:
My unfortunate eyes

O biyaakul nain abhaage

Female singer:
If my mind is so troubled now, what lies ahead?
Radha wanders alone and lost in Brij

Ab hi aisi dasha hai mann ki ka huwi hai phir aage re
Brij mein akeli Radhe khoi-khoi phirey

Male singer:
Radha wanders lost, O Krishna, appear before me

O Radhe khoi-khoi phirey, o Kanha, aan milo

वैष्णवी:
पैसा देना होगा।

बालिका पार्वती:
पैसा? पैसा तो नहीं है मेरे पास, रुपए हैं।

वैष्णव:
रुपए? चलो, बेटा, उधर चलके गाएँ।

वैष्णव गाते हैं। स्वर: गीता दत्त व मन्ना डे।

वैष्णवी:
आन मिलो आन मिलो श्याम-साँवरे आन मिलो (२)
ब्रज में अकेली राधे खोई-खोई फिरे

वैष्णव:
ओ राधे खोई-खोई फिरे, ओ कान्हा, आन मिलो

युगल:
आन मिलो आन मिलो श्याम-साँवरे आन मिलो

वैष्णवी:
बृन्दाबन की गलियन में तुम बिन जियारा न लागे

वैष्णव:
ओ जियारा न लागे

वैष्णवी:
निसदिन तुम्हरी बाट निहारे ब्याकुल नैन अभागे

वैष्णव:
ओ ब्याकुल नैन अभागे

वैष्णवी:
अब ही ऐसी दशा है मन की का हुई है फिर आगे रे
ब्रज में अकेली राधे खोई-खोई फिरे

वैष्णव:
ओ राधे खोई-खोई फिरे, ओ कान्हा, आन मिलो

ویشنوی:
پیسہ دینا ہوگا۔

کمسن پاروتی:
پیسہ؟ پیسہ تو نہیں ہے میرے پاس۔روپے ہیں۔

ویشنو:
روپے؟ چلو، بیٹا۔اُدھر چل کے گائیں۔

ویشنو گاتے ہیں۔آوازیں: گیتادت اور منّاڈے

ویشنوی:
آن ملو، آن ملو، شیام سانورے، آن ملو (۲)
برج میں اکیلی رادھے کھوئی کھوئی پھرے

ویشنو:
او، رادھے کھوئی کھوئی پھرے، او کانہا، آن ملو

دونوں:
آن ملو، آن ملو، شیام سانورے، آن ملو

ویشنوی:
بندرابن کی گلین میں تم بن جیارا نہ لاگے

ویشنو:
او جیارا نہ لاگے

ویشنوی:
نِسدن تمری باٹ نہارے ویاکل نین ابھاگے

ویشنو:
او ویاکل نینا ابھاگے

ویشنوی:
اب ہی ایسی دشا ہے من کی کا ہوئی ہے پھر آگے رے
برج میں اکیلی رادھے کھوئی کھوئی پھرے

ویشنو:
او رادھے کھوئی کھوئی پھرے۔او کانہا، آن ملو

Together:
Beloved Lord Krishna, appear before me

Aan milo aan milo Shyam-saanwaare aan milo

Female singer:
Lord, there is no word from You (2)

Ajhoon jo na bejhe Mohan taine koi khabariya (2)

Male singer:
No word from You

O taine koi khabariya

Female singer:
The weeping daughter of Brij is losing her mind

Ho jaiyhe ik Brij ki baala ro-ro kar baanwariya

Male singer:
Losing her mind

O ro-ro kar baanwariya

Female singer:
Console me
Console me, O playful beloved
Radha wanders alone and lost in Brij

Dheer bandha ja…
Dheer bandha ja mukh dikhla ja nat-naagar saanwariya re
Brij mein akeli Radhe khoi-khoi phirey

Male singer:
Radha wanders lost, O Krishna

O Radhe khoi-khoi phirey, o Kanha

Together:
Beloved Lord Krishna, appear before me

Aan milo aan milo Shyam-saanwaare aan milo

Parvati wipes away a tear from her eye as the song ends. She is sitting on a tree branch.

Young Parvati:
What a wonderful song. It has brought tears to my eyes.

Wah, kitna pyaara geet tha. Sunte-sunte aankhon mein aansu aa gaye.

युगलः
ओ आन मिलो आन मिलो श्याम-साँवरे आन मिलो

वैष्णवीः
अजहूँ जो ना भेजे मोहन तैने कोई खबरिया (२)

वैष्णवः
ओ तैने कोई खबरिया

वैष्णवीः
हो जइहे इक ब्रज की बाला रो-रो कर बावरिया

वैष्णवः
ओ रो-रो कर बावरिया

वैष्णवीः
धीर बँधा जा...
धीर बँधा जा मुख दिखला जा नट-नागर साँवरिया रे
ब्रज में अकेली राधे खोई-खोई फिरे

वैष्णवः
ओ राधे खोई-खोई फिरे, ओ कान्हा

युगलः
आन मिलो आन मिलो श्याम-साँवरे आन मिलो

गीत समाप्त होता है। पार्वती अपने आँसू पोंछती है। वह पेड़ की एक डाली पर बैठी हुई है।

बालिका पार्वतीः
वाह, कितना प्यारा गीत था। सुनते-सुनते आँखों में आँसू आ गए।

دونوں:
آن ملو،آن ملو،شیام سانورے،آن ملو

ویشنوی:
اجھوں جو نہ بھیجے موہن تَے نے کوئی خبریا (۲)

ویشنو:
او، تَے نے کوئی خبریا

ویشنوی:
ہو جیہے اک برج کی بالا رو رو کے باؤریا

ویشنو:
او رو رو کر باؤریا

ویشنوی:
دھیر بندھا جا۔۔۔
دھیر بندھا جا، مکھ دکھلا جا، نٹ ناگر سانوریا رے
برج میں اکیلی رادھے کھوئی کھوئی پھرے

ویشنو:
او رادھے کھوئی کھوئی پھرے۔ او کانہا!

دونوں:
آن ملو،آن ملو،شیام سانورے،آن ملو

گیت ختم ہوتا ہے۔ پاروتی آنکھ سے آنسو پونچھتی ہے۔ وہ ایک درخت کی شاخ پر بیٹھی ہوئی ہے۔

کمسن پاروتی:
واہ کتنا پیارا گیت تھا۔ سنتے سنتے آنکھوں میں آنسو آ گئے۔

Female singer:
Of course, it would. It's a sad song. One day Lord Krishna was nowhere to be found. Radha looked for Him everywhere, but could not find Him. Overcome with sadness, she sang this song.

Aansu kyun na aa jaayen, beti? Geet hi aisa hai. Ek din Shri Krishna alop ho gaye thay, jab bahot dhoondne pe bhi na miley toh Radha ne biyakul ho kar ye geet gaaya tha.

Young Parvati *(handing them the rupee coins):*
Here. One, two, three.

Ye lo. Ek, do, teen.

Male singer:
Three rupees? Who do they belong to?

Teen rupaiye? Kis ke hain?

Young Parvati:
Devdas.

Devdas ke.

Male singer:
Won't he hit you?

Vo tumhen maarenge nahin?

Young Parvati:
No. He has gone to Calcutta. Did you all get your share?

Nahin. Vo to Kalkatta chale gaye hain. Tum teenon ko theek-theek hissa mil gaya na?

Female singer:
Yes. You are a lucky child. We will pray to God that some day you'll marry a king and live as a queen.

Haan, beti, mil gaya. Tere haath bade daani hain. Hum aashirwaad karte hain Bhagwan tujhe kisi raja ki raani banaaye.

Male singer:
Let's go.

Chalo.

Dissolve to Parvati's house. Her mother is entering a room from the inner courtyard.

Young Parvati:
Mother, I'll go to school tomorrow. I don't like being alone.

Ma. Ma, main kal se phir paathshaala mein jaaya karungi. Mujhe akele mein kuch acha nahin lagta.

Parvati's mother:
Very well.

Theek hai, chali jaana.

वैष्णवीः
आँसू क्यों न आ जाएँ, बेटी? गीत ही ऐसा है। एक दिन श्रीकृष्ण अलोप हो गए थे जब बहुत ढूँढ़ने पे भी न मिले तो राधा ने व्याकुल हो कर यह गीत गाया था।

ویشنوی:
آنسو کیوں نہ آ جائیں بیٹی، گیت ہی ایسا ہے۔ ایک دن شری کرشن الوپ ہوگئے تھے۔ جب بہت ڈھونڈ نے پہ بھی نہ ملے تو رادھا نے بیاکل ہو کر یہ گیت گایا تھا۔

बालिका पार्वती *(उन्हें सिक्के देते हुए):*
यह लो। एक, दो, तीन।

کمسن پاروتی (سکّے دیتے ہوئے):
یہ لو۔ ایک، دو، تین۔

वैष्णवः
तीन रुपए? किसके हैं?

ویشنو:
تین روپے۔ کس کے ہیں؟

बालिका पार्वतीः
देवदास के।

کمسن پاروتی:
دیوداس کے۔

वैष्णवः
वह तुम्हें मारेंगे नहीं?

ویشنو:
وہ تمھیں ماریں گے نہیں؟

बालिका पार्वतीः
नहीं। वह तो कलकत्ता चले गए हैं। तुम तीनों को ठीक-ठीक हिस्सा मिल गया ना?

کمسن پاروتی:
نہیں۔ وہ تو کلکتے چلے گئے ہیں۔ تم تینوں کو ٹھیک ٹھیک حصہ مل گیا نا؟

वैष्णवीः
हाँ, बेटी, मिल गया। तेरे हाथ बड़े दानी हैं। हम आशीर्वाद करते हैं भगवान तुझे किसी राजा की रानी बनाए।

ویشنوی:
ہاں، بیٹی، مل گیا۔ تیرے ہاتھ بڑے دانی ہیں۔ ہم آشیرواد کرتے ہیں بھگوان تجھے کسی راجا کی رانی بنائے۔

वैष्णवः
चलो।

ویشنو:
چلو۔

वैष्णव चले जाते हैं। पार्वती के घर का दृश्य। उसकी माँ आँगन से कमरे में प्रवेश कर रही है।

ویشنو چلے جاتے ہیں۔ پاروتی کے گھر کا منظر۔ اُس کی ماں برآمدے سے ایک کمرے میں داخل ہو رہی ہے۔

बालिका पार्वतीः
माँ। माँ, मैं कल से फिर पाठशाला में जाया करूँगी। मुझे अकेले में कुछ अच्छा नहीं लगता।

کمسن پاروتی:
ماں۔ ماں، میں کل سے پھر پاٹھ شالا میں جایا کروں گی۔ مجھے اکیلے میں کچھ اچھا نہیں لگتا۔

पार्वती की माँः
ठीक है, चली जाना।

پاروتی کی ماں:
ٹھیک ہے، چلی جانا۔

(she stops and turns to her daughter)
Will you do something for me? Take the water pot and fetch some water.

Sunn, ek kaam toh kar. Ye ghada le ja aur taal se paani bhar la.

Young Parvati:
All right.

Acha.

Young Parvati climbs down the steps to the village pond. She fills the pot with water. A panning shot of the pond stops on a lotus bud. Dissolve. Time has passed. The lotus is now in full bloom. The action moves from childhood to adulthood. A slow panning shot back to Parvati's water pot. A tilt up reveals Parvati, now a beautiful young woman. Her friend Manorama arrives.

Manorama *(actress Kammo):*
Paro, did you hear? Your Devdas is back from Calcutta.

Arey Paro, kuch suna bhi? Tera Devdas Kalkatte se aaya hai.

Parvati *(actress Suchitra Sen):*
Who told you, Mano didi?

Tumhen kisne kaha, Mano didi?

Manorama:
The wind. I just saw him with my own eyes. A cane in his hand, a wrist watch, gold cuff-links, a chain — he's become the real gentleman. He used to come home every holiday, then for the last three years he started going to Nainital and Mussoorie. I wonder why he has come back to the village now. Maybe he has returned because he was missing you. Let's go.
(as they climb the steps, Parvati stops to look at a bird perched on a branch)
What are you looking at, Paro?

Hawa ne. Arey maine khud usay gaadi mein aate huey dekha hai. Haath mein chhadi, kalaayi mein ghadi, button, chain, poora babu saaheb ban gaya hai. Pehle toh har saal chhuttiyon mein gaaon aaya karta tha, phir do-teen saal se doston ke saath kabhi Nainitaal kabhi Mussoorie jaane laga, aur ab na jaane gaaon phir kyun aaya hai. Shaayad teri yaad kheench laayi. Chal.

Kya dekh rahi hai, Paro?

(रुकती है, बेटी की ओर मुड़ कर)
सुन, एक काम तो कर। यह घड़ा ले जा और ताल से पानी भर ला।

बालिका पार्वती:
अच्छा।

बालिका पार्वती तालाब की सीढ़ियाँ उतर रही है। वह पानी भरने आई है। कैमरा तालाब के पानी से होता हुआ एक कली पर आकर ठहरता है। अगला दृश्य। काल बदलता है। कली अब खिल कर कमल का फूल बन चुकी है। कैमरा लौट कर पार्वती की ओर आता है जो बाल अवस्था से युवा अवस्था के बीच का समय तय कर चुकी है। कैमरा सुन्दर और जवान पार्वती को दर्शाता है। उसकी सहेली मनोरमा वहाँ आती है।

मनोरमा *(अभिनेत्री कम्मो)*:
अरे पारो कुछ सुना भी? तेरा देवदास कलकत्ते से आया है।

पार्वती *(अभिनेत्री सुचित्रा सेन)*:
तुम्हें किसने कहा, मनो दीदी?

मनोरमा:
हवा ने। अरे मैंने खुद उसे गाड़ी में आते हुए देखा है। हाथ में छड़ी, कलाई में घड़ी, बटन, चेन, पूरा बाबू साहिब बन गया है। पहले तो हर साल छुट्टियों में गाँव आया करता था, फिर दो-तीन साल से दोस्तों के साथ कभी नैनीताल, कभी मसूरी जाने लगा, और अब न जाने गाँव फिर क्यों आया है। शायद तेरी याद खींच लाई। चल।
(दोनों तालाब की सीढ़ियाँ चढ़ती हैं। पार्वती रुक कर डाल पर बैठी हुई एक बुलबुल को देखती है)
क्या देख रही है, पारो?

(جاتے جاتے مڑ کر بیٹی سے کہتی ہے)
سن، ایک کام تو کر۔ یہ گھڑا لے جا اور تال سے پانی بھر لا۔

کمسن پاروتی:
اچھا۔

کمسن پاروتی پنگھٹ کی سیڑھیاں اُتر رہی ہے۔ وہ اپنا گھڑا بھرنے آئی ہے۔ کیمرا تالاب کے منظر سے ہوتا ہوا ایک کلی پر ٹھہرتا ہے۔ اگلا منظر۔ گزرتا ہوا وقت۔ کلی اب کھل کر کنول کا پھول بن چکی ہے۔ کیمرہ لوٹ کر پاروتی کی طرف آتا ہے جو بچپن سے جوانی کا سفر طے کر چکی ہے۔ کیمرے کے سامنے اب حسین اور نوجوان پاروتی گھڑا بھر رہی ہے۔ اُس کی سہیلی منورما وہاں آتی ہے۔

منورما (اداکارہ، کمو):
ارے پارو، کچھ سنا بھی؟ تیرا دیوداس کلکتے سے آیا ہے۔

پاروتی (اداکارہ، سچترا سین):
تمھیں کس نے کہا، منو دیدی؟

منورما:
ہوا نے۔ ارے میں نے خود اُسے گاڑی میں آتے ہوئے دیکھا ہے۔ ہاتھ میں چھڑی، کلائی میں گھڑی، بٹن، چین، پورا بابو صاحب بن گیا ہے۔ پہلے تو ہر سال چھٹیوں میں گاؤں آیا کرتا تھا، پھر دو تین سال سے دوستوں کے ساتھ کبھی نینی تال کبھی مسوری جانے لگا اور اب نہ جانے پھر کیوں گاؤں آیا ہے۔ شاید تیری یاد کھینچ لائی، چل۔
(پنگھٹ کی سیڑھیاں چڑھتے ہوئے پاروتی رک کر درخت کی شاخ پر بیٹھی بلبل کو دیکھنے لگتی ہے)
کیا دیکھ رہی ہے، پارو؟

Parvati:
Nothing.

Kuch nahin.

Dissolve to Parvati's house. She looks at herself in the mirror, wiping her face. Her excitement on hearing that Devdas is back is apparent. She goes to her grandmother who is sitting in the courtyard.

Parvati:
Grandma, braid my hair. Hurry.

Daadi, jhat se meri choti bana do.

Grandmother:
You mean now? It's hours before sunset.

Pagli huwi hai? Abhi saanjh honay mein toh bahot der hai, bitya.

Parvati:
So what? Please braid my hair, my lovely grandma.

Toh kya hua? Bana do na. Meri achi daadi, bana do.

Her grandmother braids Parvati's hair. Cut. From the doorway of her house, Parvati looks across the road towards Devdas's house. But there is no sign of him. Only the watchman is at the gate. Parvati goes back into the house and closes the door behind her.

Reel Four

Grandmother:
Daughter-in-law, I hear Devdas has returned from the city. He always comes to see us. Why didn't he come this time?

Bahu, suna hai Devdas shaher se aaya hai. Aage toh vo jab bhi aata, humen zaroor milta tha lekin aaj toh abhi tak nahin aaya.

Parvati's mother:
The city air has that kind of effect. It can change a man's temperament. Maybe Devdas has changed, too.

Shaher ki hawa hi aisi hoti hai. Aadmi rang badalta hai, dhang badalta hai. Shaayad Devdas bhi badal gaya hoga.

Devdas *(off-screen):*
Aunt!

Chaachi!

Parvati's mother:
That sounds like Devdas.

Ye toh Devdas ki aawaaz hai na?

पार्वती:
कुछ नहीं।

अगला दृश्य। पार्वती का घर। पार्वती दर्पण में अपना चेहरा देखती है। देवदास के गाँव आने की बात सुन कर वह बहुत प्रसन्न है। वह आँगन में बैठी अपनी दादी के पास जाती है।

पार्वती:
दादी, झट से मेरी चोटी बना दो।

दादीमाँ:
पगली हुई है? अभी साँझ होने में तो बहुत देर है, बिटिया।

पार्वती:
तो क्या हुआ? बना दो न। मेरी अच्छी दादी, बना दो।

दादीमाँ पार्वती की चोटी बना रही हैं। कट। घर के द्वार से वह सामने देवदास की हवेली की ओर देखती है। देवदास कहीं नहीं दिखाई देता है। केवल हवेली का चौकीदार फाटक पर है। पार्वती घर के अंदर आकर द्वार बंद कर लेती है।

रील चार

दादीमाँ:
बहू, सुना है देवदास शहर से आया है। आगे तो वह जब भी आता, हमें ज़रूर मिलता था लेकिन आज तो अभी तक नहीं आया।

पार्वती की माँ:
शहर की हवा ही ऐसी होती है। आदमी रंग बदलता है, ढंग बदलता है। शायद देवदास भी बदल गया होगा।

देवदास *(ऑफ़-स्क्रीन):*
चाची!

पार्वती की माँ:
यह तो देवदास की आवाज़ है ना?

پاروتی:
کچھ نہیں۔

اگلا منظر۔ پاروتی کا گھر۔ پاروتی آئینے میں اپنا چہرہ دیکھتی ہے۔ دیوداس کے لوٹ آنے کی خوشی اُس کے چہرے سے عیاں ہے۔ وہ برآمدے میں اپنی دادی کے پاس آتی ہے۔

پاروتی:
دادی، جھٹ سے میری چوٹی بنادو۔

دادی:
پگلی ہوئی ہے؟ ابھی سانجھ ہونے میں بہت دیر ہے، بٹیا۔

پاروتی:
تو کیا ہوا بنادو نا۔ میری اچھی دادی، بنادو۔

دادی اُس کی چوٹی بنا رہی ہے۔ کٹ۔ دہلیز کے پار دیوداس کے گھر کی طرف پاروتی تکے جارہی ہے لیکن دیوداس کہیں نظر نہیں آرہا ہے۔ صرف دربان کھڑا دکھائی دیتا ہے۔ پاروتی گھر میں آکر دروازہ بند کرلیتی ہے۔

ریل چار

دادی:
بہو، سنا ہے دیوداس شہر سے آیا ہے۔ آگے تو وہ جب بھی آتا، ہمیں ضرور ملتا تھا لیکن آج تو ابھی تک نہیں آیا۔

پاروتی کی ماں:
شہر کی ہوا ہی ایسی ہوتی ہے۔ آدمی رنگ بدلتا ہے، ڈھنگ بدلتا ہے۔ شاید دیوداس بھی بدل گیا ہوگا؟

دیوداس (آف اسکرین):
چاچی!

پاروتی کی ماں:
یہ تو دیوداس کی آواز ہے، نا؟

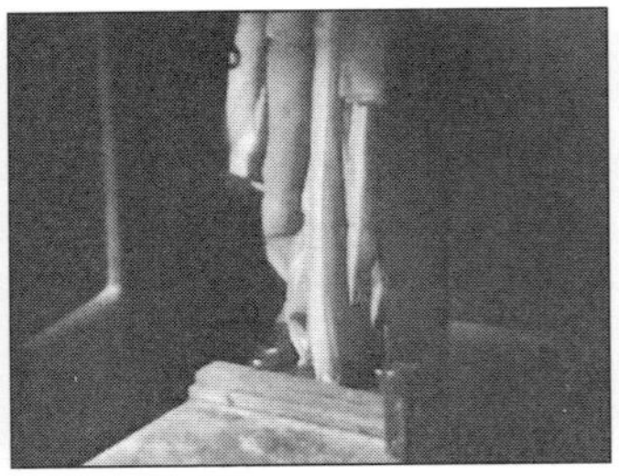

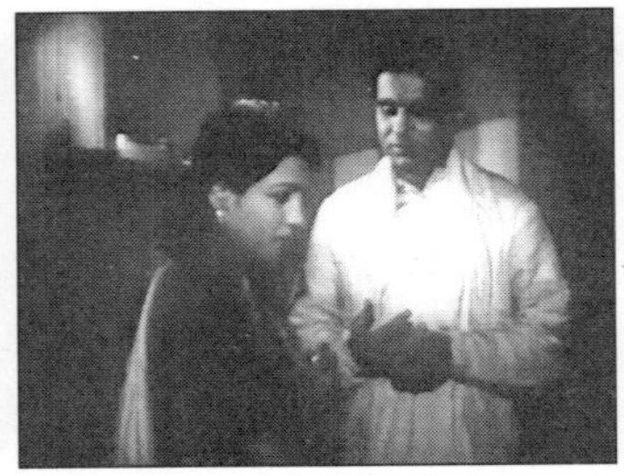

Grandmother:
Yes.

Haan.

Parvati's grandmother opens the door. The courtyard is dark. Devdas is standing outside the door. He is unseen.

Grandmother:
Devdas! You look so different. Come inside, son.
(Parvati rushes up to her room)
Bless you, son. You will live a long life. We were just talking about you.

Arey Devdas! Tumhaari toh shakal hi badal gayi. Aao, beta, andar aao.
Jeete raho, beta, badi umar hai. Abhi tumhaari hi baaten kar rahe thay.

Parvati's mother *(off-screen on shots of the smiling Parvati):*
You've changed so much, son.

Tumhaari toh shakal hi badal gayi, beta.

Devdas *(off-screen):*
You say that because you haven't seen me for a long time. Where is Paro?

Bahot dinon ke baad dekh rahi ho na, chaachi, isi liye. Paro kahaan hai?

Parvati's mother *(off-screen):*
Paro? She was right here. Maybe she's gone upstairs.

Paro? Arey abhi toh yahin thi. Shaayad upar chali gayi.

Grandmother *(off-screen):*
Paro! Look, Devdas is here.

Paro! Arey o Paro! Dekh Devdas aaya hai.

Devdas *(off-screen):*
Never mind, grandma. I'll go upstairs.

Rehne do, daadi. Main khud hi chala jaata hoon.

A nervous Parvati enters her unlit room. She hears Devdas's footsteps. Flustered, she hurriedly lights a lamp. Devdas stops at the door. He is still unseen.

दादीमाँ:
हाँ।

दादीमाँ द्वार खोलती है। आँगन में अंधेरा है। द्वार पर खड़ा देवदास दिखाई नहीं देता।

दादीमाँ:
अरे देवदास! तुम्हारी तो शक्ल ही बदल गई। आओ, बेटा, अंदर आओ।
(पार्वती ऊपर अपने कमरे में भाग जाती है)
जीते रहो, बेटा, बड़ी उमर है। अभी तुम्हारी ही बातें कर रहे थे।

पार्वती की माँ *(ऑफ़-स्क्रीन, मुस्कुराती पार्वती का शॉट):*
तुम्हारी तो शक्ल ही बदल गई, बेटा।

देवदास *(ऑफ़-स्क्रीन):*
बहुत दिनों के बाद देख रही हो ना, चाची, इसीलिए। पारो कहाँ है?

पार्वती की माँ *(ऑफ़-स्क्रीन):*
पारो? अरे अभी तो यहीं थी। शायद ऊपर चली गई।

दादीमाँ *(ऑफ़-स्क्रीन):*
पारो! अरे ओ पारो! देख, देवदास आया है।

देवदास *(ऑफ़-स्क्रीन):*
रहने दो, दादी। मैं ख़ुद ही चला जाता हूँ।

घबराई पार्वती अंधेरे कमरे में आती है। उसे सीढ़ियाँ चढ़ रहे देवदास के पैरों की आहट सुनाई देती है। गड़बड़ाकर जल्दी से एक दिया जलाती है। देवदास द्वार पर आकर रुकता है। वह अब भी नज़र नहीं आ रहा है।

دادی:
ہاں۔

پاروتی کی دادی دروازہ کھولتی ہے۔ آنگن میں اندھیرا ہے جس کی وجہ سے دہلیز پر کھڑا دیوداس دکھائی نہیں دے رہا ہے۔

دادی:
ارے دیوداس، تمہاری تو شکل ہی بدل گئی۔ آؤ، بیٹا، اندر آؤ۔
(پاروتی دوڑ کر اوپر اپنے کمرے میں چلی جاتی ہے)
جیتے رہو، بیٹا۔ بڑی عمر ہے۔ ابھی تمہاری ہی باتیں کر رہے تھے۔

پاروتی کی ماں (آف اسکرین، مسکراتی پاروتی کا شاٹ):
تمہاری تو شکل ہی بدل گئی، بیٹا۔

دیوداس (آف اسکرین):
بہت دنوں کے بعد دیکھ رہی ہو نا، چاچی، اِسی لیے۔ پارو کہاں ہے؟

پاروتی کی ماں (آف اسکرین):
پارو؟ ارے ابھی تو یہیں تھی۔ شاید اوپر چلی گئی۔

دادی (آف اسکرین):
پارو، ارے او پارو! دیکھ دیوداس آیا ہے۔

دیوداس (آف اسکرین):
رہنے دو، دادی۔ میں خود ہی چلا جاتا ہوں۔

گھبرائی ہوئی پاروتی اپنے اندھیرے کمرے میں داخل ہوتی ہے۔ سیڑھیاں چڑھ کر اوپر آتے ہوئے دیوداس کی آہٹ سنائی دے رہی ہے۔ گڑبڑا کر وہ جلدی سے ایک دِیا جلانے لگتی ہے۔ کمرے کی دہلیز پر آ کر دیوداس ٹھہر جاتا ہے۔ اب بھی اُس کا چہرہ دکھائی نہیں دے رہا ہے۔

Devdas *(actor Dilip Kumar, off-screen):*
Paro.
(Devdas comes into view, underscored by the sound of a conch)
It's you! What's going on? How you've grown.
(she shyly turns away from him)
Well, it's late. I had better go.

Paro.

Tum, kya ho raha hai? Hmm. Kitni badi ho gayi ho tum.

Acha, raat ho gayi hai. Main chalunga.

Devdas does not wait for Parvati to speak. He turns and leaves, as suddenly as he came. Parvati's grandmother is in the courtyard.

Grandmother:
What's this? You only just arrived.

Arey ye kya? Abhi aaye aur abhi chal diye?

Devdas:
The journey was tiring, thakurma. I'll come tomorrow.

Safar se aaya hoon na, thakurma. Thak gaya hoon. Kal aaunga.

Grandmother:
Very well, son.

Acha beta.

Parvati's mother *(returning to the courtyard):*
Has Devdas gone?

Chala gaya Devdas?

Grandmother:
Yes, daughter-in-law. Devdas and Paro are so close.

Haan, bahu. Acha Devdas aur Paro mein kitna sneh hai.

Parvati's mother:
It's only natural. They grew up together.

Kyun na ho? Bachpan se donon saath bade huwe hain.

Grandmother:
Paro is of age to marry. They'd make a fine couple. What do you say if we talk to Narain babu about their marriage?

Ab Paro ki umar bhi shaadi ki ho gayi. Donon ki jodi kitni achi banegi. Narain babu ke yahaan unke biyaah ki baat chalaayi jaaye toh kaisi rahe?

Parvati's mother:
What are you saying, maaji? You're reaching for the stars. They are high-caste Brahmins and rich landlords.

Kaisi baat karti ho, maaji? Tum bhi aasmaan mein thigli lagaati ho. Vo badi zaat-zamindari ke log.

देवदास *(अभिनेता दिलीप कुमार, ऑफ़-स्क्रीन):*
पारो।
(अब देवदास सामने आता हैं। पार्श्व में शंख की आवाज़)
तुम। क्या हो रहा है? हुँ। कितनी बड़ी हो गई हो तुम!
(शरमाते हुए वह घूमकर खड़ी हो जाती है)
अच्छा, रात हो गई है। मैं चलूँगा।

دیوداس (اداکار، دلیپ کمار) (آف اسکرین):
پارو۔
(دیوداس سامنے آتا ہے۔ شنکھ کی آواز)
تم، کیا ہو رہا ہے؟ ہوں، کتنی بڑی ہو گئی ہو تم۔
(شرماتے ہوئے وہ گھوم کر کھڑی ہو جاتی ہے)
اچھا، رات ہو گئی ہے۔ میں چلوں گا۔

देवदास पार्वती का उत्तर सुने बिना तुरंत वहाँ से चला जाता है। दादीमाँ उसे आँगन में मिलती है।

پاروتی کے جواب کا انتظار کیے بغیر دیوداس جیسے اچانک اُس کے سامنے آیا تھا، ویسے ہی لوٹ جاتا ہے۔ پاروتی کی دادی اُسے آنگن میں ملتی ہے۔

दादीमाँ:
अरे यह क्या? अभी आए और अभी चल दिए?

دادی:
ارے، یہ کیا؟ ابھی آئے اور ابھی چل دیے؟

देवदास:
सफ़र से आया हूँ ना, ठाकुरमाँ। थक गया हूँ। कल आऊँगा।

دیوداس:
سفر سے آیا ہوں نا، ٹھاکر ماں۔ تھک گیا ہوں۔ کل آؤں گا۔

दादीमाँ:
अच्छा बेटा।

دادی:
اچھا، بیٹا۔

पार्वती की माँ *(आँगन में लौटते हुए):*
चला गया देवदास?

پاروتی کی ماں (آنگن میں لوٹتے ہوئے):
چلا گیا دیوداس؟

दादीमाँ:
हाँ, बहू। अच्छा देवदास और पारो में कितना स्नेह है।

دادی:
ہاں، بہو۔ اچھا، دیوداس اور پارو میں کتنا سنیہہ ہے۔

पार्वती की माँ:
क्यों न हो? बचपन से दोनों साथ बड़े हुए हैं।

پاروتی کی ماں:
کیوں نہ ہو؟ بچپن سے دونوں ساتھ بڑے ہوئے ہیں۔

दादीमाँ:
अब पारो की उमर भी शादी की हो गई। दोनों की जोड़ी कितनी अच्छी बनेगी। नारायण बाबू के यहाँ उनके ब्याह की बात चलाई जाए तो कैसी रहे?

دادی:
اب پارو کی عمر بھی شادی کی ہو گئی۔ دونوں کی جوڑی کتنی اچھی بنے گی۔ نارائن بابو کے یہاں اُن کے بیاہ کی بات چلائی جائے تو کیسی رہے؟

पार्वती की माँ:
कैसी बात करती हो, माँजी? तुम भी आसमान में थिगली लगाती हो। वह बड़ी ज़ात-ज़मींदारी के लोग।

پاروتی کی ماں:
کیسی بات کرتی ہو، ماں جی؟ تم بھی آسمان میں تھگلی لگاتی ہو۔ وہ بڑی ذات زمینداری کے لوگ۔

Grandmother:
That may be so, but Paro is a great beauty. Her beauty could blind the eye. I'll speak to Devdas's mother. Let's see how she can refuse.

Zaat-zamindari badi hai toh sundarta bhi kam nahin. Aankh pade maili hoti hai apni Paro. Main zaroor Devdas ki ma ke paas jaaungi. Dekhungi vo kaise na kehti hain.

Fade out.

Fade in. Devdas's home. Dwijodas's wife comes into the room where her father-in-law is sitting on the bed, smoking a hookah. Her face is covered. She leaves something on the table as Devdas's mother enters.

Harimati Devi:
Daughter-in-law, just see if I have left the storeroom unlocked.
(to her husband)
Paro's grandmother came today to talk of Paro's marriage.

Bahu, dekhna toh main shaayad bhandaar-ghar khula hi chhod aayi hoon.
Main kehti hoon ji, aaj Parvati ki daadi ne uske biyaah ki baat chalaayi thi.

Narain:
Yes, she is of age to marry. She should get married.

Haan vo siyaani ho gayi hai. Uska biyaah toh ho jaana chaahiye.

Harimati Devi:
That's what she thinks too. Her grandmother asked me what if Devdas...

Tabhi toh usne baat chhedi thi. Kaha ki agar Devdas ke saath...

Narain *(sitting up, irritated):*
What did you say?

Phir tumne kya kaha?

Harimati Devi *(meekly):*
Me? I said no at once.

Maine? Maine wahin na keh diya.

Narain:
Good. They are Brahmins like us, but of lower-caste, and our neighbours. Don't pay any attention to their talk.

Theek kiya tumne. Ek toh hum se chhoti zaat ke Brahmin, doosre pados mein samdhiyaana. Tum unki baaton par kaan na dharna.

Cut. The next scene. Exterior. Day. Devdas comes out of his grand house. He picks a mango from the tree opposite Parvati's home and throws it onto the tin roof. She hears the sound and looks over the terrace to see

दादीमाँ:
ज़ात-ज़मींदारी बड़ी है तो सुंदरता भी कम नहीं। आँख पड़े मैली होती है अपनी पारो। मैं ज़रूर देवदास की माँ के पास जाऊँगी। देखूँगी वह कैसे ना कहती हैं।

फ़ेड आउट।

फ़ेड इन। देवदास का घर। द्विजोदास की पत्नी कमरे में आती है, जहाँ उसका ससुर बिस्तर पर बैठा हुक़्क़ा पी रहा है। द्विजोदास की पत्नी ने घूँघट निकाल रखा है। वह मेज़ पर कुछ रखती है। उसी समय देवदास की माँ कमरे में आती है।

हरिमति देवी:
बहू, देखना तो मैं शायद भंडारघर खुला ही छोड़ आई हूँ।
(अपने पति से)
मैं कहती हूँ जी, आज पार्वती की दादी ने उसके ब्याह की बात चलाई थी।

नारायण:
हाँ वह सयानी हो गई है। उसका ब्याह तो हो जाना चाहिए।

हरिमति देवी:
तभी तो उसने बात छेड़ी थी। कहा कि अगर देवदास के साथ...

नारायण *(उठ कर बैठते हुए, झुंझला कर):*
फिर तुमने क्या कहा?

हरिमति देवी *(सहम कर):*
मैंने? मैंने वहीं ना कह दिया।

नारायण:
ठीक किया तुमने। एक तो हमसे छोटी ज़ात के ब्राह्मण, दूसरे पड़ोस में समधियाना। तुम उनकी बातों पर कान ना धरना।

कट। बाहर का दृश्य। दिन। देवदास अपने बड़े घर से बाहर आता है। पार्वती के घर के बाहर लगे पेड़ से एक आम तोड़ कर उसकी छत पर फेंकता है। पार्वती आवाज़ सुन कर छज्जे से देखती है कि देवदास नीचे खड़ा है। वह तेज़ी से सीढ़ियाँ उतरती है,

دادی:
ذات زمینداری بڑی ہے تو سندرتا بھی کم نہیں۔ آنکھ پڑے میلی ہوتی ہے اپنی پارو۔ میں ضرور دیوداس کی ماں کے پاس جاؤں گی۔ دیکھوں گی وہ کیسے نا کہتی ہیں۔ فیڈ آؤٹ۔

فیڈ اِن۔ دیوداس کی حویلی۔ دویجوداس کی بیوی کمرے میں داخل ہوتی ہے جہاں اُس کا سسر بستر پر ٹکا حقہ پی رہا ہے۔ اُس نے گھونگھٹ نکال رکھا ہے۔ وہ میز پر کچھ رکھتی ہے۔ دیوداس کی ماں داخل ہوتی ہے۔

ہری متی دیوی:
بہو، دیکھنا تو میں شاید بھنڈار گھر کھلا ہی چھوڑ آئی ہوں۔
(اپنے شوہر سے)
میں کہتی ہوں جی، آج پاروتی کی دادی نے اُس کے بیاہ کی بات چلائی تھی۔

نارائن:
ہاں، وہ سیانی ہوگئی ہے۔ اُس کا بیاہ تو ہو جانا چاہیے۔

ہری متی دیوی:
تبھی تو اُس نے بات چھیڑی تھی۔ کہا کہ اگر دیوداس کے ساتھ۔۔۔

نارائن (چیں بہ جبیں ہو کر اُٹھ کر بیٹھ جاتا ہے):
پھر تم نے کیا کہا؟

ہری متی دیوی (سہم کر):
میں نے؟ میں نے وہیں نہ کہہ دیا۔

نارائن:
ٹھیک کیا تم نے۔ ایک تو ہم سے چھوٹی ذات کے برہمن۔ دوسرے پڑوس میں سمدھیانا۔ تم اُن کی باتوں پر کان نہ دھرنا۔

کٹ۔ بیرونی منظر۔ دن۔ حویلی سے نکل کر دیوداس باہر آتا ہے۔ پاروتی کے گھر کے باہر درخت سے ایک آم توڑ کر وہ اُس کی چھت پر اُچھال دیتا ہے۔ آواز سن کر پاروتی بام پر سے جھانک کر دیکھتی ہے کہ دیوداس نیچے کھڑا ہے۔ بچپن کی

Devdas standing below. She rushes down the stairs in much the same way she did as a young girl. Devdas smiles. She comes towards him. Her eyes are lowered.

Devdas:

Paro. Paro.	Paro. Paro.
(coming closer)	
Paro.	Paro.

Parvati is overcome by shyness. She looks up to see his face. Embarrassed, she turns to go back into her house and bumps into Manorama who is passing by.

Manorama:

You really have gone blind.	Arey tu toh sach-muchh andhi ho gayi.

As Parvati makes her way up the stairs to her room, her father enters the courtyard and talks to his mother. Parvati overhears their conversation.

Nilkanth *(angry):*

Who told you to go and talk of marriage to Devdas's mother? Why didn't you ask me first? So what if they are landlords or high-caste Brahmins. We may be lower-caste Brahmins, but we ask nothing of them. We don't need to beg for a suitor for Paro. On the contrary, many will beg us. So why worry?	Ma, kisne tumhen Parvati ki shaadi ki baat karne ke liye Devdas ki ma ke paas jaane ko kaha? Poocha kyun nahin mujh se? Bade aaye hain zamindar, oonchi zaat waale Brahmin, hum neechi zaat waale Brahmin hain toh unke ghar maangne nahin jaate. Ladki ka biyaah karne ke liye humen logon ke pair pakadne ki zaroorat na pade, ulta log hi humaare pair pakden. Tumhen fikr kis baat ki?

Grandmother:

Of course I worry, son.	Fikr toh hoti hai, beta.

जिस प्रकार वह बचपन में उतरा करती थी। देवदास उसे देख कर मुस्कुराता है। वह उसके निकट आती है, लज्जा से उसकी आँखें झुकी हुई हैं।

देवदासः
पारो। पारो!
(उसके और निकट आती है)
पारो।

पार्वती पर लज्जा छाती जा रही है। सर उठाकर वो उसकी ओर देखती है। अत्याधिक लजाई पार्वती गड़बड़ा कर अंदर जाते हुए सामने से आती मनोरमा से टकरा जाती है।

मनोरमाः
अरे तू तो सचमुच अंधी हो गई।

पार्वती अपने कमरे की ओर जा रही है, कि उसका पिता आँगन में आता है और अपनी माँ से कुछ कहता है। पार्वती उनकी बातें सुन लेती है।

नीलकंठ *(गुस्से से):*
माँ, किसने तुम्हें पार्वती की शादी की बात करने के लिए देवदास की माँ के पास जाने को कहा? पूछा क्यों नहीं मुझसे? बड़े आए हैं ज़मींदार, ऊँची ज़ात वाले ब्राह्मण, हम नीची ज़ात वाले ब्राह्मण हैं तो उनके घर माँगने नहीं जाते। लड़की का ब्याह करने के लिए हमें लोगों के पैर पकड़ने की ज़रूरत न पड़े, उल्टा लोग ही हमारे पैर पकड़ें। तुम्हें फ़िक्र किस बात की?

दादीमाँः
फ़िक्र तो होती है, बेटा।

طرح دوڑتی ہوئی پاروتی نیچے آتی ہے۔ دیوداس اُسے دیکھ کر مسکراتا ہے۔شرم سے نگاہیں نیچی کیے وہ اُس کی قریب آتی ہے۔

دیوداس:
پارو۔ پارو۔
(وہ اُس کے قریب آتی ہے)
پارو۔

پاروتی پر شرم غالب آتی جا رہی ہے۔ نگاہیں اُٹھا کر وہ اُسے دیکھتی ہے۔اور پھر گڑبڑا کر تیزی سے مڑتے ہوئے اپنے گھر میں داخل ہونے کی کوشش میں سامنے سے آتی منورما سے ٹکرا جاتی ہے۔

منورما:
ارے تُو تو سچ مچ اندھی ہوگئی۔

پاروتی اپنے کمرے کی طرف جا رہی ہے کہ اُس کا باپ آنگن میں داخل ہوتا ہے اور اپنی ماں سے کچھ کہنے لگتا ہے۔ پاروتی کے کان اُن کی باتوں کی طرف لگے ہوئے ہیں۔

نیل کنٹھ (غصے میں بھرا ہوا):
ماں، کس نے تمھیں پاروتی کی شادی کی بات کرنے کے لیے دیوداس کی ماں کے پاس جانے کو کہا؟ پوچھا کیوں نہیں مجھ سے؟ بڑے آئے ہیں زمیندار۔ اونچی ذات والے برہمن، ہم نیچی ذات والے برہمن ہیں تو اُن کے گھر مانگنے نہیں جاتے۔ لڑکی کا بیاہ کرنے کے لیے ہمیں لوگوں کے پیر پکڑنے کی ضرورت نہ پڑے۔ اُلٹا لوگ ہی ہمارے پیر پکڑیں۔ تمھیں فکر کس بات کی؟

دادی:
فکر تو ہوتی ہے، بیٹا۔

Nilkanth:
Not that again. You think no one has proposed? We have six proposals already. If I don't marry her to a landlord who is richer than Narain, then my name isn't Nilkanth. Her marriage will be settled within the week. The suitor does not live very far. In fact, I'll go and see him straightaway.

Phir wahi baat? Tum samajhti ho koi humen poochta nahin. Ek chhod chhe-chhe sandeshey aa chuke hain, Narain babu se bhi bade zamindar ke yahaan beti ki shaadi na ki toh Nilkanth na kehna. Main ek hafte ke andar-andar sab theek kiye deta hoon. Naai gaaon mein hi rehta hai kahin door nahin. Balki main abhi chalta hoon.

A tracking shot to Parvati who is still standing on the stairs to her room. She has a worried expression. Dissolve to the next day.

Parvati is sitting silently on her bed. She hears the sound of gunfire. She opens the window as Devdas walks by with a shotgun in his hand. It is later established through dialogue that he goes bird hunting. Parvati takes the water pot and starts to hurry out of the house.

Parvati's mother:
Paro, where are you going?

Paro, kahaan ja rahi hai?

Parvati:
To fetch water, mother.

Paani laane, ma.

Parvati's mother:
Paro, pass me the chillies on your way out.

Baahar dhoop mein mirchen sookh rahi hain, zara deti ja.

Parvati goes towards the pond looking for Devdas. A villager approaches her just as she is about to call out to Devdas who is near the pond in the distance.

Village woman *(unidentified actress):*
Paro, why have you stopped here?

Kyun, Paro, yahaan kyun ruk gayi ho?

Parvati:
No reason.

Aise hi.

Embarrassed by the villager's probing, Parvati leaves. Dissolve to the terrace of Parvati's house. Manorama is braiding Parvati's hair.

नीलकंठ:
फिर वही बात? तुम समझती हो कोई हमें पूछता नहीं। एक छोड़ छ:-छ: संदेशे आ चुके हैं। नारायण बाबू से भी बड़े ज़मींदार के यहाँ बेटी की शादी न की तो नीलकंठ न कहना। मैं एक हफ़्ते के अंदर-अंदर सब ठीक किए देता हूँ। नाई गाँव में ही रहता है, कहीं दूर नहीं। बल्कि मैं अभी चलता हूँ।

نیل کنٹھ:
پھر وہی بات؟ تم سمجھتی ہو کوئی ہمیں پوچھتا نہیں۔ ایک چھوڑ چھ چھ سندیشے آچکے ہیں۔ نارائن بابو سے بھی بڑے زمیندار کے یہاں بیٹی کی شادی نہ کی تو نیل کنٹھ نہ کہنا۔ میں ایک ہفتے کے اندر اندر سب ٹھیک کیے دیتا ہوں۔ نائی گاؤں میں ہی رہتا ہے، کہیں دور نہیں۔ بلکہ میں ابھی چلتا ہوں۔

पार्वती का ट्रैकिंग शॉट जो अभी तक अपने कमरे की सीढ़ियों पर खड़ी है। वह बहुत चिंतित है। डिज़ॉल्व। अगला दिन।

اپنے کمرے کی دہلیز پر کھڑی پاروتی کا ٹریکنگ شاٹ۔ وہ پریشان دکھائی دے رہی ہے۔ ڈزالو۔ اگلا دن۔

पार्वती अपने बिस्तर पर मौन बैठी है। वह गोली चलने की आवाज़ सुनती है। खिड़की खोल कर देखती है देवदास बंदूक़ लिए जा रहा है। बाद में आने वाले संवाद से यह बात स्पष्ट होती है कि वह कभी-कभी चिड़ियों का शिकार किया करता है। पार्वती पानी का घड़ा लेकर जल्दी से घर के बाहर निकलती है।

پاروتی اپنے بستر پر خاموش بیٹھی ہوئی ہے۔ گولی چلنے کی آواز اُس کے کانوں میں آتی ہے۔ کھڑکی سے جھانک کر وہ دیکھتی ہے کہ دیوداس ہاتھ میں بندوق لیے چلا جا رہا ہے۔ بعد کے مکالموں سے اندازہ ہوتا ہے کہ دیوداس کبھی کبھار چڑیوں کا شکار کیا کرتا ہے۔ پاروتی جلدی سے پانی کا گھڑا اُٹھا کر گھر سے باہر چل دیتی ہے۔

पार्वती की माँ:
पारो, कहाँ जा रही है?

پاروتی کی ماں:
پارو، کہاں جا رہی ہے؟

पार्वती:
पानी लाने, माँ।

پاروتی:
پانی لانے، ماں۔

पार्वती की माँ:
बाहर धूप में मिर्चें सूख रही हैं, ज़रा देती जा।

پاروتی کی ماں:
باہر دھوپ میں مرچیں سوکھ رہی ہیں، ذرا دیتی جا۔

पार्वती तालाब पर आ कर देवदास को खोजती है। दूर से देवदास को देख कर वह उसे पुकारना चाहती है लेकिन गाँव की एक महिला को निकट आते देख कर वह चुप हो जाती है।

پاروتی کی نظریں تالاب کنارے پہنچ کر دیوداس کو تلاش کر رہی ہیں۔ دور سے دیوداس کو دیکھ کر وہ اُسے پکارنا چاہتی ہے لیکن ایک عورت کو پاس آتے دیکھ کر وہ چپ ہو جاتی ہے۔

गाँव की महिला *(कलाकार अज्ञात):*
क्यों, पारो, यहाँ क्यों रुक गई हो?

گاؤں کی ایک عورت (اداکارہ، نامعلوم):
کیوں، پارو، یہاں کیوں رک گئی ہو؟

पार्वती:
ऐसे ही।

پاروتی:
ایسے ہی۔

मौक़ा न मिलने के कारण पार्वती वहाँ से चली जाती है। अगला दृश्य। पार्वती के घर की छत। मनोरमा पार्वती के बाल बना रही है।

موقع سازگار نہ پاکر پاروتی چلی جاتی ہے۔ اگلا منظر۔ پاروتی کے گھر کی چھت۔ منورما بیٹھی پاروتی کے بال سنوار رہی ہے۔

   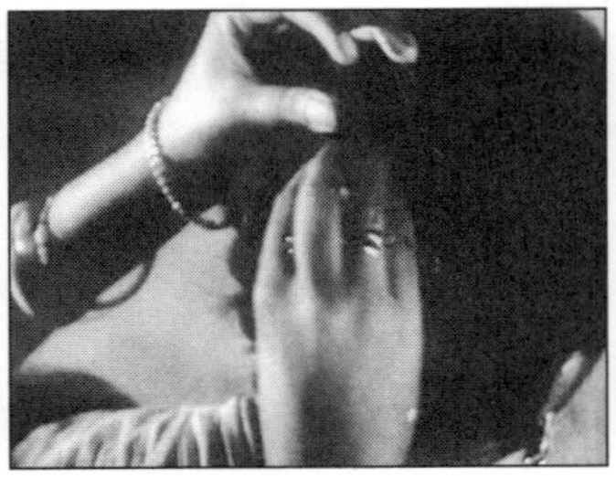 

Manorama: Paro, how old is the husband-to-be?	Acha, Paro, var ki umar kitni hogi?
Parvati: Whose husband?	Kis ke var ki?
Manorama: Yours, of course.	Tere var ki, aur kis ki?
Parvati: Twenty-three or twenty-four.	Koi taiyees-chaubees baras.
Manorama: What do you mean? I hear he is over forty.	Kya matlab? Maine toh suna hai uski umar chaalees se bhi oopar hai.
Parvati: Many suitors may be over forty, Mano didi. I don't keep count of them. All I know is that my husband-to-be is twenty-three or twenty-four.	Jaane kitnon ki umr chaalees hua karti hai, Mano didi. Main kya sab ka hisaab rakhti hoon? Main jaanti hoon toh bas itna, mere var ki umar taiyees-chaubees ki hogi.
Manorama: What is his name?	Aur naam kya hai?
Parvati: You know everything about me and you don't know that?	Arey mera khaaya-piya sab kuch jaanti hai aur ye nahin jaanti?
Manorama: How can I guess what's on your mind?	Tere mann ki baat main kaise jaanu?

मनोरमाः
अच्छा, पारो, वर की उमर कितनी होगी?

पार्वतीः
किसके वर की?

मनोरमाः
तेरे वर की, और किसकी?

पार्वतीः
कोई तेईस-चौबीस बरस।

मनोरमाः
क्या मतलब? मैंने तो सुना है, उसकी उमर चालीस से भी ऊपर है।

पार्वतीः
जाने कितनों की उमर चालीस हुआ करती है, मनो दीदी। मैं क्या सबका हिसाब रखती हूँ? मैं जानती हूँ तो बस इतना, मेरे वर की उमर तेईस-चौबीस की होगी।

मनोरमाः
और नाम क्या है?

पार्वतीः
अरे मेरा खाया-पिया सब कुछ जानती है और यह नहीं जानती?

मनोरमाः
तेरे मन की बात मैं कैसे जानूँ?

منورما:
اچھا، پارو، ور کی عمر کتنی ہوگی؟

پاروتی:
کس کے ور کی؟

منورما:
تیرے ور کی، اور کس کی؟

پاروتی:
کوئی تیئس چوبیس برس۔

منورما:
کیا مطلب؟ میں نے تو سنا ہے اُس کی عمر چالیس سے بھی اوپر ہے۔

پاروتی:
جانے کتنوں کی عمر چالیس ہوا کرتی ہے، منو دیدی۔ میں کیا سب کا حساب رکھتی ہوں؟ میں جانتی ہوں تو بس اِتنا، میرے ور کی عمر تیئس چوبیس کی ہوگی۔

منورما:
اور نام کیا ہے؟

پاروتی:
ارے میرا کھایا پیا سب کچھ جانتی ہے، اور یہ نہیں جانتی؟

منورما:
تیرے من کی بات میں کیسے جانوں؟

Parvati: Come closer. *(whispers in her ear)* Mr. Devdas.	Le sunn. Paas aa, aur paas. Shri Devdas.
Manorama: Shameless girl! Don't joke. Tell me, what's his name?	Hatt besharam! Zyaada hansi-mazaaq ki zaroorat nahin, bata seedhe-seedhe kya naam hai unka?
Parvati: I've told you.	Bata toh diya.
Manorama: But your grandmother said your marriage to the landlord of Manekpur has been settled.	Lekin maine daadi se suna hai ki tera biyaah Manekpur ke zamindar se pakka ho gaya.
Parvati: How can it be settled? I am the one marrying, not grandma.	Pakka kaise ho gaya hai? Biyaah hoga toh mere saath hi hoga. Daadi ke saath toh hoga nahin.
Manorama: Something is brewing without you knowing it. They have probably arranged the marriage in secret.	O! Maaloom hota hai andar hi andar koi khichdi pak gayi hai. Chhup-chhup ke pakka bandobast ho gaya.
Parvati: Nothing is arranged.	Kacha-pakka abhi toh kuch nahin hua hai.
Manorama: What are you talking about, Paro? I don't understand.	Tu kya kehti hai, Paro? Meri samajh mein toh kuch nahin aata.
Parvati: I'll ask Devdas. Then I'll tell you.	Toh phir Devdas se hi pooch kar batla dungi.
Manorama: What will you ask him? Whether or not he'll marry you?	Uss se kya poochegi, tujh se biyaah kare ya nahin?
Parvati: And why not?	Aur nahin toh kya?

पार्वतीः
ले सुन। पास आ, और पास।
(धीमे स्वर में उसके कान में कहती है)
श्री देवदास।

मनोरमाः
हट बेशरम! ज़्यादा हँसी-मज़ाक़ की ज़रूरत नहीं, बता सीधे-सीधे क्या नाम है उनका?

पार्वतीः
बता तो दिया।

मनोरमाः
लेकिन मैंने दादी से सुना है कि तेरा ब्याह मानेकपुर के ज़मींदार से पक्का हो गया।

पार्वतीः
पक्का कैसे हो गया है? ब्याह होगा तो मेरे साथ ही होगा। दादी के साथ तो होगा नहीं।

मनोरमाः
ओह! मालूम होता है अंदर ही अंदर कोई खिचड़ी पक गई है। छुप-छुपके पक्का बंदोबस्त हो गया।

पार्वतीः
कच्चा-पक्का अभी तो कुछ नहीं हुआ है।

मनोरमाः
तू क्या कहती है, पारो? मेरी समझ में तो कुछ नहीं आता।

पार्वतीः
तो फिर देवदास से ही पूछ कर बतला दूँगी।

मनोरमाः
उससे क्या पूछेगी, तुझसे ब्याह करे या नहीं?

पार्वतीः
और नहीं तो क्या?

پاروتی:
لے سن۔ پاس آ۔اور پاس۔
(سرگوشی میں)
شری دیوداس۔

منورما:
ہٹ بے شرم! زیادہ ہنسی مذاق کی ضرورت نہیں، بتا سیدھے سیدھے کیا نام ہے اُن کا؟

پاروتی:
بتا تو دیا۔

منورما:
لیکن میں نے دادی سے سنا ہے کہ تیرا بیاہ مانک پور کے زمیندار سے پکّا ہو گیا۔

پاروتی:
پکا کیسے ہو گیا ہے؟ بیاہ ہوگا تو میرے ہی ساتھ ہوگا۔ دادی کے ساتھ تو ہوگا نہیں۔

منورما:
اوہ! معلوم ہوتا ہے اندر ہی اندر کوئی کھچڑی پک گئی ہے۔ چھپ چھپ کے پکا بندوبست ہو گیا۔

پاروتی:
کچا پکا ابھی تو کچھ نہیں ہوا ہے۔

منورما:
تُو کیا کہتی ہے، پارو؟ میری سمجھ میں تو کچھ نہیں آتا۔

پاروتی:
تو پھر دیوداس سے ہی پوچھ کر بتلا دونگی۔

منورما:
اُس سے کیا پوچھے گی، تجھ سے بیاہ کرے یا نہیں؟

پاروتی:
اور نہیں تو کیا؟

Manorama:
Be sensible, silly girl. You mean you would ask him such a question? Won't you feel shame?

Kuch toh soch, murdi. Kya khud hi ye baat unse poochegi? Laaj na lagegi tujhe?

Parvati:
What's shameful about it? I wasn't ashamed to tell you.

Is mein laaj kaahe ki? Tumse kehne mein kya mujhe laaj aayi?

Manorama:
I am a woman and your friend. He's a man.

Main thehri aurat aur phir teri saheli lekin vo toh mard hain.

Parvati:
You are my friend and a woman, but he's hardly a stranger. Can't I tell him what I tell you? Mano didi, you're married, yet you don't know what a husband is. He is my husband. He comes before all shame and embarrassment. So why must I feel shame in front of him?

Tum saheli ho, aurat bhi ho, lekin vo kya paraaye hain? Jo baat main tumse keh sakti hoon kya unse nahin keh sakti? Mano didi, tum jhoot-moot hi maang mein sindoor lagaati ho aur ye nahin jaanti swami kisay kehte hain. Vo mere swami hain, meri lajja-sharam se parey. Unke paas meri lajja kaisi?

Parvati's mother *(off-screen):*
Manorama, someone is here from your house. They're calling you home.

Arey Manorama, tere ghar se koi bulaane aaya hai.

Manorama:
Paro, I'll come another time.

Acha, Paro, phir aaungi.

Manorama leaves. Dissolve. Night-time. Parvati gets out of bed and wrapping a shawl around her shoulders, she leaves her room.

Reel Five

From her terrace, Parvati can see the first floor of Devdas's house across the road. A light shines in his room. A dog barks in the distance. She silently enters Devdas's mansion. The watchman is singing a bhajan. He stops when he sees Parvati.

Watchman:
Who goes there?

Kaun?

Parvati:
It's me.

Main.

मनोरमाः
कुछ तो सोच, मुर्दी। क्या खुद ही यह बात उनसे पूछेगी? लाज न लगेगी तुझे?

पार्वतीः
इसमें लाज काहे की? तुमसे कहने में क्या मुझे लाज आई?

मनोरमाः
मैं ठहरी औरत और फिर तेरी सहेली लेकिन वह तो मर्द हैं।

पार्वतीः
तुम सहेली हो, औरत भी हो, लेकिन वह क्या पराए हैं? जो बात मैं तुमसे कह सकती हूँ क्या उनसे नहीं कह सकती? मनो दीदी, तुम झूठ-मूठ ही माँग में सिंदूर लगाती हो और यह नहीं जानतीं स्वामी किसे कहते हैं। वह मेरे स्वामी हैं, मेरी लज्जा-शर्म से परे। उनके पास मेरी लज्जा कैसी?

पार्वती की माँ *(ऑफ़-स्क्रीन):*
अरे मनोरमा, तेरे घर से कोई बुलाने आया है।

मनोरमाः
अच्छा, पारो, फिर आऊँगी।

मनोरमा जाती है। अगला दृश्य। रात का समय। पार्वती अपने बिस्तर से उठती है, एक शाल लपेट कर अपने कमरे से निकलती है। बाहर अंधेरा है।

रील पाँच

पार्वती अपने घर की छत से देखती है कि देवदास की हवेली के पहले माले की बत्ती जल रही है। दूर कोई कुत्ता भौंक रहा है। पारो देवदास की हवेली में चुपचाप प्रवेश करती है। दरबान भजन गा रहा है। वह पार्वती को आता देखता है।

दरबानः
कौन?

पार्वतीः
मैं।

منورما:
کچھ تو سوچ، مردی۔ کیا خود ہی یہ بات اُن سے پوچھے گی۔ لاج نہ آئے گی تجھے؟

پاروتی:
اِس میں لاج کاہے کی؟ تم سے کہنے میں کیا مجھے لاج آئی؟

منورما:
میں ٹھہری عورت اور پھر تیری سہیلی لیکن وہ تو مرد ہیں۔

پاروتی:
تم سہیلی ہو، عورت بھی ہو لیکن وہ کیا پرائے ہیں؟ جو بات میں تم سے کہہ سکتی ہوں کیا اُن سے نہیں کہہ سکتی؟ منو دیدی، تم جھوٹ موٹ ہی مانگ میں سیندور لگاتی ہو اور یہ نہیں جانتی سوامی کسے کہتے ہیں۔ وہ میرے سوامی ہیں۔ میری لجا شرم سے پرے۔ اُن کے پاس میری لجا کیسی؟

پاروتی کی ماں (آف اسکرین):
ارے منورما، تیرے گھر سے کوئی بلانے آیا ہے۔

منورما:
اچھا، پارو، پھر آؤنگی۔

منورما چلی جاتی ہے۔ اگلا منظر۔ رات۔ بستر سے اُٹھ کر پاروتی ایک شال سے خود کو لپیٹ کر اپنے کمرے سے باہر آتی ہے۔ باہر تاریکی چھائی ہوئی ہے۔

ریل پانچ

اپنی چھت پر کھڑی پاروتی دیکھتی ہے کہ دیوداس کی حویلی کی پہلی منزل پر کمرے میں روشنی ہے۔ دور کہیں ایک کتا بھونک رہا ہے۔ وہ دیوداس کی حویلی میں خاموشی داخل ہوتی ہے۔ بھجن گاتا ہوا دربان، پاروتی کو دیکھتا ہے۔

دربان:
کون؟

پاروتی:
میں۔

The watchman starts singing again. Parvati makes her way through the verandah of the house. She passes some servants who are asleep on the verandah floor.

Dissolve. She enters Devdas's room. The loud ticking of a clock can be heard. Devdas is asleep on a daybed. Parvati wakes him.

Devdas:	
Oh!	Arey!
(sitting up, surprised)	
Paro? You?	Paro, tum?
(he looks at the clock. It is 2:05 am)	
It's so late. You came alone?	Itni raat gaye akeli hi aayi ho kya?
Parvati:	
Yes.	Haan.
Devdas:	
What are you saying? Weren't you scared?	Kya keh rahi ho? Raaste mein darr bhi nahin laga?
Parvati:	
Ghosts don't frighten me.	Mujhe bhoot-voot se darr nahin lagta.
Devdas:	
Not ghosts, but surely men frighten you.	Arey bhoot se nahin par aadmi se toh darr lagta hai na?
Parvati:	
At this moment perhaps they don't either.	Shaayad is waqt uss se bhi nahin.
Devdas *(standing up):*	
How did you come inside? Did anyone see you?	Ghar ke andar kaise aayein? Kisi ne dekha?

दरबान फिर भजन गाने लगता है। पार्वती बरामदे से गुज़रती है, वहाँ कुछ सेवक सोए हुए हैं।

अगला दृश्य। वह देवदास के कमरे के अंदर जाती है। वहाँ एकदम सन्नाटा है सिवाय घड़ी की टिक-टिक के। देवदास दीवान पर सो रहा है। पार्वती उसे जगाती है।

देवदासः
अरे!
(उठ कर बैठते हुए, आश्चर्य से)
पारो, तुम?
(वह घड़ी की ओर देखता है। रात के २:०५ हुए हैं)
इतनी रात गए अकेली ही आई हो क्या?

पार्वतीः
हाँ।

देवदासः
क्या कह रही हो? रास्ते में डर भी नहीं लगा?

पार्वतीः
मुझे भूत-वूत से डर नहीं लगता।

देवदासः
अरे भूत से नहीं पर आदमी से तो डर लगता है ना?

पार्वतीः
शायद इस वक़्त उससे भी नहीं।

देवदास *(खड़े होते हुए)*:
घर के अंदर कैसे आई? किसी ने देखा?

دربان بھجن گانے میں لگا ہوا ہے۔ پاروتی برآمدے سے گزرتی ہے جہاں کچھ نوکر فرش پر سو رہے ہیں۔

اگلا منظر۔ وہ دیوداس کے کمرے میں داخل ہوتی ہے۔ گہرے سناٹے میں گھڑی کی ٹک ٹک سنائی دے رہی ہے۔ دیوداس دیوان پر دراز ہے۔ پاروتی اُسے جگا دیتی ہے۔

دیوداس:
ارے۔
(اُٹھ بیٹھتا ہے، حیرت سے)
پارو، تم؟
(گھڑی کی طرف دیکھتا ہے، رات کے ۲:۰۵ بجے ہیں)
اِتنی رات گئے اکیلی ہی آئی ہو کیا؟

پاروتی:
ہاں۔

دیوداس:
کیا کہہ رہی ہو؟ راستے میں ڈر بھی نہیں لگا؟

پاروتی:
مجھے بھوت ووت سے ڈر نہیں لگتا۔

دیوداس:
ارے بھوت سے نہیں پر آدمی سے تو ڈر لگتا ہے نا؟

پاروتی:
شاید اِس وقت اُس سے بھی نہیں۔

دیوداس (کھڑے ہوتے ہوئے):
گھر کے اندر کیسے آئیں؟ کسی نے دیکھا؟

Parvati:
The watchman.

Darbaan ne dekha tha.

Devdas:
The servants on the verandah must have seen, too.

Baraamde mein naukar-chaakar thay, unki bhi nazar padi hogi.

Parvati:
Maybe.

Shaayad padi ho.

Devdas:
Why did you do such a thing, Parvati? Won't your head hang in shame tomorrow?

Tumne aisa kyun kya, Parvati? Kal ko sharm se tumhaara sar neecha nahin hoga?

Parvati:
It would, but I know you will shield me from disgrace.

Zaroor hota agar main ye na jaanti ki meri saari lajja tum dhak loge.

Devdas:
Me? But how will I face them?

Main? Lekin main bhi kaise moonh dikhaaunga?

Parvati:
You face them? What harm will come to you? You're a man. Sooner or later any taint on you will be forgotten. No one will remember when, and on what night, the unfortunate Parvati sacrificed her all to lay herself at your feet.

Tum? Tumhaara kya hai? Tum thehre mard. Aaj nahin toh kal, kal nahin toh parson, tumhaare kalank ki baat log bhool jaayenge. Do din baad kisi ko is baat ka dhiyaan hi na reh jaayega ki kab, kis raat ko badnaseeb Parvati tumhaare charnon par sar rakhne ke liye apna sab kuch tuchh samajh kar yahaan aayi thi.

Devdas:
I was thinking of your dishonour, Paro.

Main…main tumhaare kalank ki baat soch raha tha, Paro.

Parvati:
My dishonour? I will not be dishonoured. If I am condemned for coming here in secret to you, so be it.

Mere kalank ki baat? Mujh par koi kalank nahin hai. Agar is baat ke liye meri ninda ho ki main tumhaare paas chhup kar aayi thi, toh ye ninda mujhe na lagegi.

Devdas:
Are you crying, Paro?

Arey tu ro rahi hai, Paro?

पार्वतीः
दरबान ने देखा था।

پاروتی:
دربان نے دیکھا تھا۔

देवदासः
बरामदे में नौकर-चाकर थे, उनकी भी नज़र पड़ी होगी।

دیوداس:
برآمدے میں نوکر چاکر تھے اُن کی بھی نظر پڑی ہوگی؟

पार्वतीः
शायद पड़ी हो।

پاروتی:
شاید پڑی ہو۔

देवदासः
तुमने ऐसा क्यों किया, पार्वती? कल को शर्म से तुम्हारा सर नीचा नहीं होगा?

دیوداس:
تم نے ایسا کیوں کیا، پاروتی؟ کل کو شرم سے تمہارا سر نیچا نہیں ہوگا؟

पार्वतीः
ज़रूर होता अगर मैं यह न जानती कि मेरी सारी लज्जा तुम ढँक लोगे।

پاروتی:
ضرور ہوتا اگر میں یہ نہ جانتی کہ میری ساری لجّا تم ڈھک لوگے۔

देवदासः
मैं? लेकिन मैं भी कैसे मुँह दिखाऊँगा?

دیوداس:
میں؟ لیکن میں بھی کیسے منہ دکھاؤں گا؟

पार्वतीः
तुम? तुम्हारा क्या है? तुम ठहरे मर्द। आज नहीं तो कल, कल नहीं तो परसों, तुम्हारे कलंक की बात लोग भूल जाएँगे। दो दिन बाद किसी को इस बात का ध्यान ही न रह जाएगा कि कब, किस रात को बदनसीब पार्वती तुम्हारे चरनों पर सर रखने के लिए अपना सब कुछ तुच्छ समझ कर यहाँ आई थी।

پاروتی:
تم؟ تمہارا کیا ہے؟ تم ٹھہرے مرد۔ آج نہیں تو کل، کل نہیں تو پرسوں، تمہارے کلنک کی بات لوگ بھول جائیں گے۔ دو دن کے بعد کسی کو اِس بات کا دھیان ہی نہ رہ جائے گا کہ کب، کس رات کو بدنصیب پاروتی تمہارے چرنوں پر سر رکھنے کے لیے اپنا سب کچھ تچھ سمجھ کر یہاں آئی تھی۔

देवदासः
मैं... मैं तुम्हारे कलंक की बात सोच रहा था, पारो।

دیوداس:
میں۔۔۔ میں تمہارے کلنک کی بات سوچ رہا تھا، پارو۔

पार्वतीः
मेरे कलंक की बात? मुझ पर कोई कलंक नहीं है। अगर इस बात के लिए मेरी निंदा हो कि मैं तुम्हारे पास छुप कर आई थी, तो यह निंदा मुझे न लगेगी।

پاروتی:
میرے کلنک کی بات؟ مجھ پر کوئی کلنک نہیں ہے اگر اِس بات کے لیے میری نِندا ہو کہ میں تمہارے پاس چھپ کر آئی تھی تو یہ نِندا مجھے نہ لگے گی۔

देवदासः
अरे तू रो रही है, पारो?

دیوداس:
ارے تُو رو رہی ہے، پارو؟

Parvati: There is so much water in the river. Will it not be enough to wash away my stigma?	Nadi mein kitna jal hai. Kya itne jal se bhi mera kalank na dhulega?
Devdas: You shouldn't talk like that. You know I'd do anything for you. But my parents oppose it. If I marry you against their wishes, where will that leave you?	Tumhen aisi baat nahin karni chaahiye. Main tumhaare liye sab kuch kar sakta hoon lekin...tum toh jaanti ho ki mere ma-baap is se bilkul sehmat nahin hain. Agar unki marzi ke khilaaf tumse shaadi kar loonga toh tum kahaan rahogi?
Parvati *(kneeling):* At your feet. Make a little room here for me, my lord.	Tumhaare charnon mein. Mujhe yahin thodi si jageh de do mere devta.
Dissolve. Parvati and Devdas are sitting quietly in Devdas's room. The clock chimes, suggesting it is almost daybreak.	
Devdas: Paro. Let me see you home.	Paro. Chalo tumhen ghar chhod aaun.
Parvati: Will you come with me?	Mere saath chaloge?
Devdas: What's wrong with that? If you can come here, why can't I go with you? There will be a scandal, right? That's good. It might give us a way out.	Kya harj hai? Agar tum aa sakti ho toh main nahin jaa sakta? Badnaami hogi na? Toh acha hai. Shaayad usi mein se hum donon ke liye koi raasta nikal aaye.
Parvati: So let's go.	Tabb chalo.

They leave the room. Fade out.

पार्वतीः
नदी में कितना जल है। क्या इतने जल से भी मेरा कलंक न धुलेगा?

देवदासः
तुम्हें ऐसी बात नहीं करनी चाहिए। मैं तुम्हारे लिए सब कुछ कर सकता हूँ लेकिन...तुम तो जानती हो कि मेरे माँ-बाप इससे बिल्कुल सहमत नहीं हैं। अगर उनकी मरज़ी के ख़िलाफ़ तुमसे शादी कर लूँगा तो तुम कहाँ रहोगी?

पार्वती *(उसके आगे झुकते हुए):*
तुम्हारे चरनों में। मुझे यहीं थोड़ी-सी जगह दे दो मेरे देवता।

अगला दृश्य। पार्वती और देवदास ख़ामोश बैठे हैं। घड़ियाल के घंटे बजते हैं, सवेरा होने को है।

देवदासः
पारो, चलो तुम्हें घर छोड़ आऊँ।

पार्वतीः
मेरे साथ चलोगे?

देवदासः
क्या हर्ज है? अगर तुम आ सकती हो तो मैं नहीं जा सकता? बदनामी होगी ना? तो अच्छा है। शायद उसी में से हम दोनों के लिए कोई रास्ता निकल आए।

पार्वतीः
तब चलो।

वे कमरे से बाहर आते हैं। फ़ेड आउट।

پاروتی:
ندی میں کتنا جل ہے۔کیا اِتنے جل سے بھی میرا کلنک نہ دھلے گا؟

دیوداس:
تمھیں ایسی بات نہیں کرنی چاہیے۔ میں تمہارے لیے سب کچھ کر سکتا ہوں، لیکن۔۔۔تم تو جانتی ہو کہ میرے ماں باپ اِس سے بالکل سہمت نہیں ہیں اگر اُن کی مرضی کے خلاف تم سے شادی کرلوں گا تو تم کہاں رہوگی؟

پاروتی (اُس کے سامنے جھکتے ہوئے):
تمہارے چرنوں میں ۔ مجھے یہیں تھوڑی سی جگہ دے دو میرے، دیوتا۔

اگلا منظر۔ پاروتی اور دیوداس خاموش بیٹھے ہیں۔گھڑی کے گجر سے معلوم ہوتا ہے کہ صبح ہونے کو ہے۔

دیوداس:
پارو۔ چلو تمھیں گھر چھوڑ آؤں۔

پاروتی:
میرے ساتھ چلو گے؟

دیوداس:
کیا حرج ہے؟ اگر تم آسکتی ہو تو میں نہیں جا سکتا؟ بدنامی ہوگی نا؟ تو اچھا ہے، شاید اُسی میں سے ہم دونوں کے لیے کوئی راستہ نکل آئے۔

پاروتی:
تب چلو۔

وہ کمرے سے باہر آتے ہیں۔فیڈ آؤٹ۔

Fade in. Daytime. Devdas and his mother are in his room.

Harimati Devi:
Neither your father nor brother will consent to you marrying a lower-caste Brahmin. So why are you raising a storm for such a small matter?

Neechkul ka rishta na tere pita maanenge na bhayya. Tu kyun bhid ke chhatte ko chhedta hai chhoti si baat ke liye?

Devdas:
It may be a small matter to you.

Tumhaare liye vo chhoti si baat hai na.

Dissolve to the next scene. Devdas's brother is scolding him.

Dwijodas:
I want to know how you could dare ask me that? Have you no consideration at all for tradition and family prestige?

Main poochhta hoon aisa sawaal karne ki himmat kaise padi tumhaari? Ghar ki izzat kul ki maryaada ka kuch bhi khayaal nahin raha?

Dissolve. Morning. The next scene. Devdas is with his father. It could be assumed that Devdas has been trying to persuade his father to no avail. Devdas's mother stands in the background and leaves the room silently.

Narain *(furious):*
Be silent! Stop this nonsense. If you say another word, I shall never see your face again. Get out of my sight!

Khaamosh! Bandh kar ye bakwaas. Is baare mein agar ek lafz bhi kaha toh main tera kabhi moonh nahin dekhunga. Door ho ja meri nazron ke saamne se.

Devdas enters his room and puts on his jacket. He takes a suitcase and heads out of the house. His mother tries to stop him.

Harimati Devi:
Deva, where are you going, son?

Deva, kahaan ja raha hai, beta?

फ़ेड इन। दिन का समय। देवदास और उसकी माँ कमरे में हैं।

فیڈ ان۔دن۔دیوداس اور اُس کی ماں کمرے میں ہیں۔

हरिमति देवी:
नीच कुल का रिश्ता न तेरे पिता मानेंगे न भैया। तू क्यों भिड़ के छत्ते को छेड़ता है छोटी-सी बात के लिए।

ہری متی دیوی:
نیچ کُل کا رشتہ نہ تیرے پِتا مانیں گے نہ بھیا۔ تُو کیوں بھڑ کے چھتّے کو چھیڑتا ہے چھوٹی سی بات کے لیے؟

देवदासः
तुम्हारे लिए वह छोटी-सी बात है न।

دیوداس:
تمہارے لیے وہ چھوٹی سی بات ہے نا۔

अगला दृश्य। देवदास का बड़ा भाई उसे डाँट रहा है।

اگلا منظر۔دیوداس کا بڑا بھائی اُسے ڈانٹ رہا ہے۔

द्विजोदासः
मैं पूछता हूँ ऐसा सवाल करने की हिम्मत कैसे पड़ी तुम्हारी? घर की इज़्ज़त कुल की मर्यादा का कुछ भी ख़्याल नहीं रहा?

دویجوداس:
میں پوچھتا ہوں ایسا سوال کرنے کی ہمت کیسے پڑی تمہاری؟ گھر کی عزت، کُل کی مریادا کا کچھ بھی خیال نہیں رہا۔

अगला दृश्य। सुबह। देवदास अपने पिता के साथ है। ऐसा लगता है कि देवदास ने उनको समझाने का प्रयत्न किया लेकिन बेकार। ख़ामोश-सी उसकी माँ पीछे खड़ी है। वह चुपचाप कमरे से बाहर निकल जाती है।

اگلا منظر۔دیوداس اپنے والد کے ساتھ۔منظر سے اندازہ ہوتا ہے کہ دیوداس اپنے باپ کو قائل کرنے کی کوشش کرتا رہا ہے لیکن وہ کسی صورت ماننے کو تیار نہیں ہے۔اُس کی خاموش کھڑی ماں جو وہاں موجود ہے کمرے سے باہر نکل جاتی ہے۔

नारायण *(गुस्से से):*
ख़ामोश! बंद कर यह बकवास। इस बारे में अगर एक लफ़्ज़ भी कहा तो मैं तेरा कभी मुँह नहीं देखूँगा। दूर हो जा मेरी नज़रों के सामने से।

نارائن (غصے سے):
خاموش! بند کر یہ بکواس۔اِس بارے میں اگر ایک لفظ بھی کہا تو میں تیرا کبھی منہ نہیں دیکھوں گا۔دور ہو جا میرے نظروں کے سامنے سے۔

देवदास अपने कमरे में आकर कोट पहनता है और एक सूटकेस लेकर घर से बाहर जाने के लिए निकलता है। माँ उसे रोकने का प्रयत्न करती है।

اپنے کمرے میں آکر دیوداس کوٹ پہنتا ہے، سوٹ کیس اُٹھا کر حویلی سے باہر جانے کے لیے نکلتا ہے۔اُس کی ماں اُسے روکنے کی کوشش کر رہی ہے۔

हरिमति देवी:
देवा, कहाँ जा रहा है, बेटा?

ہری متی دیوی:
دیوا! کہاں جا رہا ہے، بیٹا؟

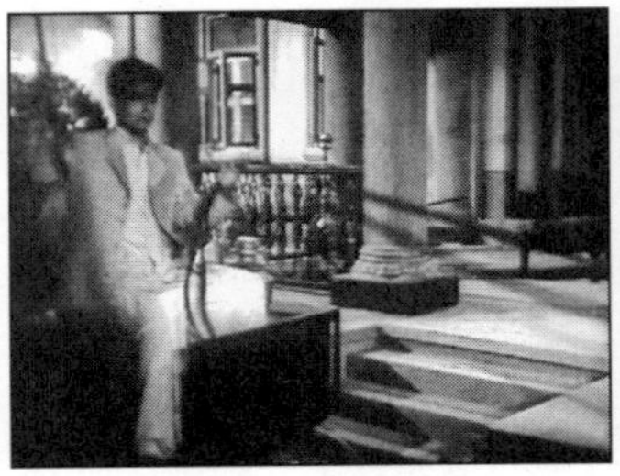    

Devdas:
I'm going to Calcutta, mother.

Kalkatte ja raha hoon, ma.

Harimati Devi:
Calcutta? Please listen to me. Devdas!

Kalkatte? Arey sunn toh sahi. Devdas!

(Devdas goes down the stairs while his mother calls after him)
Devdas. (3)

Devdas. (3)

He gets into the horse carriage and rides swiftly away.

Harimati Devi:
Deva. Deva!

Deva. Deva!

(she can't stop Devdas)
Dharamdas, Deva is upset. He's going to Calcutta. Run! Stop him! Bring him back. Tell him his mother is calling him.

Dharamdas, Deva rooth ke Kalkatte ja raha hai. Ja, ja, bhaag. Usay le aa, kehna main bula rahi hoon.

Dharamdas:
Devdas, come back! Your mother is calling you. Deva!

Arey Deva, laut aa, maaji bula rahi hain. Arey Deva.

The sound of Dharamdas's voice carries across the road. Sitting in her room, Parvati can hear the commotion and the sound of the horse carriage.

Dharamdas *(off-screen, repeating many times):*
Deva, Devdas!

Deva, Deva, o Deva, arey sunn. Deva. Deva. Devdas.

Parvati runs out of the house as Devdas drives furiously past. He does not seem to notice her. She watches Devdas disappear slowly into the distance and walks dejectedly back into her house. Dissolve. Manorama is bathing in the pond. Parvati arrives with her water pot.

देवदासः
कलकत्ते जा रहा हूँ, माँ।

हरिमति देवी:
कलकत्ते? अरे सुन तो सही। देवदास!
(देवदास सीढ़ियाँ उतरता है। पीछे से माँ आवाज़ देती है)
देवदास। (३)

वह ताँगे में बैठ कर तुरंत रवाना हो जाता है।

हरिमति देवी:
देवा। देवा!
(देवदास निकलता चला जाता है)
धरमदास, देवा रूठके कलकत्ते जा रहा है। जा, जा, भाग। उसे ले आ, कहना मैं बुला रही हूँ।

धरमदासः
अरे देवा, लौट आ, माँजी बुला रही हैं। अरे देवा।

धरमदास की आवाज़ दूर तक सुनाई देती है। अपने कमरे में बैठी पार्वती को हो-हल्ला के साथ दूर जाते ताँगे की आवाज़ भी सुनाई दे रही है।

धरमदास *(ऑफ़-स्क्रीन, पुकारते हुए):*
देवा, देवा, ओ देवा, अरे सुन। देवा। देवा। देवदास

पार्वती भागती हुई घर के बाहर आती है। गुस्से में देवदास घोड़ागाड़ी पर उसके पास से हो कर गुज़र जाता है। पेड़ के पास खड़ी पार्वती पर देवदास की नज़रें नहीं पड़ी हैं। दूर होती हुई गाड़ी को पार्वती उदास नज़रों से देखे जा रही है। निराश हो कर वह अपने घर में प्रवेश करती है। अगला दृश्य। मनोरमा तालाब में नहा रही है। पार्वती अपना घड़ा लेकर यहाँ आती है।

دیوداس:
کلکتے جا رہا ہوں، ماں۔

ہری متی دیوی:
کلکتے؟ ارے سن تو سہی۔ دیوداس۔
(دیوداس زینے اُترتا ہے۔ ماں اُسے پکارتی ہے)
دیوداس (۳)

وہ تیزی سے تانگے میں بیٹھ کر نکلتا چلا جا رہا ہے۔

ہری متی دیوی:
دیوا۔ دیوا!
(دیوداس نکلا چلا جاتا ہے)
دھرم داس، دیوا روٹھ کے کلکتے جا رہا ہے۔ جا، جا، بھاگ۔ اُسے لے آ، کہنا میں بلا رہی ہوں۔

دھرم داس:
ارے، دیوا، لوٹ آ۔ ماجی بلا رہی ہیں۔ ارے دیوا۔

دھرم داس کی آواز سنائی دے رہی ہے جو دیوداس کو پکارے جا رہا ہے۔ اپنے کمرے میں بیٹھی پاروتی کے کانوں میں اِس شور شرابے اور دور جاتے تانگے کی آوازیں گونج رہی ہیں۔

دھرم داس (آف اسکرین، پکارتے ہوئے):
دیوا، دیوا، او دیوا ارے سن۔ دیوا، دیوا، دیوداس۔

دوڑتی ہوئی پاروتی اپنے گھر سے باہر آتی ہے۔ غصے میں بھرا دیوداس گھوڑا گاڑی پر تیزی سے نکلا چلا جا رہا ہے۔ دیوداس کی نظر درخت کے پاس کھڑی پاروتی پر نہیں پڑی ہے۔ پاروتی اُسے فاصلوں میں گم ہوتا ہوا دیکھ رہی ہے۔ مایوسی سے سر جھکائے وہ اپنے گھر میں داخل ہوتی ہے۔ ڈزالو۔ منورما تالاب میں نہا رہی ہے پاروتی گھڑا اُٹھائے پنگھٹ پر آتی ہے۔

Manorama:
Paro, I hear Devdas has gone to Calcutta.

Paro, suna hai Devdas Kalkatte chala gaya?

Parvati:
Yes.

Haan.

Manorama:
What did he decide about you?

Toh phir tere baare mein kya faisla kiya?

Parvati:
He must have done something. I know him, Mano didi. I trust him completely.

Kuch toh kiya hi hoga. Main unhen jaanti hoon, Mano didi. Mujhe un par poora bharosa hai.

Dissolve. Night-time. In the Calcutta quarters where Devdas lives, his friend Chunnilal, familiarly known as "Chunni Babu" enters. He is drunk and is singing to himself. The cut here is emphasised by the word "bharosa" *(trust), which is Parvati's last word in the preceding scene and Chunni Babu's first sung word.*

Chunni Babu *(actor Motilal, singing):*
"How can one trust another (2)
When I cannot trust my own heart?"

"Bharosa kisi aur ka kya karen hum (2)
Ki khud apne dil ka bharosa nahin hai"

Chunni Babu tries to hang his cane on a hat rack, but is in fact confusing the rack with its shadow cast on the wall. He does not realise his mistake and the cane falls to the ground.

Chunni Babu *(still singing):*
"When I do not trust..."

"Bharosa nahin hai..."

(talking to some servants asleep on the floor)
These beggars insist on sleeping in the middle of the room.

Bilkul beech sadak mein sote hain. Bhikmange.

(Chunni Babu enters a room where Devdas is standing)
Devdas, when did you return? You're here one moment, vanished the next. It's so late. Why aren't you asleep?

Arey Devdas, tum kab aaye? Khair tum bhi ek chhalaawa ho. Ek minute mein dikhaayi de jaate ho, aur ek minute mein ghaayab ho jaate ho. Itni raat ho gayi, tum soye kyun nahin?

Devdas:
As though sleep came every night, Chunni babu.

Neend roz thode hi aaya karti hai, Chunni babu.

मनोरमाः
पारो, सुना है देवदास कलकत्ते चला गया?

पार्वतीः
हाँ।

मनोरमाः
तो फिर तेरे बारे में क्या फ़ैसला किया?

पार्वतीः
कुछ तो किया ही होगा। मैं उन्हें जानती हूँ, मनो दीदी। मुझे उन पर पूरा भरोसा है।

अगला दृश्य। रात का समय। कलकत्ते में जहाँ देवदास रहता है, मित्र चुन्नीलाल उर्फ़ चुन्नी बाबू अंदर आता है। वह नशे में गुनगुना रहा है। पिछले दृश्य में पार्वती का अंतिम शब्द ''भरोसा'' था और यहाँ चुन्नी बाबू का गुनगुनाया हुआ पहला शब्द।

चुन्नी बाबू *(अभिनेता मोतीलाल, गाते हुए):*
''भरोसा किसी और का क्या करें हम (२)
कि ख़ुद अपने दिल का भरोसा नहीं है''

चुन्नी बाबू अपनी छड़ी हैट रैक में टाँगने का प्रयत्न करता है। इस बात से अनजान कि वह दीवार पर पड़ रहा रैक का साया है। नशे में उसे अपनी भूल का आभास नहीं होता और अंत में छड़ी गिर जाती है।

चुन्नी बाबू *(गाते हुए):*
''भरोसा नहीं है...''
(फ़र्श पर सोए हुए नौकर से)
बिल्कुल बीच सड़क में सोते हैं। भिखमंगे।
(चुन्नी बाबू कमरे में आता है जहाँ देवदास खड़ा है)
अरे देवदास, तुम कब आए? ख़ैर तुम भी एक छलावा हो। एक मिनट में दिखाई दे जाते हो और एक मिनट में ग़ायब हो जाते हो। इतनी रात हो गई, तुम सोए क्यों नहीं?

देवदासः
नींद रोज़ थोड़े ही आया करती है, चुन्नी बाबू।

منورما:
پارو۔ سنا ہے دیوداس کلکتے چلا گیا؟

پاروتی:
ہاں۔

منورما:
تو پھر تیرے بارے میں کیا فیصلہ کیا؟

پاروتی:
کچھ تو کیا ہی ہوگا۔ میں اُنھیں جانتی ہوں، منو دیدی۔ مجھے اُن پر پورا بھروسا ہے۔

اگلا منظر۔ رات۔ کلکتے کے اُس علاقے میں جہاں دیوداس قیام کرتا ہے، اُس کا دوست چُنّی لال عرف چُنی بابو داخل ہوتے ہیں۔ وہ شراب کے نشے میں ہے اور ایک شعر گنگنا رہے ہیں جس کا پہلا لفظ 'بھروسا' ہے۔ جو پچھلے منظر میں پاروتی کا آخری لفظ تھا۔

چُنّی بابو (اداکار، موتی لال، گاتے ہوئے):
بھروسا کسی اور کا کیا کریں ہم (۲)
کہ خود اپنے دل کا بھروسا نہیں ہے

دیوار پر پڑنے والے ہیٹ اسٹینڈ کے سائے کو ہیٹ اسٹینڈ سمجھ کر چنی بابو اُس پر اپنی چھڑی لٹکانا چاہتے ہیں۔ نشے میں اُنھیں اِس غلطی کا احساس نہیں ہو پاتا اور چھڑی زمین پر گر پڑتی ہے۔

چُنّی بابو (گاتے ہوئے):
بھروسا نہیں ہے۔
(فرش پر سوئے ہوئے نوکر سے)
بالکل بیچ سڑک میں سوتے ہیں۔ بھِک منگے۔
(چُنّی بابو روم میں داخل ہوتے ہیں دیوداس سامنے ہی کھڑا ہے)
ارے دیوداس، تم کب آئے؟ خیر تم بھی ایک چھلاوا ہو۔ ایک منٹ میں دکھائی دے جاتے ہو اور ایک منٹ میں غائب ہو جاتے ہو۔ اِتنی رات ہوگئی، تم سوئے کیوں نہیں؟

دیوداس:
نیند روز تھوڑے ہی آیا کرتی ہے، چُنّی بابو۔

Chunni Babu:

You can't sleep? I thought decent boys like you never saw moonlit nights. But now I know better.

(Devdas stands at the window)

What's wrong? Why won't you speak? Is there something troubling you?

Neend nahin aati? Arey hum toh samajhte thay ki tumhaare jaise ache ladke is chandramukhi rajni ki soorat hi nahin dekhte hain. Magar aaj pata lag gaya humen.

Hmm? Kya baat hai? Tum bolte nahin? Koi takleef hai tumhen? Tumhaare mann mein kuch kalesh hai?

Devdas:

Are you never troubled, Chunni babu?

Tumhaare mann mein koi kalesh nahin, Chunni babu?

Chunni Babu:

No, never.

Nahin, bilkul nahin.

Devdas:

Have you never been unhappy?

Zindagi bhar kabhi koi dukh nahin dekha?

Chunni Babu:

Yes, I have. But that's life. Either you live it with a smile on your face or a tear in your eye. To be happy you need to deceive yourself a little. But tell me, why ask all this?

Dukh dekha toh hai, magar ye sab zindagi ka maamla hai. Ise hans kar guzaar de ya ise ro kar guzaar de. Khush rehne ke liye thoda sa apne aap ko dhoka bhi dena padta hai. Magar tum…tum ye sab kyun poochte ho?

Devdas:

I felt like hearing you.

Sirf sunne ka shauq hai.

Chunni Babu *(laughs):*

Hearing me? One day I'll tell you my story.

Sunne ka shauq hai? Toh ek din hum tumhen sunaayenge aur tum sunna.

Devdas:

Chunni babu.

Chunni babu.

Chunni Babu:

Hmm?

Hmm?

Devdas:

Where do you disappear night after night?

Ye tum raat-raat bhar kahaan ghaayab rehte ho?

Chunni Babu:

You're playing the innocent. Don't you know?

Baday bhole bante ho. Tum nahin jaante?

चुन्नी बाबू:
नींद नहीं आती? अरे हम तो समझते थे कि तुम्हारे जैसे अच्छे लड़के इस चंद्रमुखी रजनी की सूरत ही नहीं देखते हैं। मगर आज पता लग गया हमें।
(देवदास खिड़की के पास खड़ा हो जाता है)
हुँ? क्या बात है? तुम बोलते नहीं? कोई तकलीफ़ है तुम्हें? तुम्हारे मन में कुछ क्लेश है?

देवदासः
तुम्हारे मन में कोई क्लेश नहीं चुन्नी बाबू?

चुन्नी बाबू:
नहीं, बिल्कुल नहीं।

देवदासः
ज़िंदगी भर कभी कोई दु:ख नहीं देखा?

चुन्नी बाबू:
दु:ख देखा तो है, मगर यह सब ज़िंदगी का मामला है। इसे हँस कर गुज़ार दे या इसे रो कर गुज़ार दे। ख़ुश रहने के लिए थोड़ा-सा अपने आपको धोखा भी देना पड़ता है। मगर तुम...तुम यह सब क्यों पूछते हो?

देवदासः
सिर्फ़ सुनने का शौक़ है।

चुन्नी बाबू *(हँसते हुए)*:
सुनने का शौक़ है? तो एक दिन हम तुम्हें सुनाएँगे और तुम सुनना।

देवदासः
चुन्नी बाबू।

चुन्नी बाबू:
हुँ?

देवदासः
यह तुम रात-रात भर कहाँ ग़ायब रहते हो?

चुन्नी बाबू:
बड़े भोले बनते हो। तुम नहीं जानते?

چنّی بابو:
نیند نہیں آتی ؟ ارے ہم تو سمجھتے تھے کہ تمہارے جیسے اچھے لڑکے اِس چندرمکھی رجنی کی صورت ہی نہیں دیکھتے ہیں۔ مگر آج پتا لگ گیا ہمیں۔
(دیوداس کھڑکی کے پاس جا کر کھڑا ہو جاتا ہے)
ہوں؟ کیا بات ہے؟ تم بولتے نہیں۔ کوئی تکلیف ہے تمھیں؟ تمہارے من میں کچھ کلیش ہے۔

دیوداس:
تمہارے من میں کوئی کلیش نہیں، چنّی بابو؟

چنّی بابو:
نہیں، بالکل نہیں۔

دیوداس:
زندگی بھر کبھی کوئی دکھ نہیں دیکھا؟

چنّی بابو:
دکھ دیکھا تو ہے۔ مگر یہ سب زندگی کا معاملہ ہے۔ اِسے ہنس کر گزار دے یا اِسے رو کر گزار دے۔ خوش رہنے کے لیے تھوڑا سا اپنے آپ کو دھوکا بھی دینا پڑتا ہے۔ مگر تم۔۔۔ تم یہ سب کیوں پوچھتے ہو؟

دیوداس:
صرف سننے کا شوق ہے۔

چنّی بابو (ہنستے ہوئے):
سننے کا شوق ہے۔ تو ایک دن ہم تمھیں سنائیں گے اور تم سننا۔

دیوداس:
چُنّی بابو۔

چنّی بابو:
ہوں؟

دیوداس:
یہ تم رات رات بھر کہاں غائب رہتے ہو؟

چنّی بابو:
بڑے بھولے بنتے ہو۔ تم نہیں جانتے؟

  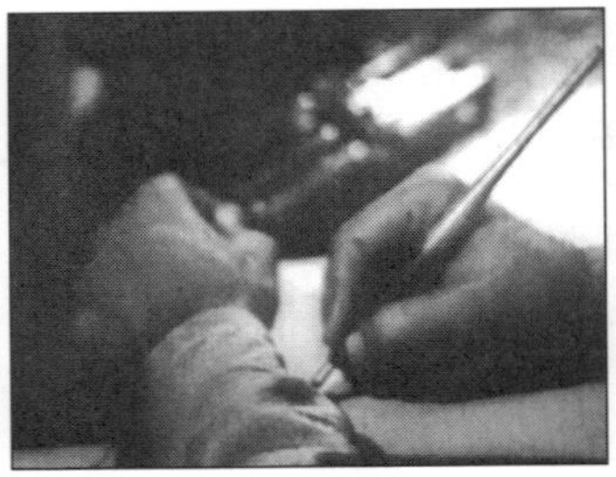  

Devdas:
I have a vague idea.

Jaanta toh hoon lekin kuch theek se nahin jaanta.

Chunni Babu:
If you really want to know, you'll have to become carefree like me.

Toh theek se jaanne ke liye tumhen mere jaisa albela banna padega.

Devdas:
I hear torment and suffering are forgotten there.

Suna hai wahaan ja kar dukh-dard sab bhool jaate hain?

Chunni Babu:
Absolutely.

Theek, bilkul theek.

Devdas:
Then take me there.

Phir mujhe bhi wahaan le chalo.

Chunni Babu:
You want to come with me? All right. I'll take you tomorrow. Sleep now.

Tum? Tum mere saath chaloge? Acha. Kal chalenge. Abhi tum so jaao. Hmm. So jaao.

Chunni Babu leaves. Devdas is writing a letter at his desk.

Reel Six

Devdas reads the letter to himself.

Devdas *(voice-over):*
"Parvati, I've been troubled by thoughts of you ever since I came here. Neither of my parents will consent to our marriage. I see no solution. If I want to make you happy then

"Parvati. Jab se main yahaan aaya hoon mujhe sirf tumhaara hi khayaal sata raha hai. Mere ma-baap mein se kisi ki bhi ye khwaahish nahin ki hum donon ka biyaah ho. Mujhe koi raasta

देवदासः
जानता तो हूँ लेकिन कुछ ठीक से नहीं जानता।

चुन्नी बाबूः
तो ठीक से जानने के लिए तुम्हें मेरे जैसा अलबेला बनना पड़ेगा।

देवदासः
सुना है वहाँ जाकर दुःख-दर्द सब भूल जाते हैं?

चुन्नी बाबूः
ठीक, बिल्कुल ठीक।

देवदासः
फिर मुझे भी वहाँ ले चलो।

चुन्नी बाबूः
तुम? तुम मेरे साथ चलोगे? अच्छा। कल चलेंगे। अभी तुम सो जाओ। हुँ। सो जाओ।

चुन्नी बाबू चला जाता है। देवदास मेज़ पर बैठा एक पत्र लिख रहा है।

रील छः

देवदास अपना लिखा हुआ पत्र पढ़ रहा है।

देवदास *(वॉइस-ओवर)*:
''पार्वती। जब से मैं यहाँ आया हूँ, मुझे सिर्फ़ तुम्हारा ही ख़्याल सता रहा है। मेरे माँ-बाप में से किसी की भी यह ख़्वाहिश नहीं कि हम दोनों का ब्याह हो। मुझे कोई रास्ता सुझाई नहीं देता। अगर तुम्हें सुखी करने का जतन करता हूँ तो माँ-बाप के जज़्बात को

دیوداس:
جانتا تو ہوں لیکن کچھ ٹھیک سے نہیں جانتا۔

چنّی بابو:
تو ٹھیک سے جاننے کے لیے تمھیں میرے جیسا البیلا بننا پڑے گا۔

دیوداس:
سنا ہے وہاں جا کر دکھ درد سب بھول جاتے ہیں؟

چنّی بابو:
ٹھیک، بالکل ٹھیک۔

دیوداس:
پھر مجھے بھی وہاں لے چلو۔

چنّی بابو:
تم ؟ تم میرے ساتھ چلو گے؟ اچھا۔ کل چلیں گے۔ ابھی تم سو جاؤ، ہوں۔ سو جاؤ۔

چنّی بابو چلے جاتے ہیں۔ دیوداس ٹیبل پر بیٹھا خط لکھ رہا ہے۔

ریل چھ

دیوداس اپنا لکھا ہوا خط پڑھ رہا ہے۔

دیوداس (بازگشت):
''پاروتی۔ جب سے میں یہاں آیا ہوں مجھے صرف تمہارا ہی خیال ستا رہا ہے۔ میرے ماں باپ میں سے کسی کی بھی یہ خواہش نہیں کہ ہم دونوں کا بیاہ ہو۔ مجھے کوئی راستا سجھائی نہیں دیتا۔ اگر تمھیں سکھی کرنے کا جتن کرتا ہوں تو ماں باپ کے جذبات پہ دھکّا پہنچتا ہے اور یہ میں کبھی سوچ بھی نہیں سکتا۔ اُس رات تم اپنا سب کچھ تج

I know how much I'll hurt my parents and I can never consider it. I feel so upset when I think of that night when you came to me with no thought of yourself. But I want to tell you, Paro, it has never crossed my mind that I loved you.
(an alarm goes off. It is 4 a.m. He puts the alarm off and continues reading in voice-over)

sujhaayi nahin deta. Agar tumhen sukhi karne ka jatan karta hoon toh ma-baap ke jazbaat ko dhakka pahonchta hai aur ye main kabhi soch bhi nahin sakta. Uss raat tum apna sab kuch tajj kar mere yahaan chali aayin, is baat ke khayaal se mujhe kitna dukh hota hai. Lekin ek baat main tumhen bata dena chaahta hoon, Paro, aur ye mere mann se kabhi nahin aayi ki main tumhen chaahta hoon.

"It grieves me to think what you will endure for my sake. Try to forget me. I shall pray to God that you will succeed."

"Mujhe dukh bhi hai toh yahi ki mere liye tum kya kuch kashth uthaaogi. Koshish kar ke tum mujhe bhool jaana. Bhagwan se meri praarthna hai ki tumhen is mein kaamyaabi ho."

Fade out.

Fade in. The next day. Devdas is sitting in a chair. He has not slept all night. He goes to find a servant.

Devdas:
Madhav.

Madhav.

Madhav *(unidentified actor):*
Sir?

Ji?

Devdas:
Please post this.

Ye chitthi toh daal aa zara.

Madhav:
Very well, sir.

Bahot acha, huzoor.

Devdas returns to his room. As he stands by the window, he hears the voice of his conscience. This scene is entirely in voice-over.

His conscience:
What have you done, Devdas?

Ye tu ne kya kiya, Devdas?

Devdas:
Why? What have I done?

Kyun? Kya kiya?

धक्का पहुँचता है और यह मैं कभी सोच भी नहीं सकता। उस रात तुम अपना सब कुछ तज कर मेरे यहाँ चली आईं, इस बात के ख़्याल से मुझे कितना दु:ख होता है। लेकिन एक बात मैं तुम्हें बता देना चाहता हूँ, पारो, और यह मेरे मन से कभी नहीं आई कि मैं तुम्हें चाहता हूँ।

(घड़ी की घंटी बजती है। प्रातः के चार बजे हैं। वह अलार्म बंद करता है। वॉइस-ओवर में पत्र पढ़ना जारी है)

''मुझे दु:ख भी है तो यही कि मेरे लिए तुम क्या कुछ कष्ट उठाओगी। कोशिश करके तुम मुझे भूल जाना। भगवान से मेरी प्रार्थना है कि तुम्हें इसमें कामयाबी हो।''

फ़ेड आउट।

फ़ेड इन। अगला दिन। देवदास रात भर सो नहीं पाया है। वह उठ कर सेवक को आवाज़ देता है।

देवदासः
माधव।

माधव *(कलाकार अज्ञात):*
जी?

देवदासः
यह चिट्ठी तो डाल आ ज़रा।

माधवः
बहुत अच्छा, हुज़ूर।

देवदास अपने कमरे में आता है। खिड़की के पास खड़े देवदास को अपनी अन्तरात्मा की आवाज़ सुनाई देती है। यह पूरा दृश्य वॉइस-ओवर में है।

उसकी अन्तरात्माः
यह तूने क्या किया, देवदास?

देवदासः
क्यों? क्या किया?

کرمیرے یہاں چلی آئیں۔اِس بات کے خیال سے مجھے کتنا دکھ ہوتا ہے۔لیکن ایک بات میں تمھیں بتا دینا چاہتا ہوں، پارو، اور یہ میرے من سے کبھی نہیں آئی کہ میں تمھیں چاہتا ہوں۔

(الارم بج اُٹھتا ہے۔صبح کے چار بجے ہیں۔وہ الارم بند کردیتا ہے۔بازگشت جاری ہے)

''مجھے دکھ بھی ہے تو یہی کہ میرے لیے تم کیا کچھ کشٹ اُٹھاؤ گی۔کوشش کر کے تم مجھے بھول جانا۔بھگوان سے میری پرارتھنا ہے کہ تمھیں اِس میں کامیابی ہو۔

فیڈ آؤٹ۔

فیڈ اِن۔اگلا دن۔دیوداس رات بھر سو نہیں پایا ہے۔وہ اُٹھ کر ملازم کو آواز دیتا ہے۔

دیوداس:
مادھو۔

مادھو (اداکار، نامعلوم):
جی؟

دیوداس:
یہ چٹھی تو ڈال آ ذرا۔

مادھو:
بہت اچھا، حضور۔

دیوداس اپنے کمرے میں واپس آتا ہے۔کھڑکی کے پاس کھڑے ہوئے دیوداس کو اُس کے ضمیر کی آواز سنائی دیتی ہے۔یہ سارا مکالمہ بازگشت جیسی آواز میں سنائی دیتا ہے۔

دیوداس کا ضمیر:
یہ تُو نے کیا کیا، دیوداس؟

دیوداس:
کیوں؟ کیا کیا؟

His conscience:
Nothing, of course. She is your childhood friend. Sacrificing her all, she came to you asking for a little space at your feet, and you say nothing to her and come running here?

Kuch kiya hi nahin? Vo bachpan ki saathi tumhaari. Apne maan, apni lajja ko chhod kar tumhaare pairon mein jagah maangne chali aayi aur tum usay kuch kahe-sune baghair yahaan bhaag kar chale aaye?

Devdas:
I had no choice. My parents opposed our marriage.

Main majboor tha, mere pita nahin chaahte, meri ma nahin chaahti.

His conscience:
But how could you tell her such a big lie? How could you write that you do not love her?

Haan, lekin itna bada jhoot kaise bol diya tumne? Kaise likh diya tum usay nahin chaahte?

Devdas:
There was no other way. But you know what a proud and stubborn girl Paro is.

Iske siwa aur koi raasta bhi toh nahin tha. Magar tum toh jaante ho ki Paro kitni abhimaani, kitni hatili ladki hai.

His conscience:
Have you thought how she'd feel when she gets your letter?

Socha bhi hai tumhaari chitthi pa kar uska kya haal hoga?

Parvati's words come back to Devdas.

Parvati *(repeat dialogue, voice-over):*
There is so much water in the river. Will it not be enough to wash away my stigma?

Nadi mein kitna jal hai. Kya itne jal se bhi mera kalank na dhulega?

Devdas rushes out of his room to find the servant to whom he gave the letter to post.

Devdas:
Madhav! (3)

Madhav! (3)

उसकी अन्तरात्माः
कुछ किया ही नहीं? वह बचपन की साथी तुम्हारी। अपने मान, अपनी लज्जा को छोड़ कर तुम्हारे पैरों में जगह माँगने चली आई और तुम उसे कुछ कहे-सुने बग़ैर यहाँ भाग कर चले आए?

देवदासः
मैं मजबूर था, मेरे पिता नहीं चाहते, मेरी माँ नहीं चाहती।

उसकी अन्तरात्माः
हाँ, लेकिन इतना बड़ा झूठ कैसे बोल दिया तुमने? कैसे लिख दिया तुम उसे नहीं चाहते?

देवदासः
इसके सिवा और कोई रास्ता भी तो नहीं था। मगर तुम तो जानते हो कि पारो कितनी अभिमानी, कितनी हठीली लड़की है।

उसकी अन्तरात्माः
सोचा भी है तुम्हारी चिट्ठी पाकर उसका क्या हाल होगा?

पार्वती के कहे हुए शब्द सुनाई देते हैं।

पार्वती *(वॉइस-ओवर में पारो के संवाद की पुनरावृत्ति):*
नदी में कितना जल है। क्या इतने जल से भी मेरा कलंक न धुलेगा?

देवदास दौड़ कर बाहर आता है कि नौकर को ख़त पोस्ट करने से रोक ले।

देवदासः
माधव! (३)

ضمیر کی آواز:
کچھ کیا ہی نہیں؟ وہ بچپن کی ساتھی تمہاری۔ اپنے مان، اپنی لجّا کو چھوڑ کر تمہارے پیروں میں جگہ مانگنے چلی آئی اور تم اُس سے کچھ کہے سنے بغیر یہاں بھاگ کر چلے آئے؟

دیوداس:
میں مجبور تھا۔ میرے پِتا نہیں چاہتے، میری ماں نہیں چاہتی۔

ضمیر کی آواز:
ہاں، لیکن اِتنا بڑا جھوٹ کیسے بول دیا تم نے؟ کیسے لکھ دیا تم اُسے نہیں چاہتے؟

دیوداس:
اِس کے سوا اور کوئی راستا بھی تو نہیں تھا۔ مگر تم تو جانتے ہو کہ پارو کتنی ابھیمانی، کتنی ہٹیلی لڑکی ہے۔

ضمیر کی آواز:
سوچا بھی ہے تمہاری چِٹھی پا کر اُس کا کیا حال ہوگا؟

پاروتی کے کہے الفاظ کی گونج۔

پاروتی (گزشتہ ڈائلاگ):
ندی میں کتنا جل ہے۔ کیا اِتنے جل سے بھی میرا کلنک نہ دھلے گا؟

دیوداس دوڑ کر باہر جاتا ہے کہ ملازم کو خط پوسٹ کرنے سے روک دے۔

دیوداس:
مادھو! (۳)

Madhav:
Coming, sir.

Ji, aaya.

Devdas:
Where is the letter I gave you?

Vo chitthi jo maine tumhen di thi, vo kahaan hai?

Madhav:
I've posted it.

Vo toh abhi main post-office mein chhod kar aaya.

Devdas decides to go back to the village at once. He is packing when Chunni Babu arrives all dressed up and ready to take Devdas out for the night.

Chunni Babu:
Devdas, aren't we going out?

Arey Devdas, jaana nahin hai?

Devdas:
That's why I'm packing.

Jaane ka hi toh bandobast kar raha hoon.

Chunni Babu:
Are you taking all your bags with you?

Ye saara ghar-baar apne saath le chaloge?

Devdas:
In whose care can I leave them?

Aur kis par chhod ke jaaunga?

Chunni Babu:
My good man, I leave my things here, too.

Arey bhale aadmi, humaara bhi toh saara saamaan yahin pada rehta hai. Hum kis par chhod jaate hain?

Devdas:
Chunni babu, I'm not coming back here again.

Chunni babu, ab main yahaan laut ke nahin aaunga.

Chunni Babu *(reciting poetry):*
"He, I was so proud of, could not do a simple thing for me
He could not keep my things, nor pay a little rent."
Come with me now. Take your bags tomorrow, if you insist.

"Hum jiske naaz uthaate hain itna bhi humaara kar na sakay
Vo bistar humaara rakh na sakay thoda sa kiraaya bhar na sakay."
Aaj toh aise chale chalo, kal agar samajh mein aaye toh bistara bhi apna saath le chalna.

माधवः
जी, आया।

مادھو:
جی، آیا۔

देवदासः
वह चिट्ठी जो मैंने तुम्हें दी थी, वह कहाँ है?

دیوداس:
وہ چٹھی جو میں نے تمھیں دی تھی، وہ کہاں ہے؟

माधवः
वह तो अभी मैं पोस्ट-ऑफ़िस में छोड़ कर आया।

مادھو:
وہ تو ابھی میں پوسٹ آفس میں چھوڑ کر آیا۔

देवदास तुरंत गाँव जाने का निश्चय करता है। वह सामान बाँध रहा है तभी सजे-बने चुन्नी बाबू, देवदास को बाहर ले जाने के लिए आते हैं।

دیوداس فوراً گاؤں جانے کا ارادہ کر لیتا ہے۔ وہ سامان باندھ رہا ہے کہ سجے بنے، چنّی بابو آ کر دیوداس کو رات گزارنے کے لیے ساتھ لے جانا چاہتے ہیں۔

चुन्नी बाबू:
अरे देवदास, जाना नहीं है?

چنّی بابو:
ارے، دیوداس، جانا نہیں ہے؟

देवदासः
जाने का ही तो बन्दोबस्त कर रहा हूँ।

دیوداس:
جانے کا ہی تو بندوبست کر رہا ہوں۔

चुन्नी बाबू:
यह सारा घर-बार अपने साथ ले चलोगे?

چنّی بابو:
یہ سارا گھر بار اپنے ساتھ لے چلو گے؟

देवदासः
और किस पर छोड़ के जाऊँगा?

دیوداس:
اور کس پر چھوڑ کے جاؤں گا؟

चुन्नी बाबू:
अरे भले आदमी, हमारा भी तो सारा सामान यहीं पड़ा रहता है। हम किस पर छोड़ जाते हैं?

چنّی بابو:
ارے، بھلے آدمی، ہمارا بھی تو سارا سامان یہیں پڑا رہتا ہے، ہم کس پر چھوڑ جاتے ہیں؟

देवदासः
चुन्नी बाबू, अब मैं यहाँ लौट के नहीं आऊँगा।

دیوداس:
چنّی بابو، اب میں یہاں لوٹ کے نہیں آؤں گا۔

चुन्नी बाबू *(एक शेर पढ़ता है):*
''हम जिसके नाज़ उठाते हैं इतना भी हमारा कर न सके
वह बिस्तर हमारा रख न सके थोड़ा सा किराया भर न सके।''
आज तो ऐसे चले चलो, कल अगर समझ में आए तो बिस्तरा भी अपना साथ ले चलना।

چنّی بابو (شعر پڑھتے ہوئے):
''ہم جس کے ناز اُٹھاتے ہیں اِتنا بھی ہمارا کر نہ سکے
وہ بستر ہمارا رکھ نہ سکے تھوڑا سا کرایہ بھر نہ سکے''
آج تو ایسے چلے چلو۔ کل اگر سمجھ میں آئے تو بستر ابھی اپنا ساتھ لے چلنا۔

Devdas:
Chunni babu, I'm going home.

Chunni babu, main ghar ja raha hoon.

Chunni Babu:
Home? When will you return?

Ghar? Phir lautoge kab?

Devdas:
I'm never coming back. If I knew that I would lose everything I cherished by coming here, I would never have come.

Ab main yahaan kabhi nahin aaunga. Agar mujhe maaloom hota ki yahaan aane se mujhe apna sab kuch kho dena padega... main is tarah lutt jaaunga toh main yahaan kabhi na aata.

Chunni Babu:
But what have you lost?

Arey bhai, magar tumne kahaan kya kho diya?

Devdas:
I'll tell you if we meet again. Here's some money. Pay any outstanding bills, and let the servants share the rest.

Phir kabhi miley toh bataaunga. Haan, ye rupay lo jiska jo mere zimme ho vo chuka dena, aur baaqi sab naukaron mein baant dena.

Devdas leaves Calcutta. Dissolve to a shot of a steam train. He arrives home and gives his suitcase to the watchman at the gate.

Devdas:
Kishan, take my bag inside. I'll be back soon.

Ye le jaao andar, Kishan, main aata hoon, acha?

Kishan:
Yes, sir.

Acha huzoor.

Devdas crosses the road to Parvati's house. Just as he nears it, he sees the postman talking to Nilkanth, Parvati's father.

Nilkanth:
Who is the letter for?

Kiski chitthi hai?

Postman:
Miss Parvati. I have given it to her.

Parvati devi ki chitthi thi, unhen dedi.

Nilkanth:
Oh.

Oh.

देवदासः
चुन्नी बाबू, मैं घर जा रहा हूँ।

चुन्नी बाबूः
घर? फिर लौटोगे कब?

देवदासः
अब मैं यहाँ कभी नहीं आऊँगा। अगर मुझे मालूम होता कि यहाँ आने से मुझे अपना सब कुछ खो देना पड़ेगा...मैं इस तरह लुट जाऊँगा तो मैं यहाँ कभी न आता।

चुन्नी बाबूः
अरे भई, मगर तुमने कहाँ क्या खो दिया?

देवदासः
फिर कभी मिले तो बताऊँगा। हाँ, यह रुपए लो जिसका जो मेरे ज़िम्मे हो वह चुका देना, और बाक़ी सब नौकरों में बाँट देना।

देवदास कलकत्ते से रवाना होता है। अगला दृश्य। भाप रेलगाड़ी का एक शॉट। देवदास घर पहुँचता है। अपना सूटकेस फाटक पर खड़े चौकीदार को देता है।

देवदासः
यह ले जाओ अंदर, किशन, मैं आता हूँ, अच्छा?

किशनः
अच्छा हुज़ूर।

देवदास पार्वती के घर की ओर जाता है। जैसे ही वह घर के निकट पहुँचता है, देखता है कि डाकिया पार्वती के पिता नीलकंठ से बात कर रहा है।

नीलकंठः
किसकी चिट्ठी है?

पोस्टमैनः
पार्वती देवी की चिट्ठी थी, उन्हें दे दी।

नीलकंठः
ओह।

دیوداس:
چُنّی بابو، میں گھر جا رہا ہوں۔

چُنّی بابو:
گھر؟ پھر لوٹو گے کب؟

دیوداس؟
اب میں یہاں کبھی نہیں آؤں گا۔ اگر مجھے معلوم ہوتا کہ یہاں آنے سے مجھے اپنا سب کچھ کھو دینا پڑے گا۔۔۔ میں اِس طرح لُٹ جاؤں گا، تو میں یہاں کبھی نہ آتا۔

چُنّی بابو:
ارے بھئی، مگر تم نے کہاں کیا کھو دیا؟

دیوداس:
پھر کبھی ملے تو بتاؤں گا۔ ہاں، یہ روپے لو جس کا جو میرے ذمے ہو وہ چکا دینا، اور باقی سب نوکروں میں بانٹ دینا۔

دیوداس کلکتے سے روانہ ہو جاتا ہے۔ اگلا منظر۔ اسٹیم ٹرین۔ دیوداس گھر پہنچ کر اپنا سوٹ کیس پھاٹک پر کھڑے دربان کے حوالے کرتا ہے۔

دیوداس:
یہ لے جاؤ اندر، کشن۔ میں آتا ہوں، اچھا؟

کشن:
اچھا، حضور۔

وہ پاروتی کے گھر کے قریب پہنچتا ہے تو دیکھتا ہے کہ ڈاکیے سے پاروتی کے والد بات کر رہے ہیں۔

نیل کنٹھ:
کس کی چِٹھی ہے؟

پوسٹ مین:
پاروتی دیوی کی چِٹھی تھی، اُنھیں دے دی۔

نیل کنٹھ:
اوہ۔

Devdas is upset. Cut to the next shot. Parvati has just finished reading his letter. She is grief stricken.

Devdas *(voice-over, letter):*
"It has never crossed my mind that I loved you."

"Ye mere mann se kabhi nahin aaya ki main tumhen chaahta hoon."

Nilkanth *(off-screen):*
Mother! Parvati's in-laws are here from Manekpur to give her their blessings.

Ma! Ma! Manekpur se Parvati ke sasuraal waale aashirwaad dene aaye hain.

Grandmother *(off-screen):*
Paro! Come down.

Paro! Arey o Paro.

Parvati tears up Devdas's letter and throws it away. Her eyes are filled with tears.

Dissolve. Devdas is sitting on the pond steps. He has a long thin rod in his hand. He looks around, hoping to see Parvati. As he climbs the steps, Parvati arrives. Her hair is untied. They look at one another. Parvati ignores him and goes down the steps to the water. She fills her water pot and starts to walk away.

Devdas:
Wait, Paro, I have come.

Thair, Paro. Main aa gaya hoon.

Parvati *(angry):*
Why?

Kyun?

Devdas:
Have you forgotten that night?

Uss raat ki baat tujhe yaad nahin kya?

देवदास परेशान है। कट। पार्वती के हाथ में देवदास का पत्र है। वह पत्र पढ़ चुकी है। उसे सदमा पहुँचा है।

देवदास *(वॉइस-ओवर, चिट्ठी):*
''यह मेरे मन से कभी नहीं आई कि मैं तुम्हें चाहता हूँ।''

नीलकंठ *(ऑफ़-स्क्रीन):*
माँ! माँ! मानेकपुर से पार्वती के ससुराल वाले आशीर्वाद देने आए हैं।

दादीमाँ *(ऑफ़-स्क्रीन):*
पारो! अरे ओ पारो!

पार्वती चिट्ठी फाड़ कर फेंक देती है। उसकी आँखों में आँसू हैं।

अगला दृश्य। देवदास तालाब की सीढ़ियों पर बैठा है। उसके हाथ में एक लम्बी छड़ी है। उसकी नज़रें पार्वती को ढूँढ़ रही हैं। जैसे ही वह तालाब की सीढ़ियाँ चढ़ता है, पार्वती अपना घड़ा उठाए पानी भरने आती है। उसके बाल खुले हैं। वे एक दूसरे को देखते हैं। पार्वती उसकी ओर ध्यान नहीं देती और पानी का घड़ा भर कर जाने लगती है।

देवदासः
ठहर, पारो। मैं आ गया हूँ।

पार्वती *(क्रोधित):*
क्यों?

देवदासः
उस रात की बात तुझे याद नहीं क्या?

دیوداس پریشان سا ہے۔ کٹ۔ پاروتی کے ہاتھ میں دیوداس کا وہ خط ہے جسے وہ پڑھ چکی ہے۔ اُس کے چہرے پر کرب کے آثار ہیں۔

دیوداس (بازگشت، خط کی):
''یہ میرے من سے کبھی نہیں آئی کہ میں تمھیں چاہتا ہوں۔''

نیل کنٹھ (آف اسکرین):
ماں! ماں! مانک پور سے پاروتی کے سسرال والے آشیرواد دینے آئے ہیں۔

دادی (آف اسکرین):
پارو! ارے او، پارو!

پاروتی خط کے پرزے کر کے پھینک دیتی ہے۔ اُس کے آنکھوں میں آنسو چھلک رہے ہیں۔

اگلا منظر۔ دیوداس پنگھٹ کی سیڑھیوں پر بیٹھا ہوا ہے۔ اُس کے ہاتھ میں ایک چھڑی ہے۔ اُس کی نظریں پاروتی کو ڈھونڈ رہی ہیں۔ سیڑھیوں سے چڑھ کر وہ اوپر آ رہا ہے جب اُس کی نظر گھڑا اُٹھائے آتی ہوئی پاروتی پر پڑتی ہے۔ اُس کے بال کھلے ہوئے ہیں۔ دونوں ایک دوسرے کو دیکھتے ہیں۔ پاروتی اُسے نظر انداز کر کے پانی بھرنے لگتی ہے۔ گھڑا بھرنے کے بعد وہ جانے کو ہوتی ہے۔

دیوداس:
ٹھیر، پارو۔ میں آ گیا ہوں۔

پاروتی (غصے سے):
کیوں؟

دیوداس:
اُس رات کی بات تجھے یاد نہیں کیا؟

Parvati:
No. Nor the letter you sent to me.

Haan. Aur vo chitthi bhi jo tumne likhi hai.

Devdas:
Forgive me, Paro. I wrote it in haste. I don't know what came over me. I didn't have the strength to think.

Mujhe maaf kar de, Paro. Vo khatt maine jaldi mein likh diya tha. Na jaane mujhe kya ho gaya tha. Sochne ki taaqat bhi nahin rahi.

Parvati:
Be quiet. I don't want to hear your excuses.

Chup raho. Main vo sab sunna nahin chaahti.

Devdas:
Listen, Parvati. I'll make my parents consent somehow.

Suno, Parvati. Jaise-kaise bhi hoga main apne maata-pita ko raazi kar loonga.

Parvati:
Your parents? And what about my parents? Is their consent not needed?

Tumhaare maata-pita hain aur mere nahin hain? Unke raazi honay aur na honay ki zaroorat nahin hai?

Devdas:
Of course. But they don't oppose our marriage.

Kyun nahin? Lekin unhen toh is baat se inkaar nahin hai na?

Parvati:
Of course they oppose it. Move aside. Let me pass.

Bilkul inkaar hai. Jaane do mujhe, raasta chhod do.

Devdas:
Paro. Have you forgotten me completely?

Paro. Kya mujhe bilkul bhool gayi ho?

पार्वतीः
हाँ। और वह चिट्ठी भी जो तुमने लिखी है।

देवदासः
मुझे माफ़ कर दे, पारो। वह ख़त मैंने जल्दी में लिख दिया था। न जाने मुझे क्या हो गया था! सोचने की ताक़त भी नहीं रही!

पार्वतीः
चुप रहो। मैं वह सब सुनना नहीं चाहती।

देवदासः
सुनो, पार्वती। जैसे-कैसे भी होगा मैं अपने माता-पिता को राज़ी कर लूँगा।

पार्वतीः
तुम्हारे माता-पिता हैं और मेरे नहीं हैं? उनके राज़ी होने और न होने की ज़रूरत नहीं है?

देवदासः
क्यों नहीं है? लेकिन उन्हें तो इस बात से इन्कार नहीं है ना?

पार्वतीः
बिल्कुल इन्कार है। जाने दो मुझे, रास्ता छोड़ दो।

देवदासः
पारो, क्या मुझे बिल्कुल भूल गई हो?

پاروتی:
ہاں۔اور وہ چٹھی بھی جو تم نے لکھی ہے۔

دیوداس:
مجھے معاف کر دے، پارو۔ وہ خط میں نے جلدی میں لکھ دیا تھا۔ نہ جانے مجھے کیا ہو گیا تھا۔ سوچنے کی طاقت بھی نہیں رہی۔

پاروتی:
چپ رہو۔ میں وہ سب سننا نہیں چاہتی۔

دیوداس:
سنو، پاروتی۔ جیسے کیسے بھی ہوگا، میں اپنے ماتا پِتا کو راضی کر لوں گا۔

پاروتی:
تمہارے ماتا پِتا ہیں اور میرے نہیں ہیں؟ اُن کے راضی ہونے اور نہ ہونے کی ضرورت نہیں ہے؟

دیوداس:
کیوں نہیں، لیکن اُنھیں تو اِس بات سے انکار نہیں ہے نا؟

پاروتی:
بالکل انکار ہے، جانے دو مجھے، راستا چھوڑ دو۔

دیوداس:
پارو۔ کیا مجھے بالکل بھول گئی ہو؟

Parvati:
I cannot trust fickle men like you. My parents have arranged my marriage. Whatever they have done is for my good. Now step aside.

Tum jaise chanchal-chit aadmi par mujhe koi vishwaas nahin. Mere maata-pita meri mangal-kaamna karte hain. Unhon ne jo kiya hai meri bhalaayi hi ke liye kiya hai. Tum raasta chhod do.

Devdas:
Such vanity?

Itna ahankaar?

Parvati:
And why not? If you can be vain, why can't I? You are handsome, but without virtue. I am beautiful and virtuous too. Your family may be rich, but my parents are not beggars.

Kyun na ho? Tum ahankaar kar sakte ho, main nahin kar sakti? Tum mein roop hai, gunn nahin. Mujh mein roop hai aur gunn bhi hai. Tum log bade aadmi ho toh mere maata-pita bhi bheek nahin maangte hain.

Devdas *(affronted):*
Paro.

Paro.

Parvati:
You think you can spoil my name? Go ahead.

Tum soch rahe ho meri badnaami karoge. Kar lo.

Devdas *(taken aback):*
Spoil your name? But how?

Main tumhaari badnaami karunga? Vo kaise?

Parvati:
I came to you alone that night, didn't I? Well, shout it from the rooftops. That will give you peace of mind.

Uss raat main tumhaare paas akeli gayi thin na? Yahi baat chau-khont phaila do. Tumhaare mann ko shaanti ho jaayegi.

Devdas:
Listen, Parvati. Your beauty...so much beauty is not right. It only fans vanity. You know how beautiful the moon is — that is why her face is scarred. Come. Let me scar your face.

Suno, Parvati. Ye roop tumhaara...itna roop acha nahin hai. Is se ahankaar bahot badh jaata hai. Jaanti ho na chaand pe bhi roop suhaaya hai. Isi liye uske chehre par daagh hai. Aao tumhaare chehre par bhi aisa hi daagh bana doon.

Devdas strikes Parvati across her forehead with the thin long rod in his hand. She falls to the ground. She looks up, saying his name softly.

Parvati:
Devdas.

Devdas.

पार्वतीः
तुम जैसे चंचल चित आदमी पर मुझे कोई विश्वास नहीं। मेरे माता-पिता मेरी मंगल-कामना करते हैं। उन्होंने जो किया है, मेरी भलाई ही के लिए किया है। तुम रास्ता छोड़ दो।

پاروتی:
تم جیسے چنچل چت آدمی پر مجھے کوئی وشواس نہیں۔ میرے ماتا پتا میری منگل کامنا کرتے ہیں۔ اُنھوں نے جو کیا ہے میری بھلائی ہی کے لیے کیا ہے۔ تم راستا چھوڑ دو۔

देवदासः
इतना अहंकार?

دیوداس:
اِتنا اہنکار؟

पार्वतीः
क्यों न हो? तुम अहंकार कर सकते हो, मैं नहीं कर सकती? तुम में रूप है, गुण नहीं। मुझ में रूप है और गुण भी है। तुम लोग बड़े आदमी हो तो मेरे माता-पिता भी भीख नहीं माँगते हैं।

پاروتی:
کیوں نہ ہو؟ تم اہنکار کر سکتے ہو، میں نہیں کر سکتی؟ تم میں روپ ہے، گُن نہیں۔ مجھ میں روپ ہے اور گُن بھی ہے۔ تم لوگ بڑے آدمی ہو تو میرے ماتا پتا بھی بھیک نہیں مانگتے ہیں۔

देवदास *(अपमानित)*:
पारो।

دیوداس (غیرت سے):
پارو:

पार्वतीः
तुम सोच रहे हो मेरी बदनामी करोगे। कर लो।

پاروتی:
تم سوچ رہے ہو، میری بدنامی کروگے۔ کرلو۔

देवदास *(आश्चर्य से)*:
मैं तुम्हारी बदनामी करूँगा? वह कैसे?

دیوداس (حیرت سے):
میں تمہاری بدنامی کروں گا؟ وہ کیسے؟

पार्वतीः
उस रात मैं तुम्हारे पास अकेली गई थी ना? यही बात चौ-खूँट फैला दो। तुम्हारे मन को शांति हो जाएगी।

پاروتی:
اُس رات میں تمہارے پاس اکیلی گئی تھی نا؟ یہی بات چوکھونٹ پھیلا دو۔ تمہارے من کو شانتی ہو جائے گی۔

देवदासः
सुनो, पार्वती। यह रूप तुम्हारा...इतना रूप अच्छा नहीं है। इससे अहंकार बहुत बढ़ जाता है। जानती हो न चाँद पे भी रूप सुहाया है। इसीलिए उसके चेहरे पर दाग़ है। आओ, तुम्हारे चेहरे पर भी ऐसा ही दाग़ बना दूँ।

دیوداس:
سنو، پاروتی۔ یہ روپ تمہارا۔۔۔ اِتنا روپ اچھا نہیں ہے۔ اِس سے اہنکار بہت بڑھ جاتا ہے۔ جانتی ہو نا چاند پہ بھی روپ سُہایا ہے۔ اِسی لیے اُس کے چہرے پر داغ ہے۔ آؤ تمہارے چہرے پر بھی ایسا ہی داغ بنادوں۔

देवदास हाथ में पकड़ी छड़ी से पार्वती के माथे पर प्रहार करता है। वह गिर जाती है। उसके मुँह से देवदास का नाम निकलता है।

دیوداس پاروتی کے ماتھے پر چھڑی مارتا ہے۔ پاروتی زمین پر گر جاتی ہے اور ہولے سے اُس کے منہ سے دیوداس کا نام نکلتا ہے۔

पार्वतीः
देवदास!

پاروتی:
دیوداس!

Devdas breaks the rod into four pieces and throws them away. Tearing a strip of cloth from his long shirt, he dampens the cloth with water from Parvati's water pot and wipes the blood from her forehead.

Parvati: What have you done, Devdas?	Ye tumne kya kiya, Devdas?
Devdas *(in a sad voice, as he bandages her head):* Don't be scared, Paro. Your wound will heal soon enough, only the scar will remain. If anyone ever asks, make up a lie, or tell the truth.	Daro nahin, Paro. Ye zakhm toh jald hi bhar jaayenge. Sirf ek daagh reh jaayega. Agar kabhi koi kuch pooche toh jhoot-moot koi baat bana ke keh dena aur nahin toh sach hi bata dena.
Parvati *(tearfully):* But, Devdas...	Lekin Devdas...
Devdas: It's nothing, Paro. It is only a mark in memory of this day of parting. So that whenever you see your face in the mirror — beautiful as the moon — maybe you will think of me. I am a foolish man, maybe our relationship has been so fated through each rebirth. You must forget me, Paro. You know I am impulsive. I can never weigh my words. You did the right thing, Paro. If you had stayed with me, perhaps you would never have been happy.	Kuch nahin, Paro. Is aakhri judayi ke din yaad rakhne ke liye sirf ek nishaan bana diya hai. Taaki ye chaand sa mukhda agar kabhi aainey mein dekho, toh shaayad tumhen meri yaad aa jaaye. Main moorakh...tera-mera shaayad janam-janam ka yahi rishta hai. Par tum mujhe bhool jao, Paro. Tum toh jaanti ho ki main naadaan hoon. Soch-samajh kar kuch baat nahin kar sakta. Tu ne acha hi kiya, Paro. Shaayad mere saath reh kar tum kabhi sukh na paao.

Parvati is silent. Cut to a shot of the sky. The sun has disappeared behind a cloud. Devdas watches Parvati as she walks further and further away.

Dissolve. The next scene. Parvati's home.

देवदास छड़ी के चार टुकडे कर देता है। वह अपने कुर्ते से एक पट्टी फाड़ कर घड़े के पानी से भिगोता है और पार्वती के माथे से बहते हुए ख़ून को पोंछता है।

دیوداس چھڑی کے چار ٹکڑے کر دیتا ہے۔ اپنے کرتے کے دامن کو پھاڑ کر وہ ایک پٹی کو پاروتی کے گھڑے کے پانی سے تر کرتے ہوئے اُس کے ماتھے سے بہتے ہوئے خون کو پونچھتا ہے۔

पार्वतीः
यह तुमने क्या किया, देवदास?

پاروتی:
یہ تم نے کیا کیا، دیوداس؟

देवदास *(सर पर पट्टी बाँधते हुए उदास स्वर में):*
डरो नहीं, पारो। यह ज़ख़्म तो जल्दी भर जाएँगे। सिर्फ़ एक दाग़ रह जाएगा। अगर कभी कोई कुछ पूछे तो झूठ-मूठ कोई बात बना के कह देना और नहीं तो सच ही बता देना।

دیوداس (پٹی باندھتے ہوئے پر تاسف لہجے میں):
ڈرو نہیں، پارو۔ یہ زخم تو جلد ہی بھر جائیں گے۔ صرف ایک داغ رہ جائے گا۔ اگر کبھی کوئی کچھ پوچھے تو جھوٹ موٹ کوئی بات بنا کے کہہ دینا۔ اور نہیں تو سچ ہی بتا دینا۔

पार्वती *(रोआंसी):*
लेकिन देवदास...

پاروتی (اشک آلود ہو کر):
لیکن، دیوداس۔۔۔

देवदासः
कुछ नहीं, पारो। इस आख़िरी जुदाई के दिन याद रखने के लिए सिर्फ़ एक निशान बना दिया है। ताकि यह चाँद-सा मुखड़ा अगर कभी आईने में देखो, तो शायद तुम्हें मेरी याद आ जाए। मैं मूर्ख...तेरा-मेरा शायद जन्म-जन्म का यही रिश्ता है। पर तुम मुझे भूल जाओ, पारो। तुम तो जानती हो कि मैं नादान हूँ। सोच-समझ कर कुछ बात नहीं कर सकता। तूने अच्छा ही किया, पारो। शायद मेरे साथ रह कर तुम कभी सुख न पाओ।

دیوداس:
کچھ نہیں، پارو۔ اِس آخری جدائی کے دن یاد رکھنے کے لیے صرف ایک نشان بنا دیا ہے۔ تاکہ یہ چاند سا مکھڑا اگر کبھی آئینے میں دیکھو تو شاید تمھیں میری یاد آ جائے۔ میں مورکھ۔۔۔ تیرا میرا شاید جنم جنم کا یہی رشتہ ہے۔ پر تم مجھے بھول جاؤ، پارو۔ تم تو جانتی ہو کہ میں نادان ہوں۔ سوچ سمجھ کر کچھ بات نہیں کر سکتا۔ تُو نے اچھا ہی کیا، پارو۔ شاید میرے ساتھ رہ کر تم کبھی سکھ نہ پاؤ۔

पार्वती चुप है। आकाश का एक शॉट। सूर्य बादलों के पीछे छिप गया है। धीरे-धीरे अपने से दूर जाती पार्वती को देवदास खड़ा देख रहा है।

پاروتی خاموش ہے۔ آسمان کا ایک شاٹ دکھائی دیتا ہے۔ سورج بادلوں کے پیچھے چھپ گیا ہے۔ پاروتی کو آہستہ آہستہ دور جاتا ہوا دیوداس کھڑا تک رہا ہے۔

डिज़ॉल्व। अगला दृश्य। पार्वती का घर।

ڈزالو۔ پاروتی کا گھر۔

Grandmother:
Paro, were you at the pond? Dreaming of your new life?
(seeing her head bandaged)
Goodness me! What happened?

Kyun, Paro? Ghaat pe kya sasuraal ke sapnay dekh...

Haaye, main mar gayi. Ye kya hua?

Parvati's mother:
Oh no! You're soon to marry. How did you get hurt?

Arey mayya ri. Tera toh biyaah honay waala hai. Ye sarwanaash kaise ho gaya?

Parvati:
It's nothing, mother. I slipped and fell on the steps.

Kuch nahin, ma. Ghaat par pair phisal gaya. Gir padi.

Fade out.

Reel Seven

Fade in. The Vaishnava singers of her childhood enter the courtyard of Parvati's house. She looks dejected.

Male singer:
Why so sad, child? I hear that you are going to marry a very rich landlord.

Kyun, beti, itni udaas si kyun baithi ho? Maine suna hai tumhaari shaadi toh kisi bahot bade zamindar se ho rahi hai.

Female singer:
Do you remember when you were a child you gave us three rupees? And I had predicted that you would marry a king and live as a queen. So didn't my words come true?

Yaad hai? Tumne bachpan mein humen teen rupay diye thay. Aur maine kaha tha tum kisi raja ki raani banogi. Theek huwi na meri baat?

Male singer:
You must reward us handsomely today.

Aaj toh tumhen ji khol ke daan dena padega, beti, haan.

The Vaishnavas start singing.

Singers: Geeta Dutt & Manna Dey

Female singer:
The young girl belongs to her beloved
Her home seems a foreign land now
O beloved

Saajan ki ho gayi gori saajan ki ho gayi
Ab ghar ka aangan bides lagay re
Saajan haaye haaye

दादीमाँ:
क्यों, पारो? घाट पे क्या ससुराल के सपने देख...
(सर पर पट्टी देख कर)
हाय! मैं मर गई। यह क्या हुआ?

पार्वती की माँ:
अरे मैया री। तेरा तो ब्याह होने वाला है। यह सर्वनाश कैसे हो गया?

पार्वती:
कुछ नहीं, माँ। घाट पर पैर फिसल गया। गिर पड़ी।

फ़ेड आउट।

रील सात

फ़ेड इन। पार्वती के बचपन वाले वैष्णव घर के आँगन में प्रवेश करते हैं। वह उदास दिखाई देती है।

वैष्णव:
क्यों, बेटी, इतनी उदास-सी क्यों बैठी हो? मैंने सुना है, तुम्हारी शादी तो किसी बहुत बड़े ज़मींदार से हो रही है।

वैष्णवी:
याद है? तुमने बचपन में हमें तीन रुपए दिये थे। और मैंने कहा था, तुम किसी राजा की रानी बनोगी। ठीक हुई न मेरी बात?

वैष्णव:
आज तो तुम्हें जी खोल के दान देना पड़ेगा, बेटी, हाँ।

वैष्णव गाते हैं।

स्वर: गीता दत्त और मन्ना डे

वैष्णवी:
साजन की हो गई गोरी साजन की हो गई
अब घर का आँगन बिदेस लागे रे
साजन हाय हाय

دادی:
کیوں، پارو۔گھاٹ پہ کیا سسرال کے سپنے دیکھ۔۔۔
(سر پر بندھی پٹی دیکھ کر)
ہائے میں مرگئی۔یہ کیا ہوا؟

پاروتی کی ماں:
ارے، میّاری۔تیرا تو بیاہ ہونے والا ہے۔یہ سروناش کیسے ہوگیا؟

پاروتی:
کچھ نہیں، ماں۔گھاٹ پر پیر پھسل گیا۔گر پڑی۔

فیڈ آؤٹ۔

ریل سات

فیڈ ان۔پاروتی کے بچپن میں ملے ویشنو اُس کے آنگن میں داخل ہوتے ہیں۔

ویشنو:
کیوں، بیٹی، اِتنی اُداس سی کیوں بیٹھی ہو؟ میں نے سنا ہے تمہاری شادی تو کسی بہت بڑے زمیندار سے ہو رہی ہے۔

ویشنوی:
یاد ہے، تم نے بچپن میں ہمیں تین روپے دیے تھے؟ اور میں نے کہا تھا، تم کسی راجہ کی رانی بنوگی۔ٹھیک ہوئی نا میری بات؟

ویشنو:
آج تو تمھیں جی کھول کے دان دینا پڑے گا، بیٹی، ہاں۔

ویشنو گاتے ہیں۔

آوازیں، گیتا دت اور منا ڈے

ویشنوی:
ساجن کی ہوگئی گوری، ساجن کی ہوگئی
اب گھر کا آنگن بدیس لاگے رے
ساجن، ہائے، ہائے

Together: The young girl belongs to her beloved	Saajan ki ho gayi gori saajan ki ho gayi
Female singer: Her parents' home seems so lonely	Sooni si laagen maike ki galiyaan
Male singer: So lonely	Sooni si laagen
Female singer: No longer pleasing No longer pleasing are her childhood friends	Bhaayen na na na Bhaayen na ab ji ko bachpan ki sakhiyaan
Male singer: No longer pleasing	Bhaayen na
Female singer: Her wedding garland sways before her eyes Thoughts of her beloved are so comforting Every breath… Every breath carries her beloved's message Her home seems a foreign land now O beloved…	Nainon mein jhoomen sehre ki ladiyaan Mann ko lubhaayen sajiya ki kaliyaan Har saans pi ka… Har saans pi ka sandes lagay re Ab ghar ka aangan bides lagay re Saajan…
Together: The young girl belongs to her beloved	Haaye haaye saajan ki ho gayi gori saajan ki ho gayi
Female singer: The flames of passion rise high	Badhti hai pal-pal agni lagan ki
Male singer: The flames of passion…	Badhti hai pal-pal…
Female singer: Love burns through her every vein	Chatkhe hai nas-nas komal badan ki
Male singer: Love burns…	Chatkhe hai nas-nas…

युगलः
साजन की हो गई गोरी साजन की हो गई

वैष्णवीः
सूनी सी लागें मैके की गलियाँ

वैष्णवः
सूनी सी लागें...

वैष्णवीः
भाएँ ना ना ना
भाएँ ना अब जी को बचपन की सखियाँ

वैष्णवः
भाएँ ना...

वैष्णवीः
नैनों में झूमें सेहरे की लड़ियाँ
मन को लुभाएँ सजिया की कलियाँ
हर साँस पी का...
हर साँस पी का संदेस लागे रे
अब घर का आँगन बिदेस लागे रे
साजन...

युगलः
हाय हाय साजन की हो गई गोरी साजन की हो गई

वैष्णवीः
बढ़ती है पल-पल अग्नि लगन की

वैष्णवः
बढ़ती है पल-पल...

वैष्णवीः
चटख़े है नस-नस कोमल बदन की

वैष्णवः
चटख़े है नस-नस...

دونوں:
ساجن کی ہوگئی گوری، ساجن کی ہوگئی

ویشنوی:
سونی سی لاگیں میکے کی گلیاں

ویشنو:
سونی سی لاگیں---

ویشنوی:
بھائیں نا، نا، نا
بھائیں نا اب جی کو بچپن کی سکھیاں

ویشنو:
بھائیں نا---

ویشنوی:
نینوں میں جھومیں سہرے کی لڑیاں
من کو لبھائیں سجیا کی کلیاں
ہر سانس پی کا---
ہر سانس پی کا سندیس لاگے رے
اب گھر کا آنگن بدیس لاگے رے
ساجن---

دونوں:
ہائے ہائے، ساجن کی ہوگئی گوری، ساجن کی ہوگئی

ویشنوی:
بڑھتی ہے پل پل اگنی لگن کی

ویشنو:
بڑھتی ہے پل پل---

ویشنوی:
چٹخے ہے نس نس کومل بدن کی

ویشنو:
چٹخے ہے نس نس---

Female singer:
I can read her every thought
She has given her heart to her beloved
Her old life…
Her old life seems so bleak

Hum jaante hain sab iske mann ki
Ab ho chuki ye apne sajan ki
Naihar ka jeevan…
Naihar ka jeevan kales lagay re

Male singer:
Her home seems a foreign land now
O beloved…

Ab ghar ka aangan bides lagay re
Saajan…

Together:
The young girl belongs to her beloved

Haaye haaye saajan ki ho gayi gori saajan ki ho gayi

Male singer:
Radha. Radha.

Radhe. Radhe.

As the song ends, Parvati enters her room and closes the door behind her. She is crying and overwhelmed with emotion. She throws herself onto her bed, sobbing. Fade out.

Fade in. Night-time. A wedding procession makes its way to Parvati's house. The groom in the palanquin is an old balding man. Manorama is sitting with Parvati inside the house.

Manorama:
I wish I could call Devdas and show him this glowing face.

Ji chaahta hai Devdas ko ek baar bula kar ye swarnmoorti dikha doon.

Parvati:
Is that possible, Mano didi? Could I anoint my brow with the dust from beneath his feet?

Kya ye ho sakta hai, Mano didi? Ek baar unke charnon ki dhool maathe par laga sakti hoon?

वैष्णवीः

हम जानते हैं सब इसके मन की
अब हो चुकी यह अपने सजन की
नैहर का जीवन...
नैहर का जीवन क्लेस लागे रे

वैष्णवः

अब घर का आँगन बिदेस लागे रे
साजन...

युगलः

हाय हाय साजन की हो गई गोरी साजन की हो गई

वैष्णवः

राधे। राधे।

गाना समाप्त होते ही पार्वती अपने कमरे में आती है। द्वार बंद करके अपने बिस्तर पर ढेर हो जाती है और सिसकियाँ लेकर रोने लगती है। फ़ेड आउट।

फ़ेड इन। रात का समय। पार्वती के घर एक बारात आ रही है। पालकी में बैठा दूल्हा एक बूढ़ा व्यक्ति है। दुल्हन बनी पार्वती के साथ उसकी सहेली मनोरमा बैठी हुई है।

मनोरमाः

जी चाहता है, देवदास को एक बार बुला कर यह स्वर्णमूर्ति दिखा दूँ।

पार्वतीः

क्या यह हो सकता है, मनो दीदी? एक बार उनके चरनों की धूल माथे पर लगा सकती हूँ?

ویشنوی:

ہم جانتے ہیں سب اِس کے من کی
اب ہو چکی یہ اپنے سجن کی
نیہر کا جیون۔۔۔
نیہر کا جیون کلیس لاگے رے

ویشنو:

اب گھر کا آنگن بدیس لاگے رے
ساجن۔۔۔

دونوں:

ہائے ہائے، ساجن کی ہوگئی گوری، ساجن کی ہوگئی

ویشنو:

رادھے۔ رادھے۔

گانا ختم ہوتے ہی پاروتی اپنے کمرے میں جا کر دروازہ بند کر لیتی ہے۔ جذبات سے مغلوب ہو کر وہ رو رہی ہے۔ سسکیاں لیتی ہوئی وہ اپنے بستر پر ڈھیر ہو جاتی ہے۔ فیڈ آؤٹ۔

فیڈ ان۔ رات۔ پاروتی کے گھر کی طرف ایک بارات آ رہی ہے۔ پالکی میں بیٹھا ہوا دولہا ایک بوڑھا شخص ہے۔ دولہن بنی پاروتی کے ساتھ منورما بیٹھی ہوئی ہے۔

منورما:

جی چاہتا ہے دیوداس کو ایک بار بلا کر یہ سورن مورتی دکھا دوں۔

پاروتی:

کیا یہ ہو سکتا ہے، منو دیدی؟ ایک بار اُن کے چرنوں کی دھول ماتھے پر لگا سکتی ہوں؟

Manorama:
Forget him, my princess. I hear that heartless man has already left for Calcutta.

Bhool ja, raani. Maine suna hai ki vo nirmohi toh Kalkatte chala gaya hai.

Tracking forward to a close-up of Parvati as she closes her eyes. Cut. Night. Devdas is sitting in a Calcutta park.

Dissolve. This scene is a continuation of the same night. Devdas returns to his room.

Chunni Babu:
Devdas? So you're back again? When did you return?

Arey Devdas, tum phir aa dhamke? Kab aaye tum?

Devdas:
Yesterday.

Kal aaya.

Chunni Babu:
Yesterday? Where were you all day? And where did you spend the night?

Kal? Phir kahaan rahe saara din? Aur kahaan bitaai saari ratiyaan?

Devdas:
In the park.

Park mein tha.

Chunni Babu:
In the park?

Park mein?

Devdas:
Hmm.

Hmm.

Chunni Babu:
Have you gone crazy? What has come over you? Did you quarrel with your father?

Tum kuch paagal ho? Kya ho gaya hai tumhen? Pitaji ke saath jhagda hua?

Devdas:
No, no.

Nahin, nahin.

Chunni Babu:
With someone else then?

Phir kisi aur ke saath jhagda hua?

मनोरमाः
भूल जा, रानी। मैंने सुना है कि वह निर्मोही तो कलकत्ते चला गया है।

منورما:
بھول جا، رانی۔ میں نے سنا ہے کہ وہ نرموہی تو کلکتے چلا گیا ہے۔

ट्रैकिंग शॉट जिसके क्लोज़-अप में पार्वती अपनी आँखें बंद कर लेती है। कट। रात। कलकत्ते के एक उद्यान में देवदास बैठा हुआ है।

ٹریکنگ شاٹ جس کے کلوز اپ میں پاروتی اپنی آنکھیں بند کر لیتی ہے۔ کٹ۔ رات۔ کلکتہ کے ایک پارک میں دیوداس بیٹھا ہوا ہے۔

डिज़ॉल्व। उसी रात का दृश्य। देवदास अपने कमरे में लौटता है।

ڈزالو۔ دیوداس اپنے کمرے میں لوٹتا ہے۔

चुन्नी बाबूः
अरे देवदास, तुम फिर आ धमके? कब आए तुम?

چنّی بابو:
ارے، دیوداس، تم پھر آ دھمکے؟ کب آئے تم؟

देवदासः
कल आया।

دیوداس:
کل آیا۔

चुन्नी बाबूः
कल? फिर कहाँ रहे सारा दिन? और कहाँ बिताई सारी रतिया?

چنّی بابو:
کل؟ پھر کہاں رہے سارا دن؟ اور کہاں بتائیں ساری رتیاں؟

देवदासः
पार्क में था।

دیوداس:
پارک میں تھا۔

चुन्नी बाबूः
पार्क में?

چنّی بابو:
پارک میں؟

देवदासः
हुँ।

دیوداس:
ہوں۔

चुन्नी बाबूः
तुम कुछ पागल हो? क्या हो गया है तुम्हें? पिताजी के साथ झगड़ा हुआ?

چنّی بابو:
تم کچھ پاگل ہو؟ کیا ہو گیا ہے تمھیں؟ پتا جی کے ساتھ جھگڑا ہوا؟

देवदासः
नहीं, नहीं।

دیوداس:
نہیں، نہیں۔

चुन्नी बाबूः
फिर किसी और के साथ झगड़ा हुआ?

چنّی بابو:
پھر کسی اور کے ساتھ جھگڑا ہوا؟

Devdas:
No.

Na.

Chunni Babu:
I forgot. You aren't even married, so how could you have quarrelled with someone else?

Main toh bhool hi gaya tha ki tumhaari shaadi hi nahin huwi. Kisi aur ke saath jhagda ho kaise sakta tha?

Devdas:
Chunni babu, do all sorrows vanish in the place where you go?

Chunni babu, tum jahaan jaate ho wahaan sach-much sab dukh door ho jaate hain na?

Chunni Babu:
They do. But it isn't a good place.

Ho toh jaate hain lekin vo jagah achi nahin hai.

Devdas:
What is good or bad? It's all nonsense. Take me with you, Chunni babu.

Acha kya aur bura kya, sab bekaar ki baatein hain. Mujhe bhi apne saath le chalo, Chunni babu.

Chunni Babu:
"O forlorn flower, let me embrace you
Like me you have withered in youth."
There's no harm in my taking you there, Devdas. But it's preferrable that you don't come with me.

"Aa ae gule-fusurda laga loon galay tujhe
Meri tarah se tu bhi luta hai shabaab mein"
Wahaan le chalne mein toh koi harj nahin, Devdas. Lekin tum na jaao toh acha hai.

Devdas:
I will most certainly go.

Main wahaan zaroor jaaunga.

Chunni Babu:
As you please. Come.

Toh tumhaari marzi. Chalo.

The same night. Parvati's father and Manorama lead the bride Parvati to the palanquin. She is going to her husband's home.

Nilkanth:
Parvati, step into the palanquin, my child.

Parvati, paalki pe chadho, beti.

Whip pan. A Calcutta street. Chunni Babu asks Devdas to alight from the horse carriage. Now married, Parvati's departure from her parents' home is cross-cut with Devdas entering the brothel.

देवदासः
ना।

चुन्नी बाबूः
मैं तो भूल ही गया था कि तुम्हारी शादी ही नहीं हुई। किसी और के साथ झगड़ा हो कैसे सकता था?

देवदासः
चुन्नी बाबू, तुम जहाँ जाते हो, वहाँ सचमुच सब दुःख दूर हो जाते हैं ना?

चुन्नी बाबूः
हो तो जाते हैं लेकिन वह जगह अच्छी नहीं है।

देवदासः
अच्छा क्या और बुरा क्या, सब बेकार की बातें हैं। मुझे भी अपने साथ ले चलो, चुन्नी बाबू।

चुन्नी बाबूः
''आ ऐ गुले-फ़ुसुर्दा लगा लूँ गले तुझे
मेरी तरह से तू भी लुटा है शबाब में''
वहाँ ले चलने में तो कोई हर्ज नहीं, देवदास। लेकिन तुम न जाओ तो अच्छा है।

देवदासः
मैं वहाँ ज़रूर जाऊँगा।

चुन्नी बाबूः
तो तुम्हारी मरज़ी। चलो।

उसी रात का दृश्य। पार्वती के पिता और मनोरमा उसे सहारा देकर सजी हुई डोली में विदा करते हैं।

नीलकंठः
पार्वती, पालकी पे चढ़ो, बेटी।

पलक झपकते ही दृश्य बदलता है। कलकत्ते की एक सड़क। चुन्नी बाबू, देवदास से कहता है कि वह घोड़ागाड़ी से उतर आए। विवाहित पार्वती की बिदाई का दृश्य और देवदास का कोठे में प्रवेश, एक साथ दिखाई दे रहे हैं।

دیوداس:
نہ۔

چنّی بابو:
میں تو بھول ہی گیا تھا کہ تمہاری شادی ہی نہیں ہوئی۔ کسی اور کے ساتھ جھگڑا ہو کیسے سکتا تھا؟

دیوداس:
چنّی بابو۔ تم جہاں جاتے ہو وہاں سچ مچ سب دکھ دور ہو جاتے ہیں نا؟

چنّی بابو:
ہو تو جاتے ہیں، لیکن وہ جگہ اچھی نہیں ہے۔

دیوداس:
اچھا کیا اور برا کیا، سب بیکار کی باتیں ہیں۔ مجھے بھی اپنے ساتھ لے چلو، چنّی بابو۔

چنّی بابو:
''آ اے گُلِ فسردہ، لگا لوں گلے تجھے
میری طرح سے تُو بھی لُٹا ہے شباب میں''
وہاں لے چلنے میں تو کوئی حرج نہیں، دیوداس۔ لیکن تم نہ جاؤ تو اچھا ہے۔

دیوداس:
میں وہاں ضرور جاؤں گا۔

چنّی بابو:
تو تمہاری مرضی۔ چلو۔

اُسی رات کا منظر۔ پاروتی کو سہارا دے کر منورما اور پاروتی کے والد سجی ہوئی ڈولی میں بٹھا کر رخصت کر رہے ہیں۔

نیل کنٹھ:
پاروتی، پالکی پہ چڑھو، بیٹی۔

پلک جھپکتے منظر بدلتا ہے۔ کلکتہ کی ایک سڑک۔ دیوداس سے چنّی بابو کہہ رہے ہیں کہ وہ گھوڑا گاڑی سے اُتر آئے۔ شادی شدہ پاروتی کی رُخصتی کا منظر اور دیوداس کے کوٹھے پر پہنچنے کے مناظر بیک وقت دکھائی دے رہے ہیں۔

Chunni Babu:
Get down, Devdas. What are you thinking?

Arey utro na, Devdas. Kya soch rahe ho?

Chunni Babu leads the reluctant Devdas towards the brothel. A drunkard bumps into him. Devdas is sickened by the atmosphere of the place. The sound of ghazal singing underscores the scene. Chunni Babu and Devdas enter a room in the brothel. Chandramukhi (actress Vyjayanthimala) is dancing for her patrons. She gives Devdas a seductive glance. He returns her look with disdain.

Devdas *(to Chunni Babu):*
What is this wretched place?

Ye kis manhoos jagah le aaye ho?

(Chandramukhi stops dancing)
It disgusts me.

Ghin aa rahi hai mujhe.

Devdas stares coldly at Chandramukhi.

Reel Eight

Unnamed client *(actor Pran):*
Who is he?

Ye kaun hai?

Second unnamed client *(comedian Johnny Walker):*
A fly in the ointment.

Kabaab mein haddi.

Chunni Babu *(to Chandramukhi):*
Oh no! Why have you stopped?
"Did you stop or did my heart stop?
Heavy with grief, the sky fell upon us."
(stopping Devdas from leaving)

Haaye haaye. Tum kyun ruk gayin?
"Tum rukein kya dil humaara ruk gaya
Gham ke maare aasmaan bhi jhuk gaya"

चुन्नी बाबू:
अरे उतरो न, देवदास। क्या सोच रहे हो?

देवदास को चुन्नी बाबू कोठे पर ले जाता है। न चाहते हुए देवदास उसके साथ चल रहा है। नशे में धुत एक शराबी उनसे टकराता है। देवदास उसे घृणा से देखता है। कहीं से ग़ज़ल गाने की आवाज़ सुनाई दे रही है। चुन्नी बाबू और देवदास कोठे के एक कमरे में पहुँचते हैं। अपने ग्राहकों के सामने नाचती हुई चंद्रमुखी (अभिनेत्री विजयंतीमाला) तिरछी नज़रों से देवदास की ओर देखती है। देवदास उससे मुँह फेर लेता है।

देवदास *(चुन्नी बाबू से):*
यह किस मनहूस जगह ले आए हो?
(चंद्रमुखी नृत्य रोक देती है)
घिन आ रही है मुझे।

उकताई हुई नज़रों से देवदास, चंद्रमुखी को देखता है।

रील आठ

ग्राहक-१ *(अभिनेता प्राण):*
यह कौन है?

ग्राहक-२ *(अभिनेता जॉनी वॉकर):*
कबाब में हड्डी।

चुन्नी बाबू *(चंद्रमुखी से):*
हाय हाय। तुम क्यों रुक गई?
''तुम रुकीं क्या दिल हमारा रुक गया
ग़म के मारे आसमाँ भी झुक गया।''
(देवदास को जाने से रोकता है)

چُنّی بابو:
ارے، اُترو، دیوداس۔ کیا سوچ رہے ہو؟

دیوداس بادلِ نخواستہ چُنی بابو کے ساتھ کوٹھے کی طرف جا رہا ہے۔ ایک شرابی نشے میں اُن سے ٹکراتا ہے۔ دیوداس کو کراہیت سی محسوس ہو رہی ہے۔ کہیں سے غزل گانے کی آواز سنائی دے رہی ہے۔ چُنی بابو اور دیوداس ایک کوٹھے پر پہنچتے ہیں۔ اپنے گاہکوں کے سامنے چندرمکھی ناچتی ہوئی (اداکارہ، وجینتی مالا) ایک نگاہِ غلط انداز دیوداس کی طرف بھی ڈالتی ہے۔ دیوداس منہ پھیر لیتا ہے۔

دیوداس (چنی بابو سے):
یہ کس منحوس جگہ لے آئے ہو؟
(ناچتی ہوئی چندرمکھی رک جاتی ہے)
گِھن آ رہی ہے مجھے۔

چندرمکھی کی طرف دیوداس سرد نگاہوں سے دیکھتا ہے۔

ریل آٹھ

گاہک ۱ (اداکار، پران):
یہ کون ہے؟

گاہک ۲ (اداکار، جانی واکر):
کباب میں ہڈی

چُنّی بابو (چندرمکھی سے):
ہائے ہائے۔ تم کیوں رک گئیں؟
''تم رکیں کیا، دل ہمارا رک گیا
غم کے مارے آسماں بھی جھک گیا''
(دیوداس کو روکتے ہوئے)

Devdas, where are you going? There's nothing to be afraid of. Come on. Sit down.

(to the tabla player)

Start playing, Ustaad.

Ae Devdas, tum kahaan chale? Ghabraane ki kya baat hai? Baitho. Baitho, baitho. Baith jaao.

Haan toh shuru ho jaao, Ustaad.

The music starts. Chandramukhi dances while she sings.

Lata Mangeshkar sings for Chandramukhi

He left his heart...
He left his heart at the feet of his beloved
As he got up to go, the distraught man said:

Dildaar ke qadmon mein
Dildaar ke qadmon mein dil daal ke nazraana
Mehfil se utha aur ye kehne laga deewaana

Unnamed client *(interrupting song):*
What?

Kya?

From now on it is your will
My beloved, my sweet love
O heartless one, it is your will
O beloved, from now on it is your will
Beloved, from now on it is your will

Ab aage teri marzi o aage teri marzi
O moray sayyaan o moray balma
Bedardi aage teri marzi
Aage teri marzi sajanwa aage teri marzi
Piharva aage teri marzi

Do not ask what makes me unhappy (2)
Why have I sacrificed my heart for you? (2)
My lips are trembling, how uneasy am I
I live in the hope that our eyes will meet

Na pooch hum se ki kyun saugwaar baithe hain (2)
Teri adaaon pe hum dil ko waar baithe hain (2)
Labon pe jaan hai aur beqaraar baithe hain
Nigaah milne ke ummeedwaar baithe hain

Unnamed client *(speaking):*
Is that right?

Sachi?

From now on it is your will
My beloved, my sweet love

Ab aage teri marzi o aage teri marzi
O moray sayyaan o moray balma

ए देवदास, तुम कहाँ चले? घबराने की क्या बात है? बैठो। बैठो, बैठो। बैठ जाओ।

(तबलची से)

हाँ तो शुरू हो जाओ, उस्ताद।

संगीत आरम्भ होता है। चंद्रमुखी नृत्य के साथ गाना गा रही है।

स्वरः लता मंगेशकर

दिलदार के क़दमों में...
दिलदार के क़दमों में दिल डाल के नज़राना
महफ़िल से उठा और यह कहने लगा दीवाना

ग्राहक *(गाने के बीच में):*
क्या?

अब आगे तेरी मरज़ी ओ आगे तेरी मरज़ी
ओ मोरे सैंया ओ मोरे बलमा
बेदर्दी आगे तेरी मरज़ी
आगे तेरी मरज़ी सजनवा आगे तेरी मरज़ी
पीहरवा आगे तेरी मरज़ी

न पूछ हमसे कि क्यों सोगवार बैठे हैं (२)
तेरी अदाओं पे हम दिल को वार बैठे हैं (२)
लबों पे जान है और बेक़रार बैठे हैं
निगाह मिलने के उम्मीदवार बैठे हैं

ग्राहक *(गाने के बीच में):*
सच्ची?

अब आगे तेरी मरज़ी ओ आगे तेरी मरज़ी
ओ मोरे सैंया ओ मोरे बलमा

اے، دیوداس۔تم کہاں چلے؟ گھبرانے کی کیا بات ہے؟ بیٹھو۔بیٹھو، بیٹھو۔بیٹھ جاؤ۔
(طبلہ نواز سے)
ہاں تو شروع ہو جاؤ، اُستاد۔

موسیقی شروع ہوتی ہے۔رقص کرتی ہوئی چندرمکھی گا رہی ہے۔

آواز، لتا منگیشکر

دلدار کے قدموں میں
دلدار کے قدموں میں دل ڈال کے نذرانہ
محفل سے اُٹھا اور یہ، کہنے لگا دیوانہ

گاہک (گانے کے درمیان تحت میں):
کیا؟

اب آگے تیری مرضی او آگے تیری مرضی
او مورے سیّاں او مورے بلما
بے دردی، آگے تیری مرضی آگے تیری مرضی
سجنوا آگے تیری مرضی
پیہروا آگے تیری مرضی

نہ پوچھ ہم سے کہ کیوں سوگوار بیٹھے ہیں (۲)
تری اداؤں پہ ہم دل کو وار بیٹھے ہیں (۲)
لبوں پہ جان ہے اور بے قرار بیٹھے ہیں
نگاہ ملنے اُمیدوار بیٹھے ہیں

گاہک (گانے کے درمیان تحت میں):
سچی؟

اب آگے تیری مرضی او آگے تیری مرضی
او مورے سیّاں او مورے بلما

O heartless one, from now on it is your will
O beloved, from now on it is your will
O fickle one, from now on it is your will

Bedardi aage teri marzi
Aage teri marzi o rasiya aage teri marzi
O chhalya aage teri marzi

Unnamed client *(Pran):*
Long life to you!

Jiyo, jiyo. Sau saal jiyo.

Second unnamed client *(Johnny Walker):*
Well done! May you have a very long life!

Wah, wah! Jitney saal ye bola utne saal jiyo.

A tempest of emotion rages in my heart
The desire to live, the desire to die
From now on it is your will
My beloved, my sweet love
O heartless one, it is your will
O cruel one, it is your will
O merciless one, it is your will
O beloved, it is your will
It is your will

Seene mein mohabbat ke jazbaat ka toofaan hai
Jeene ki bhi hasrat hai marne ka bhi armaan hai
Ab aage teri marzi o aage teri marzi
O moray sayyaan o moray balma
Bedardi aage teri marzi
Aage teri marzi o julmi
Aage teri marzi re nirdayi
Aage teri marzi o balma
Aage teri marzi

Group of men:
Long live!

Jiyo. Jiyo. Jiyo.

Unnamed client *(Pran):*
Enjoy a full life!
(handing Chandramukhi some money)
Here.

Arey jiyo jab tak ji chaahe.

Ye lo.

Second unnamed client *(Johnny Walker):*
My salaams to you.

Waalekum aadaab. Waalekum aadaab.

Chunni Babu whispers something into the client's ear. The men get up to leave.

Unnamed client *(Pran, to Chunni Babu):*
As you wish, sir. Let's go.

Oh. Tumhaari marzi. Chalo bhai, chalo sab.

Group of men:
Come on, brothers.

Chalo bhai. Chalo.

बेदर्दी आगे तेरी मरज़ी
आगे तेरी मरज़ी ओ रसिया आगे तेरी मरज़ी
ओ छलिया आगे तेरी मरज़ी

ग्राहक-१ *(प्राण):*
जियो, जियो। सौ साल जियो।

ग्राहक-२ *(जॉनी वाकर):*
वाह, वाह! जितने साल यह बोला उतने साल जियो।

सीने में मुहब्बत के जज़्बात का तूफ़ाँ है
जीने की भी हसरत है मरने का भी अरमाँ है
अब आगे तेरी मरज़ी ओ आगे तेरी मरज़ी
ओ मोरे सैंया ओ मोरे बलमा
बेदर्दी आगे तेरी मरज़ी
आगे तेरी मरज़ी ओ ज़ुल्मी
आगे तेरी मरज़ी रे निर्दयी
आगे तेरी मरज़ी ओ बलमा
आगे तेरी मरज़ी

सब लोग:
जियो। जियो। जियो।

ग्राहक-१ *(प्राण):*
अरे जियो जब तक जी चाहे।
(कुछ रुपए देते हुए)
यह लो।

ग्राहक-२*(जॉनी वाकर):*
वालैकुम आदाब। वालैकुम आदाब।

चुन्नी बाबू ग्राहक के कान में कुछ कहता है। सब जाने के लिए खड़े हो जाते हैं।

ग्राहक-१ *(प्राण, चुन्नी बाबू से):*
ओह, तुम्हारी मरज़ी। चलो भाई, चलो सब।

सब लोग:
चलो भाई। चलो।

بے دردی، آگے تیری مرضی
آگے تری مرضی اورسیا آگے تیری مرضی
او چھلیا آگے تیری مرضی

گاہک ا (پران):
جیو۔ جیو۔ سو سال جیو۔

گاہک ۲ (جانی واکر):
واہ واہ جتنے سال یہ بولا اُتنے سال جیو۔

سینے میں محبت کے جذبات کا طوفاں ہے
جینے کی بھی حسرت ہے، مرنے کا بھی ارماں ہے
اب آگے تیری مرضی او آگے تیری مرضی
او مورے سیّاں او مورے بلما
بے دردی، آگے تیری مرضی
آگے تیری مرضی او ظلمی
آگے تیری مرضی رے نردئی
آگے تیری مرضی او بلما
آگے تیری مرضی

لوگ:
جیو، جیو، جیو۔

گاہک ا (پران):
ارے، جیو جب تک دل چاہے۔
(کچھ روپے دیتے ہوئے)
یہ لو۔

گاہک ۲ (جانی واکر):
وعلیکم آداب۔ وعلیکم آداب۔

گاہک کے کان میں چُنی بابو کچھ کہتا ہے۔ سب لوگ جانے لگتے ہیں۔

گاہک ا (چنی بابو سے پران):
تمہاری مرضی۔ چلو بھئی۔ چلو سب۔

لوگ:
چلو بھئی، چلو۔

Second unnamed client *(Johnny Walker):*
Must we leave? All right, let's go.

Jaana hi padega? Aao chalo.

Chunni Babu:
Where are you going?

Arey aap kahaan chale, bhai?

Second unnamed client *(heading in the wrong direction):*
Me? I'm leaving.

Ji? Main baahar ja raha hoon.

Chunni Babu:
It's that way out.

Baahar idhar se jaayiye.

Second unnamed client:
Is there no way out here?

Kyun, idhar darwaaza nahin hai?

Chunni Babu:
No, there isn't.

Nahin. Idhar nahin hai.

Second unnamed client:
All right.

Haan toh chalo.

Chunni Babu *(to Devdas, who is about to leave):*
Where are you going? Stay here for a minute. I'll go and get some cigarettes.

Arey tum kahaan chale? Zara ek minute yahin baitho, main cigarette le ke aata hoon.

Chunni Babu leaves. Chandramukhi sits next to Devdas. He is awkward and moves away as she tries to sit closer to him. A ghazal sung by Mubarak Begum underscores the scene.

Devdas:
What an ill-mannered girl.

Kaisi bad-tameez ladki hai.

(getting up abruptly)
You take money?

Rupay leti ho na?

Chandramukhi:
The dust beneath your feet…

Aap ke charnon ki dhool jab mere ghar…

Devdas:
I'm not talking of feet. I am talking of money. You take money, don't you?

Charnon ki baat nahin karta, rupay ki baat karta hoon. Rupay leti ho na?

ग्राहक-२ *(जॉनी वाकर):*
जाना ही पड़ेगा? आओ चलो।

گاہک ۲(جانی واکر):
جانا ہی پڑے گا۔آؤ چلو۔

चुन्नी बाबू:
अरे आप कहाँ चले, भाई?

چنّی بابو:
ارے،آپ کہاں چلے،بھئی؟

ग्राहक-२ *(ग़लत दिशा में जाते हुए):*
जी? मैं बाहर जा रहा हूँ।

گاہک ۲(غلط سمت میں جاتے ہوئے):
جی؟ میں باہر جا رہا ہوں۔

चुन्नी बाबू:
बाहर इधर से जाइये।

چنّی بابو:
باہر اِدھر سے جائیے۔

ग्राहक-२:
क्यों, इधर दरवाज़ा नहीं है?

گاہک ۲:
کیا اِدھر دروازہ نہیں ہے؟

चुन्नी बाबू:
नहीं। इधर नहीं है।

چنّی بابو:
نہیں۔اِدھر نہیں ہے۔

ग्राहक-२:
हाँ तो चलो।

گاہک ۲:
ہاں تو چلو۔

चुन्नी बाबू *(देवदास से जो वहाँ से जाना चाहता है):*
अरे तुम कहाँ चले? ज़रा एक मिनट यहीं बैठो, मैं सिगरेट लेके आता हूँ।

چنّی بابو(دیوداس سے جو وہاں سے جانا چاہتا ہے):
ارے۔تم کہاں چلے؟ ذرا ایک منٹ یہاں بیٹھو۔میں سگریٹ لے کے آتا ہوں۔

चुन्नी बाबू वहाँ से चला जाता है। चंद्रमुखी देवदास के पास बैठ जाती है। जब और निकट होना चाहती है तो देवदास परे हट जाता है। पार्श्व में मुबारक बेगम की आवाज़ में एक ग़ज़ल चल रही है।

چنّی بابو جاتے ہیں۔دیوداس کے پاس چندرمکھی بیٹھ جاتی ہے۔جیسے ہی وہ مزید قریب ہونا چاہتی ہے دیوداس اور پرے کھسک جاتا ہے۔مبارک بیگم کی آواز میں غزل کا شعر گونج رہا ہے۔

देवदास:
कैसी बदतमीज़ लड़की है!
(अचानक उठ खड़ा होता है)
रुपए लेती हो ना?

دیوداس:
کیسی بدتمیز لڑکی ہے۔
(اچانک اُٹھ کھڑا ہوتا ہے)
روپے لیتی ہو نا؟

चंद्रमुखी:
आपके चरनों की धूल जब मेरे घर...

چندرمکھی:
آپ کے چرنوں کی دھول جب میرے گھر۔۔۔

देवदास:
चरनों की बात नहीं करता, रुपए की बात करता हूँ। रुपए लेती हो ना?

دیوداس:
چرنوں کی بات نہیں کرتا۔روپے کی بات کرتا ہوں۔روپے لیتی ہو نا؟

Chandramukhi:
Yes, and why not? How else would we survive if we didn't?

Ji, leti kyun nahin? Nahin toh humaara kaam kaise...

Devdas *(throwing his wallet to the floor):*
Enough! I don't want to hear any more.

Bas, bas. Main aur sunna nahin chaahta.

Chandramukhi picks up the wallet. As Devdas leaves the brothel, Chunni Babu arrives and tries to stop him.

Chunni Babu:
Devdas!

Arey Devdas!

Devdas leaves despite Chunni Babu's protests. Chunni Babu returns to Chandramukhi's room.

Chunni Babu:
Devdas has gone.

Chala gaya Devdas.

Chandramukhi *(hands him Devdas's wallet):*
Chunni babu, return this to him.

Hmm. Chunni babu, ye dekho, ye unhen lauta dena.

Chunni Babu:
Why should I? He gave it of his own free will.

Main kyun lauta doon? Vo apni marzi se de gaya hai na?

Chandramukhi:
Not really. We take money, don't we? He gave it to me in anger. Chunni babu, will you do me a favour?

Apni marzi se nahin. Hum rupay leti hain na, isi liye naaraaz ho kar de gaya hai. Chunni babu, tum mujh par ek ehsaan karoge?

Chunni Babu:
What?

Kya?

चंद्रमुखी:
जी, लेती क्यों नहीं? नहीं तो हमारा काम कैसे...

देवदास *(फर्श पर अपना बटुआ फेंकते हुए):*
बस, बस। मैं और सुनना नहीं चाहता।

चंद्रमुखी बटुआ उठा लेती है। देवदास कोठे से बाहर जा रहा है, चुन्नी बाबू उसे रोकता है।

चुन्नी बाबू:
अरे देवदास!

चुन्नी बाबू के रोकने के बावजूद देवदास चला जाता है। चुन्नी बाबू चंद्रमुखी के कमरे में वापस आता है।

चुन्नी बाबू:
चला गया देवदास।

चंद्रमुखी *(देवदास का बटुआ वापस करते हुए):*
हुँ। चुन्नी बाबू, यह देखो, यह उन्हें लौटा देना।

चुन्नी बाबू:
मैं क्यों लौटा दूँ? वह अपनी मरज़ी से दे गया है ना?

चंद्रमुखी:
अपनी मरज़ी से नहीं। हम रुपए लेती हैं ना, इसीलिए नाराज़ होकर दे गया है। चुन्नी बाबू, तुम मुझ पर एक एहसान करोगे?

चुन्नी बाबू:
क्या?

چندرمکھی:
جی۔ لیتی کیوں نہیں۔ نہیں تو ہمارا کام کیسے۔۔۔

دیوداس *(اپنا بٹوہ فرش پر پھینکتے ہوئے):*
بس، بس۔ میں اور سننا نہیں چاہتا۔

چندرمکھی بٹوہ اُٹھالیتی ہے۔ دیوداس کوٹھے سے اُتر کر جارہا ہے اور چُنّی بابو اُسے روک رہے ہیں۔

چُنّی بابو:
ارے دیوداس!

چُنّی بابو کے روکنے کے باوجود دیوداس وہاں سے چلا جاتا ہے۔ چُنّی بابو لوٹ کر چندرمکھی کے کمرے میں آتے ہیں۔

چُنّی بابو:
چلا گیا دیوداس۔

چندرمکھی *(اُسے دیوداس کا بٹوہ لوٹاتے ہوئے):*
ہوں۔ چُنّی بابو، یہ دیکھو۔ یہ اُنھیں لوٹا دینا۔

چُنّی بابو:
میں کیوں لوٹا دوں؟ وہ اپنی مرضی سے دے گیا ہے نا؟

چندرمکھی:
اپنی مرضی سے نہیں۔ ہم روپے لیتی ہیں نا۔ اِسی لیے ناراض ہو کر دے گیا ہے۔ چُنّی بابو، تم مجھ پر ایک احسان کروگے؟

چُنّی بابو:
کیا؟

Chandramukhi: Can you bring him back here some day?	Unhen phir kisi din yahaan la sakte ho?
Chunni Babu: He never comes to places like this. And I don't think he will return. But why do you want him back?	Magar vo aisi jagaahon mein kabhi aaya nahin hai aur main samajhta hoon ab vo aayega bhi nahin. Magar tum bulaana kyun chaahti ho?
Chandramukhi: No reason. I'd like to see him again.	Yunhi. Unhen phir ek baar dekhna chaahti hoon.
Chunni Babu *(laughing):* Fallen in love so soon?	Jhidki kha kar pyar ho gaya hai?
Chandramukhi: You don't know, Chunni babu, but he's the first man to give money without a motive. Do you understand?	Tum nahin jaante, Chunni babu. Ye pehla aadmi hai jo bin matlab paise de kar chala gaya. Nahin samjhe?
Chunni Babu: I understand. Many are greedy, but not you. Tell me what's really on your mind.	Samajhta hoon. Noton ka laalach karne waali koi aur, tum nahin. Magar asli baat kya hai?
Chandramukhi: Why ask? I think I like him.	Kya sochte ho? Kuch moh sa ho gaya hai.
Chunni Babu: In five minutes? *(singing)* "The moment I set eyes on him…"	Arey bas paanch minute mein? "Laage moray nain unse…"
Chandramukhi: Don't joke. You'll bring him back, won't you?	Mazaaq chhodo. Unhen zaroor laana. Laaoge na?
Chunni Babu: Who knows.	Kya maaloom.
Chandramukhi: For my sake.	Tumhen mere sar ki qasam.

चंद्रमुखीः
उन्हें फिर किसी दिन यहाँ ला सकते हो?

چندر مکھی:
اُنھیں پھر کسی دن یہاں لا سکتے ہو؟

चुन्नी बाबूः
मगर वह ऐसी जगहों में कभी आया नहीं है और मैं समझता हूँ अब वह आएगा भी नहीं। मगर तुम बुलाना क्यों चाहती हो?

چنّی بابو:
مگر وہ ایسی جگہوں میں کبھی آیا نہیں ہے۔ اور میں سمجھتا ہوں اب وہ آئے گا بھی نہیں۔ مگر تم بلانا کیوں چاہتی ہو؟

चंद्रमुखीः
यूँ ही। उन्हें फिर एक बार देखना चाहती हूँ।

چندر مکھی:
یونہی۔ اُنھیں پھر ایک بار دیکھنا چاہتی ہوں۔

चुन्नी बाबू *(हँसते हुए):*
झिड़की खाकर प्यार हो गया है?

چنّی بابو (ہنستے ہوئے):
جھڑکی کھا کر پیار ہو گیا ہے؟

चंद्रमुखीः
तुम नहीं जानते, चुन्नी बाबू। यह पहला आदमी है जो बिन मतलब पैसे देकर चला गया। नहीं समझे?

چندر مکھی:
تم نہیں جانتے، چُنّی بابو۔ یہ پہلا آدمی ہے جو بن مطلب پیسے دے کر چلا گیا۔ نہیں سمجھے؟

चुन्नी बाबूः
समझता हूँ। नोटों का लालच करने वाली कोई और, तुम नहीं। मगर असली बात क्या है?

چنّی بابو:
سمجھتا ہوں۔ نوٹوں کا لالچ کرنے والی کوئی اور، تم نہیں۔ مگر اصلی بات کیا ہے؟

चंद्रमुखीः
क्या सोचते हो? कुछ मोह सा हो गया है।

چندر مکھی:
کیا سوچتے ہو؟ کچھ موہ سا ہو گیا ہے۔

चुन्नी बाबूः
अरे बस पाँच मिनट में?
(गाते हुए)
''लागे मोरे नैन उनसे...''

چنّی بابو:
ارے بس پانچ منٹ میں؟
(گاتے ہوئے)
''لاگے مورے نین اُن سے۔۔۔''

चंद्रमुखीः
मज़ाक़ छोड़ो। उन्हें ज़रूर लाना। लाओगे ना?

چندر مکھی:
مذاق چھوڑو۔ اُنھیں ضرور لانا۔ لاؤ گے نا؟

चुन्नी बाबूः
क्या मालूम।

چنّی بابو:
کیا معلوم۔

चंद्रमुखीः
तुम्हें मेरे सर की क़सम।

چندر مکھی:
تمھیں میرے سر کی قسم۔

Chunni Babu:
I see! So it's like that? I'll do my best then.

Hein? Ye baat hai? Toh zaroor koshish karoonga.

Chunni Babu leaves the brothel. Cut. Devdas enters his Calcutta room. Dharamdas is waiting for him.

Devdas:
Dharamda?

Dharamda?

Dharamdas:
Deva. Your mother sent you a letter. You left without saying a word. She's been upset ever since.
(Devdas reads the letter. Dharamdas puts an envelope on the desk)
Here. She has sent you some money. Let's go home.

Deva. Ma ne ye chitthi de kar bheja hai mujhe. Tum bina kuch kahe-sune chale aaye jab se ma kitni ro rahi hain.

Ye lo. Rupay bheje hain. Chalo, ghar chalo.

Devdas:
You go home, Dharamda, I won't go.

Tum laut jao, Dharamda, main ghar nahin jaaunga.

Cut. Parvati's marital home. Her husband Chowdhury's family welcomes her warmly. Her widowed husband has a grown-up son and daughter from his first marriage.

Chowdhury's mother:
Welcome, daughter-in-law. Come, Lakshmi, goddess of the house. Take care of your new home.

Aao bahu. Aao Laxmi raani, sambhaalo apna ghar-baar.

Parvati's stepson, Mahendra, who is in his twenties, comes to greet Parvati on her wedding night.

Mahendra *(actor Ashim Kumar):*
Mother, I am your eldest son. Mahendra. Mother, I pay my respects to you.
(Parvati stops him from touching her feet as a gesture of respect)
It's been two years since we lost our mother. Those years have been unhappy ones for us. You are here, bless us so that we can be happy again.

Maataji, main aap ka bada ladka hoon, Mahendra. Maataji, main aap ka bada ladka hoon, pranaam karta hoon.
Aaj do baras huwe hum apni ma ko kho baithe. In do varshon se dukh museebat mein hi hum logon ke din beete hain. Ab aap aa gayin hain, ma, aashirwaad dijiye. Humaarein jivan sukhi ho jaayen.

Parvati:
Where is daughter Yashoda?

Aur beti Yashoda kahaan hai?

चुन्नी बाबूः
हैं? यह बात है? तो ज़रूर कोशिश करूँगा।

چنّی بابو:
ہیں؟---یہ بات ہے؟ تو ضرور کوشش کروں گا۔

चुन्नी बाबू चला जाता है। कट। देवदास अपने कलकत्ते वाले कमरे में आता है। धरमदास उसकी प्रतीक्षा कर रहा है।

چنّی بابو چلا جاتا ہے۔ کٹ۔ دیوداس اپنے کلکتے والے کمرے میں داخل ہوتا ہے۔ دھرم داس اُس کا انتظار کر رہا ہے۔

देवदासः
धरमदा?

دیوداس:
دھرم دا؟

धरमदासः
देवा। माँ ने यह चिट्ठी देकर भेजा है मुझे। तुम बिना कुछ कहे-सुने चले आए, जब से माँ कितनी रो रही हैं।
(देवदास चिट्ठी पढ़ता है। धरमदास एक लिफ़ाफ़ा मेज़ पर रखता है)
यह लो। रुपए भेजे हैं। चलो, घर चलो।

دھرم داس:
دیوا۔ ماں نے یہ چٹھی دے کر بھیجا ہے مجھے۔ تم بنا کچھ کہے سنے چلے آئے۔ جب سے ماں کتنی رو رہی ہیں۔
(دیوداس چٹھی پڑھتا ہے۔ دھرم داس ایک لفافہ میز پر رکھتا ہے)
یہ لو۔ روپے بھیجے ہیں۔ چلو۔ گھر چلو۔

देवदासः
तुम लौट जाओ, धरमदा, मैं घर नहीं जाऊँगा।

دیوداس:
تم لوٹ جاؤ، دھرم دا۔ میں گھر نہیں جاؤں گا۔

कट। पार्वती का ससुराल। चौधरी परिवार उसका स्वागत करता है। पार्वती के विधुर पति का एक बड़ा लड़का और एक लड़की पहली पत्नी से हैं।

کٹ۔ پاروتی کی سسرال۔ چودھری کے گھر والے اُس کا بڑی گرمجوشی کے ساتھ استقبال کرتے ہیں۔ پاروتی کے رنڈوے شوہر کا ایک نوجوان بیٹا اور ایک بیٹی پہلی بیوی سے ہیں۔

चौधरी की माँः
आओ बहू। आओ लक्ष्मी रानी, सँभालो अपना घर-बार।

چودھری کی ماں:
آؤ، بہو۔ آؤ، لکشمی رانی۔ سنبھالو اپنا گھر بار۔

पार्वती का सौतेला बेटा, महेंद्र, जो लगभग बीस वर्ष का है, उसे प्रणाम करने आता है।

پاروتی کا سوتیلا بیٹا مہندر، جس کی عمر لگ بھگ بیس سال کی ہے، اُسے سلام کرنے آتا ہے۔

महेंद्र *(अभिनेता असीम कुमार)*:
माताजी, मैं आपका बड़ा लड़का हूँ, महेंद्र। माताजी, मैं आपका बड़ा लड़का हूँ। प्रणाम करता हूँ।
(आदर से उसके पैर छूता है। पार्वती उसे ऐसा करने से रोकती है)
आज दो बरस हुए हम अपनी माँ को खो बैठे। इन दो वर्षों से दुःख मुसीबत में ही हम लोगों के दिन बीते हैं। अब आप आ गई हैं, माँ, आशीर्वाद दीजिए। हमारे जीवन सुखी हो जाएँ।

مہندر (اداکار، اشیم کمار):
ماتا جی، میں آپ کا بڑا لڑکا ہوں، مہندر۔ ماتا جی، میں آپ کا بڑا لڑکا ہوں۔ پرنام کرتا ہوں۔
(پاروتی اُسے پیر چھونے سے پہلے روک دیتی ہے۔)
آج دو برس ہوئے۔ ہم اپنی ماں کو کھو بیٹھے۔ اِن دو ورشوں سے دکھ مصیبت میں ہی ہم لوگوں کے دن بیتے ہیں۔ اب آپ آ گئیں ہیں، ماں۔ آشیرواد دیجیے۔ ہمارا جیون سکھی ہو جائے۔

पार्वतीः
और बेटी यशोदा कहाँ है?

پاروتی:
اور بیٹی یشودا کہاں ہے؟

Mahendra:
She is at her in-laws, I wrote to her. But she…was unable to come.

Ji? Ji vo apne sasuraal hai. Maine chitthi likhi bhi thi magar vo… Yashoda aa hi na saki.

Parvati:
Unable, or unwilling?

Aa hi na saki? Ya jaan boojh kar nahin aayi?

Mahendra:
I can't say, but if father went to fetch her…

Ye…ye main theek nahin jaanta, ma. Lekin pitaji ja kar le aayen toh vo…

Parvati:
No. Why should he go? Why don't we, mother and son, go together and bring her here?

Chhi. Vo kyun jaayen? Hum ma-bete kyun na ja kar le aayen?

Mahendra:
No, mother, why should you go? I will.

Nahin, ma, phir aap bhi kyun jaayen? Main khud hi ja kar le aaunga usay.

Mahendra leaves the room. Fade out.

Reel Nine

Fade in. Time has passed. Mahendra tries to persuade his sister, Yashoda, to meet their father's new wife. They are in the corridor just outside Parvati's room. She overhears them.

Mahendra:
Come on.

Chal.

Yashoda *(unidentified actress):*
No. Let go of me. I don't want to go.

Na. Chhod do mujhe, main nahin jaaungi.

Mahendra:
Why not? You shouldn't talk like that. Why won't you meet her? Come.

Kyun? Tujhe aisa nahin kehna chaahiye. Jaayegi kyun nahin? Chal.

Parvati *(stepping forward and taking the young girl into her room):*
Come, daughter. Are you cross with your mother?

Aao beti. Aao. Kyun, beti? Apni ma se kuch naaraaz ho?

महेंद्र:
जी? जी वह अपने ससुराल है। मैंने चिट्ठी लिखी भी थी मगर वह...यशोदा आ ही न सकी।

पार्वती:
आ ही न सकी? या जान-बूझकर नहीं आई?

महेंद्र:
यह...यह मैं ठीक नहीं जानता, माँ। लेकिन पिताजी जाकर ले आएँ तो वह...

पार्वती:
छी: वह क्यों जाएँ? हम माँ-बेटे क्यों न जाकर ले आएँ?

महेंद्र:
नहीं, माँ। फिर आप भी क्यों जाएँ? मैं ख़ुद ही जाकर ले आऊँगा उसे।

महेंद्र चला जाता है। फ़ेड आउट।

रील नौ

फ़ेड इन। कुछ समय बीत जाता है। महेंद्र अपनी बहन, यशोदा को सौतेली माँ से मिलाने का प्रयत्न कर रहा है। वे पार्वती के कमरे के बाहर खड़े बातें कर रहे हैं। पार्वती उनकी बातें सुन रही है।

महेंद्र:
चल।

यशोदा *(कलाकार अज्ञात):*
ना। छोड़ दो मुझे। मैं नहीं जाऊँगी।

महेंद्र:
क्यों? तुझे ऐसा नहीं कहना चाहिए। जाएगी क्यों नहीं? चल।

पार्वती *(यशोदा को अपने कमरे में ले जाती है):*
आओ बेटी। आओ। क्यों, बेटी? अपनी माँ से कुछ नाराज़ हो?

مہندر:
جی؟ جی وہ اپنے سسرال ہے۔ میں نے چٹھی لکھی بھی تھی۔ مگر وہ۔۔۔یشودا آ ہی نہ سکی۔

پاروتی:
آ ہی نہ سکی؟ یا جان بوجھ کر نہیں آئی؟

مہندر:
یہ۔۔۔یہ میں ٹھیک نہیں جانتا، ماں۔ لیکن پتاجی جا کر لے آئیں تو وہ۔۔۔

پاروتی:
چھی، وہ کیوں جائیں؟ ہم ماں بیٹے کیوں نہ جا کر لے آئیں؟

مہندر:
نہیں، ماں۔ پھر آپ بھی کیوں جائیں؟ میں خود ہی جا کر لے آؤں گا اُسے۔

مہندر کمرے سے باہر جاتا ہے۔ فیڈ آؤٹ۔

ریل نو

فیڈ اِن۔ کچھ وقت گزر جاتا ہے۔ مہندر اپنی بہن یشودا کو سوتیلی ماں پاروتی سے ملانے کی کوشش کر رہا ہے۔ وہ پاروتی کے کمرے کے باہر تکرار کر رہے ہیں جو پاروتی سن رہی ہے۔

مہندر:
چل۔

یشودا (اداکارہ، نامعلوم):
نا۔ چھوڑ دو مجھے میں نہیں جاؤں گی۔

مہندر:
کیوں؟ تجھے ایسا نہیں کہنا چاہیے۔ جائے گی کیوں نہیں؟ چل۔

پاروتی (یشودا کو اپنے کمرے میں لے جاتی ہے):
آؤ، بیٹی۔ آؤ۔ کیوں، بیٹی۔ اپنی ماں سے کچھ ناراض ہو؟

Yashoda:
No. Why should I be cross?

Nahin, nahin, main bhala naaraaz kyun honay lagi?

Parvati:
Sit down.

Baitho.

Parvati takes off her gold necklace and puts it around Yashoda's neck.

Yashoda:
What is this?

Ye kya?

Parvati:
It's nothing, just a mother's gesture. This is your father's home. How grand it is. It needs so many servants. I am nothing but a servant. Daughter, it does not befit you to be cross with a mere servant.

Kuch nahin, sirf ma ki saadh hai tumhaari. Ye tumhaare pita ka ghar hai. Kitna bada ghar, kitne naukar naukaraaniyon ki zaroorat rehti hai is mein. Main bhi toh ek daasi ke siwa aur kuch nahin hoon. Beti, tuch daas-daasiyon pe naaraaz hona kya tumhein shobha deta hai?

Yashoda:
Mother, I implore you. Take no notice of my behaviour.

Ma, main tumhaare paaon padti hoon. Mere apraadhon par dhiyaan na dena.

The smiling Yashoda leaves Parvati's room and bumps into her brother.

Mahendra:
Do you like our new mother?

Sunn, nayi ma kaise lagi?

Yashoda:
Very much.

Bahot achi.

Mahendra:
Shall I tell her what you said about her?

Hmm. Ab ma ko keh doon jo tu unke baare mein kehti rahi?

यशोदाः
नहीं, नहीं, मैं भला नाराज़ क्यों होने लगी?

یشودا:
نہیں،نہیں۔ میں بھلا ناراض کیوں ہونے لگی؟

पार्वतीः
बैठो।

پاروتی:
بیٹھو۔

पार्वती अपने गले का हार उतार कर यशोदा के गले में डालती है।

پاروتی سونے کا ہار اپنے گلے سے اُتار کر یشودا کو پہناتی ہے۔

यशोदाः
यह क्या?

یشودا:
یہ کیا؟

पार्वतीः
कुछ नहीं, सिर्फ़ माँ की साध है तुम्हारी। यह तुम्हारे पिता का घर है। कितना बड़ा घर, कितने नौकर-नौकरानियों की ज़रूरत रहती है इसमें। मैं भी तो एक दासी के सिवा और कुछ नहीं हूँ। बेटी, तुच्छ दास-दासियों पे नाराज़ होना क्या तुम्हें शोभा देता है?

پاروتی:
کچھ نہیں۔ صرف ماں کی سادھ ہے تمہاری۔ یہ تمہارے پتا کا گھر ہے۔ کتنا بڑا گھر۔ کتنے نوکر نوکرانیوں کی ضرورت رہتی ہے اس میں۔ میں بھی تو ایک داسی کے سوا اور کچھ نہیں ہوں۔ بیٹی۔ تُچھ داس داسیوں پہ ناراض ہونا کیا تمھیں شوبھا دیتا ہے؟

यशोदाः
माँ, मैं तुम्हारे पाँव पड़ती हूँ। मेरे अपराधों पर ध्यान न देना।

یشودا:
ماں۔ میں تمہارے پاؤں پڑتی ہوں۔ میرے اپرادھوں پر دھیان نہ دینا۔

यशोदा मुस्कुराती हुई पार्वती के कमरे से निकलती है और अपने भाई से टकरा जाती है।

یشودا مسکراتی ہوئی کمرے سے باہر آتے ہوئے اپنے بھائی مہندر سے ٹکرا جاتی ہے۔

महेंद्रः
सुन, नई माँ कैसी लगी?

مہندر:
سن۔ نئی ماں کیسی لگی؟

यशोदाः
बहुत अच्छी।

یشودا:
بہت اچھی۔

महेंद्रः
हुँ। अब माँ को कह दूँ जो तू उनके बारे में कहती रही?

مہندر:
ہوں۔ اب ماں کو کہہ دوں جو تُو اُن کے بارے میں کہتی رہی؟

Yashoda:
Don't, brother. I beg you. Don't tell mother anything.

Na, na, bhayya, main tumhaare paaon padti hoon. Ma ko kuch na kehna.

Dissolve. Parvati's husband, the elderly Chowdhury, is smoking a hookah in his bedroom. Parvati comes in and leaves something on the bed.

Chowdhury *(actor Moni Chatterjee):*
You have spared me great embarrassment. You have accepted my son and daughter as your own. You have also arranged Mahendra's wedding. May God bless you and shower you with happiness, Parvati.

Parvati, tumne mujhe badi bhaari lajja se mukti dedi. Beti-bete, sabhi ko apna bana liya. Mahendra ki shaadi bhi tai kar di. Bhagwan tumhaara bhala kare. Tum sada sukhi raho, Parvati.

Parvati:
Why are you saying this?

Ye aap kya kehte hain?

Chowdhury:
I wish I could explain, Parvati.
(he stands up and looks at her face)
Ah! I did wrong.

Kaash main ye baat tumhen samjha sakta, Parvati.

Ah! Ye maine acha nahin kiya.

Parvati:
What wrong did you do?

Kya acha nahin kiya ji?

Chowdhury:
What can I say, Parvati? I don't think you are suited here.

Main kya kahun, Parvati? Sochta hoon tum mere yahaan sajti nahin.

Parvati:
Why am I not suited? For us women, what does it matter if we are suited or not?

Sajti kyun nahin? Hum logon ka sajna ya na sajna kya?

Parvati goes to the mirror and combs her hair. She touches the scar on her forehead. It reminds her of Devdas.

Dissolve. Devdas is looking dejected. Dharamdas and Chunni Babu talk in the adjoining room.

Dharamdas:
What has come over Devdas?

Deva ne apni ye kya haalat bana rakhi hai?

यशोदाः
न ना, भैया, मैं तुम्हारे पाँव पड़ती हूँ। माँ को कुछ न कहना।

दृश्य समाप्त। पार्वती का अधेड़ उमर पति, चौधरी अपने कमरे में बैठा हुक़्क़ा पी रहा है। पार्वती अंदर आकर बिस्तर पर कुछ रखती है।

चौधरी *(अभिनेता मोनी चटर्जी):*
पार्वती, तुमने मुझे बड़ी भारी लज्जा से मुक्ति दे दी। बेटी-बेटे, सभी को अपना बना लिया। महेंद्र की शादी भी तय कर दी। भगवान तुम्हारा भला करे। तुम सदा सुखी रहो, पार्वती।

पार्वतीः
यह आप क्या कहते हैं?

चौधरीः
काश! मैं यह बात तुम्हें समझा सकता, पार्वती।
(खड़े होकर पार्वती को देखता है)
आह! यह मैंने अच्छा नहीं किया।

पार्वतीः
क्या अच्छा नहीं किया जी?

चौधरीः
मैं क्या कहूँ, पार्वती? सोचता हूँ, तुम मेरे यहाँ सजती नहीं।

पार्वतीः
सजती क्यों नहीं? हम लोगों का सजना या न सजना क्या?

दर्पण के सामने पार्वती अपने बाल सँवारती है। माथे का निशान उसे देवदास की याद दिलाता है।

अगला दृश्य। देवदास निरुत्साहित-सा खड़ा है। धरमदास और चुन्नी बाबू बराबर के कमरे में बातें कर रहे हैं।

धरमदासः
देवा ने अपनी यह क्या हालत बना रखी है।

یشودا:
نا، نا، بھیا۔ میں تمہارے پاؤں پڑتی ہوں۔ ماں کو کچھ نہ کہنا۔

اگلا منظر۔ پاروتی کا عمر دراز شوہر چودھری خواب گاہ میں بیٹھا حقہ پی رہا ہے۔ پاروتی اندر آکر بستر پر کچھ رکھتی ہے۔

چودھری (اداکار، مونی چٹرجی):
پاروتی، تم نے مجھے بڑی بھاری لجّا سے مُکتی دے دی۔ بیٹی بیٹے، سبھی کو اپنا بنالیا۔ مہندر کی شادی بھی طے کر دی۔ بھگوان تمہارا بھلا کرے۔ تم سدا سکھی رہو، پاروتی۔

پاروتی:
یہ آپ کیا کہتے ہیں؟

چودھری:
کاش میں یہ بات تمھیں سمجھا سکتا، پاروتی۔
(کھڑے ہوکر پاروتی کو دیکھتا ہے)
آہ۔ یہ میں نے اچھا نہیں کیا۔

پاروتی:
کیا اچھا نہیں کیا، جی۔

چودھری:
میں کیا کہوں، پاروتی۔ سوچتا ہوں، تم میرے یہاں سجتی نہیں۔

پاروتی:
سجتی کیوں نہیں؟ ہم لوگوں کا سجنا یا نہ سجنا کیا؟

آئنے کے سامنے آکر پاروتی کنگھی کرنے لگتی ہے۔ پیشانی پر لگے داغ کو دیکھتی ہے۔ دیوداس کی یاد اُسے آتی ہے۔

اگلا منظر۔ دیوداس لاتعلق سا کھڑا ہے۔ بغل کے کمرے میں چُنی لال سے دھرم داس کہہ رہا ہے۔

دھرم داس:
دیوا نے اپنی یہ کیا حالت بنا رکھی ہے۔

Chunni Babu:
Why? What's the matter?

Kyun? Kya hua?

Dharamdas:
Can't you see? He roams around all day and night like a madman. But why?

Dekhte nahin? Din raat paagalon ki tarah ghooma karte hain. Akhir ye sab kyun?

Chunni Babu:
Dharamdas, the blind asks the blind for directions. I don't understand what's troubling him. Has he quarrelled with his family by any chance?

Dharamdas, ek andha doosre andhe se raasta pooch raha hai. Meri toh samajh mein nahin aata ki usay kya hua hai. Kahin ghar-waalon se jhagada toh nahin hua hai?

Dharamdas:
No, Chunni babu, it's nothing like that.

Nahin, Chunni babu, aisa toh kuch bhi nahin hua hai.

Chunni Babu:
Then what is it?

Toh phir kya baat hai?

Dharamdas:
Sometimes I think all this started when he was separated from his childhood companion.

Kabhi-kabhi khayaal aata hai ye sab bachpan ka saathi chhoot jaane ke baad hua hai.

Chunni Babu:
I see! So Devdas and I are one of a kind.

Oho! Tabb toh Devdas bhi humaara hi bhai hai.

Dharamdas:
Why don't you make him see sense? He never listens to me. Persuade him somehow to go to his mother.

Toh aap hi jaaiye samjhaaiye usay. Meri toh sunta hi nahin. Kisi tarah mana kar ma ke paas bhej dijiye.

Chunni Babu:
Very well. I'll try my luck.

Achi baat hai. Ladaate hain koi mantar.

चुन्नी बाबू:
क्यों? क्या हुआ?

چنی بابو:
کیوں کیا ہوا؟

धरमदासः
देखते नहीं? दिन-रात पागलों की तरह घूमा करते है। आख़िर यह सब क्यों?

دھرم داس:
دیکھتے نہیں؟ دن رات پاگلوں کی طرح گھوما کرتے ہیں۔ آخر یہ سب کیوں؟

चुन्नी बाबू:
धरमदास, एक अंधा दूसरे अंधे से रास्ता पूछ रहा है। मेरी तो समझ में नहीं आता कि उसे क्या हुआ है। कहीं घर वालों से झगड़ा तो नहीं हुआ है?

چنی بابو:
دھرم داس، ایک اندھا دوسرے اندھے سے راستا پوچھ رہا ہے۔ میری تو سمجھ میں نہیں آتا کہ اُسے کیا ہوا ہے۔ کہیں گھر والوں سے جھگڑا تو نہیں ہوا ہے؟

धरमदासः
नहीं, चुन्नी बाबू, ऐसा तो कुछ भी नहीं हुआ है।

دھرم داس:
نہیں چنی بابو، ایسا تو کچھ بھی نہیں ہوا ہے۔

चुन्नी बाबू:
तो फिर क्या बात है?

چنی بابو:
تو پھر کیا بات ہے؟

धरमदासः
कभी-कभी ख़्याल आता है यह सब बचपन का साथी छूट जाने के बाद हुआ है।

دھرم داس:
کبھی کبھی خیال آتا ہے کہ یہ سب بچپن کا ساتھی چھوٹ جانے کے بعد ہوا ہے۔

चुन्नी बाबू:
ओहो! तब तो देवदास भी हमारा ही भाई है।

چنی بابو:
اوہو! تب تو دیوداس بھی ہمارا ہی بھائی ہے۔

धरमदासः
तो आप ही जाइए समझाइए उसे। मेरी तो सुनता ही नहीं। किसी तरह मना कर माँ के पास भेज दीजिए।

دھرم داس:
تو آپ ہی جایئے، سمجھایئے اُسے۔ میری تو سنتا ہی نہیں۔ کسی طرح منا کر ماں کے پاس بھیج دیجیے۔

चुन्नी बाबू:
अच्छी बात है। लड़ाते हैं कोई मंत्र।

چنی بابو:
اچھی بات ہے، لڑاتے ہیں کوئی منتر۔

Chunni Babu enters Devdas's room. Devdas is holding his head in his hands. He looks up.

Chunni Babu:
What is it, Devdas? What's come over you? | Kya baat hai, Devdas? Kya hua tumhen?

Devdas:
Nothing has come over me. | Kuch bhi toh nahin hua.

Chunni Babu:
Why don't you say something? | Kuch kaho toh.

Devdas:
There's nothing to say, Chunni babu. | Kehni si koi baat nahin, Chunni babu.

Chunni Babu:
Then take my advice. | Toh phir meri ek baat maano.

Devdas:
What? | Kya?

Chunni Babu:
Come with me. | Chalo mere saath.

Devdas:
Where to? | Kahaan chaloon?

Chunni Babu:
Where we went the other day. | Arey wahin jahaan uss roz gaye thay.

Devdas:
I don't like that place, Chunni babu. | Mujhe acha nahin lagta, Chunni babu.

Chunni Babu:
Very well. | Acha.

Devdas:
Are you going there? | Tum kya wahin ja rahe ho?

चुन्नी बाबू देवदास के कमरे में प्रवेश करता है। देवदास ने अपना सर अपने हाथों में पकड़ा हुआ है। नज़रें उठा कर वह चुन्नी बाबू को देखता है।

चुन्नी बाबू:
क्या बात है, देवदास? क्या हुआ तुम्हें?

देवदासः
कुछ भी तो नहीं हुआ।

चुन्नी बाबू:
कुछ कहो तो।

देवदासः
कहनी सी कोई बात नहीं, चुन्नी बाबू।

चुन्नी बाबू:
तो फिर मेरी एक बात मानो।

देवदासः
क्या?

चुन्नी बाबू:
चलो मेरे साथ।

देवदासः
कहाँ चलूँ?

चुन्नी बाबू:
अरे वहीं जहाँ उस रोज़ गए थे।

देवदासः
मुझे अच्छा नहीं लगता, चुन्नी बाबू।

चुन्नी बाबू:
अच्छा।

देवदासः
तुम क्या वहीं जा रहे हो?

دیوداس کے کمرے میں چُنی لال داخل ہوتے ہیں۔ دیوداس نے اپنا سر اپنے ہاتھوں سے پکڑ رکھا ہے۔ دیوداس نظریں اُٹھا کر اُسے دیکھتا ہے۔

چُنی بابو:
کیا بات ہے، دیوداس؟ کیا ہوا تمھیں؟

دیوداس:
کچھ بھی تو نہیں ہوا۔

چُنی بابو:
کچھ کہو تو؟

دیوداس:
کہنی سی کوئی بات نہیں، چُنی بابو۔

چُنی بابو:
تو پھر میری ایک بات مانو۔

دیوداس:
کیا؟

چُنی بابو:
چلو میرے ساتھ۔

دیوداس:
کہاں چلوں؟

چُنی بابو:
ارے، وہیں جہاں اُس روز گئے تھے۔

دیوداس:
مجھے اچھا نہیں لگتا، چُنی بابو۔

چُنی بابو:
اچھا۔

دیوداس:
تم کیا وہیں جا رہے ہو؟

Chunni Babu:
Yes, I am. Would you prefer I didn't?

Ja toh raha hoon. Kaho toh na jaaun?

Devdas:
No, I didn't say that. But what do you hope for by going there? What do you get out of it?

Nahin, ye main nahin kehta. Lekin kya ummeed le ke jaate ho wahaan? Kya mil jaata hai tumhen?

Chunni Babu *(laughing):*
I don't get anything. I go there to pass the time.

Milta-wilta toh kuch nahin hai. Main toh sirf apna samay bitaane jaata hoon.

Devdas:
Does time pass? Time stands still for me.

Samay beet jaata hai? Mera toh bitaaye nahin beet'ta.

Chunni Babu:
So, come with me. I will make sure that time for you doesn't just pass, but fly.

Toh tum mere saath chalo. Aisa bandobast kar deta hoon tumhaara ki samay beetega nahin balki bhaagne lagega.

Whip pan. Chandramukhi is dancing. Chunni Babu and Devdas are sitting in her room.

Lata Mangeshkar sings for Chandramukhi

You who wish to depart, stop awhile
The road is dark, beyond await a thousand sorrows
(both lines repeated)
O visitor

O aane waale ruk ja koi dam
Rasta ghere hain baahar laakhon gham

O aane waale aane waale

Come to me, I shall shelter you in my eyes
I shall hide you behind my colourful veil
(both lines repeated)
For you alone...
I'll sacrifice my life for you, O innocent one
O shy one
O shy one, stop awhile
The road is dark, beyond await a thousand sorrows
O visitor

Aa main tujhe aankhon mein basa loon
Rang bhare aanchal mein chhupa loon

Tujh pe luta doon...
Tujh pe luta doon dil-o-jaan o naadaan
O sharmaane waale
Sharmaane waale ruk ja koi dam
Rasta ghere hain baahar laakhon gham
O aane waale aane waale

चुन्नी बाबूः
जा तो रहा हूँ। कहो तो न जाऊँ?

چُنی بابو:
جاتو رہاہوں۔کہوتو نہ جاؤں؟

देवदासः
नहीं, यह मैं नहीं कहता। लेकिन क्या उम्मीद लेके जाते हो वहाँ? क्या मिल जाता है तुम्हें?

دیوداس:
نہیں۔یہ میں نہیں کہتا۔لیکن کیا اُمید لے کے جاتے ہو وہاں؟ کیا مل جاتا ہے تمھیں؟

चुन्नी बाबू *(हँसते हुए):*
मिलता-विलता तो कुछ नहीं है। मैं तो सिर्फ़ अपना समय बिताने जाता हूँ।

چُنی بابو(ہنستے ہوئے):
ملتاولتاتو کچھ نہیں ہے۔میں تو صرف اپنا سمے بتانے جاتا ہوں۔

देवदासः
समय बीत जाता है? मेरा तो बिताए नहीं बीतता।

دیوداس:
سمے بیت جاتا ہے؟ میرا تو بِتائے نہیں بیتتا۔

चुन्नी बाबूः
तो तुम मेरे साथ चलो। ऐसा बन्दोबस्त कर देता हूँ तुम्हारा कि समय बीतेगा नहीं बल्कि भागने लगेगा।

چُنی بابو:
توتم میرے ساتھ چلو۔ایسا بندوبست کر دیتا ہوں تمہارا کہ سمے بیتے گا نہیں بلکہ بھاگنے لگے گا۔

पलक झपकते ही दृश्य बदलता है। चंद्रमुखी नृत्य कर रही है। चुन्नी बाबू और देवदास उसके कमरे में बैठे हैं।

پلک جھپکتے منظر بدلتا ہے۔چندرمکھی رقص کر رہی ہے۔چُنی بابو اور دیوداس اُس کے کمرے میں بیٹھے ہوئے ہیں۔

स्वरः लता मंगेशकर

آواز،لتا منگیشکر

ओ आने वाले रुक जा कोई दम
रस्ता घेरे हैं बाहर लाखों ग़म
(दोनों पंक्तियाँ दोहराई जाती हैं)
ओ आने वाले आने वाले

آ میں تجھے آنکھوں میں بسالوں
رنگ بھرے آنچل میں چھپالوں
(दोनों पंक्तियाँ दोहराई जाती हैं)
तुझ पे लुटा दूँ...
तुझ पे लुटा दूँ दिल-ओ-जाँ ओ नादाँ
ओ शरमाने वाले
शरमाने वाले रुक जा कोई दम
रस्ता घेरे हैं बाहर लाखों ग़म
ओ आने वाले आने वाले

او،آنے والے رک جا کوئی دم
رستہ گھیرے ہیں باہر لاکھوں غم
(دونوں لائنیں دوہراتی ہے)
او،آنے والے،آنے والے

آ میں تجھے آنکھوں میں بسالوں
رنگ بھرے آنچل میں چھپالوں
(دونوں لائنیں دوہراتی ہے)
تجھ پہ لُٹا دوں۔۔۔
تجھ پہ لٹادوں دل وجاں،او،ناداں
اوشرمانے والے
شرمانے والے رک جا کوئی دم
رستہ گھیرے ہیں باہر لاکھوں غم
او،آنے والے،آنے والے

   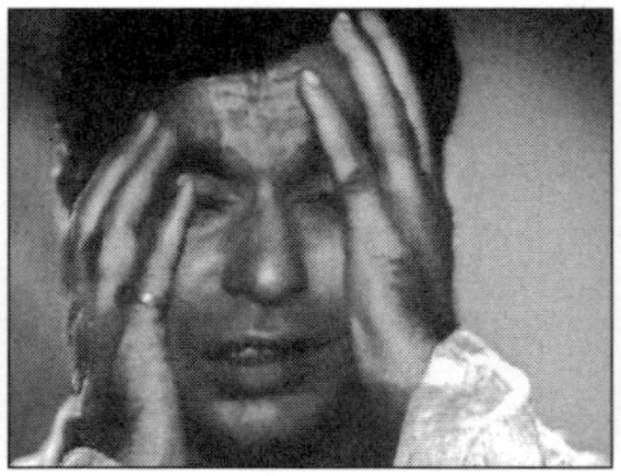 

Night's magic has filled the air
The perfume of my hair spreads
(both lines repeated)
My heart's stirring…
Heed my heart's stirring; I'd give my life for you
O tormenter
O tormenter, stop awhile
The road is dark, beyond await a thousand sorrows
O visitor

Lose yourself in the sound of my dancing bells
Lose yourself in a world of dreams
(both lines repeated)
Stay here
Stay here, listen to what we say
O tormenter
O tormenter, stop awhile
The road is dark, beyond await a thousand sorrows
O visitor
O visitor (4)

Nikhra hua hai raat ka jaadu
Bikhri huwi hai zulfon ki khushbu

Dil ka ishaara…
Dil ka ishaara pehchaan main qurbaan
O tadpaane waale
Tadpaane waale ruk ja koi damm
Rasta ghere hain baahar laakhon gham
O aane waale aane waale

Paayal ki jhankaar mein kho ja
Sapnon ke sansaar mein kho ja

Reh ja yahin pe…
Reh ja yahin pe mehmaan kaha maan
O tarsaane waale
Tarsaane waale ruk ja koi dam
Rasta ghere hain baahar laakhon gham
O aane waale aane waale
Aane waale (4)

As Chandramukhi's song builds to a crescendo, Devdas hears the wedding shehnai play in the background. He opens the window from where he sees some shehnai players sitting on a pavilion decorated for a marriage ceremony. The wedding music takes over reminding Devdas of Parvati. He is distressed and covers his face with his hands. He walks towards the table and pours himself his first drink of alcohol.

INTERVAL

निखरा हुआ है रात का जादू
बिखरी हुई है ज़ुल्फ़ों की ख़ुशबू
(दोनों पंक्तियाँ दोहराई जाती हैं)
दिल का इशारा...
दिल का इशारा पहचान मैं कुरबान
ओ तड़पाने वाले
तड़पाने वाले रुक जा कोई दम
रस्ता घेरे हैं बाहर लाखों ग़म
ओ आने वाले आने वाले

पायल की झंकार में खो जा
सपनों के संसार में खो जा
(दोनों पंक्तियाँ दोहराई जाती हैं)
रह जा यहीं पे...
रह जा यहीं पे मेहमान कहा मान
ओ तरसाने वाले
तरसाने वाले रुक जा कोई दम
रस्ता घेरे हैं बाहर लाखों ग़म
ओ आने वाले आने वाले
आने वाले (४)

चंद्रमुखी के गाने का संगीत विवाह की शहनाई की आवाज़ में ढल जाता है। देवदास खिड़की खोलता है तो उसे सजा हुआ मंडप दिखाई देता है जहाँ एक विवाह समारोह में शहनाई बज रही है। शहनाई की आवाज़ उसे पार्वती की याद दिलाती है। बेचैन होकर अपने हाथों से अपने चेहरे को छुपा लेता है। वह मेज़ की ओर बढ़ता है और पहली बार अपने लिए शराब का गिलास बनाता है।

मध्यांतर

نکھرا ہوا ہے رات کا جادو
بکھری ہوئی ہے زلفوں کی خوشبو
(دونوں لائینیں دوہراتی ہے)
دل کا اشارہ۔۔۔
دل کا اشارہ پہچان میں قربان
او تڑپانے والے
تڑپانے والے رک جا کوئی دم
رستہ گھیرے ہیں باہر لاکھوں غم
او آنے والے، آنے والے

پائل کی جھنکار میں کھو جا
سپنوں کے سنسار میں کھو جا
(دونوں لائینیں دوہراتی ہے)
رہ جا یہیں پہ۔۔۔
رہ جا یہیں پہ مہمان کہا مان
او ترسانے والے
ترسانے والے رک جا کوئی دم
رستہ گھیرے ہیں باہر لاکھوں غم
او آنے والے، آنے والے،
آنے والے (۴)

چندرمکھی کے گیت کی موسیقی بڑھ کر شہنائی کی آواز میں ڈھل جاتی ہے۔ دیوداس کھڑکی کھولتا ہے تو اُسے سجا ہوا منڈپ دکھائی دیتا ہے جہاں شہنائی نواز بیٹھے ایک شادی میں شہنائی بجا رہے ہیں۔ شہنائی کی آواز اُسے پاروتی کی یاد دلا رہی ہیں۔ بے چین ہو کر وہ اپنے چہرے کو اپنے ہاتھوں سے چھپا لیتا ہے۔ میز کی طرف بڑھتا ہے اور پہلی بار اپنے لیے شراب کا ساغر تیار کرتا ہے۔

وقفہ

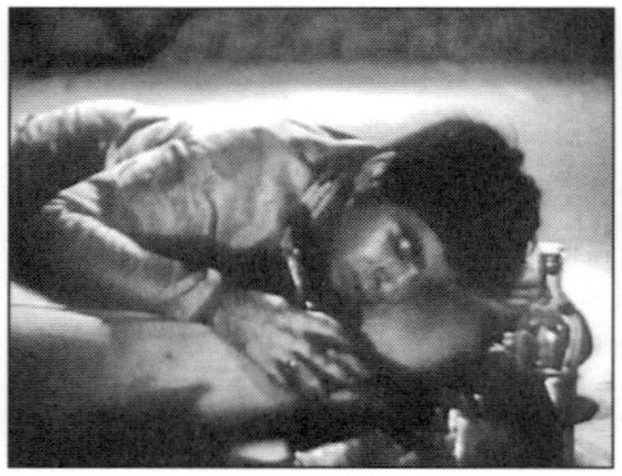

Reel 10

Fade in. Devdas's father, Narain, is ailing and lying in bed. A doctor is examining him while his wife, son Dwijodas and daughter-in-law look on. The doctor and Dwijodas then go into the adjoining room. Devdas's mother and Dwijodas's silent wife join them.

Doctor *(unidentified actor):*
What can I say? It is my duty to be honest with you. Your father is critically ill. Give him the medicine I have left for him. The rest is in God's hands.

Kya kahun, bhayya? Sach kehna mera farz hai. Babuji ki tabiyat bahot kharaab hai. Jo davaayi maine di hai vahi pilaate rahiye. Aage Ishwar ki marzi.

Harimati Devi:
Why are you waiting, son? Inform Deva at once.

Ab kaun bela dekhte ho, beta? Deva ko khabar kar do.

Dwijodas:
How can I do that, mother? No one knows where he is.

Kaise khabar kar doon, ma? Uska koi pata-thikaana bhi ho.

Harimati Devi:
Go and find him.

Tu khud ja kar le aana.

Dwijodas:
What nonsense! How can I leave father in the state he is in? Dharamdas is in Calcutta. Send him a telegram and ask him to find Devdas.

Kaisi ulti-seedhi baaten karti ho, ma? Main pitaji ko aisi haalat mein chhod kar kaise chala jaaun? Wahaan Dharamdas hai, usko taar de dete hain, kahin na kahin se dhoond kar le aayega.

Dissolve to a shot of a table with an empty bottle and a glass. Devdas is lying on the bed, humming. He is very drunk. He opens a bottle of alcohol. Chandramukhi enters into room as he hurls an empty bottle across the floor.

रील दस

फ़ेड इन। देवदास का पिता, नारायण बहुत बीमार है और बिस्तर पर लेटा हुआ है। एक डॉक्टर जाँच कर रहा है। पास में उसकी पत्नी, लड़का द्विजोदास और बहू खड़े हैं। डॉक्टर और द्विजोदास बराबर वाले कमरे में चले जाते हैं। वहाँ देवदास की माँ और द्विजोदास की पत्नी भी पहुँच जाते हैं।

डॉक्टर *(कलाकार अज्ञात)*:
क्या कहूँ, भैया? सच कहना मेरा फ़र्ज़ है। बाबूजी की तबियत बहुत ख़राब है। जो दवाई मैंने दी है, वही पिलाते रहिए। आगे ईश्वर की मरज़ी।

हरिमति देवी:
अब कौन बेला देखते हो, बेटा? देवा को ख़बर कर दो।

द्विजोदास:
कैसे ख़बर कर दूँ, माँ? उसका कोई पता-ठिकाना भी हो।

हरिमति देवी:
तू खुद जाकर ले आ ना।

द्विजोदास:
कैसी उल्टी-सीधी बातें करती हो, माँ? मैं पिताजी को ऐसी हालत में छोड़ कर कैसे चला जाऊँ? वहाँ धरमदास है, उसको तार दे देते हैं, कहीं न कहीं से ढूँढ़ के ले आएगा।

अगला दृश्य। एक मेज़ पर शराब की ख़ाली बोतल और गिलास दिखाई देते हैं। गुनगुनाहट की आवाज़ सुनाई दे रही है। बिस्तर पर पड़ा देवदास दिखाई देता है। वह नशे में धुत है। शराब की बोतल खोलता है। ख़ाली बोतल उठा कर कमरे में फेंकता है कि चंद्रमुखी प्रवेश करती है।

ریل دس

فیڈ ان۔ دیوداس کے والد نارائن کی طبیعت بہت خراب ہے اور وہ بستر پر دراز ہے۔ ایک ڈاکٹر اُس کا معائنہ کر رہا ہے اور اُس کی بیوی، بیٹا دویجوداس، اور بہو دیکھ رہے ہیں۔ ڈاکٹر اور دویجوداس دوسرے کمرے میں بات کر رہے ہیں۔ دیوداس کی ماں، اور بھابھی بھی وہیں آ جاتے ہیں۔

ڈاکٹر (اداکار، نامعلوم):
کیا کہوں، بھیا؟ سچ کہنا میرا فرض ہے۔ بابو جی کی طبیعت بہت خراب ہے۔ جو دوائی میں نے دی ہے وہی پلاتے رہیے۔ آگے ایشور کی مرضی۔

ہریمتی دیوی:
اب کون بیلا دیکھتے ہو، بیٹا؟ دیوداس کو خبر کر دو۔

دویجوداس:
کیسے خبر کر دوں، ماں؟ اُس کا کوئی پتا ٹھکانہ بھی ہو۔

ہریمتی دیوی:
تُو خود جا کر لے آنا۔

دویجوداس:
یہ اُلٹی سیدھی باتیں کرتی ہو، ماں؟ میں پتا جی کو ایسی حالت میں چھوڑ کر کیسے چلا جاؤں؟ وہاں دھرم داس ہے، اُس کو تار دے دیتے ہیں، کہیں نہ کہیں سے ڈھونڈ کر لے آئے گا۔

اگلا منظر۔ ایک میز پر شراب کی خالی بوتل اور جام رکھے ہوئے ہیں۔ گنگناہٹ کی آواز سنائی دے رہی ہے۔ بستر پر پڑا دیوداس نظر آتا ہے۔ وہ شراب کے نشے میں دھت ہے۔ شراب کی بوتل کھولتا ہے۔ خالی بوتل اُٹھا کر کمرے میں پھینکتا ہے کہ چندرمکھی داخل ہوتی ہے۔

Chandramukhi:
Don't drink any more, Devdas.

Aur matt piyo, Devdas.

Devdas:
Why not?

Kyun?

Chandramukhi:
You're not used to drinking alcohol. You cannot tolerate drinking so much.

Kuch hi din huwe peena shuru ki hai, itni zyada bardaasht na kar sakoge.

Devdas:
What unlucky fool drinks to tolerate? I drink so that I may breathe. I do not even have the strength to get up and leave this place. That's why I lie here. I lie here staring at you, but I never lose all my senses. A little remains. "Tell my senses never to let me regain them."

Kaun kam-bakht hai jo bardaasht karne ke liye peeta hai? Main toh peeta hoon ki bas saans le sakoon. Aur aisi jagah se uth kar jaane ki taaqat nahin hai na. Tabhi toh yahaan pada rehta hoon. Bas dekhta rehta hoon tumhaare moonh ki taraf. Toh bhi main bilkul be-hosh nahin hota. Kuch hosh reh hi jaata hai. "Hosh se kehdo kabhi hosh na aane paaye"

Chandramukhi:
There are some men who come here who never touch alcohol, Devdas.

Yahaan aise log bhi aate hain, Devdas, jo sharaab ko chhoote bhi nahin.

Devdas *(standing near her):*
Don't touch it? If I had a gun, I'd shoot them. They are greater sinners than I, Chandramukhi. I'll never stop drinking. And if I did, I'd never come back. Never. There's a cure for me, but what will become of those men who don't drink and yet come here? Countless are the traumas I have suffered before I turned to drink.

(in close-up, he leans his head against a bannister. He struggles to stand up again. Chandramukhi tries to steady him)

Don't touch. Don't touch me, Chandramukhi. All my senses are not lost. You don't know how much I despise your kind. And I always will. Yet I still come back to you…sit with you, talk to you. What choice do I have? Can you people understand these things? Huh? People sin in the darkness of night. I drink in broad daylight.

(he smashes the empty glass in his hand onto the floor. Chandramukhi has tears in her eyes)

Chhoote bhi nahin? Mere paas bandooq ho toh main unhen goli se uda doon. Vo log mujh se bhi badey paapi hain, Chandramukhi. Pehle toh main sharaab peena chhodunga nahin. Aur agar chhod diya toh phir yahaan kabhi nahin aaunga. Kabhi nahin aaunga. Mera toh ilaaj hai lekin unn logon ka kya hoga jo peete bhi nahin aur phir bhi yahaan aate hain? Na jaane kitna dukh hua ki maine peena shuru kiya.

Matt chhuo. Haath matt lagaao mujhe, Chandramukhi. Ab bhi kuch hosh baaqi hai. Tum nahin jaantein main tum logon se kitni nafrat karta hoon aur humesha karta rahunga. Phir bhi aaunga tumhaare paas…baithunga, baaten karunga. Iske siwaaye aur upaaye bhi kya hai? Tum log kya ye baat samajh sakogi? Huh? Log andhere mein paap karte hain aur main ujaale mein yahaan aa ke sharaab peeta hoon.

चंद्रमुखीः
और मत पियो, देवदास।

देवदासः
क्यों?

चंद्रमुखीः
कुछ ही दिन हुए पीना शुरू की है, इतनी ज़्यादा बरदाश्त न कर सकोगे।

देवदासः
कौन कमबख़्त है जो बरदाश्त करने के लिए पीता है? मैं तो पीता हूँ कि बस साँस ले सकूँ। और ऐसी जगह से उठ कर जाने की ताक़त नहीं है ना। तभी तो यहाँ पड़ा रहता हूँ। बस देखता रहता हूँ तुम्हारे मुँह की तरफ़। तो भी मैं बिल्कुल बेहोश नहीं होता। कुछ होश रह ही जाता है। ''होश से कह दो, कभी होश न आने पाए।''

चंद्रमुखीः
यहाँ ऐसे लोग भी आते हैं, देवदास, जो शराब को छूते भी नहीं।

देवदास *(उसके निकट खड़े होते हुए):*
छूते भी नहीं? मेरे पास बंदूक़ हो तो मैं उन्हें गोली से उड़ा दूँ। वह लोग मुझसे भी बड़े पापी हैं, चंद्रमुखी। पहले तो मैं शराब पीना छोड़ूँगा नहीं। और अगर छोड़ दिया तो फिर यहाँ कभी नहीं आऊँगा। कभी नहीं आऊँगा। मेरा तो इलाज है लेकिन उन लोगों का क्या होगा जो पीते भी नहीं और फिर भी यहाँ आते हैं? न जाने कितना दु:ख हुआ कि मैंने पीना शुरू किया।

(क्लोज़-अप में, वह सीढ़ियों की रेलिंग से लग कर खड़ा हो जाता है। चंद्रमुखी उसे सँभालने की कोशिश करती है)

मत छुओ। हाथ मत लगाओ मुझे, चंद्रमुखी। अब भी कुछ होश बाक़ी है। तुम नहीं जानतीं, मैं तुम लोगों से कितनी नफ़रत करता हूँ और हमेशा करता रहूँगा। फिर भी आऊँगा तुम्हारे पास...बैठूँगा, बातें करूँगा। इसके सिवाए और उपाय भी क्या है? तुम लोग क्या यह बात समझ सकोगी? हँ? लोग अंधेरे में पाप करते हैं और मैं उजाले में यहाँ आके शराब पीता हूँ।

(देवदास अपना ख़ाली गिलास ज़मीन पर फेंक कर तोड़ डालता है। चंद्रमुखी की आँखों में आँसू हैं)

چندرمکھی:
اور مت پیو، دیوداس۔

دیوداس:
کیوں؟

چندرمکھی:
کچھ ہی دن ہوئے پینا شروع کی ہے، اِتنی زیادہ برداشت نہ کرسکوگے۔

دیوداس:
کون کمبخت ہے جو برداشت کرنے کے لیے پیتا ہے؟ میں تو پیتا ہوں کہ بس سانس لے سکوں۔ اور ایسی جگہ سے اُٹھ کر جانے کی طاقت نہیں ہے نا۔ تبھی تو یہاں پڑا رہتا ہوں۔ بس دیکھتا رہتا ہوں تمہارے منہ کی طرف۔ تو بھی میں بالکل بے ہوش نہیں ہوتا۔ کچھ ہوش رہ ہی جاتا ہے۔
''ہوش سے کہہ دو کبھی ہوش نہ آنے پائے۔''

چندرمکھی:
یہاں ایسے لوگ بھی آتے ہیں، دیوداس، جو شراب کو چھوتے بھی نہیں۔

دیوداس (اُس کے قریب کھڑے ہوتے ہوئے):
چھوتے بھی نہیں؟ میرے پاس بندوق ہو تو میں اُنھیں گولی سے اُڑا دوں۔ وہ لوگ مجھ سے بھی بڑے پاپی ہیں، چندرمکھی۔ پہلے تو میں شراب پینا چھوڑوں گا نہیں۔ اور اگر چھوڑ دیا تو پھر یہاں کبھی نہیں آؤں گا۔ کبھی نہیں آؤں گا۔ میرا تو علاج ہے لیکن اُن لوگوں کا کیا ہوگا جو پیتے بھی نہیں اور پھر بھی یہاں آتے ہیں؟ نہ جانے کتنا دکھ ہوا کہ میں نے پینا شروع کیا۔

(کلوزاپ، ریلنگ کے سہارے دیوداس اُٹھ کھڑا ہوتا ہے۔ چندرمکھی لڑکھڑاتے دیوداس کو سنبھالنے کی کوشش کرتی ہے)

مت چھوؤ۔ ہاتھ مت لگاؤ مجھے، چندرمکھی۔ اب بھی کچھ ہوش باقی ہے۔ تم نہیں جانتیں میں تم لوگوں سے کتنی نفرت کرتا ہوں اور ہمیشہ کرتا رہوں گا۔ پھر بھی آؤں گا تمہارے پاس۔۔۔ بیٹھوں گا، باتیں کروں گا۔ اِس کے سوائے اور اُپائے بھی کیا ہے؟ تم لوگ کیا یہ بات سمجھ سکوگی؟ ہوں؟ لوگ اندھیرے میں پاپ کرتے ہیں اور میں اُجالے میں یہاں آکے شراب پیتا ہوں۔

(دیوداس خالی گلاس فرش پر پٹخ کر توڑ دیتا ہے۔ چندرمکھی کی آنکھوں میں آنسو ہیں)

And all you women are the living examples of endurance. Chandramukhi says, "I love you." But I don't want that. No. People play-act. They paint their faces and pretend to be kings and queens. They love and create all kinds of illusions of love that appear so real. Chandramukhi play-acts too.
(she wipes her tears)

Aur tum sab sahen-shakti ki jeeti-jaagti tasvir ho. Chandramukhi kehti hai "main tumse pyar karti hoon," lekin main toh ye nahin chaahta. Main ye nahin chaahta. Nahin. Log naatak karte hain, moonh par kaalak-choona malte hain, raja bante hain, raani bante hain, pyar karte hain, pyar ke na jaane kitne dhong rachaate hain. Aur yun lagta hai jaise sab sach hai. Chandramukhi bhi naatak karti hai.

And I watch. And yet…I miss Paro so much. In an instant everything turned to dust. She took the road to a married life and I took the road to my doom. Now the charade without end has begun.

Aur main dekhta hoon. Phir bhi…phir bhi Paro ki bahot yaad aati hai. Pal bhar mein sab kuch khatam ho gaya. Vo shaadi ke raaste pe chal di aur main barbaadi ke raaste pe. Abhi kabhi na khatam honay waala naatak shuru ho gaya.

Chandramukhi:
Devdas.

Devdas.

Devdas:
Who is it? Parvati? You aren't Paro. So why are you crying? Oh! Such severe punishment for such a small mistake? Why does the memory of Paro forever torment me? Why can't I forget her?

Kaun? Parvati? Tum toh Paro nahin ho phir kyun roti ho? Uffo! Ek chhoti si bhool. Uski itni badi saza? Kyun Paro ki yaad har waqt sataati hai mujhe? Kyun main usay nahin bhula sakta?

Chandramukhi:
Devdas.

Devdas.

Devdas:
Yes?

Haan?

Chandramukhi:
Come. Get some sleep.

Chalo, chal ke so jaao.

Devdas:
Sleep? I am a drunkard and you're a…so be it. Where's the harm? I have no hope, no trust. No peace of mind and no desire. Bravo!

So jaaun? Main ek sharaabi aur ye ek…acha honay do. Yahi honay do, bura kya hai? Koi ummeed nahin, bharosa nahin, koi sukh nahin aur koi khwaahish bhi nahin. Waah, bahot ache…

He collapses onto the floor. Chandramukhi rushes to him.

और तुम सब सहन-शक्ति की जीती-जागती तस्वीर हो। चंद्रमुखी कहती है, “मैं तुमसे प्यार करती हूँ,” लेकिन मैं तो यह नहीं चाहता। मैं यह नहीं चाहता। नहीं। लोग नाटक करते हैं, मुँह पर कालक-चूना मलते हैं, राजा बनते हैं, रानी बनते हैं, प्यार करते हैं, प्यार के न जाने कितने ढोंग रचाते हैं। और यूँ लगता है जैसे सब सच है। चंद्रमुखी भी नाटक करती है।

(वह अपने आँसू पोंछती है)

और मैं देखता हूँ। फिर भी...फिर भी पारो की बहुत याद आती है। पल भर में सब कुछ ख़त्म हो गया। वह शादी के रास्ते पे चल दी और मैं बरबादी के रास्ते पे। अभी कभी ना ख़त्म होने वाला नाटक शुरू हो गया।

चंद्रमुखीः
देवदास।

देवदासः
कौन? पार्वती? तुम तो पारो नहीं हो फिर क्यों रोती हो? उफ़्फ़ो! एक छोटी-सी भूल। उसकी इतनी बड़ी सज़ा? क्यों पारो की याद हर वक़्त सताती है मुझे? क्यों मैं उसे नहीं भुला सकता?

चंद्रमुखीः
देवदास।

देवदासः
हाँ।

चंद्रमुखीः
चलो, चलके सो जाओ।

देवदासः
सो जाऊँ? मैं एक शराबी और यह एक...अच्छा होने दो। यही होने दो, बुरा क्या है? कोई उम्मीद नहीं, भरोसा नहीं, कोई सुख नहीं और कोई ख़्वाहिश भी नहीं। वाह, बहुत अच्छे...

देवदास बेसुध होकर गिर जाता है। चंद्रमुखी उसे सँभालती है।

اور تم سب سہن شکتی کی جیتی جاگتی تصویر ہو۔ چندرمکھی کہتی ہے ''میں تم سے پیار کرتی ہوں''، لیکن میں تو یہ نہیں چاہتا۔ میں یہ نہیں چاہتا۔ نہیں۔ لوگ ناٹک کرتے ہیں، منہ پر کالک چونا ملتے ہیں، راجا بنتے ہیں، رانی بنتے ہیں، پیار کرتے ہیں، پیار کے نہ جانے کتنے ڈھونگ رچاتے ہیں۔ اور یوں لگتا ہے جیسے سب سچ ہے۔ چندرمکھی بھی ناٹک کرتی ہے۔

(وہ اپنے آنسو پوچھتی ہے)

اور میں دیکھتا ہوں۔ پھر بھی۔۔۔ پھر بھی پارو کی بہت یاد آتی ہے۔ پل بھر میں سب کچھ ختم ہو گیا۔ وہ شادی کے راستے پہ چل دی اور میں بربادی کے راستے پہ۔ ابھی کبھی نہ ختم ہونے والا ناٹک شروع ہو گیا۔

چندرمکھی:
دیوداس۔

دیوداس:
کون؟ پاروتی؟ تم تو پارو نہیں ہو پھر کیوں روتی ہو؟ اُفوہ! ایک چھوٹی سی بھول۔ اُس کی اتنی بڑی سزا؟ کیوں پارو کی یاد ہر وقت ستاتی ہے مجھے؟ کیوں میں اُسے نہیں بھلا سکتا؟

چندرمکھی:
دیوداس۔

دیوداس:
ہاں؟

چندرمکھی:
چلو، چل کے سو جاؤ۔

دیوداس:
سو جاؤں؟ میں ایک شرابی اور یہ ایک۔۔۔ اچھا ہونے دو۔ یہی ہونے دو، برا کیا ہے؟ کوئی اُمید نہیں، بھروسا نہیں، کوئی سکھ نہیں اور کوئی خواہش بھی نہیں۔ واہ، بہت اچھے۔۔۔

لڑکھڑا کر وہ فرش پر ڈھیر ہو جاتا ہے۔ چندرمکھی دوڑ کر اُسے سنبھالنے جاتی ہے۔

Chandramukhi:
Devdas!

Devdas! Devdas!

Dissolve. Night-time. Chandramukhi is fanning Devdas who is asleep in her bed.

Dharamdas *(off-screen):*
Devdas. (3)

Devdas. (3)

Chandramukhi goes to the next room where Dharamdas is standing. He is curt and disapproving of her.

Dharamdas:
Is Devdas here?

Devdas hain?

Chandramukhi:
Yes, but he's asleep. You can't see him now.

Hain, magar so rahe hain. Is waqt na mil sakenge.

Dharamdas:
Why not? He will have to see me. Tell me, where have you hidden him? I will not leave him in this hell.

Mil kyun na sakenge? Usay milna hi hoga. Bataao, kahaan chupa rakkha hai usay? Main usay is nark mein nahin rehne doonga.

Devdas *(entering the room):*
Who is it?

Kaun?

Dharamdas:
Devdas!

Devdas!

Devdas:
Dharamda? How did you find me?

Dharamda? Tum yahaan kaise aaye?

चंद्रमुखीः
देवदास! देवदास!

अगला दृश्य। रात का समय। बिस्तर पर सोए देवदास को चंद्रमुखी पंखा झल रही है।

धरमदास *(ऑफ़-स्क्रीन):*
देवदास। (३)

चंद्रमुखी बाहर कमरे में आती है, धरमदास उसे मिलता है। रूखे स्वर में उससे पूछता है।

धरमदासः
देवदास हैं?

चंद्रमुखीः
हैं, मगर सो रहे हैं। इस वक़्त न मिल सकेंगे।

धरमदासः
मिल क्यों न सकेंगे? उसे मिलना ही होगा। बताओ, कहाँ छुपा रखा है उसे? मैं उसे इस नरक में नहीं रहने दूँगा।

देवदास *(कमरे में आते हुए):*
कौन?

धरमदासः
देवदास!

देवदासः
धरमदा? तुम यहाँ कैसे आए?

چندرمکھی:
دیوداس! دیوداس!

اگلا منظر۔ رات۔ بستر پر سوئے ہوئے دیوداس کو چندرمکھی پنکھا جھل رہی ہے۔

دھرم داس (آف اسکرین):
دیوداس۔ (۳)

چندرمکھی باہر کمرے میں آتی ہے جہاں دھرم داس کھڑا ہے۔ وہ چندرمکھی سے ترش لہجے میں کہتا ہے۔

دھرم داس:
دیوداس ہیں؟

چندرمکھی:
ہیں، مگر سو رہے ہیں۔ اِس وقت نہ مل سکیں گے۔

دھرم داس:
مل کیوں نہ سکیں گے؟ اُسے ملنا ہی ہوگا۔ بتاؤ، کہاں چھپا رکھا ہے اُسے؟ میں اُسے اِس نرک میں نہیں رہنے دوں گا۔

دیوداس (کمرے میں آتے ہوئے):
کون؟

دھرم داس:
دیوداس!

دیوداس:
دھرم دا؟ تم یہاں کیسے آئے؟

Dharamdas:
Chunni babu gave me the address.

Chunni babu ne mujhe yahaan ka pata…

Devdas *(angry)*:
Why are you here? Go away, Dharamda. I won't go.

Kis liye aaye ho? Chale jaao yahaan se, Dharamda. Nikal jaao baahar. Main nahin jaaunga.

Dharamdas:
Wait, Devdas. There's a telegram from home. Your father is no more.

Thairo, Devdas. Ghar se taar aaya hai. Maalik nahin rahe.

(Devdas turns towards him with a shocked expression)
He has left us. Come home now, Devdas. At least for your mother's sake. Come, Devdas.

Hum sab ko chhod kar chale gaye. Ab ghar chalo, Devdas. Kisi ke liye nahin toh apni ma ki hi khaatir chalo, Devdas.

Dissolve from a close-up of Devdas to his house in the village. Narain's unlit hookah stands in the verandah. Devdas is sitting in a corner of the room. Dwijodas enters sobbing.

Dwijodas:
Father has left me. He has gone. I don't want to live. What's the point of living now?

Haaye. Pitaji mujhe chhod kar chale gaye. Chhod do mujhe. Main nahin bachna chaahta. Ab bachne se bhi kya faayeda?

Family member:
Have faith in God.

Bhagwan par bharosa rakho.

Dwijodas:
Who will protect us now?

Ab humaara kaun sar-parast rehega?

An old neighbour is heard in the background.

Neighbour:
Narain babu was so noble…

Narain babu toh sache…

Devdas *(pointing in the direction of his brother)*:
Not here, over there.

Idhar nahin, udhar.

धरमदासः
चुन्नी बाबू ने मुझे यहाँ का पता...

देवदास *(गुस्से से)*:
किस लिए आए हो? चले जाओ यहाँ से, धरमदा। निकल जाओ बाहर। मैं नहीं जाऊँगा।

धरमदासः
ठहरो, देवदास। घर से तार आया है। मालिक नहीं रहे।
(देवदास सदमे से धरमदास को देखता है)
हम सबको छोड़ कर चले गए। अब घर चलो, देवदास। किसी के लिए नहीं तो अपनी माँ की ही ख़ातिर चलो, देवदास।

अगला दृश्य। देवदास के क्लोज़-अप से होता हुआ गाँव में उसके घर का दृश्य। नारायण का बुझा हुआ हुक़्क़ा बरामदे में रखा हुआ है। देवदास कमरे के एक कोने में अकेला बैठा है। द्विजोदास रोता हुआ अंदर आता है।

द्विजोदासः
हाय। पिताजी मुझे छोड़ कर चले गए। छोड़ दो मुझे। मैं नहीं बचना चाहता। अब बचने से भी क्या फ़ायदा?

एक पारिवारिक सदस्यः
भगवान पर भरोसा रखो।

द्विजोदासः
अब कौन मेरा सर-परस्त रहेगा?

एक बूढ़े पड़ोसी की आवाज़ सुनाई देती है।

पड़ोसीः
नारायण बाबू तो सच्चे...

देवदासः
इधर नहीं, उधर।

دھرم داس:
چُنّی بابو نے مجھے یہاں کا پتا۔۔۔

دیوداس (غصے سے):
کس لیے آئے ہو؟ چلے جاؤ یہاں سے، دھرم دا۔ نکل جاؤ باہر۔ میں نہیں جاؤں گا۔

دھرم داس:
ٹھہرو، دیوداس۔ گھر سے تار آیا ہے۔ مالک نہیں رہے۔
(دیوداس صدمے سے پلٹ کر دیکھتا ہے)
ہم سب کو چھوڑ کر چلے گئے۔ اب گھر چلو، دیوداس۔ کسی کے لیے نہیں تو اپنی ماں ہی کی خاطر چلو، دیوداس۔

اگلا منظر۔ دیوداس کے کلوز اپ سے ہوتا ہوا اُس کے گاؤں کا منظر۔ نارائن کا بجھا ہوا حقہ برآمدے میں رکھا ہوا ہے۔ دیوداس کمرے کے ایک گوشے میں بیٹھا ہے۔ آہ وزاریاں کرتا ہوا دویجوداس آتا ہے۔

دویجوداس:
ہائے۔ پتا جی مجھے چھوڑ کر چلے گئے۔ چھوڑ دو مجھے۔ میں نہیں بچنا چاہتا۔ اب بچنے سے بھی کیا فائدہ؟

ایک رشتے دار:
بھگوان پر بھروسا رکھو۔

دویجوداس:
اب ہمارا کون سرپرست رہے گا؟

ایک بوڑھے پڑوسی کی آواز سنائی دیتی ہے ۔

پڑوسی:
نارائن بابو تو سچے۔۔۔

دیوداس:
اِدھر نہیں، اُدھر۔

Reel Eleven

A palanquin, carried by four men, enters the frame. Parvati gets out of the palanquin and knocks at the door of her parents' home. When her father comes to the door, she touches his feet in respect.

Nilkanth:
Paro, what brings you here so suddenly? You didn't tell us you were coming.

Arey Paro, beti, ek damm chali aayin. Na koi paati na koi sandesa.

Parvati:
Mano didi wrote saying that uncle is unwell.

Haan, pitaji. Mano didi ka khat mila tha, likha tha taayaji bahot beemaar hain?

Nilkanth:
He is no more.

Vo toh chal bhi diye, beti.

Parvati:
He is no more? I'll go and see them, father.

Chal diye? Main udhar se ho ke aati hoon, pitaji.

Dissolve from Parvati's forlorn face. She enters Devdas's mansion. He is coming down the stairs.

Devdas:
Parvati. When did you arrive from Manekpur?

Parvati. Manekpur se kab aayin?

Parvati:
Today.

Aaj hi.

Devdas:
It's been so long since I had the pleasure of seeing you. Are you well? And your husband and his family?

Ek jugg beet gaya tumse bhent huwe. Kaho achi toh ho na? Chowdhury mahashay aur ladke-baale sab theek hain?

रील ग्यारह

चार कहार एक पालकी लिए प्रवेश करते हैं। पालकी से उतर कर पार्वती अपने पिता के घर का द्वार खटखटाती है। जब उसका पिता द्वार पर आता है तो वह आदर से उसके पैर छूती है।

नीलकंठः
अरे पारो, बेटी, एकदम चली आई। न कोई पाती न कोई संदेसा।

पार्वतीः
हाँ, पिताजी। मनो दीदी का ख़त मिला था, लिखा था तायाजी बहुत बीमार हैं?

नीलकंठः
वह तो चल भी दिये, बेटी।

पार्वतीः
चल दिये? मैं उधर से होके आती हूँ, पिताजी।

अगला दृश्य। पार्वती का उदास चेहरा। वह देवदास की हवेली में प्रवेश करती है। देवदास सीढ़ियाँ उतर कर नीचे आ रहा है।

देवदासः
पार्वती। मानेकपुर से कब आईं?

पार्वतीः
आज ही।

देवदासः
एक जुग बीत गया तुमसे भेंट हुए। कहो अच्छी तो हो ना? चौधरी महाशय और लड़के-बाले सब ठीक हैं?

ریل گیارہ

چار کہار ایک پالکی اُٹھائے داخل ہوتے ہیں۔ پالکی سے اُتر کر پاروتی اپنے میکے کے دروازے پر دستک دیتی ہے۔ جب اُس کے پِتا دروازے پر آتے ہیں تو وہ اُن کے پیر چھوتی ہے۔

نیل کنٹھ:
ارے پارو، بیٹی، ایک دم چلی آئیں۔ نہ کوئی پاتی نہ کوئی سندیسہ۔

پاروتی:
ہاں، پتاجی۔ منو دیدی کا خط ملا تھا، لکھا تھا تایاجی بہت بیمار ہیں؟

نیل کنٹھ:
وہ تو چل بھی دیے، بیٹی۔

پاروتی:
چل دیے؟ میں اُدھر سے ہو کے آتی ہوں، پتاجی۔

اگلا منظر۔ پاروتی کا اُداس چہرہ۔ وہ دیوداس کی حویلی میں داخل ہوتی ہے۔ دیوداس زینے اُتر کر نیچے آ رہا ہے۔

دیوداس:
پاروتی۔ مانک پور سے کب آئیں؟

پاروتی:
آج ہی۔

دیوداس:
ایک جُگ بیت گیا تم سے بھینٹ ہوئے۔ کہو اچھی تو ہو نا؟ چودھری مہاشے اور لڑکے بالے سب ٹھیک ہیں؟

Parvati:
They are well.

Haan, sabhi ache hain.

Devdas:
Will you stay a while?
(she nods)
Then we'll meet again.

Hmm. Abhi toh kuch din rahogi na yahaan?

Acha, acha toh phir milunga.

Devdas leaves. Parvati goes into a room where she sees Dharamdas.

Dharamdas:
Parvati, you're here. Well, I am glad of that. Perhaps you can save Devdas.

Parvati. Tum aa gayein. Chalo acha hua. Shaayad tum Devdas ko bacha sako.

Parvati:
Why? What has happened, Dharamda?

Kyun? Kya hua, Dharamda?

Dharamdas:
If only I didn't have to tell you. His father has left him a lot of money; it will mean more problems.

Kehne ki baat ho toh kahun. Maalik nahin rahe, Devdas ke haath be-hisaab rupay lag gaye, ab toh mushkil hi hai.

Parvati:
What problems? Tell me.

Kya mushkil hai? Saaf-saaf bataao na.

Dharamdas:
What can I say, Paro? I don't know what's wrong with him. He doesn't eat, or sleep. All he does is drink alcohol, bottle after bottle. He disappears for days on end. No one knows where he goes. I hear he has had a lot of jewellery made for her.

Kya bataaun, Paro? Na jaane unhen kya ho gaya hai. Na khaana hai, na sona hai. Sirf botlon pe botlen sharaab. Teen-teen chaar-chaar din na jaane kahaan pade rehte hain. Aur suna hai kayi hazaar ke toh usay gehne banwa diye hain.

Parvati:
For whom?
(looking shocked)
Oh…

Kisay?

Oh…

Cut. A wide shot of Devdas and his elder brother Dwijodas.

Devdas:
How much cash has father left?

Pitaji kul kitne naqd chhod gaye hain?

पार्वतीः
हाँ, सभी अच्छे हैं।

پاروتی:
ہاں، سبھی اچھے ہیں۔

देवदासः
हुँ। अभी तो कुछ दिन रहोगी न यहाँ?
(वह 'हाँ' में सर हिलाती है)
अच्छा, अच्छा तो फिर मिलूँगा।

دیوداس:
ہوں۔ابھی تو کچھ دن رہوگی نا یہاں؟
(اثبات میں سر ہلاتی ہے)
اچھا، اچھا تو پھر ملوں گا۔

देवदास चला जाता है। पार्वती एक कमरे में आती है। जहाँ धरमदास है।

دیوداس چلا جاتا ہے۔پاروتی ایک کمرے میں داخل ہوتی ہے جہاں دھرم داس ہے۔

धरमदासः
पार्वती। तुम आ गईं। चलो, अच्छा हुआ। शायद तुम देवदास को बचा सको।

دھرم داس:
پاروتی۔تم آ گئیں۔چلو اچھا ہوا۔شاید تم دیوداس کو بچا سکو۔

पार्वतीः
क्यों? क्या हुआ, धरमदा?

پاروتی:
کیوں؟ کیا ہوا، دھرم دا؟

धरमदासः
कहने की बात हो तो कहूँ। मालिक नहीं रहे, देवदास के हाथ बे-हिसाब रुपए लग गए, अब तो मुश्किल ही है।

دھرم داس:
کہنے کی بات ہوتو کہوں۔مالک نہیں رہے، دیوا کے ہاتھ بے حساب روپے لگ گئے، اب تو مشکل ہی ہے۔

पार्वतीः
क्या मुश्किल है? साफ़-साफ़ बताओ न?

پاروتی:
کیا مشکل ہے؟ صاف صاف بتاؤ نا۔

धरमदासः
क्या बताऊँ, पारो? न जाने उन्हें क्या हो गया है। न खाना है, न सोना है। सिर्फ़ बोतलों पे बोतलें शराब। तीन-तीन चार-चार दिन न जाने कहाँ पड़े रहते हैं? और सुना है कई हज़ार के तो उसे गहने बनवा दिए हैं।

دھرم داس:
کیا بتاؤں، پارو؟ نہ جانے اُنھیں کیا ہوگیا ہے۔نہ کھانا ہے، نہ سونا ہے۔صرف بوتلوں پہ بوتلیں شراب۔تین تین چار چار دن نہ جانے کہاں پڑے رہتے ہیں۔اور سنا ہے کئی ہزار کے تو اُسے گہنے بنوا دیے ہیں۔

पार्वतीः
किसे?
(अचंभे से)
ओह...

پاروتی:
کسے؟
(حیرت سے)
اوہ---

कट। देवदास और द्विजोदास का वाइड शॉट।

کٹ۔دیوداس اور دویجوداس کا وائڈ شاٹ۔

देवदासः
पिताजी कुल कितने नक़द छोड़ गए हैं?

دیوداس:
پتا جی کُل کتنے نقد چھوڑ گئے ہیں؟

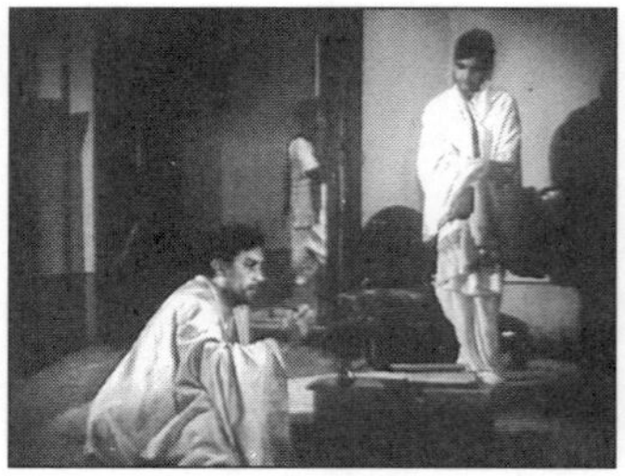

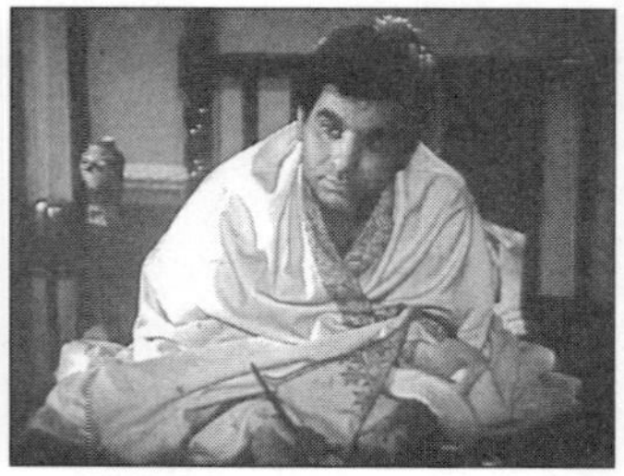

Dwijodas:
150,000 rupees.

Dedh laakh.

Devdas:
What is my share?

Uss mein se mujhe kitna milega?

Dwijodas:
We have an equal share. Seventy-five thousand each.

Aadha tumhen, aadha mujhe. Pichhat'har hazaar tumhen aur pichhat'har hazaar mujhe.

Devdas:
What about mother?

Aur ma ko?

Dwijodas *(laughing dismissively):*
Why does mother need money? She is the mistress of the house. I will look after her. I have thought it over and have decided it isn't necessary to spend more than ten thousand rupees on father's funeral expenses.

Ma ko rupay-vapay ki kya zaroorat hai? Vo toh ghar ki maalkin hai. Unki dekh-bhaal toh humen khud karni hai. Sab kuch soch-bichaar ke main is nateeje pe pohcha hoon ki pitaji ke shraadh pe das hazaar rupay se ziyaada kharch karne ki zaroorat nahin.

Devdas:
But this is father's last expense. Mother wants to feed all the villagers and give them money. I think we will need to spend at least thirty thousand.

Magar ye pitaji ka aakhri kharch hai, bhayya. Ma chaahti hain ki gaaon waalon ko khilaaya jaaye, daan diya jaaye. Main samajhta hoon kam-se kam tees hazaar rupay toh is mein lag hi jaayega.

Dwijodas:
Thirty thousand?

Tees hazaar?

Devdas:
Yes. I tell you what, take twenty-five from my share and add five thousand of yours. From my remaining fifty thousand,

Haan. Toh yun kijiye na, mere hisse se pachees hazaar kharch kar dijiye aur paanch hazaar apne se. Baaqi jo mere hisse ke

द्विजोदासः
डेढ़ लाख।

देवदासः
उसमें से मुझे कितना मिलेगा?

द्विजोदासः
आधा तुम्हें, आधा मुझे। पिछत्तर हज़ार तुम्हें और पिछत्तर हज़ार मुझे।

देवदासः
और माँ को?

द्विजोदास *(हँस कर टालते हुए):*
माँ को रुपए-वुपए की क्या ज़रूरत है? वह तो घर की मालकिन हैं। उनकी देख-भाल तो हमें खुद करनी है। सब कुछ सोच-विचार के मैं इस नतीजे पे पहुँचा हूँ कि पिताजी के श्राद्ध पे दस हज़ार रुपए से ज़्यादा ख़र्च करने की ज़रूरत नहीं।

देवदासः
मगर यह पिताजी का आख़िरी ख़र्च है, भैया। माँ चाहती हैं कि गाँव वालों को खिलाया जाए, दान दिया जाए। मैं समझता हूँ कम से कम तीस हज़ार रुपए तो इसमें लग ही जाएगा।

द्विजोदासः
तीस हज़ार?

देवदासः
हाँ। तो यूँ कीजिए न, मेरे हिस्से से पच्चीस हज़ार ख़र्च कर दीजिए और पाँच हज़ार अपने से। बाक़ी जो मेरे हिस्से के पचास हज़ार रह जाएँगे, उसमें से पच्चीस मैं ले

دویجوداس:
ڈیڑھ لاکھ۔

دیوداس:
اُس میں سے مجھے کتنا ملے گا؟

دویجوداس:
آدھا تمھیں، آدھا مجھے۔ پچھتر ہزار تمھیں، پچھتر ہزار مجھے۔

دیوداس:
اور ماں کو؟

دویجوداس (ہنس کر ٹالتے ہوئے):
ماں کو روپے وپے کی کیا ضرورت ہے؟ وہ تو گھر کی مالکن ہے۔ اُن کی دیکھ بھال تو ہمیں خود کرنی ہے۔ سب کچھ سوچ بچار کے میں اِس نتیجے پہ پہنچا ہوں کہ پتاجی کے شرادھ پہ دس ہزار روپے سے زیادہ خرچ کرنے کی ضرورت نہیں۔

دیوداس:
مگر یہ پتاجی کا آخری خرچ ہے، بھیا۔ ماں چاہتی ہیں کہ گاؤں والوں کو کھلایا جائے، دان دیا جائے۔ میں سمجھتا ہوں کم سے کم تیس ہزار روپے تو اِس میں لگ ہی جائیں گے۔

دویجوداس:
تیس ہزار؟

دیوداس:
ہاں۔ تو یوں کیجیے نا، میرے حصے سے پچیس ہزار خرچ کر دیجیے اور پانچ ہزار اپنے سے۔ باقی جو میرے حصے کے پچاس ہزار رہ جائیں گے اُس میں سے پچیس میں لے لوں گا اور باقی ماں کے نام جمع رہے۔ آپ کی کیا

I will take half and leave the rest in mother's name. What do you say?

pachaas hazaar reh jaayenge uss mein se pachees main le lunga aur baaqi ma ke naam jama rahe. Aap ki kya raaye hai?

Dwijodas:
Fine. You know I'm married with children. I must worry about their marriage. Shall we sign an agreement?

Hmm. Theek hai. Tum toh jaante ho main baal-bache waala aadmi hoon, unki shaadi-biyaah…toh phir likha-padhi ho jaaye?

Devdas:
Where's the need? It doesn't seem right.

Iski kya zaroorat hai? Acha nahin lagta.

Dwijodas:
No, brother. Later it might…

Nahin, bhai. Baad mein phir…shaayad…

Devdas:
All right. I'll put something down in writing.

Acha toh likh doonga.

Devdas leaves the room. Dissolve. Later that same day, Devdas is sitting on his bed and writing. Parvati comes in and locks the door behind her.

Devdas:
What if I maligned you now?

Ab agar tumhen bad-naam karun toh?

(Parvati looks away. Devdas is playful and then turns serious)

You feel shame, right, Paro? But where's the shame? We made a childish mistake and look at what's happened since. In your anger, you said whatever you felt like saying, and I scarred your forehead.

Hein? Kyun lajja aati hai na, Paro? Par is mein lajja ki kya baat hai? Do janay mil kar ek ladakpan kar baithe, aur phir dekho na, beech mein kya kuch ho gaya hai. Tumne bhi ghusse mein aa ke jo chaaha vo kaha, aur maine bhi maathe pe vo nishaan bana diya.

Parvati *(voice-over):*
This scar is my only joy and peace. It gives me the only support I have.

Yahi nishaan toh meri sukh-sampatti hai. Yahi toh sahaara hai.

Devdas:
Why don't you speak? You make me very angry, Paro.

Kuch bolti kyun nahin? Mujhe tujh pe bahot ghussa aata hai, Paro.

(in a sad voice)

Father is no more. These are difficult times for me. Would I suffer as much if you were with me? You know my sister-in-law and brother well. Nothing is hidden from you. Where

Babuji nahin rahe. Ye mere liye kitne dukh ke din hain. Agar tu hoti toh ye sab dukh rehta? Bhabhi ko toh tu jaanti hai, aur bhayya ka svabhaav bhi kuch tujh se chhupa hua toh nahin.

लूँगा और बाक़ी माँ के नाम जमा रहे। आपकी क्या राय है?

رائے ہے؟

द्विजोदासः
हुँ। ठीक है। तुम तो जानते हो, मैं बाल-बच्चे वाला आदमी हूँ, उनकी शादी-ब्याह... तो फिर लिखा-पढ़ी हो जाए?

دویجوداس:
ہوں۔ ٹھیک ہے۔تم تو جانتے ہو میں بال بچے والا آدمی ہوں، اُن کی شادی بیاہ۔ ۔۔تو پھر لکھا پڑھی ہوجائے؟

देवदासः
इसकी क्या ज़रूरत है? अच्छा नहीं लगता।

دیوداس:
اِس کی کیا ضرورت ہے؟ اچھا نہیں لگتا۔

द्विजोदासः
नहीं भाई। बाद में फिर...शायद...

دویجوداس:
نہیں بھائی۔ بعد میں پھر۔۔۔شاید۔۔۔

देवदासः
अच्छा तो लिख दूँगा।

دیوداس:
اچھا تو لکھ دوں گا۔

देवदास कमरे से चला जाता है। अगला दृश्य। उसी दिन थोड़ी देर बाद। देवदास अपने बिस्तर पर बैठा कुछ लिख रहा है। पार्वती अंदर आकर द्वार बंद कर लेती है।

دیوداس چلا جاتا ہے۔ اگلا منظر۔ اُسی دن اگلے پہر۔ دیوداس اپنے بستر پر بیٹھا کچھ لکھ رہا ہے۔ پاروتی کمرے میں آکر دروازہ بند کرلیتی ہے۔

देवदासः
अब अगर तुम्हें बदनाम करूँ तो?
(पार्वती दूसरी ओर देखने लगती है। देवदास मस्ती करते हुए गंभीर हो जाता है)
हैं? क्यों लज्जा आती है न, पारो? पर इसमें लज्जा की क्या बात है? दो जने मिल कर एक लड़कपन कर बैठे, और फिर देखो न, बीच में क्या कुछ हो गया है। तुमने भी गुस्से में आके जो चाहा वह कहा, और मैंने भी माथे पे वह निशान बना दिया।

دیوداس:
اب اگر تمھیں بدنام کروں تو؟
(پاروتی نظریں چرا لیتی ہے۔شوخی کرتا ہوا دیوداس سنجیدہ ہوجاتا ہے)
ہَیں؟ کیوں لجّا آتی ہے نا، پارو؟ پر اِس میں لجّا کی کیا بات ہے؟ دو جنے مل کر ایک لڑکپن کر بیٹھے، اور پھر دیکھو نا، بیچ میں کیا کچھ ہوگیا ہے۔تم نے بھی غصے میں آکے جو چاہا وہ کہا، اور میں نے بھی ماتھے پہ وہ نشان بنا دیا۔

पार्वती *(वॉइस-ओवर):*
यही निशान तो मेरी सुख-संपत्ति है। यही तो सहारा है।

پاروتی (بازگشت):
یہی نشان تو میری سکھ سمپتی ہے۔یہی تو سہارا ہے۔

देवदासः
कुछ बोलती क्यों नहीं? मुझे तुझपे बहुत गुस्सा आता है, पारो।
(दु:खी स्वर में)
बाबूजी नहीं रहे। यह मेरे लिए कितने दु:ख के दिन हैं। अगर तू होती तो यह सब दु:ख रहता? भाभी को तो तू जानती है, और भैया का स्वभाव भी कुछ तुझसे

دیوداس:
کچھ بولتی کیوں نہیں؟ مجھے تجھ پہ بہت غصہ آتا ہے، پارو۔
(دکھ بھرے لہجے میں)
بابو جی نہیں رہے۔ یہ میرے لیے کتنے دکھ کے دن ہیں اگر تُو ہوتی تو یہ سب دکھ رہتا؟ بھابھی کو تو تُو جانتی ہے، اور بھیا کا سوبھاؤ بھی کچھ تجھ سے چھپا ہوا تو نہیں۔ ایسے میں بھلا بتا میں اپنی ماں کو لے کر کہاں جاؤں گا؟ اور

can I take mother under these circumstances? I don't know what will become of me. If you were here, I'd give you all my troubles, and no longer need to worry. What's this? You're crying, Paro? Never mind. Let's stop talking of all this.

Aise mein bhala bata main apni ma ko le kar kahaan jaaunga? Aur phir mera kya hoga, ye bhi toh kuch samajh mein nahin aata. Tu hoti toh sabhi kuch tujhi ko saunp kar khud be-fikar ho…arey tu ro rahi hai, Paro? Acha jaane de, ye baat yahin khatam ho gayi.

Parvati *(has her back to him as she wipes away her tears):*
No, don't stop.

Nahin, tum kaho.

Devdas *(half-smiling):*
I hear you're a model housewife, mistress of a large house and estate. Mother to grown children and wife of a rich man. Yes? Could you do me a favour?

Suna hai tu badi pakki girahstan ho gayi hai? Khoob bada makaan, badi zamindari, bade-bade ladke ladkiyaan. Aur Chowdhury mahashay, vo bhi bade. Aur sabhi kuch bade. Haan? Ek upkaar kar sakegi mujh par?

Parvati *(coming towards him):*
What?

Kya?

Devdas:
Can you find me a wife in your village? I feel like settling down.

Idhar teri taraf koi ladki mil sakegi? Ji chaahta hai main bhi grihasth ban jaaun.

Parvati:
You want a beautiful wife?

Bahot sundar chaahiye na?

Devdas:
Yes, just like you.

Haan. Bilkul teri tarah.

Parvati:
Good-natured?

Bhali maanus ho?

Devdas:
No, bad-natured. Someone who can argue with me like you.

Nahin, balki dusht. Jo teri tarah mere saath jhagda kar sakey.

Parvati:
There are thousands like me who would fall at your feet and think themselves lucky.

Main moonh jali. Meri jaisi na jaane kayi hazaar tumhaare charno mein aa kar apne aap ko dhanya samjhengi.

छुपा हुआ तो नहीं। ऐसे में भला बता मैं अपनी माँ को लेकर कहाँ जाऊँगा? और फिर मेरा क्या होगा, यह भी तो कुछ समझ में नहीं आता। तू होती तो सभी कुछ तुझी को सौंप कर ख़ुद बे-फ़िक्र हो...अरे तू रो रही है, पारो? अच्छा जाने दे, यह बात यहीं ख़त्म हो गई।

पार्वती *(उसकी पीठ देवदास की ओर है। वह अपने आँसू पोंछती है):*
नहीं, तुम कहो।

देवदास *(फीकी मुस्कुराहट से):*
सुना है तू बड़ी पक्की गृहस्थन हो गई है? ख़ूब बड़ा मकान, बड़ी ज़मींदारी, बड़े-बड़े लड़के-लड़कियाँ। और चौधरी महाशय, वह भी बड़े। और सभी कुछ बड़े। हाँ? एक उपकार कर सकेगी मुझ पर?

पार्वती *(उसके निकट आते हुए):*
क्या?

देवदास:
इधर तेरी तरफ़ कोई लड़की मिल सकेगी? जी चाहता है, मैं भी गृहस्थ बन जाऊँ।

पार्वती:
बहुत सुंदर चाहिए ना?

देवदास:
हाँ। बिल्कुल तेरी तरह।

पार्वती:
भली मानुस हो?

देवदास:
नहीं, बल्कि दुष्ट। जो तेरी तरह मेरे साथ झगड़ा कर सके।

पार्वती:
मैं मुँहजली। मेरी जैसी न जाने कई हज़ार तुम्हारे चरनों में आकर अपने आपको धन्य समझेंगी।

پھر میرا کیا ہوگا، یہ بھی تو کچھ سمجھ میں نہیں آتا۔تُو ہوتی تو سبھی کچھ تجھی کو سونپ کر خود بے فکر ہو۔۔۔ارے تُو رو رہی ہے، پارو؟ اچھا جانے دے، یہ بات یہیں ختم ہوگئی۔

پاروتی (پاروتی کی پیٹھ دیوداس کی طرف ہے۔وہ اپنے آنسو پونچھتی ہے۔):
نہیں، تم کہو۔

دیوداس (نیم تبسم کے ساتھ):
سنا ہے تُو بڑی پکّی گرہستن ہوگئی ہے؟ خوب بڑا مکان، بڑی زمینداری، بڑے بڑے لڑکے لڑکیاں۔اور چودھری مہاشے، وہ بھی بڑے۔اور سبھی کچھ بڑے۔ہاں؟ ایک اُپکار کر سکے گی مجھ پر؟

پاروتی (پاس آتے ہوئے):
کیا؟

دیوداس:
اِدھر تیری طرف کوئی لڑکی مل سکے گی؟ جی چاہتا ہے میں بھی گرہست بن جاؤں۔

پاروتی:
بہت سندر چاہیے نا؟

دیوداس:
ہاں۔بالکل تیری طرح۔

پاروتی:
بھلی مانس ہو؟

دیوداس:
نہیں، بلکہ دُشٹ۔جو تیری طرح میرے ساتھ جھگڑا کر سکے۔

پاروتی:
میں منہ جلی۔میری جیسی نہ جانے کئی ہزار تمہارے چرنوں میں آ کر اپنے آپ کو دھنیہ سمجھیں گی۔

Devdas:
Not thousands. One will do.

Hazaar nahin abhi toh ek hi kaafi hogi.

Parvati:
Devdas.

Devdas.

Devdas:
Hmm?

Hmm?

Parvati:
May I say something?

Ek baat kahun?

Devdas:
Yes.

Kaho.

Parvati:
Why have you started drinking?

Tumne sharaab peene ki aadat kyun daali?

Devdas:
Who told you that?

Tumse kis ne kaha?

Parvati:
Never mind. Is it true?

Chaahe koi kahe. Kya ye sach hai?

Devdas:
Yes. It's true.

Haan. Sach hai.

Parvati:
I hear you have had a lot of jewellery made for her?

Aur usay kayi hazaar ke gehne banwa diye?

Devdas *(smiles):*
I haven't given it yet. Do you want it?

Abhi sirf banwaaye hain, diye nahin. Tu legi?

Parvati:
Yes. Look. I have no adornments.

Laao do. Dekho, mere badan pe gehne nahin hain.

Devdas:
Doesn't your husband give you any jewellery?

Toh kya tujhe Chowdhury mahashay ne nahin banwa ke diye?

देवदासः
हज़ार नहीं अभी तो एक ही काफ़ी होगी।

دیوداس:
ہزار نہیں ابھی تو ایک ہی کافی ہوگی۔

पार्वतीः
देवदास।

پاروتی:
دیوداس

देवदासः
हुँ?

دیوداس:
ہوں؟

पार्वतीः
एक बात कहूँ?

پاروتی:
ایک بات کہوں؟

देवदासः
कहो।

دیوداس:
کہو۔

पार्वतीः
तुमने शराब पीने की आदत क्यों डाली?

پاروتی:
تم نے شراب پینے کی عادت کیوں ڈالی؟

देवदासः
तुमसे किसने कहा?

دیوداس:
تم سے کس نے کہا؟

पार्वतीः
चाहे कोई कहे। क्या यह सच है?

پاروتی:
چاہے کوئی کہے۔ کیا یہ سچ ہے؟

देवदासः
हाँ। सच है।

دیوداس:
ہاں۔ سچ ہے۔

पार्वतीः
और उसे कई हज़ार के गहने बनवा दिए?

پاروتی:
اور اُسے کئی ہزار کے گہنے بنوا دیے؟

देवदास *(मुस्कुराते हुए):*
अभी सिर्फ़ बनवाए हैं, दिए नहीं। तू लेगी?

دیوداس (مسکراتے ہوئے):
ابھی صرف بنوائے ہیں، دیے نہیں، تُو لے گی؟

पार्वतीः
लाओ दो। देखो मेरे बदन पे गहने नहीं हैं।

پاروتی:
لاؤ دو، دیکھو، میرے بدن پہ گہنے نہیں ہیں۔

देवदासः
तो क्या तुझे चौधरी महाशय ने नहीं बनवा के दिए?

دیوداس:
تو کیا تجھے چودھری مہاشے نے نہیں بنوا کے دیے؟

Parvati:
Yes, he does. But I gave them to his daughter.

Diye thay lekin maine vo sab unki ladki ko de diye.

Devdas:
Perhaps you have no need of jewellery, Paro. What you hear are lies, Paro. I do not love any woman.

Tujhe shaayad unki zaroorat hi nahin, Paro. Aur vo jo tu ne baat suni hai, vo jhoot hai, Paro. Main kisi aurat se bhi pyar nahin karta.

Parvati:
Promise me one thing: never drink alcohol again.

Acha. Ek baat ki pratigya karo, ab kabhi sharaab nahin piyoge.

Devdas:
I can't promise that, Paro.

Main ye nahin kar sakta, Paro.

Parvati:
Why not?

Kyun?

Devdas:
Can you promise never to think of me again?
(she sighs)
I have work downstairs, Paro. I'll go.

Kya tu ye pratigya kar sakti hai ki ek baar bhi mujhe yaad nahin karegi?
Mujhe neeche kaam hai, Paro. Main chalta hoon.

Parvati *(standing against the door so he cannot leave):*
No. First promise me.

Nahin. Pehle tum vaada karo.

Devdas:
I can't, Paro.

Main nahin kar sakta, Paro.

Parvati:
Why not?

Kyun nahin kar sakte?

Devdas:
Can people do whatever they want?

Kya sabhi log sab kuch kar sakte hain?

Parvati:
If they want it, yes.

Koi karna chaahe toh zaroor kar sakta hai.

Devdas:
So, could you run away with me tonight?

Toh kya aaj raat tu mere saath bhaag ke ja sakegi?

पार्वतीः
दिए थे लेकिन मैंने वह सब उनकी लड़की को दे दिए।

देवदासः
तुझे शायद उनकी ज़रूरत ही नहीं, पारो। और वह जो तूने बात सुनी है, वह झूठ है, पारो। मैं किसी औरत से भी प्यार नहीं करता।

पार्वतीः
अच्छा। एक बात की प्रतिज्ञा करो, अब कभी शराब नहीं पियोगे।

देवदासः
मैं यह नहीं कर सकता, पारो।

पार्वतीः
क्यों?

देवदासः
क्या तू यह प्रतिज्ञा कर सकती है कि एक बार भी मुझे याद नहीं करेगी?
(पार्वती आह भरती है)
मुझे नीचे काम है, पारो। मैं चलता हूँ।

पार्वती *(द्वार पर खड़ी होकर उसका रास्ता रोक लेती है)*:
नहीं। पहले तुम वादा करो।

देवदासः
मैं नहीं कर सकता, पारो।

पार्वतीः
क्यों नहीं कर सकते?

देवदासः
क्या सभी लोग सब कुछ कर सकते हैं?

पार्वतीः
कोई करना चाहे तो ज़रूर कर सकता है।

देवदासः
तो क्या आज रात तू मेरे साथ भाग के जा सकेगी?

پاروتی:
دیے تھے لیکن میں نے وہ سب اُن کی لڑکی کو دے دیے۔

دیوداس:
تجھے شاید اُن کی ضرورت ہی نہیں، پارو۔ اور وہ جو تُو نے بات سنی ہے وہ جھوٹ ہے، پارو۔ میں کسی عورت سے بھی پیار نہیں کرتا۔

پاروتی:
اچھا۔ ایک بات کی پرتگیا کرو اب کبھی شراب نہیں پیو گے۔

دیوداس:
میں یہ نہیں کر سکتا، پارو۔

پاروتی:
کیوں؟

دیوداس:
کیا تُو یہ پرتگیا کر سکتی ہے کہ ایک بار بھی مجھے یاد نہیں کرے گی؟
(پاروتی آہ بھرتی ہے)
مجھے نیچے کام ہے، پارو۔ میں چلتا ہوں۔

پاروتی (دہلیز پر اُس کا راستہ روک لیتی ہے):
نہیں۔ پہلے تم وعدہ کرو۔

دیوداس:
میں نہیں کر سکتا، پارو۔

پاروتی:
کیوں نہیں کر سکتے؟

دیوداس:
کیا سبھی لوگ سب کچھ کر سکتے ہیں؟

پاروتی:
کوئی کرنا چاہے تو ضرور کر سکتا ہے۔

دیوداس:
تو کیا آج رات تُو میرے ساتھ بھاگ کے جا سکے گی؟

   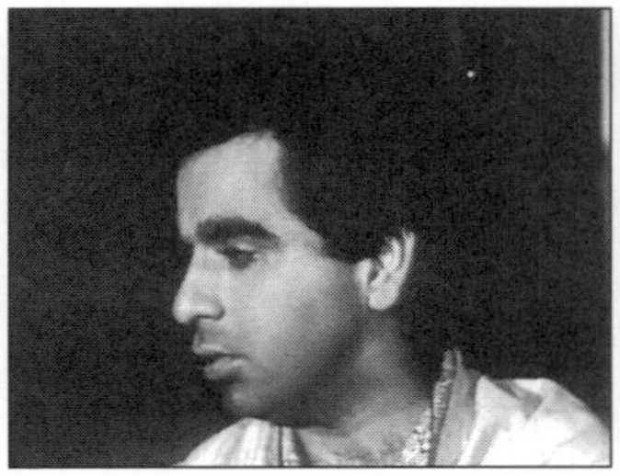 

Parvati *(taken aback):*
Devdas!

Devdas!

He smiles at her. The clock strikes seven (evening).

Devdas:
It's late. Go home, Paro.

Saanjh ho gayi, ab ghar ja, Paro.

Parvati:
First promise me.

Pehle pratigya karo.

Devdas:
Is it right to force a promise out of someone? I may not be able to keep my word later. Open the door, Paro.
(she is crying)
Parvati!

Yun zabardasti pratigya karana koi achhi baat hai kya? Mumkin hai aaj ke baad kal na rakh sakoon. Darwaaza khol de, Paro.

Parvati!

Parvati:
Devdas, I feel suffocated.

Devdas, mera damm ghutt raha hai.

Devdas:
Don't I know that?

Main kya nahin jaanta?

Parvati:
I feel as though I were dying, Devdas. I couldn't look after you. Come to my house. There's no one here to take care of you.

Main mari ja rahi hoon, Devdas. Main tumhaari sewa na kar saki. Mere yahaan chalo, yahaan tumhen dekhne-waala koi nahin.

Devdas:
Come to your house? You'll look after me?

Tere ghar chalun? Tu meri sewa karegi?

पार्वती *(चौंक कर):*
देवदास!

वह मुस्करा कर उसे देखता है। घड़ियाल के घंटे संध्या के सात बजाते हैं।

देवदासः
साँझ हो गई, अब घर जा, पारो।

पार्वतीः
पहले प्रतिज्ञा करो।

देवदासः
यूँ ज़बरदस्ती प्रतिज्ञा कराना कोई अच्छी बात है क्या? मुमकिन है आज के बाद कल न रख सकूँ। दरवाज़ा खोल दे पारो।
(वह रो रही है)
पार्वती!

पार्वतीः
देवदास, मेरा दम घुट रहा है।

देवदासः
मैं क्या नहीं जानता?

पार्वतीः
मैं मरी जा रही हूँ, देवदास। मैं तुम्हारी सेवा न कर सकी। मेरे यहाँ चलो। यहाँ तुम्हें देखने वाला कोई नहीं।

देवदासः
तेरे घर चलूँ? तू मेरी सेवा करेगी?

پاروتی (چونک کر):
دیوداس۔

وہ اُسے دیکھ کر مسکراتا ہے۔ گھڑی کا گجر شام کے سات بجاتا ہے۔

دیوداس:
سانجھ ہوگئی، اب گھر جا، پارو۔

پاروتی:
پہلے پرتگیا کرو۔

دیوداس:
یوں زبردستی پرتگیا کرانا کوئی اچھی بات ہے کیا؟ ممکن ہے آج کے بعد کل نہ رکھ سکوں۔ دروازہ کھول دے، پارو۔
(اُس کے آنسو نکل پڑتے ہیں)
پاروتی!

پاروتی:
دیوداس، میرا دم گھٹ رہا ہے۔

دیوداس:
میں کیا نہیں جانتا؟

پاروتی:
میں مری جا رہی، دیوداس۔ میں تمہاری سیوا نہ کر سکی۔ میرے یہاں چلو۔ یہاں تمھیں دیکھنے والا کوئی نہیں۔

دیوداس:
تیرے گھر چلوں؟ تُو میری سیوا کرے گی؟

Parvati:
That is all I have ever wanted, my lord. Give me the chance. I shall die with no regrets. Come with me.

Ye toh mere janam bhar ki saadhya hai mere devta. Meri ye saadhya poori kar do. Iske baad main mar bhi jaaun toh koi dukh nahin. Mere ghar chalo.

Devdas:
I shall come.

Acha chalunga.

Parvati:
Take an oath and tell me that you will come. Will you come?

Mujhe chhu kar meri saugandh le kar kaho, aaoge?

Devdas:
I shall never forget, Paro. If looking after me will lessen your sorrow, then I shall come. Before I die, I shall come to you.

Ye baat main kabhi nahin bhoolunga, Paro. Agar meri sewa karne se tera dukh kam hota hai toh main aaunga. Marne se pehle ek baar zaroor aaunga.

Devdas walks away as Parvati turns to open the door. Fade out.

Reel Twelve

Fade in. Mahendra and his wife arrive home in a bridal palanquin. Parvati welcomes the new bride into the house.

Parvati:
Come, daughter-in-law. The goddess of our house.

Aao, bahu. Aao grahalakshmi.

Dissolve. The next day. Mahendra comes to Parvati. He passes his wife in the corridor who covers her face.

Mahendra:
Mother, the beggars are making a fuss downstairs. Many have received no clothes as yet.

Ma, neeche bhikaari log shor macha rahe hain. Unn mein se sau ek ko kapde nahin mile hain.

Parvati:
Why not? They shall all get their share. Tell the manager to make the arrangements.

Kyun nahin miley? Jab sab ko miley hain toh unhen bhi milney chaahiye. Jao, Munimji se keh do bandobast kar denge.

Mahendra:
Very well, mother.

Acha ma.

पार्वतीः
यह तो मेरे जन्म भर की साध्य है मेरे देवता। मेरी यह साध्य पूरी कर दो। इसके बाद मैं मर भी जाऊँ तो कोई दुःख नहीं। मेरे घर चलो।

پاروتی:
یہ تو میرے جنم بھر کی سادھیہ ہے میرے دیوتا۔ میری یہ سادھ پوری کر دو۔ اِس کے بعد میں مر بھی جاؤں تو کوئی دکھ نہیں۔ میرے گھر چلو۔

देवदासः
अच्छा चलूँगा।

دیوداس:
اچھا چلوں گا۔

पार्वतीः
मुझे छूकर मेरी सौगंध लेकर कहो, आओगे?

پاروتی:
مجھے چھوکر میری سوگند لے کر کہو۔ آؤ گے؟

देवदासः
यह बात मैं कभी नहीं भूलूँगा, पारो। अगर मेरी सेवा करने से तेरा दुःख कम होता है तो मैं आऊँगा। मरने से पहले एक बार ज़रूर आऊँगा।

دیوداس:
یہ بات میں کبھی نہیں بھولوں گا، پارو۔ اگر میری سیوا کرنے سے تیرا دکھ کم ہوتا ہے تو میں آؤں گا۔ مرنے سے پہلے ایک بار ضرور آؤں گا۔

देवदास चला जाता है। पार्वती द्वार की ओर बढ़ती है। फ़ेड आउट।

دیوداس چلا جاتا ہے۔ پاروتی دروازے کی طرف رخ کر لیتی ہے۔ فیڈ آؤٹ۔

रील बारह

ریل بارہ

फ़ेड इन। महेंद्र और उसकी पत्नी एक सजी हुई डोली में आते हैं। पार्वती नई दुल्हन का स्वागत करती है।

فیڈ اِن۔ مہندر اور اُس کی بیوی ایک سجی ہوئی ڈولی میں آتے ہیں۔ پاروتی دہلیز پر دولہن کا استقبال کرتی ہے۔

पार्वतीः
आओ, बहू। आओ गृहलक्ष्मी।

پاروتی:
آؤ، بہو۔ آؤ گرہ لکشمی۔

डिज़ॉल्व। अगला दिन। महेंद्र, पार्वती के पास आता है। उसे देखकर राहदारी में उसकी पत्नी घूँघट काढ़ लेती है।

ڈزالو۔ اگلا دن۔ پاروتی کے پاس مہندر آتا ہے۔ اُسے دیکھ کر راہ داری میں اُس کی بیوی گھونگھٹ کاڑھ لیتی ہے۔

महेंद्रः
माँ, नीचे भिखारी लोग शोर मचा रहे हैं। उनमें से सौ एक को कपड़े नहीं मिले हैं।

مہندر:
ماں، نیچے بھکاری لوگ شور مچا رہے ہیں۔ اُن میں سے کئی سو ایک کو کپڑے نہیں ملے ہیں۔

पार्वतीः
क्यों नहीं मिले? जब सबको मिले हैं तो उन्हें भी मिलने चाहिए। जाओ मुनीमजी से कह दो, बन्दोबस्त कर देंगे।

پاروتی:
کیوں نہیں ملے؟ جب سب کو ملے ہیں تو اُنھیں بھی ملنے چاہییں۔ جاؤ، منیم جی سے کہہ دو بندوبست کر دیں گے۔

महेंद्रः
अच्छा माँ।

مہندر:
اچھا ماں۔

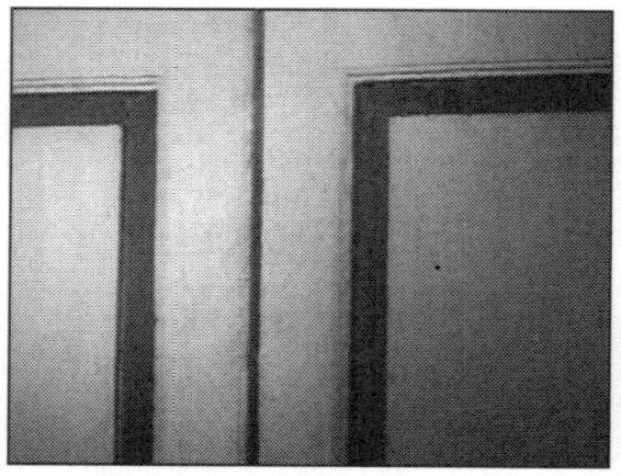

Cut. Exterior. Day. A crowd of beggars stand near the gate.

Munimji:
Silence! The mistress of the house has ordered that you shall be given clothes.

Khaamosh, khaamosh, khaamosh. Raani ma ne kaha hai sab ko kapde milenge.

Crowd:
May she live long! (6)

Raani ma ki jai! (6)

Parvati comes onto the balcony to hear the crowd applaud her generosity. Dissolve. Devdas knocks at Chandramukhi's door. A woman, whose face is covered, opens the door.

Devdas:
Does a woman called Chandramukhi...

Suniye, yahaan Chandramukhi naam ki koi...

Chandramukhi *(face covered):*
Yes. Come in.

Haan, andar aao.

Devdas:
What has happened to this room? Where is Chandramukhi?
(the woman turns to face him. She is dressed plainly)
It's you? What has happened to you?

Arey ye kamra aisa kyun? Chandramukhi kahaan hai?

Tum? Ye kya haal ho gaya hai tumhaara?

Chandramukhi:
Happened to me? I believe my fate has turned for the better. You've forgotten me so quickly?

Haal kaisa? Main toh samajhti hoon qismat jaag gayi meri. Itni jaldi bhool gaye mujhe?

Devdas:
You look thin. Have you been unwell?

Tum kuch dubli maaloom ho rahi ho. Beemaar thein kya?

कट। बाहर। दिन। भिखारी दान माँग रहे हैं।

मुनीमजीः
ख़ामोश, ख़ामोश, ख़ामोश। रानी-माँ ने कहा है, सबको कपड़े मिलेंगे।

जन समूहः
रानी-माँ की जय! (६)

पार्वती छज्जे पर आती है। भीड़ उसकी दयालुता की जय-जयकार कर रही है। डिज़ॉल्व। देवदास चंद्रमुखी का द्वार खटखटाता है। पल्लू निकाले एक महिला द्वार खोलती है।

देवदासः
सुनिए, यहाँ चंद्रमुखी नाम की कोई...

चंद्रमुखी *(पल्लू निकाले):*
हाँ अंदर आओ।

देवदासः
अरे यह कमरा ऐसा क्यों? चंद्रमुखी कहाँ है?
(वह महिला घूमती है। वह चंद्रमुखी है जिसने सादे कपड़े पहने हुए हैं)
तुम? यह क्या हाल हो गया है तुम्हारा?

चंद्रमुखीः
हाल कैसा? मैं तो समझती हूँ, क़िस्मत जाग गई मेरी। इतनी जल्दी भूल गए मुझे?

देवदासः
तुम कुछ दुबली मालूम हो रही हो। बीमार थीं क्या?

کٹ۔ بیرونِ خانہ۔ دن۔ فقیروں کا ایک گروہ دان مانگ رہا ہے۔

منیم جی:
خاموش، خاموش، خاموش۔ رانی ماں نے کہا ہے سب کو کپڑے ملیں گے۔

بھکاری:
رانی ماں کی جے (۶)

پاروتی جھروکے میں آتی ہے جسے دیکھ کر فقیروں کا ٹولہ اُس کی تعریف میں نعرے لگاتا ہے۔ ڈزالو۔ چندر مکھی کے دروازے پر دیوداس دستک دیتے ہوئے۔ پلّو نکالے ایک عورت دروازہ کھولتی ہے۔

دیوداس:
سنیے، یہاں چندر مکھی نام کی کوئی۔۔۔

چندر مکھی (گھونگھٹ نکالے):
ہاں اندر آؤ۔

دیوداس:
ارے یہ کمرا ایسا کیوں؟ چندر مکھی کہاں ہے؟
(وہ عورت گھومتی ہے۔ وہ چندر مکھی ہے جس نے سادا سے کپڑے پہن رکھے ہیں)
تم؟ یہ کیا حال ہو گیا ہے تمہارا؟

چندر مکھی:
حال کیسا؟ میں تو سمجھتی ہوں قسمت جاگ گئی میری۔ اتنی جلدی بھول گئے مجھے؟

دیوداس:
تم کچھ دبلی معلوم ہو رہی ہو۔ بیمار تھیں کیا؟

Chandramukhi:
Not physically.

Shareer ki toh bimaari koi nahin.

Devdas:
You're wearing no jewellery. The house is empty. Where has everything gone?

Badan pe koi gehna nahin? Ghar mein koi maal-asbaab nahin, vo sab kya hua?

Chandramukhi:
I sold everything.

Bech daala.

Devdas:
And the musicians and the musical instruments?

Aur gaane-bajaane ka vo sab saaz-o-saamaan?

Chandramukhi:
I've given everything up.

Gaana-bajaana sab chhod diya.

Devdas:
The outer room has completely changed.

Tumhaara ye baahar ka kamra toh bilkul badal gaya hai.

A shot of the empty room. A devotional tune underscores the scene.

Chandramukhi:
Everything has changed. The inner room, too. Come.

Sirf baahar nahin, andar bhi. Aao..

Devdas enters the bedroom to find a lamp burning in front of a statuette of Lord Krishna and Radha. Chandramukhi lowers her eyes.

Devdas:
Does Chunni babu stop by?

Chunni babu nahin aate?

Chandramukhi:
No. He came about two months ago, argued and left. I hear he works away from Calcutta now.

Nahin. Koi do maheene huwe aaye thay, jhagda kar ke chale gaye. Suna hai Kalkatte se baahar koi naukri kar li hai.

Devdas:
What did you argue about?

Jhagda kis baat pe hua tha?

Chandramukhi:
He came with an offer. I threw him out.

Dalaali karne aaye thay. Maine nikaal diya.

चंद्रमुखीः
शरीर की तो बीमारी कोई नहीं।

چندر مکھی:
شریر کی تو بیماری کوئی نہیں۔

देवदासः
बदन पे कोई गहना नहीं? घर में कोई माल-असबाब नहीं, वह सब क्या हुआ?

دیوداس:
بدن پہ کوئی گہنا نہیں؟ گھر میں کوئی مال اسباب نہیں، وہ سب کیا ہوا؟

चंद्रमुखीः
बेच डाला।

چندر مکھی:
بیچ ڈالا۔

देवदासः
और गाने-बजाने का वह सब साज़-ओ-सामान?

دیوداس:
اور گانے بجانے کا وہ سب ساز وسامان؟

चंद्रमुखीः
गाना-बजाना सब छोड़ दिया।

چندر مکھی:
گانا بجانا سب چھوڑ دیا۔

देवदासः
तुम्हारा यह बाहर का कमरा तो बिल्कुल बदल गया है।

دیوداس:
تمہارا یہ باہر کا کمرا تو بالکل بدل گیا ہے۔

ख़ाली कमरे का एक शॉट। भक्ति संगीत सुनाई दे रहा है।

خالی کمرے کا ایک شاٹ۔ بھگتی دھن بجتی ہوئی سنائی دیتی ہے۔

चंद्रमुखीः
सिर्फ़ बाहर नहीं, अंदर भी। आओ।

چندر مکھی:
صرف باہر نہیں، اندر بھی۔ آؤ۔

देवदास शयनकक्ष में प्रवेश करता है। भगवान कृष्ण और राधा की मूर्ति के आगे एक दिया जल रहा है। चंद्रमुखी अपनी आँखें झुका लेती है।

دیوداس خواب گاہ میں داخل ہوتا ہے جہاں رادھا کرشن کی مورتی کے سامنے ایک دِیا روشن ہے۔ چندر مکھی نظریں جھکا لیتی ہے۔

देवदासः
चुन्नी बाबू नहीं आते?

دیوداس:
چُنّی بابو نہیں آتے؟

चंद्रमुखीः
नहीं। कोई दो महीने हुए आए थे, झगड़ा करके चले गए। सुना है कलकत्ते से बाहर कोई नौकरी कर ली है।

چندر مکھی:
نہیں۔ کوئی دو مہینے ہوئے، آئے تھے، جھگڑا کر کے چلے گئے۔ سنا ہے کلکتے سے باہر کوئی نوکری کر لی ہے۔

देवदासः
झगड़ा किस बात पे हुआ था?

دیوداس:
جھگڑا کس بات پہ ہوا تھا؟

चंद्रमुखीः
दलाली करने आए थे। मैंने निकाल दिया।

چندر مکھی:
دلالی کرنے آئے تھے۔ میں نے نکال دیا۔

Devdas:
An offer? For what?

Dalaali kaahe ki?

Chandramukhi *(laughs):*
For wheat! You're so naive. He brought a rich client with him, offering me five hundred rupees a month, a lot of jewellery. And a watchman, too.

Gehoon ki! Tum bhi toh bas samjhte hi nahin. Kisi bade raees ko pakad ke le aaye thay. Paanch sau rupay maheena, dher saare gehne, darwaaze pe rakhwaali ke liye sipaahi.

Devdas:
But where is everything? There's nothing here.

Magar kahaan hai vo sab? Dikhaayi toh koi nahin deta.

Chandramukhi:
If I had agreed, you'd see everything. I chased them away.

Rehne deti toh dekhte. Maine sab ko bhaga diya.

Devdas:
What was their fault?

Unka qusoor?

Chandramukhi:
No fault. I just didn't like the idea. No one has come here since you left.

Qusoor toh kuch nahin, mujhe acha nahin laga. Jab se tum gaye ho yahaan koi nahin aaya.

Devdas:
So, you've closed shop?

Toh tumne dukaan-daari se utha diye?

Chandramukhi:
Yes. I have nothing now.

Haan. Diwaaliye jo ho gaye.

Devdas:
How will you manage?

Toh ab guzar kaise ho ga?

Chandramukhi:
If I stayed in the city, I couldn't. I was thinking of moving somewhere less expensive.

Shaher mein rehne se toh hoga nahin, sochti hoon kisi sasti jageh mein chali jaaun.

Devdas:
So why didn't you leave?

Toh pehle kyun nahin chali gayein?

Chandramukhi:
I was waiting in the hope of seeing you. I knew you would come back one day.

Sirf tumhen dekh paane ki aas mein padi rahi. Jaanti thi ek din tum zaroor aaoge.

देवदासः
दलाली काहे की?

चंद्रमुखी *(हँसते हुए):*
गेहूँ की! तुम भी तो बस समझते ही नहीं। किसी बड़े रईस को पकड़ के ले आए थे। पाँच सौ रुपए महीना, ढेर सारे गहने, दरवाज़े पे रखवाली के लिए सिपाही।

देवदासः
मगर कहाँ हैं वह सब? दिखाई तो कोई नहीं देता।

चंद्रमुखीः
रहने देती तो देखते। मैंने सबको भगा दिया।

देवदासः
उनका क़ुसूर?

चंद्रमुखीः
क़ुसूर तो कुछ नहीं, मुझे अच्छा नहीं लगा। जब से तुम गए हो यहाँ कोई नहीं आया।

देवदासः
तो तुमने दुकानदारी से उठा दिए?

चंद्रमुखीः
हाँ। दिवालिये जो हो गए।

देवदासः
तो अब गुज़र कैसे होगा?

चंद्रमुखीः
शहर में रहने से तो होगा नहीं, सोचती हूँ किसी सस्ती जगह में चली जाऊँ।

देवदासः
तो पहले क्यों नहीं चली गईं?

चंद्रमुखीः
सिर्फ़ तुम्हें देख पाने की आस में पड़ी रही। जानती थी, एक दिन तुम ज़रूर आओगे।

دیوداس:
دلالی کاہے کی؟

چندرمکھی (ہنستے ہوئے):
گیہوں کی! تم بھی تو بس سمجھتے ہی نہیں۔ کسی بڑے رئیس کو پکڑ کے لے آئے تھے۔ پانچ سو روپے مہینہ، ڈھیر سارے گہنے، دروازے پہ رکھوالی کے لیے سپاہی۔

دیوداس:
مگر کہاں ہے وہ سب؟ دکھائی تو کوئی نہیں دیتا۔

چندرمکھی:
رہنے دیتی تو دیکھتے۔ میں نے سب کو بھگا دیا۔

دیوداس:
اُن کا قصور؟

چندرمکھی:
قصور تو کچھ نہیں، مجھے اچھا نہیں لگا۔ جب سے تم گئے ہو یہاں کوئی نہیں آیا۔

دیوداس:
تو تم نے دکان داری سے اُٹھا دیے؟

چندرمکھی:
ہاں۔ دیوالیے جو ہو گئے۔

دیوداس:
تو اب گزر کیسے ہوگا؟

چندرمکھی:
شہر میں رہنے سے تو ہوگا نہیں، سوچتی ہوں کسی سستی جگہ میں چلی جاؤں۔

دیوداس:
تو پہلے کیوں نہیں چلی گئیں؟

چندرمکھی:
صرف تمھیں دیکھ پانے کی آس میں پڑی رہی۔ جانتی تھی ایک دن تم ضرور آؤ گے۔

Devdas *(softly):*

In the hope of seeing me? Why?

Sirf mujhe dekh paane ki aas mein? Kyun?

Chandramukhi:

You used to despise me so much. No one has ever hated me as much. I don't know how many have come here and gone. But I never found the kind of inner glow that you have. From the moment I saw you, I can't explain the effect you had on me, Devdas. I have completely changed.

Tum mujh se bahot nafrat karte thay na? Itni nafrat kabhi aur kisi ne mujh se nahin ki. Tumse pehle na jaane kitne log yahaan aaye aur chale gaye. Lekin maine kisi ke andar vo tej na dekha jo tum mein tha. Tumne aate hi jaane kya kar diya, Devdas. Jab se main bilkul hi badal gayi.

(a shot of the statuette of Krishna and Radha is inserted here)

I see everything with new eyes now.

In aankhon se mujhe har cheez aur hi dikhaayi dene lagi.

(cut back to Chandramukhi and Devdas)

Then you took to drink. I hate alcohol. It angers me to see how people misbehave when they're drunk. But when you were drunk, I would cry. One day you said how much we women endure. From that day I began to believe in myself and left my old life behind.

Phir tumne sharaab peena shuru kar diya. Sharaab se mujhe bahot nafrat hai. Koi sharaab pi kar matwaala hota hai toh mujhe bahot ghussa aata hai. Lekin jab tum matwaale hote thay toh main ro deti thi. Ek din tumne kaha hum log kitna sahen karte hain. Usi din mujhe apne aap par abhimaan paida ho gaya aur maine sab kuch chhod diya.

Devdas:

You gave it all up, Chandramukhi, but the heart of a woman is so whimsical.

Chhod toh diya, Chandramukhi, lekin auraton ka mann bada chanchal hota hai.

Chandramukhi:

Devdas, did Parvati hurt you deeply?

Devdas, kya Parvati ne tumhaare mann ko bahot thes lagaayi?

Devdas:

Why do you ask?

Ye kyun poochhti ho?

Chandramukhi:

I have been in the business of love for many years, Devdas, but have loved only once. Love is one thing, attraction

Maine zindagi mein prem ka karobaar bahot dinon tak kiya hai, Devdas, lekin prem sirf ek baar. Prem karna aur baat hai,

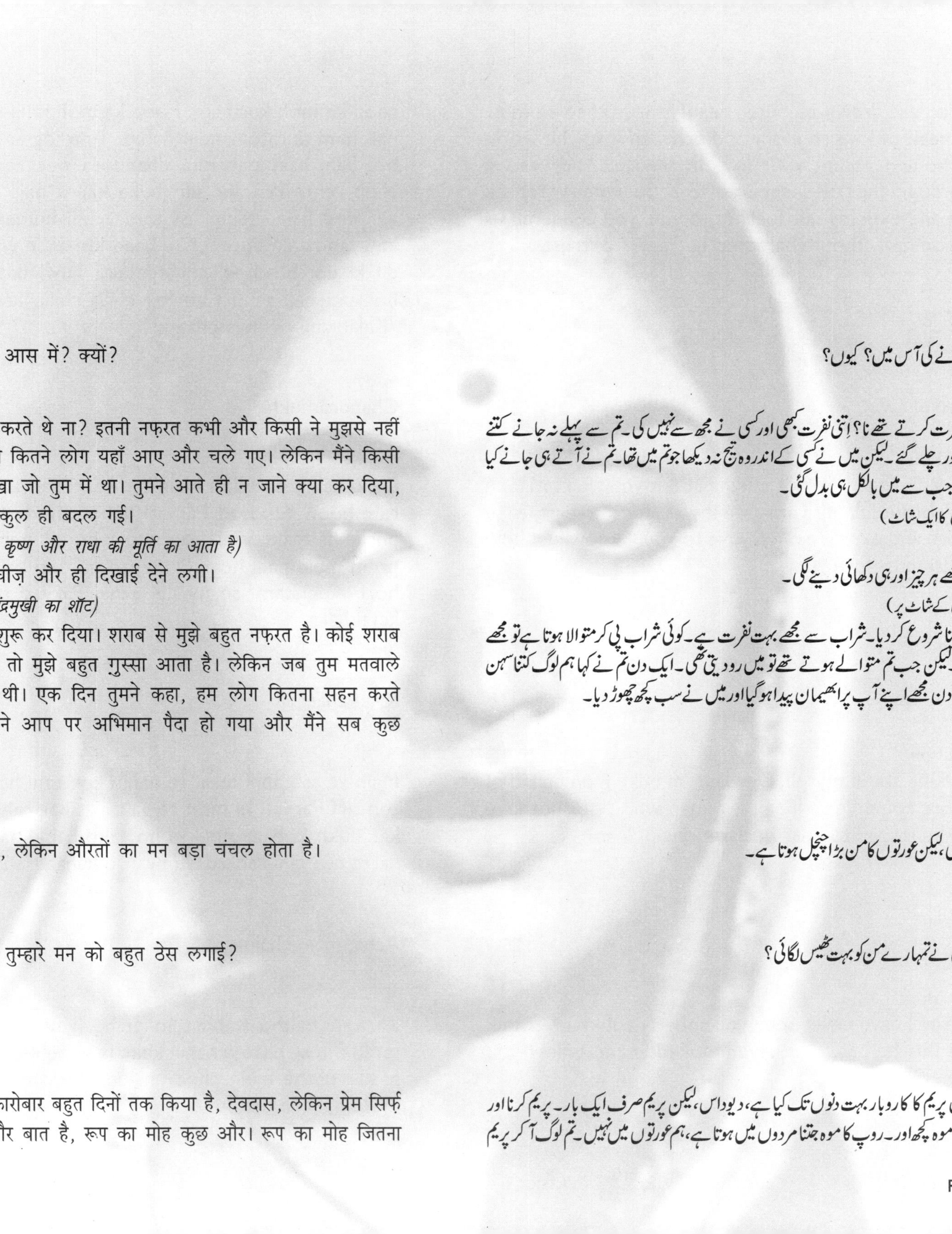

देवदास *(नरमी से)*:
सिर्फ़ मुझे देख पाने की आस में? क्यों?

चंद्रमुखीः
तुम मुझसे बहुत नफ़रत करते थे ना? इतनी नफ़रत कभी और किसी ने मुझसे नहीं की। तुमसे पहले न जाने कितने लोग यहाँ आए और चले गए। लेकिन मैंने किसी के अंदर वह तेज न देखा जो तुम में था। तुमने आते ही न जाने क्या कर दिया, देवदास। जब से मैं बिल्कुल ही बदल गई।
(बीच में एक शॉट भगवान कृष्ण और राधा की मूर्ति का आता है)
इन आँखों से मुझे हर चीज़ और ही दिखाई देने लगी।
(कट बैक। देवदास और चंद्रमुखी का शॉट)
फिर तुमने शराब पीना शुरू कर दिया। शराब से मुझे बहुत नफ़रत है। कोई शराब पीकर मतवाला होता है तो मुझे बहुत ग़ुस्सा आता है। लेकिन जब तुम मतवाले होते थे तो मैं रो देती थी। एक दिन तुमने कहा, हम लोग कितना सहन करते हैं। उसी दिन मुझे अपने आप पर अभिमान पैदा हो गया और मैंने सब कुछ छोड़ दिया।

देवदासः
छोड़ तो दिया, चंद्रमुखी, लेकिन औरतों का मन बड़ा चंचल होता है।

चंद्रमुखीः
देवदास, क्या पार्वती ने तुम्हारे मन को बहुत ठेस लगाई?

देवदासः
यह क्यों पूछती हो?

चंद्रमुखीः
मैंने ज़िंदगी में प्रेम का कारोबार बहुत दिनों तक किया है, देवदास, लेकिन प्रेम सिर्फ़ एक बार। प्रेम करना और बात है, रूप का मोह कुछ और। रूप का मोह जितना

دیوداس (نرمی سے):
صرف مجھے دیکھ پانے کی آس میں؟ کیوں؟

چندرمکھی:
تم مجھ سے بہت نفرت کرتے تھے نا؟ اِتنی نفرت کبھی اور کسی نے مجھ سے نہیں کی۔ تم سے پہلے نہ جانے کتنے لوگ یہاں آئے اور چلے گئے۔ لیکن میں نے کسی کے اندر وہ تیج نہ دیکھا جو تم میں تھا۔ تم نے آتے ہی جانے کیا کر دیا، دیوداس۔ جب سے میں بالکل ہی بدل گئی۔
(رادھا کرشن کی مورتی کا ایک شاٹ)

اِن آنکھوں سے مجھے ہر چیز اور ہی دکھائی دینے لگی۔
(چندرمکھی اور دیوداس کے شاٹ پر)
پھر تم نے شراب پینا شروع کر دیا۔ شراب سے مجھے بہت نفرت ہے۔ کوئی شراب پی کر متوالا ہوتا ہے تو مجھے بہت غصہ آتا ہے۔ لیکن جب تم متوالے ہوتے تھے تو میں رو دیتی تھی۔ ایک دن تم نے کہا ہم لوگ کتنا سہن کرتے ہیں۔ اُسی دن مجھے اپنے آپ پر ابھیمان پیدا ہو گیا اور میں نے سب کچھ چھوڑ دیا۔

دیوداس:
چھوڑ تو دیا، چندرمکھی، لیکن عورتوں کا من بڑا چنچل ہوتا ہے۔

چندرمکھی:
دیوداس، کیا پاروتی نے تمہارے من کو بہت ٹھیس لگائی؟

دیوداس:
یہ کیوں پوچھتی ہو؟

چندرمکھی:
میں نے زندگی میں پریم کا کاروبار بہت دنوں تک کیا ہے، دیوداس، لیکن پریم صرف ایک بار۔ پریم کرنا اور بات ہے، روپ کا موہ کچھ اور۔ روپ کا موہ جتنا مردوں میں ہوتا ہے، ہم عورتوں میں نہیں۔ تم لوگ آ کر پریم

another. Men are drawn to outer beauty more than women. You men speak of love so easily and boast of it to the world while we women accept your love in silence. And yet we fail to understand the true meaning of love. But when we speak out of turn and express our feelings to you, you condemn us calling us women without character, betrayers of trust.

roop ka moh kuch aur. Roop ka moh jitna mardon mein hota hai, hum auraton mein nahin. Tum log aa kar prem jatlaate ho, baat-baat par iska dhandora peet'te ho, jab bhi hum chup rehti hain aur sar jhuka kar is nayi zindagi ko svikaar kar lete hain. Lekin uss samay bhi humen prem ke akshar ka gyan nahin hota. Uske baad kisi aade waqt mein humaare dil ki koi bhadaas, chhatpataati huwi baahar aa kar khadi ho jaati hai, tabb tum log chilla-chilla kar kehne lagte ho: "Kalankani, vishwasghaatni."

Devdas:
Chandramukhi.

Chandramukhi.

Chandramukhi:
Don't worry, Devdas. I'm not talking about your Parvati. She may be very beautiful, but I am sure it was she who first fell in love with you and expressed her love to you. I know just how much Parvati must love you.

Daro nahin, Devdas. Main tumhaari Parvati ki baat nahin keh rahi hoon. Shaayad Parvati bahot ziyada roopvati hai, lekin phir bhi main yahi jaan paayi hoon, pehle vahi tumhaare prem mein padi hogi. Pehle usi ne tum par ye baat zaahir ki hogi. Apni taraf se maine jaana, Parvati tumhen kitna pyar karti hai.

Devdas:
What did you say?

Kya kaha?

Chandramukhi:
I am not talking about myself, Devdas. I'm talking on behalf of Parvati. What could be sadder for a man who does not love another to be forced to hear declarations of love?

Main ye sab apni taraf se nahin keh rahi hoon, Devdas. Main toh sirf Parvati ki taraf se vakaalat kar rahi hoon. Is se badh kar dukh ki baat aur kya ho sakti hai ki aadmi jis se pyar na karta ho, vahi zabardasti pyar ki kahaani sunaane baith jaaye.

Devdas:
I must go.

Acha, main chalunga.

Chandramukhi:
Sit for a while. I have never seen you sober. I could never talk to you like this before. You never looked at me unless you were completely drunk.

Zara aur baitho. Kabhi tumhen hosh mein nahin paaya, kabhi is tarah tumse baaten nahin kein. Is se pehle jab tak tum sharaab pi kar nashe mein choor nahin ho jaate thay, tab tak mera moonh nahin dekhte thay.

मर्दों में होता है, हम औरतों में नहीं। तुम लोग आकर प्रेम जतलाते हो, बात-बात पर इसका ढिंढोरा पीटते हो, जब भी हम चुप रहती हैं और सर झुका कर इस नई ज़िंदगी को स्वीकार कर लेते हैं। लेकिन उस समय भी हमें प्रेम के अक्षर का ज्ञान नहीं होता। उसके बाद किसी आड़े वक़्त में हमारे दिल की कोई भड़ास, छटपटाती हुई बाहर आकर खड़ी हो जाती है, तब तुम लोग चिल्ला-चिल्ला कर कहने लगते हो: "कलंकनी, विश्वासघातिनी"।

جتلاتے ہو، بات بات پر اِس کا ڈھنڈورا پیٹتے ہو، جب بھی ہم چپ رہتی ہیں اور سر جھکا کر اِس نئ زندگی کو سویکار کر لیتے ہیں۔ لیکن اُس سمے بھی ہمیں پریم کے اکشر کا گیان نہیں ہوتا۔ اُس کے بعد کسی آڑے وقت میں ہمارے دل کی کوئی بھڑاس، چھٹپٹاتی ہوئی باہر آ کر کھڑی ہو جاتی ہے تب تم لوگ چلاّ چلاّ کر کہنے لگتے ہو، ''کلکنی، وشواس گھاتنی''۔

देवदासः
चंद्रमुखी।

دیوداس:
چندر مکھی

चंद्रमुखीः
डरो नहीं, देवदास। मैं तुम्हारी पार्वती की बात नहीं कह रही हूँ। शायद पार्वती बहुत ज़्यादा रूपवती है, लेकिन फिर भी मैं यही जान पाई हूँ, पहले वही तुम्हारे प्रेम में पड़ी होगी। पहले उसी ने तुम पर यह बात ज़ाहिर की होगी। अपनी तरफ़ से मैंने जाना, पार्वती तुम्हें कितना प्यार करती है।

چندر مکھی:
ڈرو نہیں، دیوداس۔ میں تمہاری پاروتی کی بات نہیں کہہ رہی ہوں۔ شاید پاروتی بہت زیادہ روپ وتی ہے، لیکن پھر بھی میں یہی جان پائی ہوں پہلے وہی تمہارے پریم میں پڑی ہوگی۔ پہلے اُسی نے تم پر یہ بات ظاہر کی ہوگی۔ اپنی طرف سے میں نے جانا پاروتی تمھیں کتنا پیار کرتی ہے۔

देवदासः
क्या कहा?

دیوداس:
کیا کہا؟

चंद्रमुखीः
मैं यह सब अपनी तरफ़ से नहीं कह रही हूँ, देवदास। मैं तो सिर्फ़ पार्वती की तरफ़ से वकालत कर रही हूँ। इससे बढ़ कर दु:ख की बात और क्या हो सकती है कि आदमी जिससे प्यार न करता हो, वही ज़बरदस्ती प्यार की कहानी सुनाने बैठ जाए।

چندر مکھی:
میں یہ سب اپنی طرف سے نہیں کہہ رہی ہوں، دیوداس۔ میں تو صرف پاروتی کی طرف سے وکالت کر رہی ہوں۔ اِس سے بڑھ کر دکھ کی بات کیا ہو سکتی ہے کہ آدمی جس سے پیار نہ کرتا ہو، وہی زبردستی پیار کی کہانی سنانے بیٹھ جائے۔

देवदासः
अच्छा, मैं चलूँगा।

دیوداس:
اچھا، میں چلوں گا۔

चंद्रमुखीः
ज़रा और बैठो। कभी तुम्हें होश में नहीं पाया, कभी इस तरह तुमसे बातें नहीं कीं। इससे पहले जब तक तुम शराब पीकर नशे में चूर नहीं हो जाते थे, तब तक मेरा मुँह नहीं देखते थे।

چندر مکھی:
ذرا اور بیٹھو۔ کبھی تمھیں ہوش میں نہیں پایا، کبھی اِس طرح تم سے باتیں نہیں کیں۔ اِس سے پہلے جب تک تم شراب پی کر نشے میں چور نہیں ہو جاتے تھے، تب تک میرا منہ نہیں دیکھتے تھے۔

Devdas:
I cannot drink for another year. My father has died.

Ab toh yun bhi main ek baras tak sharaab ko chhu bhi nahin sakta. Mere pita ki mrityu ho gayi hai na.

Chandramukhi:
Will you drink again?

Phir piyoge?

Devdas:
I can't say.

Keh nahin sakta.

Chandramukhi:
Give it up, if you can. Do not destroy your beautiful life.

Ho sakay toh sada ke liye chhod do. Dekho aise sundar pran nashth na karo.

Devdas:
I had better go.

Acha main jaata hoon.

Chandramukhi:
Give me your blessings so I may stay well.

Aashirwaad do, main sukhi rahoon.

Devdas:
Chandramukhi, let me know where you are. Don't hesitate to ask if you need anything.

Jahaan bhi jaao, Chandramukhi, mujhe khabar zaroor karna. Aur agar kabhi koi zaroorat ho toh sankoch matt karna.

Devdas pauses for a moment and walks out. Fade out.

Reel Thirteen

Fade in. Day. Manorama is walking on a village path near the pond. She is carrying a water pot under her arm. She hears a gun shot. Devdas approaches her.

Devdas *(he looks lost):*
Manorama. Are you well, sister?

Manorama, achi toh ho, bahen?

Manorama:
Yes.

Haan.

देवदासः
अब तो यूँ भी मैं एक बरस तक शराब को छू भी नहीं सकता। मेरे पिता की मृत्यु हो गई है ना।

चंद्रमुखीः
फिर पियोगे?

देवदासः
कह नहीं सकता।

चंद्रमुखीः
हो सके तो सदा के लिए छोड़ दो। देखो ऐसे सुंदर प्राण नष्ट न करो।

देवदासः
अच्छा मैं जाता हूँ।

चंद्रमुखीः
आशीर्वाद दो, मैं सुखी रहूँ।

देवदासः
जहाँ भी जाओ, चंद्रमुखी, मुझे ख़बर ज़रूर करना। और अगर कभी कोई ज़रूरत हो तो संकोच मत करना।

एक पल को देवदास रुकता है, फिर निकल जाता है। फ़ेड आउट।

रील तेरह

फ़ेड इन। दिन। तालाब के निकट गाँव की एक पगडंडी पर मनोरमा पानी का घड़ा लिए जा रही है। एक बंदूक़ के चलने की आवाज़ सुनती है। देवदास उसके निकट आता है।

देवदास *(खोया-सा):*
मनोरमा अच्छी तो हो, बहन?

मनोरमाः
हाँ।

دیوداس:
اب تو یوں بھی میں ایک برس تک شراب کو چھو بھی نہیں سکتا۔ میرے پتا کی مرتیو ہوگئی ہے نا۔

چندرمکھی:
پھر پیوگے؟

دیوداس:
کہہ نہیں سکتا۔

چندرمکھی:
ہو سکے تو سدا کے لیے چھوڑ دو۔ دیکھو ایسے سندر پران نشٹ نہ کرو۔

دیوداس:
اچھا میں جاتا ہوں۔

چندرمکھی:
آشیرواد دو، میں سکھی رہوں۔

دیوداس:
جہاں بھی جاؤ، چندرمکھی، مجھے خبر ضرور کرنا۔ اور اگر کبھی کوئی ضرورت ہو تو سنکوچ مت کرنا۔

ایک پل کو دیوداس ٹھہرتا ہے اور پھر باہر نکل جاتا ہے۔ فیڈ آوٹ۔

ریل تیرہ

فیڈ اِن۔ دن۔ گاؤں کے راستے پر، تالاب کنارے، گھڑا اُٹھائے منورما چلی جا رہی ہے۔ اُسے بندوق چلنے کی آواز سنائی دیتی ہے۔ دیوداس اُس کے قریب آتا ہے۔

دیوداس (کھویا کھویا سا):
منورما، اچھی تو ہو، بہن؟

منورما:
ہاں۔

Devdas:

I am so happy to see you all. Stay well.

Tum logon ko dekhne se bada aanand milta hai. Acha, sukhi raho.

Devdas walks towards the pond.

Dissolve. Manorama is sitting on a bed, writing a letter. Dissolve to Parvati reading Manorama's letter.

Manorama *(voice-over):*

"Since you married and left, Paro, the village has completely changed. Devdas's mother is now living in Banaras. He often comes here to quarrel with his brother and ask for money. As soon as he gets it, he leaves. In the two and a half years since Devdas's father died, he has squandered half his inheritance. I thank God, Paro, that He saved you from marrying him. Devdas is back in the village now. He spends all day long with a shotgun in his hand, shooting birds. When it is very hot, he sits quietly under some tree, deep in thought. It seems as if he were yearning for a lost love."

"Jab se tumhaari doli gayi hai, Paro, gaaon ka naqsha hi badal gaya hai. Zamindarni Kashi padhaar gayin. Devdas aksar yahaan aata hai lekin sirf apne bhai se jhagda karne aur rupay lene. Udhar rupay milte hain, idhar chal deta hai. Uske pita ko maray dhaayi saal ho gaye, lekin itney hi arsay mein usne aadhi daulat uda daali. Main toh kehti hoon, Paro, Bhagwan ne acha hi kiya jo tumhaari shaadi uss se na honay di. Vo in dinon phir gaaon aaya hua hai. Din bhar bandooq haath mein liye chidiyaan maara karta hai. Jab bahot dhoop se sar bol uth'ta hai toh kisi ped ke neeche chup-chaap baith kar kuch socha karta hai. Lagta hai jaise koi birhi hai."

As the letter ends, from afar, Devdas's song starts.

Talat Mahmood sings for Devdas

Devdas:

O beloved friend *(over a shot of Parvati)*

Mitwa, mitwa

Dissolve to a panning shot of the sky and trees. A storm is brewing. Dissolve to a wide shot of Devdas, back to camera. He is sitting on the steps of the pond with his shotgun balanced on his lap.

देवदासः
तुम लोगों को देखने से बड़ा आनंद मिलता है। अच्छा, सुखी रहो।

देवदास तालाब की ओर जाता है।

अगला दृश्य। मनोरमा अपने बिस्तर पर बैठी एक पत्र लिख रही है। अगला दृश्य। पार्वती मनोरमा का पत्र पढ़ रही है।

मनोरमा *(वॉइस-ओवर):*
''जब से तुम्हारी डोली गई है, पारो, गाँव का नक़्शा ही बदल गया है। ज़मींदारनी काशी पधार गईं। देवदास अकसर यहाँ आता है लेकिन सिर्फ़ अपने भाई से झगड़ा करने और रुपए लेने। उधर रुपए मिलते हैं, इधर चल देता है। उसके पिता को मरे ढाई साल हो गए, लेकिन इतने ही अर्से में उसने आधी दौलत उड़ा डाली। मैं तो कहती हूँ, पारो, भगवान ने अच्छा ही किया जो तुम्हारी शादी उससे न होने दी। वह इन दिनों फिर गाँव आया हुआ है। दिन भर बंदूक़ हाथ में लिए चिड़ियाँ मारा करता है। जब बहुत धूप से सर बोल उठता है तो किसी पेड़ के नीचे चुपचाप बैठ कर कुछ सोचा करता है। लगता है जैसे कोई बिरही है।''

पत्र समाप्त होते ही, दूर से देवदास के गाने की आवाज़ सुनाई देती है।

स्वरः तलत महमूद

देवदासः
मितवा, मितवा *(पार्वती के शॉट पर)*

डिज़ॉल्व। आकाश और पेड़ दिखाई देते हैं। लगता है कोई तूफ़ान आने वाला है। डिज़ॉल्व। गोद में बंदूक़ लिए देवदास तालाब की सीढ़ियों पर बैठा हुआ है। उसकी पीठ दिखाई दे रही है।

دیوداس:
تم لوگوں کودیکھنے سے بڑا آنند ملتا ہے۔اچھا، سکھی رہو۔

دیوداس تالاب کی طرف جاتا ہے۔

اگلا منظر۔منورما اپنے بستر پر بیٹھی خط لکھ رہی ہے۔
اگلا منظر۔منورما کا خط پڑھتی ہوئی پاروتی۔

منورما (بازگشت):
''جب سے تمہاری ڈولی گئی ہے، پارو، گاؤں کا نقشہ ہی بدل گیا ہے۔زمیندارنی کاشی پدھار گئیں۔دیوداس اکثر یہاں آتا ہے لیکن صرف اپنے بھائی سے جھگڑا کرنے اور روپیہ لینے۔اُدھر روپے ملتے ہیں، اِدھر چل دیتا ہے۔اُس کے پتا کو مرے ڈھائی سال ہو گئے، لیکن اِتنے ہی عرصے میں اُس نے آدھی دولت اُڑا ڈالی۔میں تو کہتی ہوں، پارو، بھگوان نے اچھا ہی کیا جو تمہاری شادی اُس سے نہ ہونے دی۔وہ اِن دنوں پھر گاؤں آیا ہوا ہے۔دن بھر بندوق ہاتھ میں لیے چڑیاں مارا کرتا ہے۔جب بہت دھوپ سے سر بول اُٹھتا ہے تو کسی پیڑ کے نیچے چپ چاپ بیٹھ کر کچھ سوچا کرتا ہے۔لگتا ہے جیسے کوئی برہی ہے۔''

خط ختم ہوتے ہی، دور سے دیوداس کے گانے کی آواز سنائی دیتی ہے۔

آواز، طلعت محمود:

دیوداس:
متوا، متوا (پاروتی کے منظر پر)

ڈزالو۔درخت اور آسمان دکھائی دیتے ہیں۔کوئی طوفان آنے کو ہے۔ڈزالو۔گود میں بندوق لیے دیوداس تالاب کنارے بیٹھا ہوا ہے۔اُس کی پشت دکھائی دے رہی ہے۔

O beloved friend
(cut to Devdas in mid-shot)
What is this undying fire that consumes me?
O beloved friend
My beloved friend does not come
What is this undying...

Mitwa

Laagi re ye kaisi an-bujh aag
Mitwa, mitwa
Mitwa nahin aaye
Laagi re ye kaisi...

Restless is my spirit, restless are my eyes (2)
A hundred laments in every silence
Tears are left behind, the song is over
O beloved friend (4)

Biyakul jiyara biyakul naina (2)
Ik-ik chup mein sau-sau baina
Reh gaye aansu lutt gaye raag
Mitwa (4)

A slow panning shot across the landscape. Dissolve to Parvati. She is as we left her at the beginning of the song, sitting on her bed with Manorama's letter in her hand. The song ends. A tracking shot pulls away from her. She stirs from her reverie and leaves the letter on the bed. With new determination, she goes in search of her stepson.

Parvati:
Mahendra.

Mahendra, Mahendra.

Mahendra:
What is it, mother?

Kya, ma?

Parvati:
Arrange a palanquin for me. I'll leave at once for Talsonapur.

Ek paalki aur kahaaron ka bando-bast karo. Aaj hi, isi waqt main Talsonapur jaaungi.

Mahendra:
Father is visiting the estate. Tomorrow is Lord Ram's birthday.

Magar, ma, pitaji ilaaqe par gaye huwe hain. Kal Ram-naumi ka vrat hai aur braahmanon ko newta bhi...

मितवा

(कट। देवदास मिड शॉट)

लागी रे यह कैसी अन-बुझ आग
मितवा, मितवा
मितवा नहीं आए
लागी रे यह कैसी...

ब्याकुल जियरा ब्याकुल नैना (२)
इक-इक चुप में सौ-सौ बैना
रह गए आँसू लुट गए राग
मितवा (४)

अगला दृश्य। दूर तक हरियाली दिखाई दे रही है। पार्वती दिखाई देती है। वह वहीं पर दिखाई देती है जहाँ वह गीत के आरम्भ में थी। मनोरमा का पत्र हाथ में लिए बिस्तर पर बैठी है। गीत समाप्त होता है। ट्रैकिंग शॉट में दृश्य उससे दूर हो जाता है। जैसे किसी सपने से जागती है। वह बिस्तर पर पत्र रख कर उठ जाती है। एक नए इरादे से अपने सौतेले बेटे को ढूँढ़ती है।

पार्वतीः
महेंद्र, महेंद्र।

महेंद्रः
क्या, माँ?

पार्वतीः
एक पालकी और कहारों का बन्दोबस्त करो। आज ही, इसी वक़्त मैं ताल सोनापुर जाऊँगी।

महेंद्रः
मगर, माँ, पिताजी इलाक़े पर गए हुए हैं। कल राम-नौमी का व्रत है और ब्राह्मणों को न्योता भी...

متوا۔

(کٹ۔ دیوداس۔ مڈشاٹ)

لاگی رے یہ کیسی اَن بجھ آگ
متوا، متوا
متوانہیں آئے
لاگی رے یہ کیسی۔۔۔

بیاکل جیارا بیاکل نینا (۲)
اِک اِک چپ میں سَو سَو بینا
رہ گئے آنسولٹ گئے راگ
متوا (۴)

اگلا منظر۔ دور تک ہریالی کا منظر دکھائی دے رہا ہے۔ پاروتی نظر آتی ہے۔ وہ وہیں نظر آ رہی ہے جہاں گیت کی شروعات میں دکھائی دی تھی، منورما کا خط ہاتھ میں لیے اپنے بستر پر بیٹھی ہوئی ہے۔ گیت ختم ہوتا ہے۔ ٹریکنگ شاٹ میں منظر اُس سے دور ہو جاتا ہے اور جیسے وہ کسی خواب سے جاگ پڑتی ہے۔ وہ بستر پر خط رکھ کر اُٹھ جاتی ہے۔ ایک نئے ارادے کے ساتھ اپنے سوتیلے بیٹے کو تلاش کرتی ہے۔

پاروتی:
مہندر، مہندر۔

مہندر:
کیا، ماں؟

پاروتی:
ایک پالکی اور کہاروں کا بندوبست کرو۔ آج ہی، اِسی وقت میں تال سونا پور جاؤں گی۔

مہندر:
مگر، ماں، پتاجی علاقے پر گئے ہوئے ہیں۔ کل رام نومی کا ورَت ہے اور باہمنوں کو نیوتا بھی۔۔۔

Parvati:
Don't argue. I know all that. Just do as I say. It is urgent that I leave at once..

Bahes matt karo, main sab jaanti hoon. Is waqt jo main kehti hoon wahi karo. Mera jaana bahot zaroori hai.

Mahendra:
Very well, mother.

Acha ma.

Dissolve from Parvati's home to the road that leads to the village. Parvati is in a palanquin carried by four men.

Parvati:
Faster! Hurry.

Aur jaldi chalo, paalki-waale.

Dissolve. Parvati arrives at her parents' home. She does not go inside but crosses the road towards Devdas's house. She meets Dharamdas on the verandah.

Parvati:
Dharamdas, where is Devdas?

Dharamdas, Devdas kahaan hai?

Dharamdas:
I tried very hard to stop him. But he wouldn't listen to me and left for Calcutta by the morning train.

Maine kitna mana kiya par meri ek na maana aur aaj subha ki gaadi se Kalkatte chala gaya.

Parvati *(crestfallen):*
He's gone?

Chale gaye?

Cut to Chandramukhi who sits up with a start. She is now living in a small village. A milkman enters the courtyard where Chandramukhi is watering a tulsi plant.

Chandramukhi:
Bhairo, did you go to the post office?

Kyun, Bhairo? Daak-khaane se ho aaye?

Bhairo *(unidentified actor):*
Yes, but there was no letter.

Haan, maaji, par koi chitthi nahin aayi.

Chandramukhi *(to herself):*
Three months have passed. He has not written nor answered my letters.

Teen maheene honay ko aaye. Na koi khat likha unhone na jawaab diya.

पार्वती:
बहस मत करो, मैं सब जानती हूँ। इस वक़्त जो मैं कहती हूँ वही करो। मेरा जाना बहुत ज़रूरी है।

महेंद्र:
अच्छा माँ।

अगला दृश्य पार्वती के घर से होता हुआ उस रास्ते की ओर जाता है जो गाँव की ओर जा रहा है। चार कहार पार्वती की पालकी लिए जा रहे हैं।

पार्वती:
और जल्दी चलो, पालकी वाले।

अगला दृश्य। पार्वती अपने मायके पहुँचती है। वह घर के अंदर न जाकर रास्ता पार करके देवदास की हवेली की ओर जाती है। बरामदे में धरमदास उसे मिलता है।

पार्वती:
धरमदास, देवदास कहाँ है?

धरमदास:
मैंने कितना मना किया पर मेरी एक न माना और आज सुबह की गाड़ी से कलकत्ते चला गया।

पार्वती *(निराश)*:
चले गए?

कट। चंद्रमुखी घबरा कर उठ बैठती है। वह एक छोटे-से गाँव में रहने लगी है। एक ग्वाला आँगन में आता है, चंद्रमुखी तुलसी के पौधे को पानी दे रही है।

चंद्रमुखी:
क्यों, भैरव? डाक-ख़ाने से हो आए?

भैरव *(कलाकार अज्ञात)*:
हाँ, माँजी, पर कोई चिट्ठी नहीं आई।

चंद्रमुखी *(अपने आपसे)*:
तीन महीने होने को आए। न कोई ख़त लिखा उन्होंने न जवाब दिया।

پاروتی:
بحث مت کرو، میں سب جانتی ہوں۔ اِس وقت جو میں کہتی ہوں وہی کرو۔ میرا جانا بہت ضروری ہے۔

مہندر:
اچھا ماں۔

اگلا منظر پاروتی کے گھر سے ہوتا ہوا اُس راستے کی طرف جاتا ہے جو گاؤں کی طرف جا رہا ہے۔ چار کہار پاروتی کی پالکی کو اُٹھائے لیے جا رہے ہیں۔

پاروتی:
اور جلدی چلو، پالکی والے۔

اگلا منظر۔ پاروتی اپنے میکے پہنچتی ہے۔ اپنے باپ کے گھر میں داخل ہونے کی بجائے وہ راستہ پار کر کے دیوداس کے گھر کی طرف جاتی ہے۔ برآمدے میں دھرم داس اُس سے ملتا ہے۔

پاروتی:
دھرم دا، دیوداس کہاں ہے؟

دھرم داس:
میں نے کتنا منع کیا پر میری ایک نہ مانا اور آج صبح کی گاڑی سے کلکتے چلا گیا۔

پاروتی (مایوسی سے):
چلے گئے؟

کٹ۔ چندرمکھی گھبرا کر اُٹھ بیٹھتی ہے۔ وہ ایک چھوٹے سے گاؤں میں رہنے لگی ہے۔ گوالہ آنگن میں آتا ہے، چندرمکھی، تلسی کے پودے کو پانی دے رہی ہے۔

چندرمکھی:
کیوں، بھیرو؟ ڈاک خانے سے ہو آئے؟

بھیرو (اداکار، نامعلوم):
ہاں، ماجی، پر کوئی چٹھی نہیں آئی۔

چندرمکھی (خودکلامی):
تین مہینے ہونے کو آئے۔ نہ کوئی خط لکھا اُنھوں نے نہ جواب دیا۔

Chandramukhi feeds the calf in the courtyard and then turns to the milkman who is still nearby.

Chandramukhi:
Bhairo, how far to the house of Talsonapur's landlord?

Bhairo, Talsonapur ke zamindar ka makaan yahaan se kitni door hai?

Bhairo:
About a mile. The landlord is no more; his two sons live there now. Dwijodas and Devdas.

Bas koi kos-bhar hai, maaji. Zamindarji ka toh svargwaas ho gaya, ab unke do ladke hain, Dwijodas babu aur Devdas babu.

Chandramukhi:
Can you take me there?

Mujhe wahaan le ja sakte ho?

Bhairo:
Of course, whenever you wish.

Kyun nahin? Jis din aap ka ji chaahe.

Chandramukhi:
We'll go there now. Get ready.

Jis din nahin, abhi chalenge. Tum tayyaar ho jao.

Bhairo:
Very well.

Acha, maaji.

Dissolve. Chandramukhi and Bhairo walk on the road to Talsonapur. The road is filled with puddles. It is an overcast day. As they walk along the path, we see Parvati in her palanquin. She is returning from Devdas's house as Chandramukhi makes her way there.

Background song: Mohammed Rafi & chorus

Chorus:
Many roads lead to one's destination
Some are joyful, others sorrowful
Many roads lead to one's destination

Manzil ki chaah mein rahi ke vaaste
Sukh ke bhi raaste, dukh ke bhi raaste
Manzil ki chaah mein…

Some have soothing shade
Others are scorching hot
This is one form
That is another

Kahin ghani chhaon hai
Kahin kadi dhoop hai
Ye bhi ek roop hai
Vo bhi ek roop hai

आँगन में बछड़े को चारा देने के बाद चंद्रमुखी ग्वाले से कहती है।

بچھڑے کو چارہ دینے کے بعد چندر مکھی گوالے سے کہتی ہے۔

चंद्रमुखी:
भैरव, तालसोनापुर के ज़मींदार का मकान यहाँ से कितनी दूर है?

چندر مکھی:
بھیرو، تال سونا پور کے زمیندار کا مکان یہاں سے کتنی دور ہے؟

भैरव:
बस कोई कोस भर है, माँजी। ज़मींदारजी का तो स्वर्गवास हो गया, अब उनके दो लड़के हैं, द्विजोदास बाबू और देवदास बाबू।

بھیرو:
بس کوئی کوس بھر ہے، ماجی۔ زمیندار جی کا تو سورگواس ہوگیا، اب اُن کے دو لڑکے ہیں، دویجوداس بابو اور دیوداس بابو۔

चंद्रमुखी:
मुझे वहाँ ले जा सकते हो?

چندر مکھی:
مجھے وہاں لے جا سکتے ہو؟

भैरव:
क्यों नहीं? जिस दिन आपका जी चाहे।

بھیرو:
کیوں نہیں؟ جس دن آپ کا جی چاہے۔

चंद्रमुखी:
जिस दिन नहीं, अभी चलेंगे। तुम तैयार हो जाओ।

چندر مکھی:
جس دن نہیں، ابھی چلیں گے۔ تم تیار ہو جاؤ۔

भैरव:
अच्छा, माँजी।

بھیرو:
اچھا، ماجی۔

अगला दृश्य। चंद्रमुखी और भैरव तालसोनापुर गाँव के रास्ते पर चले जा रहे हैं। घने बादल घिरे हुए हैं। रास्ते पर जगह जगह गढ़ों में पानी भरा हुआ है। वे रास्ते पर चले जा रहे हैं जबकि पार्वती की पालकी देवदास के घर से वापस लौट रही है। चंद्रमुखी वहाँ से गुज़र रही है।

اگلا منظر۔ چندر مکھی اور بھیرو تال سونا پور گاؤں کے راستے پر چلے جا رہے ہیں۔ گھنے بادل گھرے ہوئے ہیں۔ راستے پر جگہ جگہ گڑھوں میں پانی بھرا ہوا ہے۔ وہ راستے پر چلے جا رہے ہیں جبکہ پاروتی کی پالکی دیوداس کے گھر سے واپس لوٹ رہی ہے۔ چندر مکھی وہاں سے گزر رہی ہے۔

स्वर: मुहम्मद रफ़ी और कोरस (बैक ग्राउंड गाना)

محمد رفیع اور کورس (بیک گراؤنڈ گیت)

मंज़िल की चाह में राही के वास्ते
सुख के भी रास्ते, दु:ख के भी रास्ते
मंज़िल की चाह में...

منزل کی چاہ میں راہی کے واسطے
سکھ کے بھی راستے دکھ کے بھی راستے
منزل کی چاہ میں ---

कहीं घनी छाँव है
कहीं कड़ी धूप है
यह भी एक रूप है
वह भी एक रूप है

کہیں گھنی چھاؤں ہے
کہیں کڑی دھوپ ہے
یہ بھی ایک روپ ہے
وہ بھی ایک روپ ہے

Many will lose here
Others will win
Travellers
Many will leave
Others will arrive
O travellers
(Chandramukhi and Parvati exchange a long look as they cross one another)
Many will leave
Others will arrive
O travellers

Kayi yahaan khoyenge
Kayi yahaan paayenge
Raahi
Kayi abhi jaayenge
Kayi abhi aayenge
O raahi

Kayi abhi jaayenge
Kayi abhi aayenge
Raahi o raahi

The last shot of the song has Chandramukhi and Bhairo, back to camera, walking into the distance.

Dissolve. A maid is applying "alta" *on the feet of Dwijodas's wife. She is the new mistress of the house since Devdas's mother, Harimati Devi, is now living in Banaras.*

Dwijodas's wife *(actress Praveen Pal):*
Why did you miss work for the past two days?

Tu parson kyun nahin aayi thi?

Maid:
My child was unwell, mistress.

Mera bachcha bimaar tha, raniji.

Devdas's sister-in-law is scolding the maid as Chandramukhi arrives.

Dwijodas's wife:
There's always someone unwell in your family. Who will get the work done? Don't you dare take any more time off.

Tere ghar mein toh humesha bimaariyan lagi rahengi lekin humaara kaam yahaan kaun karega? Khabar-daar jo phir kabhi ek din ki bhi chhutti ki.

कई यहाँ खोएँगे
कई यहाँ पाएँगे
राही
कई अभी जाएँगे
कई अभी आएँगे
ओ राही
(रास्ते से गुज़रते हुए एक स्थान पर चंद्रमुखी और पार्वती एक दूसरे की ओर देखते हैं।)
कई अभी जाएँगे
कई अभी आएँगे
राही ओ राही

गीत के अंतिम शॉट में चंद्रमुखी और भैरव की पीठ दिखाई दे रही है जो दूर चले जा रहे हैं।

अगला दृश्य। एक नौकरानी द्विजोदास की पत्नी के पैरों पर अल्ता लगा रही है। देवदास की माँ के बनारस चले जाने के बाद अब वही घर की मालकिन है।

द्विजोदास की पत्नी *(अभिनेत्री प्रवीण पाल)*:
तू परसों क्यों नहीं आई थी?

दासीः
मेरा बच्चा बीमार था, रानीजी।

देवदास की भाभी नौकरानी को डाँट-डपट रही होती है, तभी चंद्रमुखी आती है।

द्विजोदास की पत्नीः
तेरे घर में तो हमेशा बीमारियाँ लगी रहेंगी लेकिन हमारा काम यहाँ कौन करेगा? ख़बरदार जो फिर कभी एक दिन की भी छुट्टी की।

کئی یہاں کھوئیں گے
کئی یہاں پائیں گے
راہی
کئی ابھی جائیں گے
کئی ابھی آئیں گے
او راہی
(راستے سے گزرتے ہوئے پاروتی اور چندرمکھی ایک دوسری کی طرف دیکھتی ہیں)
کئی ابھی جائیں گے
کئی ابھی آئیں گے
راہی او راہی

گیت کے آخری شاٹ پر چندرمکھی اور بھیرو کی پشت دکھائی دے رہی ہے جو دور چلے جا رہے ہیں۔

اگلا منظر۔ایک ملازمہ دویجوداس کی بیوی کے پیروں پر آٹا لگا رہی ہے۔دیوداس کی ماں کے بنارس چلے جانے کے بعد اب گھر کی مالکن وہی بن گئی ہے۔

دویجوداس کی بیوی (اداکارہ پروین پال)
تُو پرسوں کیوں نہیں آئی تھی؟

نوکرانی:
میرا بچہ بیمار تھا، رانی جی۔

دیوداس کی بھابھی ملازمہ کو لعن طعن کر رہی ہوتی ہے جب چندرمکھی داخل ہوتی ہے۔

دویجوداس کی بیوی:
تیرے گھر میں تو ہمیشہ بیماریاں لگی رہیں گی لیکن ہمارا کام یہاں کون کرے گا؟ خبردار جو پھر کبھی ایک دن کی بھی چھٹی کی۔

Chandramukhi:
My respects, maaji.

Pranam, maaji.

Dwijodas's wife:
Now who are you?

Tum kaun ho ji?

Chandramukhi:
A tenant. I have brought the rent.

Aap ki praja hoon, maaji. Lagaan le ke aayi hoon.

Dwijodas's wife:
Sit down. Where do you live?

Baitho. Kahaan rehti ho?

Chandramukhi:
In Ashathjhuri, in a village on your estate. Maaji, tell me, don't two landlords share this property?

Aap hi ke raaj, Ashathjhuri gaaon. Kyun, maaji? Maalik toh do hisse-daar hain na?

Dwijodas's wife:
Yes, but soon everything will belong to us. The young master has wasted his share in Calcutta, spent a fortune on drink and prostitutes. He has squandered everything.

Haan, beti, lekin do din mein sab humaara hi ho jaayega. Chhote babu ne toh lutiya dubo di. Kalkatte mein sharaab aur vaishiya hi unhein le mari hain. Na jaane kitna rupya udaaya, kuch hisaab hai!

Chandramukhi:
Doesn't the young master ever come home?

Toh kya chhote babu kabhi ghar nahin aate?

Dwijodas's wife:
He was here the other day. He fought with my husband and took about a thousand rupees and left.

Uss din toh aaye thay. Bade bhai se jhagda kar ke paanch ek hazaar rupay liye aur kal chale gaye.

Chandramukhi:
When will he return?

Toh ab phir kab aayenge?

Dwijodas's wife:
Who knows if he ever will. He has a hundred ailments. They say he won't last long.

Pata nahin aayenge bhi ki nahin aayenge. Na jaane kya-kya bimaariyaan laga rakkhi hain. Aur ab toh bachne ki bhi koi ummeed nahin hai.

Chandramukhi:
Where does he stay in Calcutta?

Vo Kalkatte mein kahaan rehte hain?

चंद्रमुखीः
प्रणाम, माँजी।

چندرمکھی:
پرنام، ماجی۔

द्विजोदास की पत्नीः
तुम कौन हो जी?

دویجوداس کی بیوی:
تم کون ہو جی؟

चंद्रमुखीः
आपकी प्रजा हूँ, माँजी। लगान लेके आई हूँ।

چندرمکھی:
آپ کی پرجا ہوں، ماجی۔ لگان لے کے آئی ہوں۔

द्विजोदास की पत्नीः
बैठो। कहाँ रहती हो?

دویجوداس کی بیوی:
بیٹھو۔ کہاں رہتی ہو؟

चंद्रमुखीः
आप ही के राज अशथझुरी गाँव। क्यों माँजी? मालिक तो दो हिस्सेदार हैं ना?

چندرمکھی:
آپ ہی کے راج اشتھ جھوری گاؤں۔ کیوں ماجی؟ مالک تو دو حصے دار ہیں نا؟

द्विजोदास की पत्नीः
हाँ, बेटी, लेकिन दो दिन में सब हमारा ही हो जाएगा। छोटे बाबू ने तो लुटिया डुबो दी। कलकत्ते में शराब और वेश्या ही उन्हें ले मरी हैं। न जाने कितना रुपया उड़ाया, कुछ हिसाब है!

دویجوداس کی بیوی:
ہاں، بیٹی، لیکن دو دن میں سب ہمارا ہی ہو جائے گا۔ چھوٹے بابو نے تو لٹیا ڈبو دی۔ کلکتے میں شراب اور ویشیا ہی اُنھیں لے مری ہیں۔ نہ جانے کتنا روپیہ اُڑایا، کچھ حساب ہے!

चंद्रमुखीः
तो क्या छोटे बाबू कभी घर नहीं आते?

چندرمکھی:
تو کیا چھوٹے بابو کبھی گھر نہیں آتے؟

द्विजोदास की पत्नीः
उस दिन तो आए थे। बड़े भाई से झगड़ा करके पाँच एक हज़ार रुपए लिए और कल चले गए।

دویجوداس کی بیوی:
اُس دن تو آئے تھے۔ بڑے بھائی سے جھگڑا کر کے پانچ ایک ہزار روپے لیے اور کل چلے گئے۔

चंद्रमुखीः
तो अब फिर कब आएँगे?

چندرمکھی:
تو اب پھر کب آئیں گے؟

द्विजोदास की पत्नीः
पता नहीं आएँगे भी कि नहीं आएँगे। न जाने क्या-क्या बीमारियाँ लगा रखी हैं। और अब तो बचने की भी कोई उम्मीद नहीं है।

دویجوداس کی بیوی:
پتا نہیں آئیں گے بھی کہ نہیں آئیں گے۔ نہ جانے کیا کیا بیماریاں لگا رکھی ہیں۔ اور اب تو بچنے کی بھی کوئی اُمید نہیں ہے۔

चंद्रमुखीः
वह कलकत्ते में कहाँ रहते हैं?

چندرمکھی:
وہ کلکتے میں کہاں رہتے ہیں؟

Dwijodas's wife:

It's anyone's guess. He eats in restaurants and wanders about, spending the night in some friend or the other's house. Only he knows and the Lord of Death knows.

Jaane jooti kahaan rehte hain. Kahin kisi hotel mein kha-pi lete hain, jis-tis ke ghar paday rehte hain aur kya kar sakte hain? Vo jaanen unka yam jaane.

Chandramukhi:

Very well, maaji. I had better go.

Acha, maaji, main jaati hoon.

Dwijodas's wife *(to her maid):*

Take her to the office so she can leave the rent.

Arey inhen lagaan dena hai zara kachehri mein le ja.

Chandramukhi:

No, maaji. I'll find my own way.

Nahin, maaji, main aap hi chali jaaungi.

Chandramukhi leaves. Fade out.

Reel Fourteen

Fade in. Parvati is locking her cupboard and her husband is lying on the bed, smoking a hookah.

Chowdhury:

Parvati, I've been meaning to say something to you for a long time now.

Parvati, kitne hi dinon se main tumse kuch kehna chaahta hoon.

Parvati:

Yes?

Kahiye.

Chowdhury:

You have so many beautiful sarees, so much jewellery. Why do you dress in such simple clothes, Parvati?

Tumhaare paas itni achi-achi saadiyaan hain, itne ache-ache pehnaave hain phir bhi tum ye maamooli se kapde kyun pehne rehti ho, Parvati?

Parvati:

No reason.

Aise hi.

Chowdhury:

What about all your jewellery? Who is that for?

Aur vo itne gehne, aakhir vo kis liye rakkhe hain?

Parvati:

I gave it to your daughter.

Gehne toh maine Yashoda ko de diye.

द्विजोदास की पत्नीः
जाने जूती कहाँ रहते हैं। कहीं किसी होटल में खा-पी लेते हैं, जिस-तिस के घर पड़े रहते हैं और क्या कर सकते हैं? वह जानें उनका यम जाने।

चंद्रमुखीः
अच्छा, माँजी, मैं जाती हूँ।

द्विजोदास की पत्नी *(नौकरानी से):*
अरे इन्हें लगान देना है ज़रा कचहरी में ले जा।

चंद्रमुखीः
नहीं, माँजी, मैं आप ही चली जाऊँगी।

चंद्रमुखी वहाँ से जाती है। फ़ेड आउट।

रील चौदह

फ़ेड इन। पार्वती अपनी अलमारी बंद करती है। चौधरी बिस्तर पर लेटा हुक़्क़ा पी रहा है।

चौधरीः
पार्वती, कितने ही दिनों से मैं तुमसे कुछ कहना चाहता हूँ।

पार्वतीः
कहिए।

चौधरीः
तुम्हारे पास इतनी अच्छी-अच्छी साड़ियाँ हैं, इतने अच्छे-अच्छे पहनावे हैं फिर भी तुम यह मामूली से कपड़े क्यों पहने रहती हो, पार्वती?

पार्वतीः
ऐसे ही।

चौधरीः
और वह इतने गहने, आख़िर वह किसलिए रखे हैं?

पार्वतीः
गहने तो मैंने यशोदा को दे दिए।

دوبجوداس کی بیوی:
جانے جوتی کہاں رہتے ہیں۔ کہیں کسی ہوٹل میں کھا پی لیتے ہیں، جس تِس کے گھر پڑے رہتے ہیں اور کیا کر سکتے ہیں۔ وہ جانیں اُن کا یم جانے۔

چندرمکھی:
اچھا، ماجی، میں جاتی ہوں۔

دوبجوداس کی بیوی (نوکرانی سے):
ارے اِنھیں لگان دینا ہے ذرا کچہری میں لے جا۔

چندرمکھی:
نہیں، ماجی، میں آپ ہی چلی جاؤں گی۔

چندرمکھی وہاں سے اُٹھ آتی ہے۔ فیڈ آؤٹ۔

ریل چودہ

فیڈ اِن۔ پاروتی الماری بند کر رہی ہے اور اُس کا شوہر بستر پر نیم دراز حقے سے شوق کر رہا ہے۔

چودھری:
پاروتی، کتنے ہی دنوں سے میں تم سے کچھ کہنا چاہتا ہوں۔

پاروتی:
کہیے۔

چودھری:
تمہارے پاس اِتنی اچھی اچھی ساڑیاں ہیں، اِتنے اچھے اچھے پہناوے ہیں پھر بھی تم یہ معمولی سے کپڑے کیوں پہنے رہتی ہو، پاروتی؟

پاروتی:
ایسے ہی۔

چودھری:
اور وہ اِتنے گہنے، آخر وہ کس لیے رکھے ہیں؟

پاروتی:
گہنے تو میں نے یشودا کو دے دیے۔

Chowdhury:
You did well, but I had more made for you. So why do you insist on living like an ascetic and dress so austerely, Parvati?

Vo toh acha hi kiya magar maine toh tumhen dobaara banwa diye thay, phir bhi tum ye jogan ka bhes kyun bana rakkhi ho, Parvati?

Parvati:
What do you mean? You live simply. I do the same.

Jogan ka bhes kaisa? Aap jaise seedhe-saade rehte hain waise hi main bhi rehti hoon.

Chowdhury:
Never mind me. I am old. You are not old. You should wear some ornaments.

Meri baat chhodo, main toh boodha hoon. Tum toh boodhi nahin ho. Zara gehne-wehne pehna karo.

Parvati:
I don't like ornaments.

Ji gehne achhe nahin lagte.

Cut to a shot of a jewellery box. Chandramukhi takes out a necklace from the box and puts it around her neck. She is sitting in front of a mirror and is all dressed up. A friend, another prostitute, enters.

Chameli *(actress Vimla):*
Sister?

Didi?

Chandramukhi:
Chameli? Come in. Close the door behind you.

Kaun? Chameli? Aa. Darwaaza bandh karti aa.

Chameli:
How beautiful you are! You'll charm them all. But what's this? One day you leave everything for a spirtiual life, and now? Who is this finery for?

Arey baap re, itni khoobsurat! Aaj toh bijli hi gira rahi ho. Aakhir baat kya hai? Ek din sab kuch chhod jogan ban chali gayi, aaj phir ye haar-singaar kaisa?

चौधरीः
वह तो अच्छा ही किया मगर मैंने तो तुम्हें दोबारा बनवा दिए थे, फिर भी तुम यह जोगन का भेस क्यों बना रखी हो, पार्वती?

چودھری:
وہ تو اچھا ہی کیا مگر میں نے تو تمھیں دوبارہ بنوا دیے تھے، پھر بھی تم یہ جوگن کا بھیس کیوں بنا رکھی ہو، پاروتی؟

पार्वतीः
जोगन का भेस कैसा? आप जैसे सीधे-सादे रहते हैं वैसे ही मैं भी रहती हूँ।

پاروتی:
جوگن کا بھیس کیسا؟ آپ جیسے سیدھے سادے رہتے ہیں ویسے ہی میں بھی رہتی ہوں۔

चौधरीः
मेरी बात छोड़ो, मैं तो बूढ़ा हूँ। तुम तो बूढ़ी नहीं हो। ज़रा गहने-वहने पहना करो।

چودھری:
میری بات چھوڑو، میں تو بوڑھا ہوں۔ تم تو بوڑھی نہیں ہو، ذرا گہنے وہنے پہنا کرو۔

पार्वतीः
जी गहने अच्छे नहीं लगते।

پاروتی:
جی گہنے اچھے نہیں لگتے۔

कट। गहनों का डिब्बा। एक हार निकाल कर चंद्रमुखी अपने गले में पहनती है। वह दर्पण के सामने सजी-बनी बैठी है। उसकी एक साथी प्रवेश करती है।

کٹ۔ زیورات کا ڈبہ۔ ایک ہار نکال کر چندرمکھی اپنے گلے میں پہنتی ہے۔ آئینے کے سامنے وہ سجی بنی بیٹھی ہے۔ اُس کی ایک ساتھی طوائف داخل ہوتی ہے۔

चमेली *(अभिनेत्री विमला):*
दीदी?

چمیلی (اداکار، وملا):
دیدی؟

चंद्रमुखीः
कौन? चमेली? आ। दरवाज़ा बंद करती आ।

چندرمکھی:
کون؟ چمیلی؟ آ۔ دروازہ بند کرتی آ۔

चमेलीः
अरे बाप रे, इतनी ख़ूबसूरत! आज तो बिजली ही गिरा रही हो। आख़िर बात क्या है? एक दिन सब कुछ छोड़ जोगन बन चली गई, आज फिर यह हार-सिंगार कैसा?

چمیلی:
ارے باپ رے، اتنی خوبصورت! آج تو بجلی ہی گرا رہی ہو۔ آخر بات کیا ہے؟ ایک دن سب کچھ چھوڑ جوگن بن چلی گئی، آج پھر یہ ہار سنگار کیسا؟

Chandramukhi:
I'm looking for my husband.

Main apne var ko dhoondne ja rahi hoon.

Chameli:
What husband?

Var? Kaun var?

Chandramukhi:
You'll find out when he comes.

Aayega jabhi pata chalega.

Chameli *(hearing a knock at the door):*
I get it. Maybe that's him. I'll go.

Oh, samjhi. Lo, vo shaayad yahin aa gaye. Main jaati hoon.

Unnamed client *(Johnny Walker, drunk and staggering):*
Here I am.

Lo, hum aa gaye.

Chandramukhi:
Who are you?

Kaun ho tum?

Unnamed client:
I wasn't looking for you, but you're lovely too. Very nice!

Hein? Arey arey tum toh doosri ho magar tumhaara bhi jawaab nahin. Waah-waah, bahot ache!

Chandramukhi:
Get out!

Chale jao yahaan se.

Unnamed client:
What did you say?

Kya kaha aap ne?

Chandramukhi:
I told you to get out.

Main kehti hoon nikal jao yahaan se.

Unnamed client:
Out?

Oh? Baahar?

(stepping outside the door)
I'm out now. But may I ask why I'm being turned out? There must be a reason. What is it?
(Chandramukhi shuts the door on him. Off-screen, he calls out)
You're something else…

Ye lo baahar aa gaye. Ab main kuch pooch sakta hoon ki main kis liye baahar nikaala gaya? Nahin nahin, ek baat hai. Kya baat kya hai? Bahot achhe.
Jawaab nahin aap ka…

चंद्रमुखी:
मैं अपने वर को ढूँढ़ने जा रही हूँ।

चमेली:
वर? कौन वर?

चंद्रमुखी:
आएगा जभी पता चलेगा।

चमेली *(दरवाज़े पर दस्तक सुन कर):*
ओह, समझी। लो, वह शायद यहीं आ गए। मैं जाती हूँ।

ग्राहक *(नशे में लड़खड़ाता हुआ, जॉनी वॉकर):*
लो हम आ गए।

चंद्रमुखी:
कौन हो तुम?

ग्राहक:
हैं? अरे अरे तुम तो दूसरी हो मगर तुम्हारा भी जवाब नहीं। वाह वाह, बहुत अच्छे।

चंद्रमुखी:
चले जाओ यहाँ से।

ग्राहक:
क्या कहा आपने?

चंद्रमुखी:
मैं कहती हूँ निकल जाओ यहाँ से।

ग्राहक:
ओह, बाहर?
(कमरे के बाहर खड़ा हो जाता है)
यह लो बाहर आ गए। अब मैं कुछ पूछ सकता हूँ कि मैं किसलिए बाहर निकाला गया? नहीं नहीं, एक बात है। क्या बात क्या है? बहुत अच्छे।
(चंद्रमुखी द्वार बंद कर लेती है। ऑफ़-स्क्रीन कहता है)
जवाब नहीं आपका...

چندرمکھی:
میں اپنے ور کو ڈھونڈنے جارہی ہوں

چمیلی:
ور؟ کون ور؟

چندرمکھی:
آئے گا جبھی پتا چلے گا۔

چمیلی (دروازے پر دستک سن کر):
اوہ، سمجھی۔ لو، وہ شاید یہیں آگئے۔ میں جاتی ہوں۔

گاہک (جانی واکر، نشے میں دھت):
لو ہم آگئے۔

چندرمکھی:
کون ہو تم؟

گاہک:
ہیں؟ ارے ارے تم تو دوسری ہو مگر تمہارا بھی جواب نہیں۔ واہ واہ، بہت اچھے۔

چندرمکھی:
چلے جاؤ یہاں سے۔

گاہک:
کیا کہا آپ نے؟

چندرمکھی:
میں کہتی ہوں نکل جاؤ یہاں سے۔

گاہک:
اوہ، باہر؟
(دروازے کی چوکھٹ پر کھڑا ہو کر)
یہ لو باہر آگئے۔ اب میں کچھ پوچھ سکتا ہوں کہ میں کس لیے باہر نکالا گیا؟ نہیں نہیں، ایک بات ہے۔ کیا بات کیا ہے؟ بہت اچھے۔
(چندرمکھی دروازہ بند کر دیتی ہے۔ آف اسکرین کہتا ہے)
جواب نہیں آپ کا۔۔۔

Chandramukhi looks disturbed. Dissolve. Night-time. A shot of a dark lane in the red-light area of Calcutta. A woman stands on a balcony. Chandramukhi arrives.

Chandramukhi:
Mohana, does a man called Devdas come here?

Kyun, Mohana, koi Devdas naam ka aadmi yahaan aata hai?

Mohana *(unidentified actress):*
Devdas?

Devdas? Kaun Devdas?

Chandramukhi:
Fair-skinned, heavy eyebrows and shining eyes. He is an important man and spends lavishly.

Khula rang, ghani bhawen, tej bhari aankhen. Bahot baday aadmi hain, jab aate hain bahot maal lutaate hain.

Mohana:
No, sister, it is not our fortune to meet a man like him.

Nahin bahen, aisa humaari qismat mein kahaan hai?

Dissolve. Night-time. Chandramukhi is in a horse carriage. She is roaming the streets, looking for Devdas. The sound of ghazal singing, off-screen, underscores the scene.

Talat Mahmood sings for Devdas

"Who would have ever known, who would ever believe…

"Kisko khabar thi kisko yaqeen tha…"

Chandramukhi:
Stop. Coachman, stop the carriage.

Roko. Gaadi-waale, gaadi roko.

Chandramukhi alights from the carriage and follows the sound of Devdas's voice through the dark alley.

Devdas *(singing off-screen):*
"…such days would come."

"…aise bhi din aayenge"

Chandramukhi:
Devdas.

Devdas.

Lying drunk in the alley, Devdas continues singing.

चंद्रमुखी परेशान है। अगला दृश्य। रात का समय। कलकत्ते की एक बदनाम बस्ती में एक महिला छज्जे पर खड़ी है। चंद्रमुखी उसके पास आती है।

चंद्रमुखीः
क्यों, मोहना, कोई देवदास नाम का आदमी यहाँ आता है?

मोहना *(कलाकार अज्ञात):*
देवदास? कौन देवदास?

चंद्रमुखीः
खुला रंग, घनी भौंहें, तेज भरी आँखें। बहुत बड़े आदमी हैं, जब आते हैं, बहुत माल लुटाते हैं।

मोहनाः
नहीं बहन, ऐसा हमारी क़िस्मत में कहाँ है?

अगला दृश्य। रात का समय। चंद्रमुखी एक घोड़ागाड़ी में बैठ कर शहर में देवदास को ढूँढ़ने निकली है। दृश्य में अलग-अलग ग़ज़लों के शेर सुनाई देते हैं।

देवदास गाता है। स्वरः तलत महमूद

''किसको ख़बर थी किसको यक़ीं था...''

चंद्रमुखीः
रोको। गाड़ी वाले, गाड़ी रोको।

चंद्रमुखी गाड़ी से उतर कर देवदास की आवाज़ का पीछा करती है।

देवदास *(ऑफ़-स्क्रीन गाता है):*
''...ऐसे भी दिन आएँगे''

चंद्रमुखीः
देवदास।

सड़क पर नशे में धुत पड़ा देवदास गाता रहता है।

چندرمکھی کا مزاج مکدر ہے۔ اگلا منظر۔ رات۔ کلکتہ کے ایک بدنام علاقے میں ایک عورت چھجے پر کھڑی ہے۔ چندر مکھی اُس کے پاس آتی ہے۔

چندرمکھی:
کیوں، موہنا، کوئی دیوداس نام کا آدمی یہاں آتا ہے؟

موہنا (اداکارہ، نامعلوم):
دیوداس؟ کون دیوداس؟

چندرمکھی:
کھلا رنگ، گھنی بھنویں، تیج بھری آنکھیں۔ بہت بڑے آدمی ہیں، جب آتے ہیں بہت مال لٹاتے ہیں۔

موہنا:
نہیں بہن، ایسا ہماری قسمت میں کہاں ہے؟

اگلا منظر۔ رات۔ گھوڑا گاڑی میں سوار چندرمکھی۔ وہ دیوداس کی تلاش میں ہے۔ منظر نامے میں مختلف غزل کے اشعار گونجتے ہوئے سنائی دیتے ہیں۔

آواز، طلعت محمود

''کس کو خبر تھی کس کو یقین تھا۔۔۔''

چندرمکھی:
روکو۔ گاڑی والے، گاڑی روکو۔

دیوداس کی آواز کے تعاقب میں چندرمکھی گھوڑا گاڑی سے اُتر پڑتی ہے۔

دیوداس (آف اسکرین گاتے ہوئے):
''۔۔۔ایسے بھی دن آئیں گے''

چندرمکھی:
دیوداس:

سڑک پر نشے میں چور پڑا دیوداس گارہا ہے۔

Devdas *(singing):* "Who would have ever known, who would ever believe… *(laughs)* "…such days would come."	"Kisko khabar thi kisko yaqeen tha… "…aise bhi din aayenge…haaye"
Chandramukhi: Devdas.	Devdas.
Devdas *(singing):* "Living would be a hard task And dying beyond my reach."	"Jeena bhi mushkil hoga Aur marne bhi na paayenge…haaye"
Chandramukhi: Devdas.	Devdas.
Devdas: Hmm?	Ein?
Chandramukhi: Why are you lying here? Come. Let's go home.	Yahaan kyun paday ho? Chalo, ghar chalo.
Devdas *(singing):* "For the broken hearted There's little difference between living and… …dying Today I leave this gathering Tomorrow I leave this world."	"Hum jaise barbaad dilon ka Jeena kya aur… …marna kya Aaj teri mehfil se uthe Kal duniya se uth jaayenge…haaye"
Chandramukhi: Do you want a drink?	Sharaab piyoge?

देवदास *(गाते हुए)*:
''किसको ख़बर थी किसको यक़ीं था...
(हँसता है)
''...ऐसे भी दिन आएँगे...हाय''

चंद्रमुखीः
देवदास।

देवदास *(गाते हुए)*:
''जीना भी मुश्किल होगा और
मरने भी न पाएँगे...हाय''

चंद्रमुखीः
देवदास।

देवदासः
ऐं?

चंद्रमुखीः
यहाँ क्यों पड़े हो? चलो, घर चलो।

देवदास *(गाते हुए)*:
''हम जैसे बरबाद दिलों का
जीना क्या...
और...मरना क्या
आज तेरी महफ़िल से उठे
कल दुनिया से उठ जाएँगे...हाय''

चंद्रमुखीः
शराब पियोगे?

دیوداس (گاتے ہوئے):
''کس کو خبر تھی کس کو یقیں تھا---
(ہنستا ہے)
''---ایسے بھی دن آئیں گے---ہائے''

چندرمکھی:
دیوداس:

دیوداس (گاتے ہوئے):
''جینا بھی مشکل ہوگا
اور مرنے بھی نہ پائیں گے---ہائے''

چندرمکھی:
دیوداس:

دیوداس:
ایں؟

چندرمکھی:
یہاں کیوں پڑے ہو؟ چلو، گھر چلو۔

دیوداس (گاتے ہوئے):
''ہم جیسے برباد دلوں کا جینا کیا---
اور---مرنا کیا
آج تیری محفل سے اُٹھے
کل دنیا سے اُٹھ جائیں گے---ہائے''

چندرمکھی:
شراب پیوگے؟

Devdas:
Yes. Where can I find one?

Haan, haan. Kahaan milegi?

Chandramukhi:
Come with me. I'll get you a drink.

Chalo, main bando-bast kar doongi.

Devdas:
Where have you come from, my friend? You're very beautiful. Very beautiful.

Arey tum kahaan se aa gayin, meri mitra? Waah, bahot sundar, bahot sundar ho.

Chandramukhi *(helping him to stand up):*
Yes, I am. Let's go. Come.

Haan, sundar hoon. Chalo, chalo.

Devdas:
Do you even know me, lovely lady?

Tum mujhe pehchaanti bhi ho, sundari?

Chandramukhi:
Yes, I know you. Let's go.

Haan, pehchaanti hoon. Chalo.

Chandramukhi helps the drunk Devdas to walk. Dissolve. They arrive at Chandramukhi's rooms. She makes him sit on the bed. He still does not remember who she is.

Devdas:
Where am I? Where's the liquor?

Ye kahaan le aayi ho, bhai? Acha laao, sharaab laao.

Chandramukhi:
There isn't any.

Sharaab nahin hai.

Devdas:
No liquor? Then why did you bring me here? Why did you lie to me? Get me something to drink!

Nahin hai? Toh phir yahaan kyun laayi ho mujhe? Yahi dhoka diya? Jahaan se bhi ho, laao. Laao.

Chandramukhi:
You shouldn't drink.

Tumhen peena nahin chaahiye.

Devdas:
Who are you to lecture me? Give me a drink otherwise I am leaving.

Ye tum mujhe naseehat karne-waali kaun ho ji? Laao, nahin toh main yahaan se chala.

देवदासः
हाँ, हाँ। कहाँ मिलेगी?

دیوداس:
ہاں، ہاں۔ کہاں ملے گی؟

चंद्रमुखीः
चलो, मैं बन्दोबस्त कर दूँगी।

چندرمکھی:
چلو، میں بندوبست کر دوں گی۔

देवदासः
अरे तुम कहाँ से आ गईं मेरी मित्र? वाह, बहुत सुंदर, बहुत सुंदर हो।

دیوداس:
ارے تم کہاں سے آ گئیں، میری متر؟ واہ، بہت سندر، بہت سندر ہو۔

चंद्रमुखी *(उसे सहारा देकर खड़ा करती है):*
हाँ, सुंदर हूँ। चलो, चलो।

چندرمکھی (چندرمکھی اُسے سہارا دے کر کھڑا کرتی ہے):
ہاں، سندر ہوں۔ چلو، چلو۔

देवदासः
तुम मुझे पहचानती भी हो, सुंदरी?

دیوداس:
تم مجھے پہچانتی بھی ہو، سندری؟

चंद्रमुखीः
हाँ, पहचानती हूँ। चलो।

چندرمکھی:
ہاں، پہچانتی ہوں۔ چلو۔

नशे में चूर देवदास को चंद्रमुखी सहारा देती है। अगला दृश्य। वह चंद्रमुखी के कमरे पर पहुँचते हैं। वह उसे बिस्तर पर बिठाती है। अब तक देवदास उसे पहचान नहीं सका है।

چندرمکھی نشے میں چور دیوداس کو سہارا دے کر لے جاتی ہے۔ اگلا منظر۔ وہ چندرمکھی کے کمرے پر پہنچتے ہیں۔ وہ اُسے بستر پر بٹھاتی ہے۔ اب تک اُس نے چندرمکھی کو پہچانا نہیں ہے۔

देवदासः
यह कहाँ ले आई हो, भई? अच्छा लाओ, शराब लाओ।

دیوداس:
یہ کہاں لے آئی ہو، بھئی؟ اچھا لاؤ، شراب لاؤ۔

चंद्रमुखीः
शराब नहीं है।

چندرمکھی:
شراب نہیں ہے۔

देवदासः
नहीं है? तो फिर यहाँ क्यों लाई हो मुझे? यही धोखा दिया? जहाँ से भी हो, लाओ। लाओ!

دیوداس:
نہیں ہے؟ تو پھر یہاں کیوں لائی ہو مجھے؟ یہی دھوکہ دیا؟ جہاں سے بھی ہو، لاؤ۔ لاؤ!

चंद्रमुखीः
तुम्हें पीना नहीं चाहिए।

چندرمکھی:
تمھیں پینا نہیں چاہیے۔

देवदासः
यह तुम मुझे नसीहत करने वाली कौन हो जी? लाओ, नहीं तो मैं यहाँ से चला।

دیوداس:
یہ تم مجھے نصیحت کرنے والی کون ہو جی؟ لاؤ نہیں تو میں یہاں سے چلا۔

Chandramukhi:
Don't go. You aren't well.

Matt jaao. Tumhaari tabiyat theek nahin.

Devdas:
What business is it of yours whether I go to hell or die? "You aren't well." Ha!

Arey mar jaaunga, jahannum mein chala jaaunga. Tum ko is se kya hai? Tabiyat theek nahin!

Chandramukhi:
Sit down, I'll order some liquor. Watch my dance till it comes.

Zara baitho toh sahi, main abhi mangva deti hoon. Baitho. Tabb tak mera naach toh dekho.

Devdas:
Watch you dance?

Naach dekhoon?

Chandramukhi starts to dance. Devdas is in a drunken daze.

Reel Fifteen

Lata Mangeshkar sings for Chandramukhi

Where do I find a graceful way that's acceptable to you?
Where do I find the song that charms you?
Where do I find a graceful way...

Jisay tu qubool kar le vo ada kahaan se laaun
Tere dil ko jo lubha le vo sada kahaan se laaun
Jisay tu qubool kar le...

I am that flower crushed underfoot by all
My youth has been washed away in my tears
(both lines repeated)
Where do I find the cloud that brings Spring?
Where do I find the song that charms you?
Where do I find a graceful way...

Main vo phool hoon ki jisko gaya har koi masal ke
Meri umr beh gayi hai mere aansuon mein dhal ke

Jo bahaar ban ke barse vo ghata kahaan se laaun
Tere dil ko jo lubha le vo sada kahaan se laaun
Jisay tu qubool kar le...

You desire another, I desire only you
Your heart is filled with sadness, my heart is filled with you
(both lines repeated)
Where do I find the cure that heals hearts?
Where do I find the song that charms you?
Where do I find a graceful way...

Tujhe aur ki tamanna mujhe teri aarzu hai
Tere dil mein gham hi gham hai mere dil mein tu hi tu hai

Jo dilon ko chain de de vo dawa kahaan se laaun
Tere dil ko jo lubha le vo sada kahaan se laaun
Jisay tu qubool kar le...

चंद्रमुखीः
मत जाओ। तुम्हारी तबियत ठीक नहीं।

देवदासः
अरे मर जाऊँगा, जहन्नुम में चला जाऊँगा। तुमको इससे क्या है? तबियत ठीक नहीं!

चंद्रमुखीः
ज़रा बैठो तो सही, मैं अभी मँगवा देती हूँ। बैठो। तब तक मेरा नाच तो देखो।

देवदासः
नाच देखूँ?

चंद्रमुखी नाचना आरम्भ करती है। देवदास नशे में उसे देख रहा है।

रील पन्द्रह

चंद्रमुखी गाती है। स्वरः लता मंगेशकर

जिसे तू क़बूल कर ले वह अदा कहाँ से लाऊँ
तेरे दिल को जो लुभा ले वह सदा कहाँ से लाऊँ
जिसे तू क़बूल कर ले...

मैं वह फूल हूँ कि जिसको गया हर कोई मसल के
मेरी उम्र बह गई है मेरे आँसुओं में ढल के
(दोनों पंक्तियाँ दोहराई जाती हैं)
जो बहार बनके बरसे वह घटा कहाँ से लाऊँ
तेरे दिल को जो लुभा ले वह सदा कहाँ से लाऊँ
जिसे तू क़बूल कर ले...

तुझे और की तमन्ना मुझे तेरी आरज़ू है
तेरे दिल में ग़म ही ग़म है मेरे दिल में तू ही तू है
(दोनों पंक्तियाँ दोहराई जाती हैं)
जो दिलों को चैन दे दे वह दवा कहाँ से लाऊँ
तेरे दिल को जो लुभा ले वह सदा कहाँ से लाऊँ
जिसे तू क़बूल कर ले...

چندرمکھی:
مت جاؤ۔تمہاری طبعیت ٹھیک نہیں۔

دیوداس:
ارے مرجاؤں گا،جہنم میں چلا جاؤں گا۔تم کو اِس سے کیا ہے؟طبعیت ٹھیک نہیں!

چندرمکھی:
ذرا بیٹھوتو سہی، میں ابھی منگوادیتی ہوں۔بیٹھو۔تب تک میرا ناچ تو دیکھو۔

دیوداس:
ناچ دیکھوں؟

چندرمکھی رقص شروع کرتی ہے۔دیوداس نشے کی حالت میں اُسے دیکھ رہا ہے۔

ریل پندرہ

چندرمکھی گاتی ہے۔آواز،لتا منگیشکر

جسے تُو قبول کرلے وہ ادا کہاں سے لاؤں
تیرے دل کو جولُبھالے وہ صدا کہاں سے لاؤں
جسے تُو قبول کرلے۔۔۔

میں وہ پھول ہوں کہ جس کو گیا ہر کوئی مسل کے
میری عمر بہہ گئی ہے میرے آنسوؤں میں ڈھل کے
(دونوں لائنیں دوہراتی ہے)
جو بہار بن کے برسے وہ گھٹا کہاں سے لاؤں
تیرے دل کو جولُبھالے وہ صدا کہاں سے لاؤں
جسے تُو قبول کرلے۔۔۔

تجھے اور کی تمنا مجھے تیری آرزو ہے
تیرے دل میں غم ہی غم ہے میرے دل میں تُو ہی تُو ہے
(دونوں لائنیں دوہراتی ہے)
جودلوں کو چین دے دے وہ دوا کہاں سے لاؤں
تیرے دل کو جولُبھالے وہ صدا کہاں سے لاؤں
جسے تُو قبول کرلے۔۔۔

My sighs have little effect, my helplessness shows
If I were to ask for death, I would not find it at his threshold
(both lines repeated)
Where do I find the answer to my prayers?
Where do I find the song that charms you?
Where do I find a graceful way that's acceptable to you?
Where do I find the song that charms you?
Where do I find a graceful way…

Meri be-basi hai zaahir meri aahe-be-asar se
Kabhi maut bhi jo maangi toh na paayi uske dar se

Jo muraad le ke aaye vo dua kahaan se laaun
Tere dil ko jo lubha le vo sada kahaan se laaun
Jisay tu qubool kar le vo ada kahaan se laaun
Tere dil ko jo lubha le vo sada kahaan se laaun
Jisay tu qubool kar le…

Devdas has fallen asleep by the end of the song. Chandramukhi smiles. Fade out.

Fade in. Day. Devdas is asleep on the bed. He wakes up, unsure of where he is. He now recognises Chandramukhi when she enters.

Devdas *(smiling)*:
Where did you kidnap me?

Ye kal kahaan se chura laayin tum mujhe, hein?

Chandramukhi:
I didn't kidnap you. You were lying in an alley. I only brought you here.

Chura ke nahin laayi. Raaste mein pada paaya, sirf utha laayi hoon.

Devdas *(seeing her jewellery)*:
Have you gone back to your old life? You look like a new bride, bedecked with jewellery. Who gave them to you?

Aur ye sab tumne phir se kya shuru kar diya hai? Gehnon se ladi huwi ho, nayi-naveli dulhan ki tarah. Kisne diye?

Chandramukhi:
Not that again.

Phir?

Devdas:
I was only joking.

Main bhi yunhi mazaaq kar raha tha.

मेरी बे-बसी है ज़ाहिर मेरी आहे बे-असर से
कभी मौत भी जो माँगी तो न पाई उसके दर से
(दोनों पंक्तियाँ दोहराई जाती हैं)
जो मुराद लेके आए वह दुआ कहाँ से लाऊँ
तेरे दिल को जो लुभा ले वह सदा कहाँ से लाऊँ
जिसे तू क़बूल कर ले वह अदा कहाँ से लाऊँ
तेरे दिल को जो लुभा ले वह सदा कहाँ से लाऊँ
जिसे तू क़बूल कर ले...

गाना समाप्त होते-होते देवदास सो जाता है। चंद्रमुखी उसे सोता देख मुस्कुरा देती है। फ़ेड आउट।

फ़ेड इन। दिन। देवदास बिस्तर पर सोया हुआ है। जागने पर उसे आश्चर्य होता है कि वह कहाँ है। चंद्रमुखी को देख कर पहचान जाता है।

देवदास *(मुस्कुराते हुए):*
यह कल कहाँ से चुरा लाईं तुम मुझे, हैं?

चंद्रमुखीः
चुरा के नहीं लाई। रास्ते में पड़ा पाया, सिर्फ़ उठा लाई हूँ।

देवदास *(गहनों को देखते हुए):*
और यह सब तुमने फिर से क्या शुरू कर दिया है? गहनों से लदी हुई हो, नई-नवेली दुल्हन की तरह। किसने दिये?

चंद्रमुखीः
फिर?

देवदासः
मैं भी यूँ ही मज़ाक़ कर रहा था।

میری بے بسی ہے ظاہر میری آہِ بے اثر سے
کبھی موت بھی جو مانگی تو نہ پائی اُس کے در سے
(دونوں لائنیں دوہراتی ہے)
جو مراد لے کے آئے وہ دعا کہاں سے لاؤں
تیرے دل کو جو لُبھا لے وہ صدا کہاں سے لاؤں
جسے تُو قبول کر لے وہ ادا کہاں سے لاؤں
تیرے دل کو جو لُبھا لے وہ صدا کہاں سے لاؤں
جسے تُو قبول کر لے۔۔۔

گیت ختم ہوتے ہوتے دیوداس سو جاتا ہے۔ چندرمکھی اُسے سوتا دیکھ کر مسکرا دیتی ہے۔ فیڈ آؤٹ۔

فیڈ اِن۔ دن۔ دیوداس بستر پر سو رہا ہے۔ جاگنے پر اُسے حیرت ہوتی ہے کہ وہ کہاں ہے۔ چندرمکھی کو دیکھ کر پہچان جاتا ہے۔

دیوداس (مسکراتے ہوئے):
یہ کل کہاں سے چرا لائیں تم مجھے، ہیں؟

چندرمکھی:
چرا کے نہیں لائی۔ راستے میں پڑا پایا، صرف اُٹھا لائی ہوں۔

دیوداس (سجی بنی چندرمکھی کو دیکھ کر):
اور یہ سب تم نے پھر سے کیا شروع کر دیا ہے؟ گہنوں سے لدی ہوئی ہو، نئی نویلی دلہن کی طرح۔ کس نے دیے؟

چندرمکھی:
پھر؟

دیوداس:
میں بھی یونہی مذاق کر رہا تھا۔

Chandramukhi:
No one gave them to me, nor did I have them made. They're imitation. I have been living here for a month, waiting for you. I rented this room and bought these trinkets. I've wasted a lot of money for you — and you, you didn't even recognise me.

Na kisi ne diye, na banvaaye, sab naqli hain. Ek mahine se tumhaare liye yahaan aa ke padi hoon. Makaan liya, kiraaya bhara, ye sab zevar kharide. Be-kaar kitne rupay kharch karne pade tumhaare liye, aur ek tum ho jo kal mujhe pehchaan bhi na sakay.

Devdas:
No, I didn't recognise you. But your voice did sound familiar. I kept thinking to myself — who else but my Chandramukhi would look after me like this?

Pehchaan nahin saka lekin tumhaari aawaaz sunn kar kabhi-kabhi shak zaroor hua. Aur baar-baar yahi sochta raha ki kaun itni sewa kar sakta hai siwaaye meri Chandramukhi ke?

Chandramukhi is overwhelmed with emotion.

Chandramukhi:
Devdas, do you still despise me?

Devdas, kya ab bhi tum mujh se utni hi nafrat karte ho?

Devdas:
No, Chandramukhi, in fact, I love you.

Nahin, Chandramukhi, balki pyar karta hoon.

Unable to contain her happiness, she goes to the adjoining room.

Chandramukhi *(to herself):*
"My Chandramukhi." God.

"Meri Chandramukhi." Bhagwan.

Lata Mangeshkar sings a cappella (off-screen) for Chandramukhi over a shot of Devdas.

My destiny smiles on me (2)
My beloved has come home (2)

Dhan-dhan bhaag jaage moray (2)
Piya ghar aaye ri (2)

चंद्रमुखीः
न किसी ने दिये न बनवाए, सब नक़ली हैं। एक महीने से तुम्हारे लिए यहाँ आके पड़ी हूँ। मकान लिया, किराया भरा, यह सब ज़ेवर ख़रीदे। बेकार कितने रुपए ख़र्च करने पड़े तुम्हारे लिए, और एक तुम हो जो कल मुझे पहचान भी न सके।

देवदासः
पहचान नहीं सका लेकिन तुम्हारी आवाज़ सुन कर कभी-कभी शक ज़रूर हुआ। और बार-बार यही सोचता रहा कि कौन इतनी सेवा कर सकता है सिवाए मेरी चंद्रमुखी के?

चंद्रमुखी भावुक हो जाती है।

चंद्रमुखीः
देवदास, क्या अब भी तुम मुझसे उतनी ही नफ़रत करते हो?

देवदासः
नहीं, चंद्रमुखी, बल्कि प्यार करता हूँ।

अपनी प्रसन्नता छिपाने के लिए वह दूसरे कमरे में चली जाती है।

चंद्रमुखी *(अपने-आपसे):*
''मेरी चंद्रमुखी।'' भगवान!

कट। देवदास का शॉट। चंद्रमुखी एक दोहा गुनगुनाते हुए। लता मंगेशकर की आवाज़।

धन धन भाग्य जागे मोरे (२)
पिया घर आए री (२)

چندرمکھی:
نہ کسی نے دیے نہ بنوائے، سب نقلی ہیں۔ ایک مہینے سے تمہارے لیے یہاں آکے پڑی ہوں۔ مکان لیا، کرایہ بھرا، یہ سب زیور خریدے۔ بے کار کتنے روپے خرچ کرنے پڑے تمہارے لیے، اور ایک تم ہو جو کل مجھے پہچان بھی نہ سکے۔

دیوداس:
پہچان نہیں سکا لیکن تمہاری آواز سن کر کبھی کبھی شک ضرور ہوا۔ اور بار بار یہی سوچتا رہا کہ کون اِتنی سیوا کر سکتا ہے سوائے میری چندرمکھی کے؟

چندرمکھی جذبات سے مغلوب ہو جاتی ہے۔

چندرمکھی:
دیوداس، کیا اب بھی تم مجھ سے اُتنی ہی نفرت کرتے ہو؟

دیوداس:
نہیں، چندرمکھی، بلکہ پیار کرتا ہوں۔

اپنی خوشی کو چھپانے کے لیے وہ دوسرے کمرے میں چلی جاتی ہے۔

چندرمکھی (خودکلامی):
''میری چندرمکھی۔'' بھگوان۔

لتا منگیشکر، چندرمکھی کے لیے ایک دوہا گنگناتے ہوئے، دیوداس کا شاٹ۔

دھن دھن بھاگ جاگے مورے (۲)
پیا گھر آئے ری (۲)

Devdas smiles hearing Chandramukhi sing. He suddenly doubles up with pain. The glass of tea in his hands smashed to the ground. Hearing the sound of the shattering glass, Chandramukhi rushes to him.

Chandramukhi:
What's wrong? What's happened to you? Are you in pain? Is it your liver?

Kya hua? Kya hua tumhen? Kahin sarvanash toh nahin kar diya? Jigar ka dard toh nahin hai?

Devdas:
I think so.

Kuch aisa hi maaloom hota hai mujhe.

Chandramukhi *(helping him to lie on the bed):*
Lie down. I'll call the doctor.

Tum lait jaao. Lait jaao. Main abhi doctor ko le kar aati hoon.

She leaves the room. Fade out.

Fade in. Day. A tracking shot pulls back to reveal a table full of medicine bottles. The doctor sits near Devdas, who is lying in bed, looking stronger. Chandramukhi stands behind him.

Doctor *(unidentified actor):*
It looks like you're getting better.

Maaloom hota hai ab aap ki tabiyat kuch theek hui.

Devdas:
Thanks to your medicine, doctor.

Aap ki dawa ne acha kar diya hai, doctor saaheb.

Doctor *(laughs):*
My medicine didn't help — it was her prayers and her day and night care. But don't think you're strong and healthy again. You must be very careful. Alcohol is a poison for you. Leave Calcutta if you can. A change of climate will help.

Meri dawa ne nahin, inki dua ne, din-raat ki sewa ne. Magar ye matt samajhiye ki aap ek damm tandurust ho gaye. Aap ko apni sehat ka bahot khayaal rakhna padega. Sharaab aap ke liye zaher hai. Ho sakay toh Kalkatte se baahar kahin aab-o-hawa badalne chale jaaiye. Acha.

The doctor leaves.

Chandramukhi:
The doctor said you should leave the city for awhile.

Doctor ne kaha hai tumhen kuch din ke liye kahin jaana chaahiye.

चंद्रमुखी को गाता सुन कर देवदास मुस्कुरा देता है। अचानक उसे बहुत ज़ोर की पीड़ा होती है। चाय का गिलास उसके हाथ से छूट कर गिर पड़ता है और टूट जाता है। गिलास टूटने की आवाज़ सुन कर चंद्रमुखी भाग कर आती है।

चंद्रमुखीः
क्या हुआ? क्या हुआ तुम्हें? कहीं सर्वनाश तो नहीं कर दिया? जिगर का दर्द तो नहीं है?

देवदासः
कुछ ऐसा ही मालूम होता है मुझे।

चंद्रमुखी *(उसे सहारा देकर बिस्तर पर लिटाती है):*
तुम लेट जाओ। लेट जाओ। मैं अभी डॉक्टर को लेकर आती हूँ।

वह कमरे के बाहर जाती है। फ़ेड आउट।

फ़ेड इन। दिन। दूर होते हुए ट्रैकिंग शॉट में मेज़ पर दवाएँ रखी दिखाई देती हैं। डॉक्टर देवदास के निकट बिस्तर पर बैठता है, जिसकी दशा पहले से अच्छी है। चंद्रमुखी उसके पीछे खड़ी हुई है।

डॉक्टर *(कलाकार अज्ञात):*
मालूम होता है अब आपकी तबियत कुछ ठीक हुई।

देवदासः
आपकी दवा ने अच्छा कर दिया है, डॉक्टर साहिब।

डॉक्टर *(हँसता है):*
मेरी दवा ने नहीं, इनकी दुआ ने, दिन-रात की सेवा ने। मगर यह मत समझिए कि आप एकदम तंदुरुस्त हो गए। आपको अपनी सेहत का बहुत ख़्याल रखना पड़ेगा। शराब आपके लिए ज़हर है। हो सके तो कलकत्ते से बाहर कहीं आब-ओ-हवा बदलने चले जाइए। अच्छा।

डॉक्टर चला जाता है।

चंद्रमुखीः
डॉक्टर ने कहा है, तुम्हें कुछ दिन के लिए कहीं जाना चाहिए।

چندرمکھی کو گاتا سن کر دیوداس مسکرا رہا ہے۔ اچانک ہی اپنا پہلو پکڑ کر درد سے وہ دوہرا ہو جاتا ہے۔ چائے کا گلاس چھوٹ کر ہاتھ سے فرش پر گر کر ٹوٹ جاتا ہے۔ گلاس ٹوٹنے کی آواز سن کر چندرمکھی اُس کی طرف لپکتی ہے۔

چندرمکھی:
کیا ہوا؟ کیا ہوا تمھیں؟ کہیں سروناش تو نہیں کر دیا؟ جگر کا درد تو نہیں ہے؟

دیوداس:
کچھ ایسا ہی معلوم ہوتا ہے مجھے۔

چندرمکھی (اُسے لیٹنے میں مدد کرتی ہے):
تم لیٹ جاؤ۔ لیٹ جاؤ۔ میں ابھی ڈاکٹر کو لے کر آتی ہوں۔

وہ کمرے سے باہر نکل جاتی ہے۔ فیڈ آؤٹ۔

فیڈ اِن۔ دن۔ دور ہوتے ہوئے ٹریکنگ شاٹ میں ایک میز پر دوائیں رکھی دکھائی دیتی ہیں۔ دیوداس کے قریب ڈاکٹر بیٹھا ہوا ہے جو بستر پر دراز ہے لیکن اب کچھ بہتر نظر آ رہا ہے۔ چندرمکھی اُس کے پیچھے کھڑی ہوئی ہے۔

ڈاکٹر (اداکار، نامعلوم):
معلوم ہوتا ہے اب آپ کی طبعیت کچھ ٹھیک ہوئی۔

دیوداس:
آپ کی دوا نے اچھا کر دیا ہے، ڈاکٹر صاحب۔

ڈاکٹر (ہنستے ہوئے):
میری دوا نے نہیں، اِنکی دعا نے، دن رات کی سیوا نے۔ مگر یہ مت سمجھیے کہ آپ ایک دم تندرست ہو گئے۔ آپ کو اپنی صحت کا بہت خیال رکھنا پڑے گا۔ شراب آپ کے لیے زہر ہے۔ ہو سکے تو کلکتے سے باہر کہیں آب و ہوا بدلنے چلے جایئے۔ اچھا۔

ڈاکٹر چلا جاتا ہے۔

چندرمکھی:
ڈاکٹر نے کہا ہے تمھیں کچھ دن کے لیے کہیں جانا چاہیے۔

Devdas:
What am I to you, Chandramukhi? Why do you look after me so well?

Tum meri kaun hoti ho, Chandramukhi, jo itni sewa kar rahi ho?

Chandramukhi:
Do you still not understand?

Kya ab bhi ye samajh na sakay?

Devdas:
Yes, but what's the use? How much I love Parvati, and how much she loved me. But society opposed it. What did I gain? Only sorrow. After suffering so much, I thought I'd never fall into this trap again. I wasn't ensnared of my own free will. Why did you do this, Chandramukhi? Why have you tied me to you? Perhaps you'll have to endure the same sorrow as Parvati. You are so different, yet so alike. She is dignified and whimsical, and you are tranquil and thoughtful. She cannot endure anything, and you endure everything. She is so respected, and you are so dishonoured. Everyone loves her, and people despise you. But I don't hate you, Chandramukhi. I can never do that.

Samajh toh liya lekin is se bhi kya hota hai? Dekho na main Parvati ko kitna chaahta hoon aur vo bhi mujhe kitna chaahti thi, lekin samaaj ne nahin chaaha. Siwaaye dukh ke aur kya mila? Itna dukh pa ke socha tha kabhi in phandon mein nahin phansunga, aur apni marzi se phansa bhi nahin. Tumne aisa kyun kiya, Chandramukhi? Kyun is tarah baandh liya mujhe? Shaayad tum bhi Parvati ki tarah hi dukh jhelogi. Tum donon mein kitna farq hai aur phir bhi tum kitni ek si ho. Ek badi khud-daar aur chanchal doosri shaant aur gambheer. Vo kuch bhi nahin seh sakti, aur tum sab kuch seh guzarti ho. Uski kitni izzat hai aur tum kitni bad-naam ho. Usay sabhi pyar karte hain, aur tumse nafrat. Lekin main tumse nafrat nahin karta, Chandramukhi. Kar hi nahin sakta.

Chandramukhi:
That is enough for me. I want nothing else.

Mere liye yahi bahot hai. Mujhe aur kuch nahin chaahiye.

Chandramukhi leaves his side. She is crying. Dissolve. Day. Chandramukhi is packing some bags for Devdas.

Servant:
Maaji, the carriage is here.

Maaji, gaadi aa gayi.

Chandramukhi:
Take the bedding.

Bistar le jaao.

The servant takes Devdas's bag.

देवदासः
तुम मेरी कौन होती हो, चंद्रमुखी, जो इतनी सेवा कर रही हो?

دیوداس:
تم میری کون ہوتی ہو، چندرمکھی، جو اِتنی سیوا کر رہی ہو؟

चंद्रमुखीः
क्या अब भी यह समझ न सके?

چندرمکھی:
کیا اب بھی یہ سمجھ نہ سکے؟

देवदासः
समझ तो लिया लेकिन इससे भी क्या होता है? देखो न मैं पार्वती को कितना चाहता हूँ और वह भी मुझे कितना चाहती थी, लेकिन समाज ने नहीं चाहा। सिवाए दुःख के और क्या मिला? इतना दुःख पाके सोचा था कभी इन फंदों में नहीं फँसूँगा, और अपनी मरज़ी से फँसा भी नहीं। तुमने ऐसा क्यों किया चंद्रमुखी? क्यों इस तरह बाँध लिया मुझे? शायद तुम भी पार्वती की तरह ही दुःख झेलोगी। तुम दोनों में कितना फ़र्क़ है और फिर भी तुम कितनी एक सी हो। एक बड़ी ख़ुद्दार और चंचल, दूसरी शांत और गंभीर। वह कुछ भी नहीं सह सकती और तुम सब कुछ सह गुज़रती हो। उसकी कितनी इज़्ज़त है और तुम कितनी बदनाम हो। उसे सभी प्यार करते हैं और तुमसे नफ़रत। लेकिन मैं तुमसे नफ़रत नहीं करता, चंद्रमुखी। कर ही नहीं सकता।

دیوداس:
سمجھ تو لیا لیکن اِس سے بھی کیا ہوتا ہے؟ دیکھو نا میں پاروتی کو کتنا چاہتا ہوں اور وہ بھی مجھے کتنا چاہتی تھی، لیکن سماج نے نہیں چاہا۔ سوائے دکھ کے اور کیا ملا؟ اِتنا دکھ پا کے سوچا تھا کبھی اِن پھندوں میں نہیں پھنسوں گا، اور اپنی مرضی سے پھنسا بھی نہیں۔ تم نے ایسا کیوں کیا، چندرمکھی؟ کیوں اِس طرح باندھ لیا مجھے؟ شاید تم بھی پاروتی کی طرح ہی دکھ جھیلوگی۔ تم دونوں میں کتنا فرق ہے اور پھر بھی تم کتنی ایک سی ہو۔ ایک بڑی خوددار اور چنچل، دوسری شانت اور گمبھیر۔ وہ کچھ بھی نہیں سہہ سکتی اور تم سب کچھ سہہ گزرتی ہو۔ اُس کی کتنی عزت ہے اور تم کتنی بدنام ہو۔ اُسے سبھی پیار کرتے ہیں اور تم سے نفرت۔ لیکن میں تم سے نفرت نہیں کرتا، چندرمکھی۔ کر ہی نہیں سکتا۔

चंद्रमुखीः
मेरे लिए यही बहुत है। मुझे और कुछ नहीं चाहिए।

چندرمکھی:
میرے لیے یہی بہت ہے۔ مجھے اور کچھ نہیں چاہیے۔

चंद्रमुखी उसके पास से उठ जाती है। उसकी आँखों में आँसू हैं। अगला दृश्य। दिन। वह सामान बाँध रही है।

چندرمکھی اُس کے پہلو سے اُٹھ جاتی ہے۔ اُس کی آنکھوں میں آنسو ہیں۔
اگلا منظر۔ دن۔ وہ سامان باندھ رہی ہے۔

सेवकः
माँजी, गाड़ी आ गई।

نوکر:
ماجی، گاڑی آ گئی۔

चंद्रमुखीः
बिस्तर ले जाओ।

چندرمکھی:
بستر لے جاؤ۔

सेवक देवदास का बैग उठा लेता है।

ملازم دیوداس کا بیگ اُٹھا لیتا ہے۔

Reel Sixteen

Cut. Devdas enters the room.

Devdas:
Where did I leave my muffler?

Vo muffler na jaane kahaan rakh diya maine?

Chandramukhi:
On the chair.

Kursi pe hai.

Devdas:
Hmm?

Hmm?

(seeing her wipe away her tears)
You're crying, Chandramukhi?

Tum ro rahi ho, Chandramukhi?

Chandramukhi:
No.

Nahin toh.

Devdas:
Look up. Come on.

Zara moonh toh uthaao. Uthaao moonh.

Chandramukhi *(looking up, feigning a smile):*
See?

Dekho?

Devdas:
I don't need so many clothes and so much bedding.

Ye itne kapde-latte peti-bistar ki zaroorat toh nahin thi mujhe.

Chandramukhi:
I know whether or not you need them.

Zaroorat thi ya nahin, ye main tumse ziyaada jaanti hoon.

(coming towards him)
Listen…

Suno…

Devdas:
Hmm?

Hmm?

Chandramukhi:
You'll need someone to look after you. Take me with you.

Pardes mein ek daasi ki toh zaroorat hogi, mujhe bhi saath le chalo.

रील सोलह

देवदास कमरे में प्रवेश करता है।

देवदासः
वह मफ़लर न जाने कहाँ रख दिया मैंने?

चंद्रमुखीः
कुर्सी पे है।

देवदासः
हुँ?
(उसे आँसू पोंछते देख लेता है)
तुम रो रही हो, चंद्रमुखी?

चंद्रमुखीः
नहीं तो।

देवदासः
ज़रा मुँह तो उठाओ। उठाओ मुँह।

चंद्रमुखी *(ऊपर देखती है, फीकी मुस्कुराहट से):*
देखो?

देवदासः
यह इतने कपड़े-लत्ते पेटी-बिस्तर की ज़रूरत तो नहीं थी मुझे।

चंद्रमुखीः
ज़रूरत थी या नहीं। यह मैं तुमसे ज़्यादा जानती हूँ।
(वह उसके पास जाती है)
सुनो...

देवदासः
हुँ?

चंद्रमुखीः
परदेस में एक दासी की तो ज़रूरत होगी, मुझे भी साथ ले चलो।

ریل سولہ

کٹ۔ دیوداس کمرے میں داخل ہوتا ہے۔

دیوداس:
وہ مفلر نہ جانے کہاں رکھ دیا میں نے؟

چندرمکھی:
کرسی پہ ہے۔

دیوداس:
ہوں۔
(اُسے آنسو پونچھتا ہوا دیکھ لیتا ہے)
تم رو رہی ہو، چندرمکھی؟

چندرمکھی:
نہیں تو۔

دیوداس:
ذرا منہ تو اُٹھاؤ۔ اُٹھاؤ منہ۔

چندرمکھی (مسکرانے کی کوشش کرتے ہوئے سر اُٹھاتی ہے):
دیکھو۔

دیوداس:
یہ اِتنے کپڑے لتے، پیٹی بستر کی ضرورت تو نہیں تھی مجھے۔

چندرمکھی:
ضرورت تھی یا نہیں۔ یہ میں تم سے زیادہ جانتی ہوں۔
(چندرمکھی اُس کی طرف آتی ہے)
سنو۔۔۔

دیوداس:
ہوں؟

چندرمکھی:
پردیس میں ایک داسی کی تو ضرورت ہوگی، مجھے بھی ساتھ لے چلو۔

Devdas:
That is impossible, Chandramukhi. People will point fingers at you and I shan't be able to tolerate that.

Ye ho hi nahin sakta, Chandramukhi. Duniya tum par ungliyaan uthaayegi aur ye main bardaasht nahin kar sakunga.

Chandramukhi:
I'm very worried. You aren't well. How will you travel alone? How will you manage?

Magar mujhe bahot fikr ho rahi hai. Tumhaari tabiyat achi nahin. Pardes mein akele kaise jaaoge? Kaise rahoge?

Devdas:
I have written to Dharamdas. He'll meet me at the station.

Maine Dharamdas ko khat likh diya hai. Vo station pe mujhe mil jaayega.

Chandramukhi:
Will you promise me something?

Mujhe ek vardaan doge?

Devdas:
What is it?

Kya?

Chandramukhi:
Never drink again.

Ab kabhi sharaab nahin piyoge.

Devdas:
I can't promise that, Chandramukhi. But I will not forget what you ask.

Vaada toh nahin karta, Chandramukhi, lekin tumhaari baat yaad zaroor rakhunga.

Chandramukhi:
Listen.

Suno.

(holding his hands)
Wherever you are, if you fall ill, let this servant know.

Jahaan bhi raho agar tumhaara shareer zara bhi kharaab ho, toh is daasi ko zaroor khabar de dena.

Devdas *(giving her a bundle of notes):*
Chandramukhi, keep this.

Acha, Chandramukhi. Dekho, ye…ye rakh lo apne paas.

Chandramukhi:
No. It isn't necessary. I don't need it.

Nahin, nahin. Ab iski zaroorat nahin.

Devdas:
Let me be the judge of that. Look, Chandramukhi, life is unpredictable. Do you want to end up destitute? Keep it. Don't say another word.

Zaroorat hai ya nahin ye toh main jaanta hoon. Dekho, Chandramukhi, jeene ka toh koi bharosa nahin, tum kya manjdhaar mein doobogi? Ye apne paas rakh lo aur kuch matt kaho.

देवदासः
यह हो ही नहीं सकता, चंद्रमुखी। दुनिया तुम पर उँगलियाँ उठाएगी और यह मैं बरदाश्त नहीं कर सकूँगा।

चंद्रमुखीः
मगर मुझे बहुत फ़िक्र हो रही है। तुम्हारी तबियत अच्छी नहीं। परदेस में अकेले कैसे जाओगे, कैसे रहोगे?

देवदासः
मैंने धरमदास को ख़त लिख दिया है। वह स्टेशन पे मुझे मिल जाएगा।

चंद्रमुखीः
मुझे एक वरदान दोगे?

देवदासः
क्या?

चंद्रमुखीः
अब कभी शराब नहीं पियोगे।

देवदासः
वादा तो नहीं करता, चंद्रमुखी, लेकिन तुम्हारी बात याद ज़रूर रखूँगा।

चंद्रमुखीः
सुनो।
(उसके हाथ पकड़ कर)
जहाँ भी रहो, अगर तुम्हारा शरीर ज़रा भी ख़राब हो, तो इस दासी को ज़रूर ख़बर दे देना।

देवदास *(उसे नोटों का बंडल देते हुए):*
अच्छा, चंद्रमुखी। देखो। यह...यह रख लो अपने पास।

चंद्रमुखीः
नहीं, नहीं। अब इसकी ज़रूरत नहीं।

देवदासः
ज़रूरत है या नहीं, यह तो मैं जानता हूँ। देखो, चंद्रमुखी, जीने का तो कोई भरोसा नहीं। तुम क्या मँझधार में डूबोगी? यह अपने पास रख लो और कुछ मत कहो।

دیوداس:
یہ ہو ہی نہیں سکتا، چندرمکھی۔ دنیا تم پر اُنگلیاں اُٹھائے گی اور یہ میں برداشت نہیں کر سکوں گا۔

چندرمکھی:
مگر مجھے بہت فکر ہو رہی ہے۔ تمہاری طبعیت اچھی نہیں۔ پردیس میں اکیلے کیسے جاؤ گے، کیسے رہو گے؟

دیوداس:
میں نے دھرم داس کو خط لکھ دیا ہے۔ وہ اسٹیشن پہ مجھے مل جائے گا۔

چندرمکھی:
مجھے ایک وردان دو گے؟

دیوداس:
کیا؟

چندرمکھی:
اب کبھی شراب نہیں پیو گے۔

دیوداس:
وعدہ تو نہیں کرتا، چندرمکھی، لیکن تمہاری بات یاد ضرور رکھوں گا۔

چندرمکھی:
سنو۔
(اُس کے ہاتھ تھام کر)
جہاں بھی رہو اگر تمہارا شریر ذرا بھی خراب ہو، تو اِس داسی کو ضرور خبر دے دینا۔

دیوداس (اُسے نوٹوں کا بنڈل دیتے ہوئے):
اچھا، چندرمکھی۔ دیکھو۔ یہ۔۔۔ یہ رکھ لو اپنے پاس۔

چندرمکھی:
نہیں، نہیں۔ اب اِس کی ضرورت نہیں۔

دیوداس:
ضرورت ہے یا نہیں یہ تو میں جانتا ہوں۔ دیکھو، چندرمکھی، جینے کا تو کوئی بھروسا نہیں۔ تم کیا منجدھار میں ڈوبو گی؟ یہ اپنے پاس رکھ لو اور کچھ مت کہو۔

She holds the money in her hand. Devdas is about to leave.

Chandramukhi:
Wait.

Zara thehro.

(she touches his feet in a sign of respect)
When will we meet again?

Ab phir kab milna hoga?

The scene is underscored by a ghazal sung by Mubarak Begum.

"He will never return, no matter how many times I call
Tell my desires to forget this dream."

"Vo na aayenge palat kar unhen laakh hum bulaayen
Meri hasraton se keh do ki ye khwaab bhool jaayen"

Devdas:
Who knows? But as long as I shall live, Chandramukhi, I will never forget you. I will always want to see you again. I don't know what the guardians of morality may say about you, but if there is union after death, I shall never be able to stay apart from you.

Kaun jaane? Par jab tak main zinda hoon, Chandramukhi, main tumhen kabhi nahin bhool sakunga. Tumhen dekhne ki pyaas kabhi nahin bujhegi. Na jaane paap aur punn ke vichaar karne waale tumhaare baare mein kya faisla karen, lekin agar marne ke baad mel hota hai toh main tumse kabhi door nahin reh paaunga.

Chandramukhi *(to herself):*
I shall spend this life in the hope of such a rebirth.

Usi ek janam ke intezaar mein ye zindagi guzaar doongi.

Background song sung by Mubarak Begum.

"If ever you should meet the Creator of this world
Ask Him what crime deserved such punishment (2)
He will never return, no matter how many times I call" (2)

"Agar is jahaan ka maalik kahin mil sakay toh poochen
Mili kaun si khata par humen is qadar sazaayen (2)
Vo na aayenge palat kar unhen laakh hum bulaayen"(2)

A background song underscores the scene. Devdas makes his way down the stairs. He pauses for a brief moment and then walks on. Tearful, Chandramukhi looks over her balcony. She goes into her room and closes the door behind her. Fade out.

नोटों का बंडल उसके हाथ में है। देवदास जाने वाला है।

चंद्रमुखीः
ज़रा ठहरो।
(श्रद्धा से उसके पैर छूकर हाथ माथे से लगाती है)
अब फिर कब मिलना होगा?

बैक ग्राउंड गीत में मुबारक बेगम की आवाज़।

''वह न आएँगे पलट कर उन्हें लाख हम बुलाएँ
मेरी हसरतों से कह दो कि यह ख़्वाब भूल जाएँ...''

देवदासः
कौन जाने? पर जब तक मैं ज़िंदा हूँ, चंद्रमुखी, मैं तुम्हें कभी नहीं भूल सकूँगा। तुम्हें देखने की प्यास कभी नहीं बुझेगी। न जाने पाप और पुण्य के विचार करने वाले तुम्हारे बारे में क्या फ़ैसला करें, लेकिन अगर मरने के बाद मेल होता है तो मैं तुमसे कभी दूर नहीं रह पाऊँगा।

चंद्रमुखी *(स्वयं से):*
उसी एक जन्म के इंतिज़ार में यह ज़िंदगी गुज़ार दूँगी।

स्वरः मुबारक बेगम। बैक ग्राउंड गीत

''अगर इस जहाँ का मालिक कहीं मिल सके तो पूछें
मिली कौन सी ख़ता पर हमें इस क़दर सज़ाएँ (२)
वह न आएँगे पलट कर उन्हें लाख हम बुलाएँ...'' (२)

देवदास नीचे उतरता है। एक पल के लिए ठहरता है फिर चला जाता है। अपने छज्जे से चंद्रमुखी उसे जाता देख रही है। उसकी आँखों में आँसू हैं। वह अपने कमरे में जाकर द्वार बंद कर लेती है। फ़ेड आउट।

وہ پیسے ہاتھوں میں تھامے کھڑی ہے۔ دیوداس روانہ ہونے کو ہو۔

چندرمکھی:
ذرا ٹھہرو۔
(چندرمکھی اُس کے پیر چھوتی ہے)
اب پھر کب ملنا ہوگا؟

منظرنامے میں مبارک بیگم کی آواز میں غزل۔

''وہ نہ آئیں گے پلٹ کر اُنھیں لاکھ ہم بلائیں
میری حسرتوں سے کہہ دو کہ یہ خواب بھول جائیں''

دیوداس:
کون جانے؟ پر جب تک میں زندہ ہوں، چندرمکھی، میں تمھیں کبھی نہیں بھول سکوں گا۔ تمھیں دیکھنے کی پیاس کبھی نہیں بجھے گی۔ نہ جانے پاپ اور پُن کے وچار کرنے والے تمہارے بارے میں کیا فیصلہ کریں، لیکن اگر مرنے کے بعد میل ہوتا ہے تو میں تم سے کبھی دور نہیں رہ پاؤں گا۔

چندرمکھی (خودکلامی):
اُسی ایک جنم کے انتظار میں یہ زندگی گزار دوں گی۔

آواز مبارک بیگم، بیک گراؤنڈ

''اگر اِس جہاں کا مالک کہیں مل سکے تو پوچھیں
ملی کون سی خطا پر ہمیں اِس قدر سزائیں (۲)
وہ نہ آئیں گے پلٹ کر اُنھیں لاکھ ہم بلائیں'' (۲)

دیوداس سیڑھیوں سے نیچے جا رہا ہے۔ ایک پل کے لیے وہ ٹھہرتا ہے پھر چلا جاتا ہے۔ بام پر سے چندرمکھی اُسے دیکھ رہی ہے۔ اُس کی آنکھوں میں آنسو ہیں۔ وہ اپنے کمرے میں جا کر دروازہ بند کر لیتی ہے۔ فیڈ آؤٹ۔

Fade in. A shot of a train tearing through the night. Dissolve. Dharamdas and Devdas are in their compartment.

Dharamdas:
Have you decided where we are going?

Kahaan jaana hai, kuch tai kiya?

Devdas:
No, I haven't decided anything.

Nahin abhi kuch tai nahin kiya.

Dharamdas:
Let us go to your mother in Banaras.

Toh phir Kashi chalo na ma ke paas.

Devdas:
No, Dharamda, I won't go to Banaras. I want to go somewhere far away.

Nahin, Dharamda, main Kashi nahin jaunga. Main kahin bahot door jaana chaahta hoon.

Dissolve from a mid-shot of Devdas to a montage of railway tracks and views from the window of a moving train. The signboards of many cities — Delhi, Madras, Bombay, Lahore — are superimposed on the images.

The montage ends in a dissolve. Night-time. A troubled Devdas is sitting in a train compartment. His memories haunt him.

Chandramukhi *(voice-over, repeat dialogue):*
"I know just how much Parvati must love you."

"Apni taraf se maine jaana Parvati tumhen kitna pyar karti hai."

Parvati *(voice-over, repeat dialogue):*
"If I am condemned for coming here in secret to you, then so be it."

"Agar is baat ke liye meri ninda ho ki main tumhaare paas chhup kar aayi thi, toh ye ninda mujhe na lagegi."

Night-time. A trail of steam-train smoke fills the sky. The train pulls into a station.

फ़ेड इन। रेलगाड़ी का एक शॉट जो रात के अंधेरे को चीरती हुई चली जा रही है। अगला दृश्य। धरमदास और देवदास डिब्बे में बैठे हैं।

धरमदासः
कहाँ जाना है, कुछ तय किया?

देवदासः
नहीं, अभी कुछ तय नहीं किया।

धरमदासः
तो फिर काशी चलो न माँ के पास।

देवदासः
नहीं, धरमदा, मैं काशी नहीं जाऊँगा। मैं कहीं बहुत दूर जाना चाहता हूँ।

अगले दृश्य में देवदास से होकर मिड-शॉट में रेल की पटरियाँ दिखाई दे रही हैं। एक मोनटाज में रेल की पटरियाँ चलती हुई रेलगाड़ी की खिड़की से दिखाई दे रही हैं। गुज़रते हुए शहरों दिल्ली, मदरास, बम्बई, लाहौर के नाम की तख़्तियाँ दिखाई देती हैं।

मोनटाज समाप्त होता है। अगला दृश्य। रात। रेल के डिब्बे में देवदास बेचैन-सा बैठा हुआ है। बीती यादें उसे सता रही हैं।

चंद्रमुखी *(वॉइस-ओवर, संवाद पुनरावृत्ति):*
''अपनी तरफ़ से मैंने जाना पार्वती तुम्हें कितना प्यार करती है।''

पार्वती *(वॉइस-ओवर, संवाद पुनरावृत्ति):*
''अगर इस बात के लिए मेरी निंदा हो कि मैं तुम्हारे पास छुप कर आई थी, तो यह निंदा मुझे न लगेगी।''

रात का समय। रेलगाड़ी से निकलता हुआ धुआँ आकाश पर छाता जा रहा है। गाड़ी एक स्टेशन पर रुकती है।

فیڈ اِن۔رات کی تاریکی میں ایک ٹرین چلی جارہی ہے۔
اگلا منظر۔دھرم داس اور دیوداس ایک ڈبے میں نظر آرہے ہیں۔

دھرم داس:
کہاں جانا ہے کچھ طے کیا؟

دیوداس:
نہیں ابھی کچھ طے نہیں کیا۔

دھرم داس:
تو پھر کاشی چلو نا ماں کے پاس۔

دیوداس:
نہیں، دھرم دا، میں کاشی نہیں جاؤں گا۔میں کہیں بہت دور جانا چاہتا ہوں۔

اگلے منظر میں دیوداس سے ہوکر مڈ شاٹ ریل کی پٹریاں نظر آرہی ہیں۔ایک مونتاج میں ریل کی پٹریاں چلتی ہوئی کھڑکی سے نظر آرہی ہیں۔گزرتے ہوئے شہروں، دہلی، مدراس، بمبئی، لاہور کے نام کی تختیاں نظر آتے ہیں۔

مونتاج کا اختتام ہوتا ہے۔اگلا منظر۔رات۔ٹرین کے ڈبے میں دیوداس بے چین سا بیٹھا ہوا ہے۔گزری ہوئی یادیں اُسے ستارہی ہیں۔

چندرمکھی (بازگشت، گزشتہ ڈائلاگ):
''اپنی طرف سے میں نے جانا پاروتی تمھیں کتنا پیار کرتی ہے۔''

پاروتی (بازگشت، گزشتہ ڈائلاگ):
''اگر اِس بات کے لیے میری نِندا ہو کہ میں تمہارے پاس چھپ کر آئی تھی، تو یہ نِندا مجھے نہ لگے گی۔''

رات۔ٹرین کے انجن سے نکلتا ہوا دھواں آسماں پر چھاتا جارہا ہے۔ٹرین ایک اسٹیشن پر رکتی ہے۔

Dharamdas *(exasperated)*:
Just tell me where you want to go.

Mujhe sirf itna bata do ki aakhir tum jaana kahaan chaahte ho?

Devdas:
I want to run away from myself, Dharamda.

Main apne aap se kahin bhaag jaana chaahta hoon, Dharamda.

Dharamdas:
I don't understand such senseless talk.

Tumhaari ye be-sar-pair ki baaten meri samajh mein nahin aati.

Devdas:
Dharamda.

Dharamda.

Dharamdas:
Yes?

Haan?

Devdas:
I won't eat. Buy yourself some food at the station.

Main khaana nahin khaaunga. Tum station se apne liye kuch le lo.

Dharamdas *(affectionately)*:
Why won't you eat? Have you a temperature again?

Tum khaana kyun nahin khaaoge? Phir bukhaar aa gaya kya?

Devdas *(pushing Dharamdas's hand away like a child)*:
No.

Nahin.

Dharamdas *(irritated again)*:
I'm not surprised you have a fever. What else do you expect, if you torture yourself like this? Deva, I warn you, continue this aimless wandering and I'll go home.

Bukhaar kyun na ho? Apne aap par itna zulm karoge toh aur kya hoga? Deva, main kahe deta hoon agar isi tarah tum din-raat ghoomte rahe toh main gaaon waapas laut jaaunga.

Devdas *(taunting, childlike)*:
Go! Go home, if you can.

Toh jaao. Ja sakte ho, toh jaao.

Dharamdas *(emotionally)*:
Yes. You know I can't leave you alone, that's why you taunt me. But I won't listen to you anymore. Tomorrow, at the next station, I will find you a doctor. Such fevers are bad.

Haan. Tum jaante ho na ki main tumhen akela chhod kar nahin ja sakta, isi liye tum mujhe sata rahe ho. Lekin main tumhaari ek baat nahin maanunga. Kal subha kisi bhi baday station par utar kar tumhen doctor ko dikhlaaunga. Ye roz-roz ka bukhaar aana acha nahin hai.

धरमदास *(झुँझला कर):*
मुझे सिर्फ़ इतना बता दो कि आख़िर तुम जाना कहाँ चाहते हो?

دھرم داس (جھنجھلا کر):
مجھے صرف اِتنا بتا دو کہ آخر تم جانا کہاں چاہتے ہو؟

देवदासः
मैं अपने आपसे कहीं भाग जाना चाहता हूँ, धरमदा।

دیوداس:
میں اپنے آپ سے کہیں بھاگ جانا چاہتا ہوں، دھرم دا۔

धरमदासः
तुम्हारी यह बे-सर-पैर की बातें मेरी समझ में नहीं आतीं।

دھرم داس:
تمہاری یہ بے سر پیر کی باتیں میری سمجھ میں نہیں آتیں۔

देवदासः
धरमदा।

دیوداس:
دھرم دا۔

धरमदासः
हाँ?

دھرم داس:
ہاں؟

देवदासः
मैं खाना नहीं खाऊँगा। तुम स्टेशन से अपने लिए कुछ ले लो।

دیوداس:
میں کھانا نہیں کھاؤں گا۔ تم اسٹیشن سے اپنے لیے کچھ لے لو۔

धरमदास *(स्नेह से):*
तुम खाना क्यों नहीं खाओगे? फिर बुख़ार आ गया क्या?

دھرم داس (شفقت سے):
تم کھانا کیوں نہیں کھاؤ گے؟ پھر بخار آ گیا کیا؟

देवदास *(बच्चे की भाँति उसका हाथ हटा देता है):*
नहीं।

دیوداس (بچوں کی طرح اُس کا ہاتھ ہٹا دیتا ہے):
نہیں۔

धरमदास *(चिढ़ कर):*
बुख़ार क्यों न हो? अपने आप पर इतना ज़ुल्म करोगे तो और क्या होगा? देवा, मैं कहे देता हूँ, अगर इसी तरह तुम दिन-रात घूमते रहे तो मैं गाँव वापस लौट जाऊँगा।

دھرم داس (پھر جھنجھلا کر):
بخار کیوں نہ ہو؟ اپنے آپ پر اِتنا ظلم کرو گے تو اور کیا ہوگا؟ دیوا، میں کہے دیتا ہوں اگر اِسی طرح تم دن رات گھومتے رہے تو میں گاؤں واپس لوٹ جاؤں گا۔

देवदास *(बच्चे की भाँति इठला कर):*
तो जाओ। जा सकते हो, तो जाओ।

دیوداس (بچوں کی طرح اِٹھلا کر):
تو جاؤ، جا سکتے ہو، تو جاؤ۔

धरमदास *(भावुक होकर):*
हाँ। तुम जानते हो न कि मैं तुम्हें अकेला छोड़ कर नहीं जा सकता, इसीलिए तुम मुझे सता रहे हो। लेकिन मैं तुम्हारी एक बात नहीं मानूँगा। कल सुबह किसी भी बड़े स्टेशन पर उतर कर तुम्हें डॉक्टर को दिखलाऊँगा। यह रोज़-रोज़ का बुख़ार आना अच्छा नहीं है।

دھرم داس (جذباتی ہو کر):
ہاں۔ تم جانتے ہو نا کہ میں تمھیں اکیلا چھوڑ کر نہیں جا سکتا، اِسی لیے تم مجھے ستا رہے ہو۔ لیکن میں تمہاری ایک بات نہیں مانوں گا۔ کل صبح کسی بھی بڑے اسٹیشن پر اُتر کر تمھیں ڈاکٹر کو دکھلاؤں گا۔ یہ روز روز کا بخار آنا اچھا نہیں ہے۔

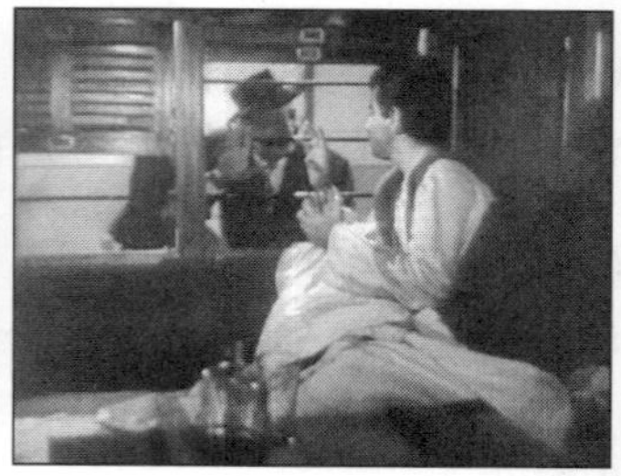

Devdas:
Dharamda, just switch off the light.

Dharamda, ye batti zara bujha dena.

Dharamdas:
All right. It's late. Sleep now. I'll go to my compartment.

Acha. Raat ziyaada ho gayi ab aaraam se so jaao. Main apne dabbe mein jaata hoon.

Devdas lies down as Dharamdas leaves. Just as the train is about to pull out of the station, a man enters Devdas's unlit compartment. The light is switched on, waking Devdas. He looks up and is surprised to see his old friend.

Chunni Babu:
Devdas!

Arey Devdas!

Devdas:
Chunni babu, it's you?

Arey Chunni babu, tum?

Chunni Babu:
What has happened to you? I could hardly recognise you. So, what news?

Ye kya soorat bana rakkhi hai? Pehchaane bhi nahin jaate. Kya khabar hai?

Devdas *(sitting up. He is pleased to see Chunni Babu):*
The only news is that I'm still alive. And you?

Khabar bas yahi hai ki zinda hain. Tum yahaan kaise?

Chunni Babu:
Calcutta didn't suit me. I'm working in Delhi now. I'm travelling on business. Here today, gone tomorrow. But where are you going?

Bhai, Kalkatta humen raas nahin aaya. Dilli mein ek naukri kar rakkhi hai, uss silsilay mein daure par ja rahe hain. Aaj yaahan, kal wahaan. Tum kahaan ja rahe ho?

Devdas:
I haven't decided yet.

Ye abhi kuch tai nahin kiya.

देवदासः
धरमदा, यह बत्ती ज़रा बुझा देना।

धरमदासः
अच्छा। रात ज़्यादा हो गई। अब आराम से सो जाओ। मैं अपने डब्बे में जाता हूँ।

धरमदास चला जाता है। रेलगाड़ी सीटी के साथ रवाना होती है। एक व्यक्ति अंधेरे डिब्बे में प्रवेश करता है। बत्ती के जलते ही देवदास की आँख खुल जाती है। उसे यह देख कर आश्चर्य होता है कि वह व्यक्ति उसका पुराना मित्र है।

चुन्नी बाबूः
अरे देवदास!

देवदासः
अरे चुन्नी बाबू, तुम?

चुन्नी बाबूः
यह क्या सूरत बना रखी है? पहचाने भी नहीं जाते। क्या ख़बर है?

देवदास *(बैठते हुए। चुन्नी बाबू को देख कर धीरे से मुस्कुराता है)*:
ख़बर बस यही है कि ज़िंदा हैं। तुम यहाँ कैसे?

चुन्नी बाबूः
भाई, कलकत्ता हमें रास नहीं आया। दिल्ली में एक नौकरी कर रखी है। उस सिलसिले में दौरे पर जा रहे हैं। आज यहाँ, कल वहाँ। तुम कहाँ जा रहे हो?

देवदासः
यह अभी कुछ तय नहीं किया।

دیوداس:
دھرم دا، یہ بتّی ذرا بجھا دینا۔

دھرم داس:
اچھا۔ رات زیادہ ہوگئی ہے اب آرام سے سو جاؤ۔ میں اپنے ڈبّے میں جاتا ہوں۔

دھرم داس چلا جاتا ہے۔ سیٹی بجاتی ہوئی ٹرین اسٹیشن سے روانہ ہونے کو ہوتی ہے کہ ایک شخص تاریک ڈبے میں داخل ہوتا ہے۔ بتی جلانے پر دیوداس کی آنکھ کھل جاتی ہے۔ اُسے یہ دیکھ کر حیرت ہوتی ہے کہ وہ شخص اُس کا پرانا دوست ہے۔

چُنّی بابو:
ارے دیوداس!

دیوداس:
ارے چُنّی بابو، تم؟

چُنّی بابو:
یہ کیا صورت بنا رکھی ہے؟ پہچانے بھی نہیں جاتے۔ کیا خبر ہے؟

دیوداس (اُٹھ کر بیٹھ جاتا ہے۔ چنّی بابو کو دیکھ کر ہلکے سے مسکراتا ہے):
خبر بس یہی ہے کہ زندہ ہیں۔ تم یہاں کیسے؟

چُنّی بابو:
بھئی، کلکتہ ہمیں راس نہیں آیا۔ دلّی میں ایک نوکری کر رکھی ہے، اُس سلسلے میں دورے پر جا رہے ہیں۔ آج یہاں، کل وہاں۔ تم کہاں جا رہے ہو؟

دیوداس:
یہ ابھی کچھ طے نہیں کیا۔

Chunni Babu:
Why not?

Maqsad?

Devdas:
Life has no purpose for me, Chunni babu.

Zindagi mein ab koi maqsad hi nahin raha, Chunni babu.

Chunni Babu *(smiling):*
You're the same Devdas. We're meeting after so long, we have to celebrate. What do you say?
(he pours two drinks)
I drink it neat now. Why waste money on soda? But it may be too strong for you. Shall I add some water?

Tum rahe vahi Devdas. Acha, thehro. Itne dinon ke baad mile hain mulaaqaat ko rangeen kiya jaaye. Kya khayaal hai?

Ab toh hum soda milaane ke bhi qaayel nahin rahe. Kyun fuzool soday pe paisa zaaye kiya jaayen? Lekin tumhen takleef hogi, thoda paani mila doon?

Devdas:
I've stopped drinking, Chunni babu.

Maine peena chhod diya hai, Chunni babu.

Chunni Babu:
Did someone make you promise?

Kisi ne apne sar ki qasam toh nahin dila di?

Devdas:
Nothing like that. I just don't drink.

Aisi koi baat nahin hai. Main bas nahin piyunga.

Chunni Babu:
Where are you taking that glass? I'll drink it for you. Is it an old affliction or a new one? Why won't you say anything?

Arey arey! Magar ye glass kahaan le jaate ho? Tum nahin piyoge toh main pi loonga. Acha ye vo puraana maraz hai ya koi naya rog laga liya? Arey kuch kehte kyun nahin?

Devdas:
What can I say, Chunni babu? Nothing pleases me. I have come to like this state of mind in which nothing pleases.

Kya kahun, Chunni babu? Mujhe toh kuch bhi acha nahin lagta. Ab toh bas yahi acha lagta hai ki kuch bhi acha na lagay.

Chunni Babu:
I understand what you're going through, Devdas. Don't think you are the only victim of such suffering. When heartache overwhelms, this is the only refuge.
(he pours himself another drink. Tempted, Devdas looks at the glass)
This alone puts out that fire. There is no other way.

Tumhen kya dukh hai main achi tarah samajhta hoon, Devdas. Lekin ye na samjho ki sirf tumhin is dukh ke shikaar ho. Jab is dukh ki aag seene mein bhadakti hai toh isi ka sahaara lena padta hai.
Isi aag se uss aag ko bujhaaya ja sakta hai, aur koi chaara nahin.

चुन्नी बाबू:
मक़सद?

देवदास :
ज़िंदगी में अब कोई मक़सद ही नहीं रहा, चुन्नी बाबू।

चुन्नी बाबू *(मुस्कुराते हुए):*
तुम रहे वही देवदास। अच्छा ठहरो। इतने दिनों के बाद मिले हैं मुलाक़ात को रंगीन किया जाए। क्या ख़्याल है?
(दो गिलासों में शराब डालता है)
अब तो हम सोडा मिलाने के भी क़ायल नहीं रहे। क्यों फ़ुज़ूल सोडे पे पैसा ज़ाए किया जाए? लेकिन तुम्हें तकलीफ़ होगी, थोड़ा पानी मिला दूँ?

देवदास:
मैंने पीना छोड़ दिया है, चुन्नी बाबू।

चुन्नी बाबू:
किसी ने अपने सर की क़सम तो नहीं दिला दी?

देवदास:
ऐसी कोई बात नहीं है, मैं बस नहीं पिऊँगा।

चुन्नी बाबू:
अरे अरे! मगर यह गिलास कहाँ ले जाते हो? तुम नहीं पियोगे तो मैं पी लूँगा। अच्छा यह वह पुराना मर्ज़ है या कोई नया रोग लगा लिया? अरे कुछ कहते क्यों नहीं?

देवदास:
क्या कहूँ, चुन्नी बाबू? मुझे तो कुछ भी अच्छा नहीं लगता। अब तो बस यही अच्छा लगता है कि कुछ भी अच्छा न लगे।

चुन्नी बाबू:
तुम्हें क्या दु:ख है मैं अच्छी तरह समझता हूँ, देवदास। लेकिन यह न समझो कि सिर्फ़ तुम ही इस दु:ख के शिकार हो। जब इस दु:ख की आग सीने में भड़कती है तो इसी का सहारा लेना पड़ता है।
(वह अपने लिए दूसरा गिलास तैयार करता है, देवदास ललचाई हुई नज़रों से गिलास देख रहा है)
इसी आग से उस आग को बुझाया जा सकता है, और कोई चारा नहीं।

چُنّی بابو:
مقصد؟

دیوداس:
زندگی میں اب کوئی مقصد ہی نہیں رہا، چُنّی بابو۔

چُنّی بابو (مسکراتے ہوئے):
تم رہے وہی دیوداس۔ اچھا ٹھہرو۔ اِتنے دنوں کے بعد ملے ہیں ملاقات کو رنگین کیا جائے۔ کیا خیال ہے؟
(دو گلاسوں میں شراب اُنڈیلتا ہے)
اب تو ہم سوڈا ملانے کے بھی قائل نہیں رہے۔ کیوں فضول سوڈے پہ پیسے ضائع کیے جائیں؟ لیکن تمھیں تکلیف ہوگی، تھوڑا پانی ملا دوں؟

دیوداس:
میں نے پینا چھوڑ دیا ہے، چُنّی بابو۔

چُنّی بابو:
کسی نے اپنے سر کی قسم تو نہیں دلا دی؟

دیوداس:
ایسی کوئی بات نہیں ہے، میں بس نہیں پیوں گا۔

چُنّی بابو:
ارے ارے مگر یہ گلاس کہاں لے جاتے ہو؟ تم نہیں پیوگے تو میں پی لوں گا۔ اچھا یہ وہ پرانا مرض ہے یا کوئی نیا روگ لگا لیا؟ ارے کچھ کہتے کیوں نہیں؟

دیوداس:
کیا کہوں، چُنّی بابو؟ مجھے تو کچھ بھی اچھا نہیں لگتا۔ اب تو بس یہی اچھا لگتا ہے کہ کچھ بھی اچھا نہ لگے۔

چُنّی بابو:
تمھیں کیا دکھ ہے میں اچھی طرح سمجھتا ہوں، دیوداس۔ لیکن یہ نہ سمجھو کہ صرف تم ہی اس دکھ کے شکار ہو۔ جب اِس دکھ کی آگ سینے میں بھڑکتی ہے تو اِسی کا سہارا لینا پڑتا ہے۔
(وہ اپنے لیے دوسرا جام تیار کرتا ہے، دیوداس للچائی ہوئی نظروں سے جام کو تک رہا ہے۔)
اِسی آگ سے اُس آگ کو بجھایا جا سکتا ہے، اور کوئی چارہ نہیں۔

Devdas cannot stop himself. He takes the glass and gulps the drink down. Cut. The train driver adds coal to the burning furnace. Cut. The train makes its way through the night. Dissolve.

The next day. The train is at a station. Chunni Babu and Devdas are drunk and half-asleep. The guard on the platform blows a whistle. Chunni Babu wakes up with a start.

Chunni Babu:
Devdas, have some more. Ah! This is where I'm supposed to get off. I'll leave the bottle.

Arey Devdas, thodi aur piyo na yaar. Aur piyo. Arey hum ko toh yahin utarna tha. Ye botal yahin chhode jaata hoon.

Devdas:
Oh...

Arey...

Chunni Babu:
If we live, we'll meet again, friend.

Zinda rahenge toh phir milenge, dost.

Chunni Babu alights the train. He smiles at Devdas through the window and disappears. Devdas is alone in the compartment.

Devdas *(to himself):*
Why does this thirst never get quenched? This never-ending thirst.

Ye pyaas kyun nahin bujhti? Ye kabhi na khatam honay waali pyaas.

Devdas reaches for the bottle of alcohol that Chunni Babu has left behind and collapses onto the compartment floor. Fade out.

Reel Seventeen

Fade in. Dawn. The train pulls into a small-town station. Dharamdas sees Devdas lying on the floor of the compartment. He rushes in.

Dharamdas:
Devdas! What's wrong, Devdas? What happened?
(Devdas struggles to sit up)
Deva, have you been drinking again?

Devdas. Devdas! Kya hua, Devdas? Kya hua?

Deva, kya tumne sharaab pi li? Hein? Phir pi li?

Devdas:
I couldn't help it, Dharamda.

Mujh se raha nahin gaya, Dharamda.

देवदास अपने आप को रोक नहीं पाता। वह गिलास उठा कर पी जाता है। कट। इंजन चालक भट्टी में और कोयला झोंकता है। कट। रात के अंधेरे में रेलगाड़ी चली जा रही है।

डिज़ॉल्व। अगला दिन। एक स्टेशन पर रेलगाड़ी रुकती है। चुन्नी बाबू और देवदास नशे और नींद में हैं। प्लेटफ़ॉर्म पर खड़े गार्ड की सीटी पर चुन्नी बाबू चौंक कर उठता है।

चुन्नी बाबूः
अरे देवदास, थोड़ी और पियो न यार। और पियो। अरे हमको तो यहीं उतरना था। यह बोतल यहीं छोड़े जाता हूँ।

देवदासः
अरे...

चुन्नी बाबूः
ज़िंदा रहेंगे तो फिर मिलेंगे, दोस्त।

चुन्नी बाबू ट्रेन से उतर कर मुस्कुराता हुआ चला जाता है। देवदास अपने डिब्बे में अकेला है।

देवदास *(अपने-आप से):*
यह प्यास क्यों नहीं बुझती? यह कभी न ख़त्म होने वाली प्यास।

बोतल की ओर हाथ बढ़ाते हुए देवदास डिब्बे के फ़र्श पर निढाल होकर गिर पड़ता है। फ़ेड आउट।

रील सत्रह

अगला दृश्य। प्रातः। रेलगाड़ी एक छोटे स्टेशन पर रुकती है। देवदास को डिब्बे के फ़र्श पर पड़ा देख कर धरमदास तुरंत अंदर आता है।

धरमदासः
देवदास। देवदास! क्या हुआ, देवदास? क्या हुआ?
(देवदास उठने का प्रयत्न करता है)
देवा, क्या तुमने शराब पी ली? हैं? फिर पी ली?

देवदासः
मुझसे रहा नहीं गया, धरमदा।

دیوداس اپنے آپ کو روک نہیں پاتا۔ وہ گلاس اُٹھا کر پی جاتا ہے۔ کٹ۔ ٹرین ڈرائیور جلتے ہوئے انجن میں کوئلے جھونک رہا ہے۔ کٹ۔ رات کی تاریکی میں ٹرین چلی جا رہی ہے۔ ڈزالو۔

ڈزالو۔ اگلا دن۔ ٹرین ایک اسٹیشن پر رکتی ہے۔ چنی بابو اور دیوداس نشے اور غنودگی کی حالت میں ہیں۔ پلیٹ فارم پر کھڑے گارڈ کی سیٹی کی آواز پر چُنی بابو چونک کر جاگ جاتا ہے۔

چُنی بابو:
ارے دیوداس، تھوڑی اور پیو نا یار۔ اور پیو۔ ارے ہم کو تو یہیں اُترنا تھا۔ یہ بوتل یہیں چھوڑے جاتا ہوں۔

دیوداس:
ارے۔۔۔

چُنی بابو:
زندہ رہیں گے تو پھر ملیں گے، دوست۔

چُنی بابو ٹرین سے اُتر کر مسکراتا ہوا چلا جاتا ہے۔ دیوداس اپنے ڈبے میں تنہا ہے۔

دیوداس (خودکلامی):
یہ پیاس کیوں نہیں بجھتی؟ یہ کبھی نہ ختم ہونے والی پیاس۔

بوتل کی طرف ہاتھ بڑھاتے ہوئے دیوداس ڈبے کے فرش پر گر جاتا ہے۔ فیڈ آؤٹ۔

ریل سترہ

اگلا منظر۔ صبح صادق۔ ٹرین ایک چھوٹے سے اسٹیشن پر رکتی ہے۔ دیوداس کو ڈبے کے فرش پر پڑا دیکھ کر دھرم داس تیزی سے اندر آتا ہے۔

دھرم داس:
دیوداس۔ دیوداس! کیا ہوا، دیوداس؟ کیا ہوا؟
(دیوداس مشکل سے اُٹھتا ہے)
دیوا، کیا تم نے شراب پی لی؟ ہوں؟ پھر پی لی؟

دیوداس:
مجھ سے رہا نہیں گیا، دھرم دا۔

 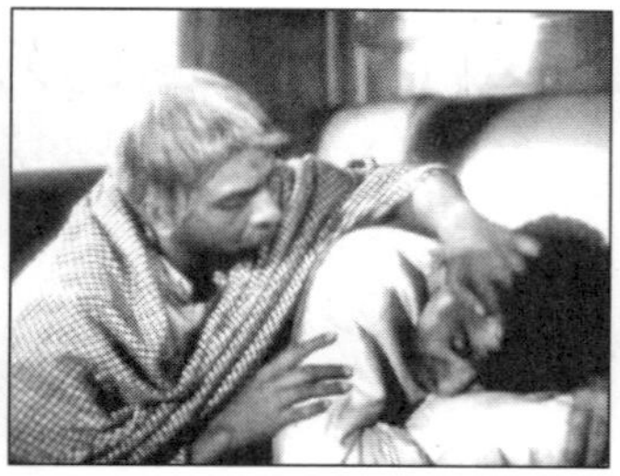 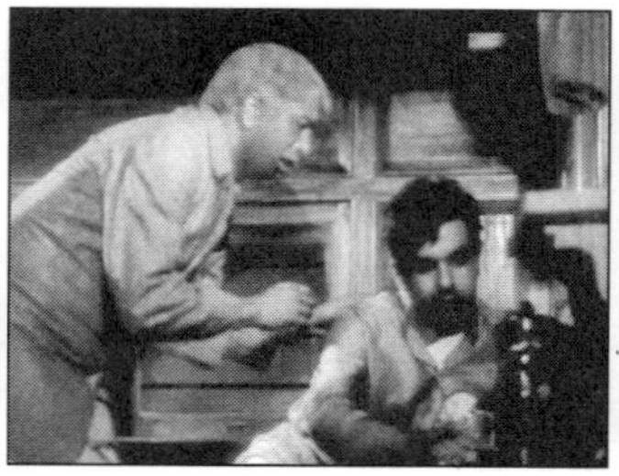  

Dharamdas: Oh no! You're burning with fever. Come on. Let's get down here. I'll get you a doctor.	Uff, tumhaara badan kitna jal raha hai. Chalo, isi station par utar chalen. Main tumhen kisi doctor ko dikhlaaunga.
Devdas: No, don't stop me, Dharamda. Let me keep going.	Nahin, mujhe roko matt, Dharamda. Mujhe chalne do.
Cut. A wide-shot of a moving train.	
Dharamdas: Don't drink anymore, Devdas. The doctor has warned you. You'll die if you drink another drop.	Ab matt piyo, Devdas. Doctor ne mana nahin kiya tha? Ek ghoont bhi sharaab pi toh mar jaaoge.
Devdas: I'll die whether or not I drink, Dharamda.	Nahin piyunga toh bhi mar jaaunga, Dharamda.
Shots of the train travelling relentlessly through night and day.	
Dharamdas: How is the fever, Deva?	Bukhaar kaisa hai, Deva?
Devdas: Hmm?	Hmm?
Dharamdas: How is the fever?	Bukhaar kaisa hai?
Devdas *(delirious with a fever):* Very…	Bahot…
Cut. The moving train.	

धरमदासः
उफ़! तुम्हारा बदन कितना जल रहा है। चलो, इसी स्टेशन पर उतर चलें। मैं तुम्हें किसी डॉक्टर को दिखलाऊँगा।

देवदासः
नहीं, मुझे रोको मत, धरमदा। मुझे चलने दो।

कट। चलती हुई रेलगाड़ी का वाइड-शॉट।

धरमदासः
अब मत पियो, देवदास। डॉक्टर ने मना नहीं किया था? एक घूँट भी शराब पी तो मर जाओगे।

देवदासः
नहीं पिऊँगा तो भी मर जाऊँगा, धरमदा।

दिन-रात रेलगाड़ी चलती चली जा रही है।

धरमदासः
बुख़ार कैसा है, देवा?

देवदासः
हुँ?

धरमदासः
बुख़ार कैसा है?

देवदास *(बुख़ार से तपते हुए):*
बहुत...

कट। रेलगाड़ी चली जा रही है।

دھرم داس:
اُف! تمہارا بدن کتنا جل رہا ہے۔ چلو، اِسی اسٹیشن پر اُتر چلیں۔ میں تمھیں کسی ڈاکٹر کو دکھلاؤں گا۔

دیوداس:
نہیں، مجھے روکو مت، دھرم دا۔ مجھے چلنے دو۔

کٹ۔ چلتی ہوئی ٹرین کا ایک وائڈ شاٹ۔

دھرم داس:
اب مت پیو، دیوداس۔ ڈاکٹر نے منع نہیں کیا تھا۔ ایک گھونٹ بھی شراب پی تو مر جاؤ گے۔

دیوداس:
نہیں پیوں گا تو بھی مر جاؤں گا، دھرم دا۔

رات اور دن ٹرین چلتی چلی جا رہی ہے۔

دھرم داس:
بخار کیسا ہے، دیوا؟

دیوداس:
ہوں؟

دھرم داس:
بخار کیسا ہے؟

دیوداس (بخار کی شدت میں):
بہت ۔۔۔

کٹ۔ ٹرین چلی جا رہی ہے۔

Dharamdas:
What can I do, Deva? The fever won't come down.

Main kya karoon, Deva? Tumhaara bukhaar toh utarta hi nahin hai.

Devdas:
My time has come to go, Dharamda.

Mere jaane ka waqt aa gaya hai, Dharamda.

Dharamdas:
Go where?

Kahaan jaane ka?

Devdas:
From this world.

Is duniya se.

Dharamdas:
Don't say that. For God's sake, don't say such things, Deva.

Matt kaho aisi baaten. Bhagwan ke liye aisi baaten matt kaho, Deva.

Devdas:
Why cry now, Dharamda?

Abhi se kyun rote ho, Dharamda?

Dharamdas:
If I don't cry, what else can I do? Do you think I have a heart of stone? I beg you, Deva, let's go back.

Rouon na toh aur kya karoon? Tum samajhte ho mera dil patthar ka hai. Tumhaare paaon padta hoon, Deva, laut chalo.

Devdas:
Where? To whom, Dharamda? Who do I have in this world to call my own?

Kahaan? Kis ke paas, Dharamda? Kaun hai mera is duniya mein?

Dharamdas:
What are you saying, Deva? You have so many.

Kya keh rahe ho, Deva? Tumhaara sab koi hai.

Devdas:
Yes. I have many. But I belong to no one, Dharamda.

Haan. Mera sab koi hai. Main hi kisi ka nahin, Dharamda.

Dharamdas:
I can't bear hearing you say that. Mogulsarai isn't far. We'll get down there and go to Banaras, to your mother.

Aise matt kaho, mujh se nahin suna jaata. Saamne Mogulsarai hai, wahin utar ke Kashi chale jaayenge ma ke paas.

धरमदासः
मैं क्या करूँ, देवा? तुम्हारा बुख़ार तो उतरता ही नहीं है।

دھرم داس:
میں کیا کروں، دیوا؟ تمہارا بخار تو اُترتا ہی نہیں ہے۔

देवदासः
मेरे जाने का वक़्त आ गया है, धरमदा।

دیوداس:
میرے جانے کا وقت آ گیا ہے، دھرم دا۔

धरमदासः
कहाँ जाने का?

دھرم داس:
کہاں جانے کا؟

देवदासः
इस दुनिया से।

دیوداس:
اِس دنیا سے۔

धरमदासः
मत कहो ऐसी बातें। भगवान के लिए ऐसी बातें मत कहो, देवा।

دھرم داس:
مت کہو ایسی باتیں، بھگوان کے لیے ایسی باتیں مت کہو، دیوا۔

देवदासः
अभी से क्यों रोते हो, धरमदा?

دیوداس:
ابھی سے کیوں روتے ہو، دھرم دا؟

धरमदासः
रोऊँ न तो और क्या करूँ? तुम समझते हो, मेरा दिल पत्थर का है? तुम्हारे पाँव पड़ता हूँ, देवा, लौट चलो।

دھرم داس:
روؤں نہ تو اور کیا کروں؟ تم سمجھتے ہو میرا دل پتھر کا ہے۔ تمہارے پاؤں پڑتا ہوں، دیوا، لوٹ چلو۔

देवदासः
कहाँ? किसके पास, धरमदा? कौन है मेरा इस दुनिया में?

دیوداس:
کہاں؟ کس کے پاس، دھرم دا؟ کون ہے میرا اِس دنیا میں؟

धरमदासः
क्या कह रहे हो, देवा? तुम्हारा सब कोई है।

دھرم داس:
کیا کہہ رہے ہو، دیوا؟ تمہارا سب کوئی ہے۔

देवदासः
हाँ। मेरा सब कोई है। मैं ही किसी का नहीं, धरमदा।

دیوداس:
ہاں۔ میرا سب کوئی ہے۔ میں ہی کسی کا نہیں، دھرم دا۔

धरमदासः
ऐसे मत कहो, मुझसे नहीं सुना जाता। सामने मुग़लसराय है, वहीं उतर के काशी चले जाएँगे माँ के पास।

دھرم داس:
ایسے مت کہو، مجھ سے نہیں سنا جاتا۔ سامنے مغل سرائے ہے، وہیں اُتر کے کاشی چلے جائیں گے ماں کے پاس۔

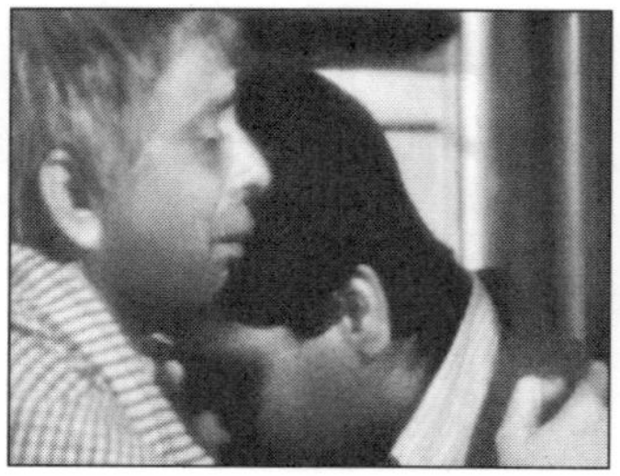  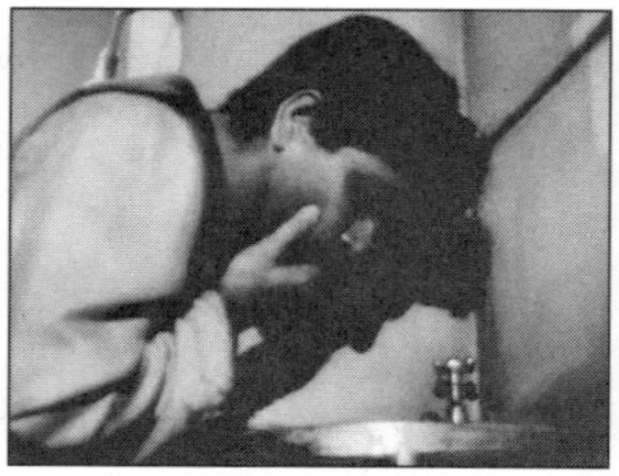 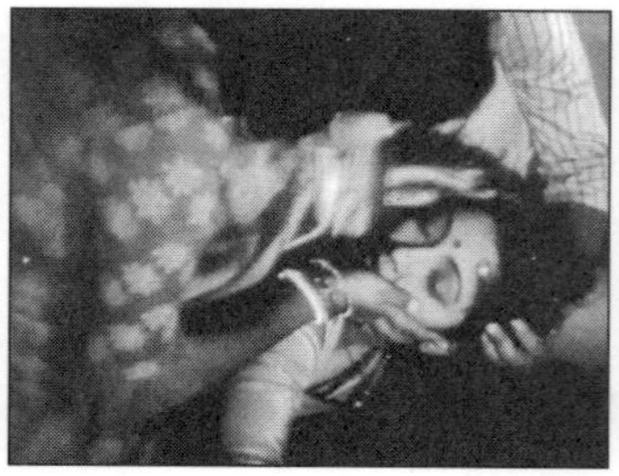 

Devdas:
To mother?

Ma?

Dharamdas:
Yes, to mother.

Haan, ma ke paas.

Devdas:
I'm a drunkard, a good-for-nothing, debauched…I will not show my disgraceful face to her.

Main ek sharaabi, bad-kaar, bad-chalan…ma ko ye kaala moonh nahin dikhaaunga, Dharamda.

Dharamdas *(holding the weak and ailing Devdas in his arms):*
Deva.

Deva.

Devdas:
Hmm?

Hmm?

Dharamdas:
Shall we go back to the village?

Phir gaaon hi laut chal.

Devdas:
To the village? Yes, that would be right. This empty shell of a body is of that soil, isn't it, Dharamda? Take it there.

Gaaon? Haan. Ye theek hai. Ye khokhla badan bhi toh wahin ki mitti hai na, Dharamda? Isay…isay wahin le chalo.

Cut. Night shots of the moving train against the sky. Devdas has a coughing fit in the middle of the night. He goes to the sink and spits blood.

Devdas:
Blood.

Khoon.

Whip pan. Parvati slips and falls.

Mahendra's wife:
Mother!

Ma!

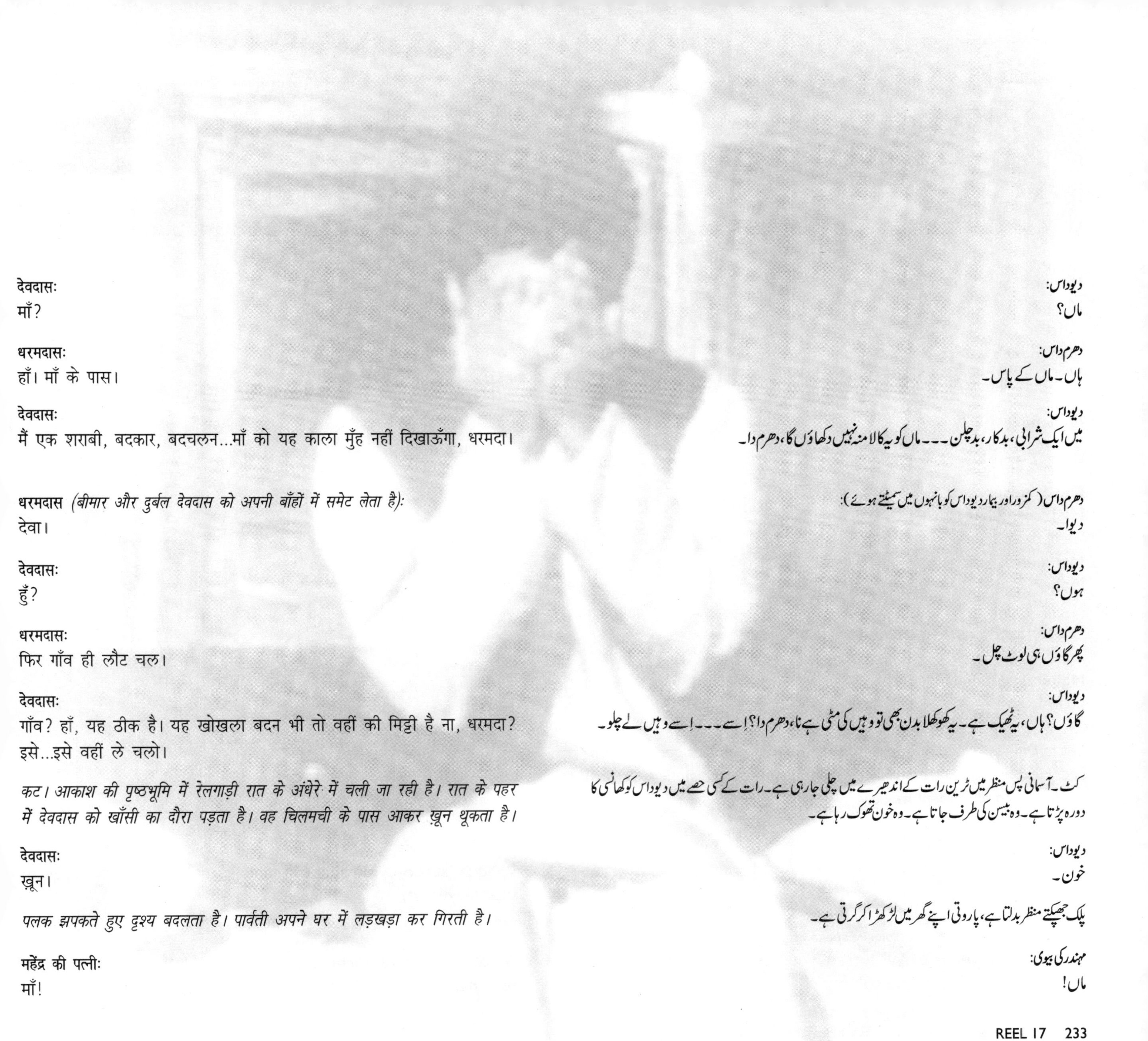

देवदासः
माँ?

धरमदासः
हाँ। माँ के पास।

देवदासः
मैं एक शराबी, बदकार, बदचलन...माँ को यह काला मुँह नहीं दिखाऊँगा, धरमदा।

धरमदास *(बीमार और दुर्बल देवदास को अपनी बाँहों में समेट लेता है):*
देवा।

देवदासः
हुँ?

धरमदासः
फिर गाँव ही लौट चल।

देवदासः
गाँव? हाँ, यह ठीक है। यह खोखला बदन भी तो वहीं की मिट्टी है ना, धरमदा? इसे...इसे वहीं ले चलो।

कट। आकाश की पृष्ठभूमि में रेलगाड़ी रात के अंधेरे में चली जा रही है। रात के पहर में देवदास को खाँसी का दौरा पड़ता है। वह चिलमची के पास आकर खून थूकता है।

देवदासः
खून।

पलक झपकते हुए दृश्य बदलता है। पार्वती अपने घर में लड़खड़ा कर गिरती है।

महेंद्र की पत्नीः
माँ!

دیوداس:
ماں؟

دھرم داس:
ہاں۔ماں کے پاس۔

دیوداس:
میں ایک شرابی، بدکار، بدچلن۔۔۔ماں کو یہ کالا منہ نہیں دکھاؤں گا، دھرم دا۔

دھرم داس (کمزور اور بیمار دیوداس کو بانہوں میں سمیٹتے ہوئے):
دیوا۔

دیوداس:
ہوں؟

دھرم داس:
پھر گاؤں ہی لوٹ چل۔

دیوداس:
گاؤں؟ ہاں، یہ ٹھیک ہے۔یہ کھوکھلا بدن بھی تو وہیں کی مٹی ہے نا، دھرم دا؟ اِسے۔۔۔اِسے وہیں لے چلو۔

کٹ۔آسمانی پس منظر میں ٹرین رات کے اندھیرے میں چلی جا رہی ہے۔رات کے کسی حصے میں دیوداس کو کھانسی کا دورہ پڑتا ہے۔وہ بیسن کی طرف جاتا ہے۔وہ خون تھوک رہا ہے۔

دیوداس:
خون۔

پلک جھپکتے منظر بدلتا ہے، پاروتی اپنے گھر میں لڑکھڑا کر گرتی ہے۔

مہندر کی بیوی:
ماں!

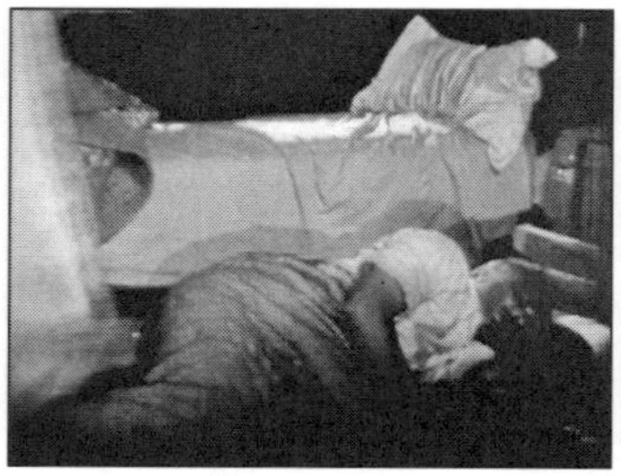
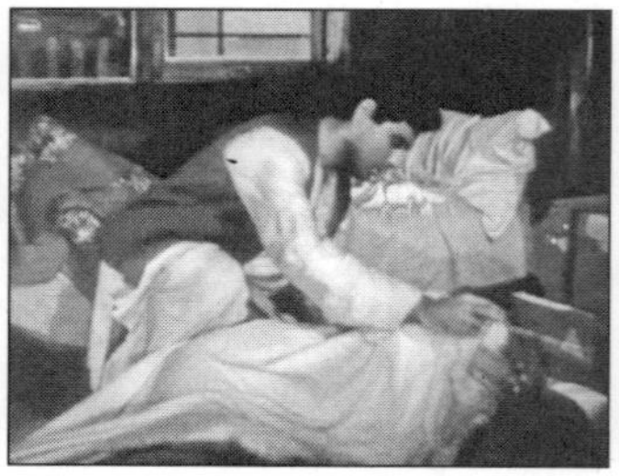

Mahendra:
Ma.

Ma!

Mahendra's wife:
Ma!

Ma!

Mahendra:
What's wrong, mother?

Kya hua, ma?

Old maidservant:
Mistress, what is it?

Maalkin, kya hua?

Mahendra:
Ma!

Ma!

The scar on Parvati's forehead starts to bleed.

Mahendra's wife:
Blood.

Khoon.

Cut to Devdas. The train whistles loudly. Devdas stumbles back onto his bed. He is in pain. Dissolve. Night. The train arrives at a station. Devdas sits by the compartment window.

Railway guard on the platform:
Pandua station. Alight here for Mirpur, Mirganj, Manekpur. (3)

Pandua station. Mirpur, Mirganj, Manekpur ki sawaariyaan utar jaayen. (3)

Devdas *(voice-over, repeat dialogue spoken to Parvati):*
"If looking after me will lessen your sorrow, I shall come. Before I die, I shall come to you."

"Agar meri sewa karne se tera dukh kam hota hai toh main tere haan aaunga. Marne se pehle ek baar zaroor aaunga."

महेंद्रः
माँ!

महेंद्र की पत्नीः
माँ!

महेंद्रः
क्या हुआ, माँ?

बूढ़ी सेविकाः
मालकिन, क्या हुआ?

महेंद्रः
माँ!

पार्वती के माथे के निशान से ख़ून बहने लगता है।

महेंद्र की पत्नीः
ख़ून।

कट। रेलगाड़ी की तेज़ सीटी सुनाई देती है। देवदास लड़खड़ा कर अपने बिस्तर पर गिर जाता है। वह बहुत पीड़ा में है। अगला दृश्य। रात। रेलगाड़ी एक स्टेशन पर रुक रही है। देवदास डिब्बे की खिड़की से लगा बैठा है।

रेल्वे का गार्डः
पांडुआ स्टेशन। मीरपुर, मीरगंज, मानेकपुर की सवारियाँ उतर जाएँ। (३)

देवदास *(वॉइस-ओवर, संवाद पुनरावृत्ति, जो देवदास ने पार्वती से कहे थे)*
''अगर मेरी सेवा करने से तेरा दुःख कम होता है तो मैं तेरे यहाँ आऊँगा। मरने से पहले एक बार ज़रूर आऊँगा।''

مہندر:
ماں!

مہندر کی بیوی:
ماں!

مہندر:
کیا ہوا، ماں؟

بوڑھی نوکرانی:
مالکن، کیا ہوا؟

مہندر:
ماں!

پاروتی کے ماتھے کے نشان سے خون بہہ رہا ہے

مہندر کی بیوی:
خون۔

کٹ۔ دیوداس۔ ٹرین کی تیز سیٹی سنائی دے رہی ہے۔ دیوداس لڑکھڑا کر اپنے بستر پر گر جاتا ہے۔ وہ سخت تکلیف میں ہے۔ اگلا منظر۔ رات۔ ٹرین ایک اسٹیشن پر رک رہی ہے۔ دیوداس ڈبے کی کھڑکی سے لگا بیٹھا ہے۔

ریلوے گارڈ:
پانڈوا اسٹیشن، میر پور، میر گنج، مانک پور کی سواریاں اُتر جائیں۔ (۳)

دیوداس (پاروتی سے کہی ہوئی باتوں کی بازگشت):
''اگر میری سیوا کرنے سے تیرا دکھ کم ہوتا ہے تو میں تیرے ہاں آؤں گا۔ مرنے سے پہلے ایک بار ضرور آؤں گا''۔

Devdas takes off his shawl and gently covers Dharamdas who is fast asleep on the compartment floor. He puts on his coat and gets off the train. Dissolve.

Devdas walks with great difficulty. He makes his way out of the deserted Pandua station. He sees a bullock cart driver asleep in his cart.

Devdas:
Driver! Brother…

Gaadi-waale! O bhai, gaadi-waale.

Driver *(unidentified actor):*
Hmm?

Hmm?

Devdas:
Will you take me to Manekpur?

Manekpur chaloge?

Driver *(still lying down):*
Manekpur? Sir, it's far away, and the road is very bad. I won't go in this dark night. Sleep here tonight. I'll take you in the morning.

Manekpur? Vo toh yahaan se bahot door hai, babuji, aur raasta bhi bada kharaab hai. Main toh is andheri raat mein nahin jaaunga. Raat ko yahin so jaayiye, kal subha le chalunga.

Devdas:
I haven't that much time, brother.

Mere paas itna waqt nahin hai, bhai.

Driver:
What, sir?

Ji?

Devdas:
I have to go there. I'll give you lots of money. Take me there.

Dekho, mujhe wahaan jaana hi hai. Main tumhen bahot se paise doonga, mujhe wahaan le chalo.

Driver *(getting up quickly):*
Sir, come. Sit at the back.

Aayiye, aayiye, aayiye, babuji. Baithiye, baithiye. Aayiye, baithiye.

Dissolve. The bullock cart makes its way to Manekpur. It is a dark night. A lantern swings at the back of the cart, throwing dappled light onto Devdas's face.

देवदास अपना शाल उतार कर डिब्बे के फ़र्श पर गहरी नींद सोए धरमदास पर प्यार से डालता है। कोट पहन कर रेलगाड़ी से उतर जाता है।

دیوداس اپنی شال اُتار کر پیار سے فرش پر گہری نیند سوئے ہوئے دھرم داس کو اُڑھا دیتا ہے۔ کوٹ پہن کر وہ ٹرین کے ڈبے سے اُتر جاتا ہے۔ ڈزالو۔ بڑی مشکلوں سے چلتا ہوا دیوداس ویران پانڈوا اسٹیشن سے باہر نکل آتا ہے۔ ایک بیل گاڑی میں گاڑی بان گہری نیند سو رہا ہے۔

डिज़ॉल्व। बड़ी कठिनाई से, लड़खड़ाता हुआ वह वीरान पांडुआ स्टेशन से बाहर निकल आता है। उसे एक बैलगाड़ी दिखाई देती है। कोचवान सोया हुआ है।

देवदासः
गाड़ीवाले! ओ भाई, गाड़ीवाले।

دیوداس:
گاڑی والے! او بھائی، گاڑی والے۔

गाड़ीवाला *(कलाकार अज्ञात):*
हुँ?

گاڑی والا (اداکار، نامعلوم):
ہوں؟

देवदासः
मानेकपुर चलोगे?

دیوداس:
مانک پور چلو گے؟

गाड़ीवाला *(लेटे-लेटे):*
मानेकपुर? वह तो यहाँ से बहुत दूर है, बाबूजी, और रास्ता भी बड़ा ख़राब है। मैं तो इस अँधेरी रात में नहीं जाऊँगा। रात को यहीं सो जाइए, कल सुबह ले चलूँगा।

گاڑی والا (لیٹے ہوئے):
مانک پور؟ وہ تو یہاں سے بہت دور ہے، بابو جی، اور راستہ بھی بڑا خراب ہے۔ میں تو اِس اندھیری رات میں نہیں جاؤں گا۔ رات کو یہیں سو جایئے، کل صبح لے چلوں گا۔

देवदासः
मेरे पास इतना वक़्त नहीं है, भाई।

دیوداس:
میرے پاس اِتنا وقت نہیں ہے، بھائی۔

गाड़ीवालाः
जी?

گاڑی والا:
جی؟

देवदासः
देखो, मुझे वहाँ जाना ही है। मैं तुम्हें बहुत से पैसे दूँगा, मुझे वहाँ ले चलो।

دیوداس:
دیکھو، مجھے وہاں جانا ہی ہے۔ میں تمھیں بہت سے پیسے دوں گا، مجھے وہاں لے چلو۔

गाड़ीवाला *(तुरंत उठ कर):*
आइए, आइए, आइए, बाबूजी। बैठिए, बैठिए, आइए। बैठिए।

گاڑی والا (اُٹھ بیٹھتا ہے):
آیئے، آیئے، آیئے، بابو جی، بیٹھیے، بیٹھیے، آیئے۔ بیٹھیے۔

अगला दृश्य। बैलगाड़ी मानेकपुर की ओर चली जा रही है। बहुत अंधेरी रात है। गाड़ी के पीछे एक लालटेन लटक रही है, जिसकी रोशनी उसके चेहरे पर पड़ती है।

اگلا منظر۔ بیل گاڑی مانک پور کی طرف چلی جا رہی ہے۔ رات تاریک ہے۔ گاڑی کے پیچھے ایک لالٹین لٹک رہی ہے جس کی روشنی کی چھوٹ اُس کے چہرے پر پڑ رہی ہے۔

Devdas:
How much longer, driver?

Aur kitni der hai, bhai gaadi-waale?

Driver:
We've just started, sir. We have a long way to go.

Babuji, abhi-abhi toh aap gaadi pe baithe hain. Abhi toh bahot door jaana hai.

Devdas drifts in and out of sleep. He hears voices from his past.

Young Parvati *(voice-over, repeat dialogue):*
Devdas. Devdas!

Devdas. Devdas!

The first superimposed flashback: Young Devdas is being taken to Calcutta for the first time. Young Parvati stands by the tree watching his horse carriage disappear into the distance.

Young Devdas *(repeat dialogue):*
Paro, I'll be back as soon as the holidays start.

Paro, chhuttiyaan hote hi main waapas chala aaunga.

When the flashback fades away, another flashback (superimposed images) unfolds in which Devdas and Parvati meet for the first time as adults.

Devdas *(repeat dialogue):*
How you've grown.

Kitni badi ho gayi ho tum.

They continue travelling into the night. Devdas has fallen asleep. His mother's voice wakes him.

Harimati Devi *(voice-over, repeat dialogue):*
Devdas!

Devdas!

देवदासः
और कितनी देर है, भाई गाड़ीवाले?

गाड़ीवालाः
बाबूजी, अभी-अभी तो आप गाड़ी पे बैठे हैं। अभी तो बहुत दूर जाना है।

देवदास सोता जागता रहता है। पिछली बातें उसके मस्तिष्क में गूँज रही हैं।

बालिका पार्वती *(वॉइस-ओवर, संवाद पुनरावृत्ति):*
देवदास। देवदास!

पहला फ़्लैश बैकः बाल देवदास को पहली बार कलकत्ता ले जा रहे हैं। बालिका पार्वती रास्ते के किनारे पेड़ों के झुंड में खड़ी उसकी घोड़ागाड़ी को दूर जाता देख रही है।

बाल देवदास *(संवाद पुनरावृत्ति):*
पारो, छुट्टियाँ होते ही मैं वापस चला आऊँगा।

फ़्लैश बैक के समाप्त होते ही दूसरा फ़्लैश बैक दिखाई देता है जिसमें जवान पार्वती से देवदास मिल रहा है।

देवदास *(संवाद पुनरावृत्ति):*
कितनी बड़ी हो गई हो तुम!

रात के अंधेरे में उसकी यात्रा जारी है। देवदास सोया-सा है। माँ की आवाज़ की गूँज पर उसकी आँख खुलती है।

हरिमति देवी *(वॉइस-ओवर, संवाद पुनरावृत्ति):*
देवदास!

دیوداس:
اور کتنی دیر ہے، بھائی گاڑی والے؟

گاڑی والا:
بابو جی، ابھی ابھی تو آپ گاڑی پہ بیٹھے ہیں۔ ابھی تو بہت دور جانا ہے۔

دیوداس سوتا جاگتا رہا ہے۔ ماضی کی آوازیں اُس کے ذہن میں گونج رہی ہیں۔

کمسن پاروتی (گزری ہوئی باتوں کی بازگشت):
دیوداس۔ دیوداس!

پہلا فلیش بیک: کمسن دیوداس کو پہلی بار کلکتہ لے جا رہے ہیں۔ کم عمر پاروتی درختوں کے جھنڈ میں کھڑی اُس کی گھوڑا گاڑی کو دور جاتا دیکھ رہی ہے۔

کمسن دیوداس (بازگشت):
پارو، چھٹیاں ہوتے ہی میں واپس چلا آؤں گا۔

فلیش بیک کے ختم ہوتے ہی دوسرا فلیش بیک نظر آتا ہے جس میں نوجوان پاروتی سے دیوداس کی ملاقات ہو رہی ہے۔

دیوداس (گزشتہ ڈائلاگ):
کتنی بڑی ہو گئی ہو تم۔

رات کے اندھیرے میں اُس کا سفر جاری ہے۔ دیوداس پر غنودگی طاری ہے۔ ماں کی آواز کی گونج پر اُس کی آنکھ کھلتی ہے۔

ہری متی دیوی (گزشتہ ڈائلاگ کی بازگشت):
دیوداس!

 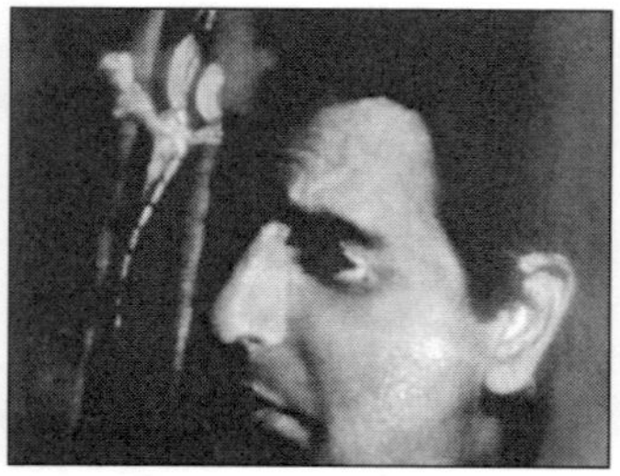 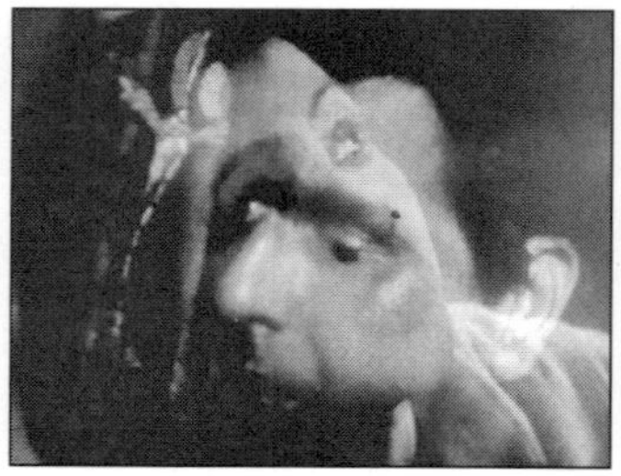  

Devdas:
Hmm?

Hmm?

The third flashback: Devdas realises he cannot persuade his parents to let him marry Parvati and so leaves for Calcutta. His mother tries to stop him.

Harimati Devi *(repeat dialogue):*
Devdas. Deva, where are you going, son?

Devdas. Deva, kahaan ja raha hai, beta?

Devdas *(repeat dialogue):*
I'm going to Calcutta, mother.

Kalkatte ja raha hoon, ma.

Harimati Devi *(calling after him, repeat dialogue):*
Devdas.

Devdas.

The fourth flashback: Chandramukhi sits at his feet, looking up at him. This was the last time they had met.

Chandramukhi *(repeat dialogue):*
When will we meet again?

Ab phir kab milna hoga?

The image of Chandramukhi fades. The fifth flashback shows the night Parvati came to him. She is kneeling at his feet, looking up at him.

Parvati *(repeat dialogue):*
Make a little room here for me, my lord.

Mujhe yahin thodi si jageh de do, mere devta.

Devdas:
Brother, will this road never end?

Arey bhai, ye raasta kya kabhi khatm nahin hoga?

देवदासः
हुँ?

तीसरा फ़्लैश बैकः देवदास के माता-पिता पार्वती से उसके विवाह के लिए तैयार नहीं हैं इसलिए वह कलकत्ते जा रहा है। उसकी माँ उसे रोक रही है।

हरिमति देवी *(संवाद पुनरावृत्ति):*
देवदास। देवा, कहाँ जा रहा है, बेटा?

देवदास *(संवाद पुनरावृत्ति):*
कलकत्ते जा रहा हूँ, माँ।

हरिमति देवी *(पुकारते हुए, संवाद पुनरावृत्ति):*
देवदास!

चौथा फ़्लैश बैकः चंद्रमुखी उसके चरनों में बैठी उसे ताक रही है। चंद्रमुखी से अंतिम भेंट।

चंद्रमुखी *(संवाद पुनरावृत्ति):*
अब फिर कब मिलना होगा?

चंद्रमुखी का चित्र लुप्त हो जाता हैं। पाँचवा फ़्लैश बैकः रात। पार्वती उसके पास आई है। घुटनों पर झुकी उसके चेहरे को ताक रही है।

पार्वती *(संवाद पुनरावृत्ति):*
मुझे यहीं थोड़ी-सी जगह दे दो, मेरे देवता।

देवदासः
अरे भाई, यह रास्ता क्या कभी ख़त्म नहीं होगा?

دیوداس:
ہوں؟

تیسرا فلیش بیک: دیوداس کے والدین پاروتی سے اُس کی شادی کے لیے راضی نہیں ہیں اس لیے وہ کلکتہ جا رہا ہے۔ اُس کی ماں اُسے روک رہی ہے۔

ہری متی دیوی *(گزشتہ ڈائلاگ کی بازگشت):*
دیوداس۔ دیوا، کہاں جا رہا ہے، بیٹا؟

دیوداس *(گزشتہ ڈائلاگ بازگشت):*
کلکتے جا رہا ہوں، ماں۔

ہری متی دیوی *(پکارتے ہوئے، گزشتہ ڈائلاگ، بازگشت):*
دیوداس!

چوتھا فلیش بیک: چندرمکھی اُس کے قدموں میں بیٹھی اُسے تک رہی ہے۔ آخری مرتبہ جب وہ ملے۔

چندرمکھی *(فلیش بیک، چندرمکھی سے آخری ملاقات کی بازگشت):*
اب پھر کب ملنا ہوگا؟

چندرمکھی کی تصویر مدغم ہو جاتی ہے۔ پانچواں فلیش بیک: رات۔ جب پاروتی اُس کے پاس آئی تھی۔ گھٹنوں پر جھکی وہ اُس کے چہرے کو دیکھ رہی ہے۔

پاروتی *(گزشتہ ڈائلاگ، بازگشت):*
مجھے یہیں تھوڑی سی جگہ دے دو، میرے دیوتا۔

دیوداس:
ارے بھائی، یہ راستہ کیا کبھی ختم نہیں ہوگا؟

  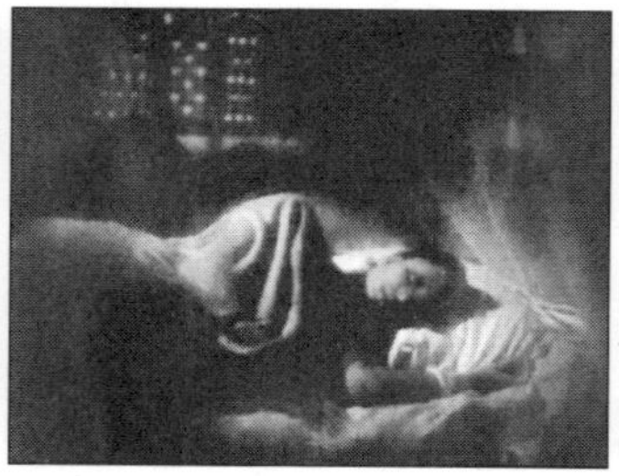  

Driver:
It will, sir. Of course it will end.

Hoga hujoor, jaroor khatm hoga.

The bullock cart moves slowly along the uneven road. Devdas is lying down. He looks up when he hears the sound of a shehnai and watches a wedding procession pass by. He falls asleep again.

Dissolve. They arrive in Manekpur at the home of Parvati's husband. The driver stops in front of the grand mansion near a tall tree. It is late at night.

Driver:
We've arrived at Manekpur, sir. This is the landlord's house. Where do you need to go? Have you fallen asleep? Sir!
(the driver gets down and tries to wake Devdas)
Sir, have you fallen asleep?
(Devdas is barely breathing)
We're at Manekpur. Which house do you want, sir?
(Devdas weakly hands him some money)
Why won't you speak? What's wrong, sir?

Babuji, Manekpur toh pahonch gaye. Ye raha zamindar saaheb ka makaan. Aap ko kahaan jaana hai? Arey so gaye, babuji, kya? Babuji!
Babuji, aap so gaye hain kya?

Babuji, hum Manekpur aa gaye. Aap ko kis ke ghar jaana hai, babuji?
Aap bolte kyun nahin? Kya hua, babuji?

Reel Eighteen

Parvati is lying awake in bed. She hears Devdas's whisper.

Devdas *(off-screen):*
Paro. Paro, I have come. I have come, Paro.
(she sits up. A shot of Devdas is inserted here. His lips are not moving. Cut back to Parvati)
Paro, I have come.

Paro. Paro, main aa gaya hoon. Main aa gaya hoon, Paro.

Paro, main aa gaya hoon.

The bedroom door gently rattles as though someone were knocking.

गाड़ीवालाः
होगा हुज़ूर, ज़रूर ख़त्म होगा

ऊबड़-खाबड़ रास्ते पर बैलगाड़ी हिचकोले लेती चली जा रही है। देवदास लेटा हुआ है। शहनाई और बारात की आवाज़ पर आँख उठा कर देखता है और फिर सो जाता है।

अगला दृश्य। अंत में बैलगाड़ी मानेकपुर पार्वती के पति के घर पहुँच जाती है। एक ऊँचे पेड़ के पास जहाँ हवेली है, गाड़ी ठहरती है। अब भी रात है।

गाड़ीवालाः
बाबूजी, मानेकपुर तो पहुँच गए। यह रहा ज़मींदार साहिब का मकान। आपको कहाँ जाना है? अरे सो गए, बाबूजी, क्या? बाबूजी!
(गाड़ीवाला उतर कर देवदास को जगाने आता है)
बाबूजी, आप सो गए हैं क्या?
(देवदास की साँसें रुक-रुक कर चल रही हैं)
बाबूजी, हम मानेकपुर आ गए। आपको किसके घर जाना है, बाबूजी?
(देवदास दुर्बल हाथों से उसे कुछ पैसे देता है)
आप बोलते क्यों नहीं? क्या हुआ, बाबूजी?

रील अठारह

बिस्तर पर पार्वती लेटी जाग रही है। उसके कानों में देवदास की आवाज़ आ रही है।

देवदास *(ऑफ-स्क्रीन)*:
पारो। पारो, मैं आ गया हूँ। मैं आ गया हूँ, पारो।
(वह बिस्तर पर उठ बैठती है। देवदास के शॉट दिखाई देते हैं लेकिन उसके होंठ नहीं हिल रहे हैं। कट। पार्वती)
पारो, मैं आ गया हूँ।

शयनकक्ष का द्वार जैसे कोई धीरे-धीरे खटखटा रहा है।

گاڑی والا:
ہوگا جور، جرور ختم ہوگا۔

اوبڑکھابڑ راستوں پر بیل گاڑی ہچکولے لیتی چلی جارہی ہے۔ دیوداس لیٹا ہوا ہے۔ شہنائی اور بارات کی آواز پر وہ آنکھ اُٹھا کر دیکھتا ہے اور پھر غنودگی کے عالم میں ڈوب جاتا ہے۔

اگلا منظر۔ آخرکار بیل گاڑی مانک پور پاروتی کے شوہر کے گھر پہنچ جاتی ہے۔ ایک اونچے درخت کے پاس جہاں حویلی ہے گاڑی ٹھہرتی ہے۔ اب بھی رات باقی ہے۔

گاڑی والا:
بابو جی، مانک پور تو پہنچ گئے۔ یہ رہا زمیندار صاحب کا مکان۔ آپ کو کہاں جانا ہے؟ ارے سو گئے، بابو جی، کیا؟ بابو جی!
(بیل گاڑی سے اُتر کر گاڑی والا اُسے جگانے آتا ہے)
بابو جی، آپ سو گئے ہیں کیا؟
(دیوداس کی سانسیں رک رک کر چل رہی ہیں)
بابو جی، ہم مانک پور آ گئے۔ آپ کو کس کے گھر جانا ہے، بابو جی؟
(دیوداس لرزتے ہاتھوں سے اُسے کچھ روپے دیتا ہے)
آپ بولتے کیوں نہیں؟ کیا ہوا، بابو جی؟

ریل اٹھارہ

بستر پر پاروتی پڑی جاگ رہی ہے۔ اُس کے کانوں میں دیوداس کی آواز آ رہی ہے۔

دیوداس (آف اسکرین):
پارو۔ پارو، میں آ گیا ہوں۔ میں آ گیا ہوں، پارو۔
(وہ بستر پر اُٹھ بیٹھتی ہے۔ دیوداس کے شاٹس دکھائی دیتے ہیں لیکن اُس کے ہونٹ ساکت ہیں۔ کٹ۔)
پارو، میں آ گیا ہوں۔

خواب گاہ کا دروازہ جیسے کوئی ہولے ہولے کھٹکھٹا رہا ہے۔

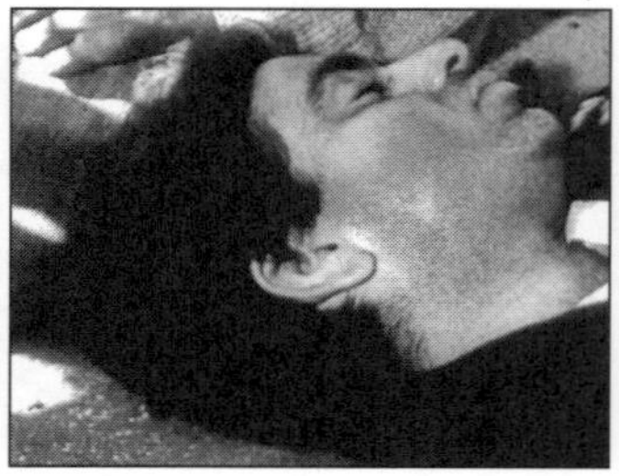

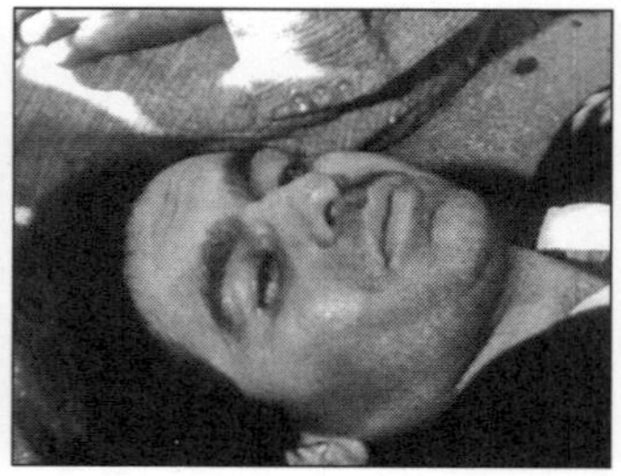

Parvati:
Who is it?

Kaun?

Devdas *(whisper, off-screen):*
Paro.

Paro.

Parvati goes to the balcony. It is a windy night. She looks into the distance but can see nothing. Her husband joins her.

Chowdhury:
Why are you standing here, Parvati?

Yahaan aa kar kyun khadi ho gayi, Parvati?

Parvati:
Someone called me.

Kisi ne mujhe pukaara na.

Chowdhury:
What are you saying? Who would call you at this hour?

Kya keh rahi ho? Itni raat mein kaun tumhen pukaarne aayega?

Parvati:
So, who…

Toh phir…

She turns and goes back into her room. Fade out.

Fade in. Day. Devdas has been made to lie on the stone seat around the tree outside Parvati's house. A villager comes and looks at him. The cart driver returns with a constable.

Driver:
It isn't my fault, I didn't want to bring him here…he was coughing all night.

Dekhiye sarkar, mera qusoor nahin. Main toh…ye raat ko bahot khaansi-waasi huwi.

पार्वती:
कौन?

देवदास *(ऑफ़-स्क्रीन):*
पारो।

पार्वती छज्जे पर आती है। तेज़ हवा चल रही है। वह बाहर देखने का प्रयत्न करती है, लेकिन कुछ दिखाई नहीं देता। उसका पति उसके पास आता है।

चौधरी:
यहाँ आकर क्यों खड़ी हो गई, पार्वती?

पार्वती:
किसी ने मुझे पुकारा ना।

चौधरी:
क्या कह रही हो? इतनी रात में कौन तुम्हें पुकारने आएगा?

पार्वती:
तो फिर...

वह मुड़ कर अपने कमरे में चली जाती है। फ़ेड आउट।

फ़ेड इन। दिन। पार्वती के घर के बाहर पेड़ के जगत पर देवदास को लिटा दिया गया है। एक गाँववाला आकर उसे देखता है। गाड़ीवाला एक हवलदार के साथ आता है।

गाड़ीवाला:
देखिए सरकार, मेरा क़सूर नहीं। मैं तो...यह रात को बहुत खाँसी-वाँसी हुई।

پاروتی:
کون؟

دیوداس (سرگوشی، آف اسکرین):
پارو۔

پاروتی جھروکے میں آتی ہے۔ تیز ہوائیں چل رہی ہیں۔ وہ باہر دیکھنے کی کوشش کرتی ہے مگر کچھ دکھائی نہیں دیتا۔ اُس کا شوہر اُس کے پاس آتا ہے۔

چودھری:
یہاں آکر کیوں کھڑی ہوگئی، پاروتی؟

پاروتی:
کسی نے مجھے پکارا نا۔

چودھری:
کیا کہہ رہی ہو؟ اتنی رات میں کون تمھیں پکارنے آئے گا؟

پاروتی:
تو پھر۔۔۔

وہ مڑکر اپنے کمرے میں چلی جاتی ہے۔ فیڈ آؤٹ۔

فیڈ ان۔ دن۔ پاروتی کے گھر کے باہر درخت کی جگت پر دیوداس کو لٹا دیا گیا ہے۔ ایک دیہاتی آکر اُسے دیکھتا ہے۔ گاڑی بان ایک حولدار کے ساتھ آتا ہے۔

گاڑی والا:
دیکھیے سرکار، میرا قصور نہیں میں۔۔۔ یہ رات کو بہت کھانسی واسی ہوئی۔

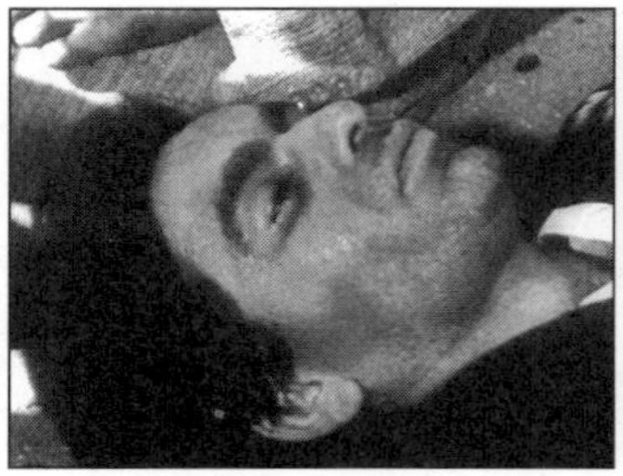   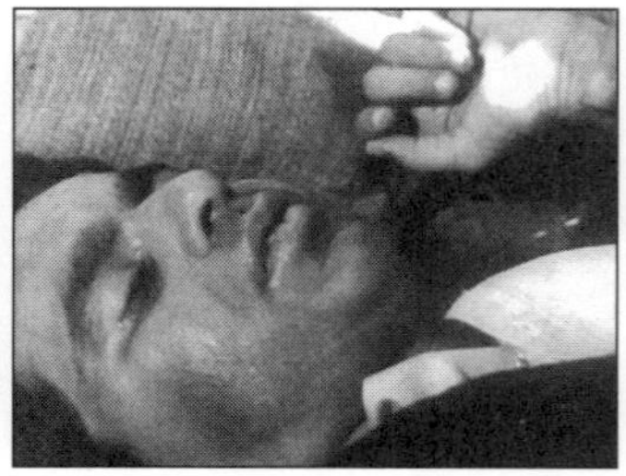 

Dissolve. Many villagers surround Devdas. Parvati comes to the balcony and sees the crowd. A maid enters.

Parvati:
Why are so many people gathered outside the gate?

Shyamu ki ma, baahar phaatak ke paas itne aadmi kyun jama huwe hain?

Maid:
I hear an ailing stranger has been lying near the gate all night. He is breathing his last.

Suna hai ki koi bimaar pardesi raat bhar phaatak ke paas pada hai. Bas ab do-chaar saansen aur lega.

Parvati:
Aah!

Aah!

Cut to a close-up of Devdas. He is in the throes of death. He looks up barely distinguishing the faces of the villagers who stare down at him. Throughout the scene prayers are chanted (off-screen). A single tear falls from Devdas's eye. Cut. Parvati is in her prayer room. She is uneasy and troubled. She hears a sound.

Parvati:
Who is it?

Kaun?

Mahendra's wife:
What is it, mother?

Kya hua, ma?

Parvati:
Nothing.

Kuch nahin.

अगला दृश्य। गाँववालों की भीड़ देवदास को घेरे हुए है। मंत्रों की ध्वनि सुनाई दे रही है। पार्वती छज्जे पर आती है और लोगों की भीड़ को देखती है। एक नौकरानी अंदर आती है।

पार्वतीः
श्यामू की माँ, बाहर फाटक के पास इतने आदमी क्यों जमा हुए हैं?

दासीः
सुना है कि कोई बीमार परदेसी रात भर फाटक के पास पड़ा रहा है। बस अब दो-चार साँसें और लेगा।

पार्वतीः
आह!

कट। देवदास का क्लोज़-अप। वह मौत की अंतिम हिचकियाँ ले रहा है। वह अपने चारों ओर खड़े गाँववालों को देखने का प्रयत्न करता है। ऑफ़-स्क्रीन, मंत्रों का जाप, दृश्य में सुनाई दे रहा है। उसकी आँखों से एक आँसू टपक पड़ता है। कट। पार्वती अपने पूजा के कमरे में है। उसे बेचैनी हो रही है। उसे एक आवाज़ सुनाई देती है।

पार्वतीः
कौन?

महेंद्र की पत्नीः
क्या हुआ, माँ?

पार्वतीः
कुछ नहीं।

اگلا منظر۔ دیہاتیوں کی بھیڑ دیوداس کے اطراف لگ گئی ہے۔ اشلوکوں کی آواز سنائی دے رہی ہے۔ پاروتی اپنے جھرونکے سے بھیڑ کو دیکھتی ہے۔ ایک ملازمہ آتی ہے۔

پاروتی:
شیاموکی ماں، باہر پھاٹک کے پاس اِتنے آدمی کیوں جمع ہوئے ہیں؟

نوکرانی:
سنا ہے کوئی بیمار پردیسی رات بھر پھاٹک کے پاس پڑا ہے۔ بس اب دو چار سانسیں اور لے گا۔

پاروتی:
آہ!

کٹ۔ دیوداس کا کلوزاپ۔ وہ موت کی آخری ہچکیاں لے رہا ہے۔ اپنے چاروں طرف کھڑے دیہاتیوں کو دیکھنے کی کی کوشش کرتا ہے۔ اشلوکوں کی آواز، آف اسکرین، منظرنامے میں سنائی دے رہی ہے۔ اُس کی آنکھوں سے ایک آنسو ٹپک پڑتا ہے۔ کٹ۔ پاروتی اپنے پوجا کے کمرے میں ہے۔ اُسے بے چینی محسوس ہو رہی ہے۔ اُسے آواز سنائی دیتی ہے۔

پاروتی:
کون؟

مہندر کی بیوی:
کیا ہوا، ماں؟

پاروتی:
کچھ نہیں۔

Mahendra's wife:
You seem unwell. Why don't you go upstairs and rest?

Aaj aap ki tabiyat theek nahin maaloom hoti. Jaayiye upar ja kar aaraam kijiye.

Parvati leaves the prayer room and goes upstairs to her room. She overhears two servants talking.

First servant:
Who knows if he was from here in a previous lifetime — but it seems as if the poor man came here only to die.

Na jaane punar-janam ki mitti kahaan ki thi, sirf yahaan marne ke liye be-chaara chala aaya tha.

Second servant:
Have you any idea where he was from?

Kuch pata chala, kahaan ka rehne waala tha?

First servant:
I hear he was from Talsonapur.

Suna hai vo Talsonapur ka rehne waala tha.

Parvati:
Who was from Talsonapur?

Kaun Talsonapur ka rehne waala tha?

First servant:
Mistress, a man has just died outside the gate. We were talking about him.

Maalkin, abhi-abhi baahar ek aadmi mar gaya. Usi ki baat kar raha hoon.

Parvati:
What was his name?

Kya naam tha?

First servant:
I don't know. Mahendra babu is coming back inside the house, he might know.

Mujhe maaloom nahin. Vo Mahendra babu wahin se aa rahe hain, shaayad unhen pata ho.

Parvati *(as Mahendra arrives):*
Mahendra, who has just died?

Mahendra, baahar kaun mara hai?

Mahendra:
I don't know for sure, mother, but the man who just died could be someone from your village — a Devdas Mukherjee.

Theek-theek toh pata nahin chala, ma, lekin shak hota hai aap ke gaaon ka koi Devdas Mukherjee mara hai.

Parvati *(ashen):*
Who?

Kaun?

महेंद्र की पत्नीः
आज आपकी तबियत ठीक नहीं मालूम होती। जाइए ऊपर जाकर आराम कीजिए।

مہندر کی بیوی:
آج آپ کی طبیعت ٹھیک نہیں معلوم ہوتی۔ جائیے اوپر جا کر آرام کیجیے۔

पार्वती पूजा के कमरे से निकल कर ऊपर अपने कमरे में जाती है। वह दो नौकरों को बात करते हुए सुनती है।

پوجا کے کمرے سے نکل کر پاروتی اوپر اپنے کمرے کی طرف جاتی ہے۔ دو ملازموں کو باتیں کرتے ہوئے وہ سنتی ہے۔

पहला सेवकः
न जाने पूर्व जन्म की मिट्टी कहाँ की थी। सिर्फ़ यहाँ मरने के लिए बेचारा चला आया था।

پہلا نوکر:
نہ جانے پورو جنم کی مٹی کہاں کی تھی، صرف یہاں مرنے کے لیے بے چارہ چلا آیا تھا۔

दूसरा सेवकः
कुछ पता चला, कहाँ का रहने वाला था?

دوسرا نوکر:
کچھ پتا چلا کہاں کا رہنے والا تھا؟

पहला सेवकः
सुना है वह तालसोनापुर का रहने वाला था।

پہلا نوکر:
سنا ہے وہ تال سونا پور کا رہنے والا تھا۔

पार्वतीः
कौन तालसोनापुर का रहने वाला था?

پاروتی:
کون تال سونا پور کا رہنے والا تھا؟

पहला सेवकः
मालकिन, अभी-अभी बाहर एक आदमी मर गया, उसी की बात कर रहा हूँ।

پہلا نوکر:
مالکن، ابھی ابھی باہر ایک آدمی مر گیا، اُسی کی بات کر رہا ہوں۔

पार्वतीः
क्या नाम था?

پاروتی:
کیا نام تھا؟

पहला सेवकः
मुझे मालूम नहीं। वह महेंद्र बाबू वहीं से आ रहे हैं। शायद उन्हें पता हो।

پہلا نوکر:
مجھے معلوم نہیں۔ وہ مہندر بابو وہیں سے آ رہے ہیں شاید اُنھیں پتا ہو۔

पार्वती *(महेंद्र को देख कर):*
महेंद्र, बाहर कौन मरा है?

پاروتی (مہندر کو دیکھ کر):
مہندر، باہر کون مرا ہے؟

महेंद्रः
ठीक-ठीक तो पता नहीं चला, माँ, लेकिन शक होता है, आपके गाँव का कोई देवदास मुखर्जी मरा है।

مہندر:
ٹھیک ٹھیک تو پتا نہیں چلا، ماں لیکن شک ہوتا ہے آپ کے گاؤں کا کوئی دیوداس مکھرجی مرا ہے۔

पार्वती *(ठंडी पड़ जाती है):*
कौन?

پاروتی (چہرے کا رنگ اُڑ جاتا ہے):
کون؟

Mahendra *(voice with echo-effect):* Devdas, from your village.	Aap ke gaaon ka Devdas.
Underscoring the scene is ominous drumming which soon develops into dramatic background music.	
Parvati: How do you know?	Kaise jaana?
Mahendra: There were two letters in his pocket, one letter was from Dwijodas Mukherjee…	Jaib mein do chitthiyaan thein. Ek Dwijodas Mukherjee ki…
Parvati: Yes, his elder brother.	Haan, unke bade bhai.
Mahendra: The other from Harimati Devi in Banaras.	Doosri Kashi se Harimati Devi.
Parvati: Yes, his mother.	Haan, unki ma.
Mahendra: He was wearing a blue stone ring.	Haath mein neelam ki anguthi thi.
Parvati: Yes, yes, his father gave it to him. I am going.	Haan, haan, taayaji ne di thi. Main jaa rahi hoon.
Mahendra: Where to? They must have taken him away by now.	Aap kahaan ja rahi hain? Ab tak toh log usay le bhi gaye honge.

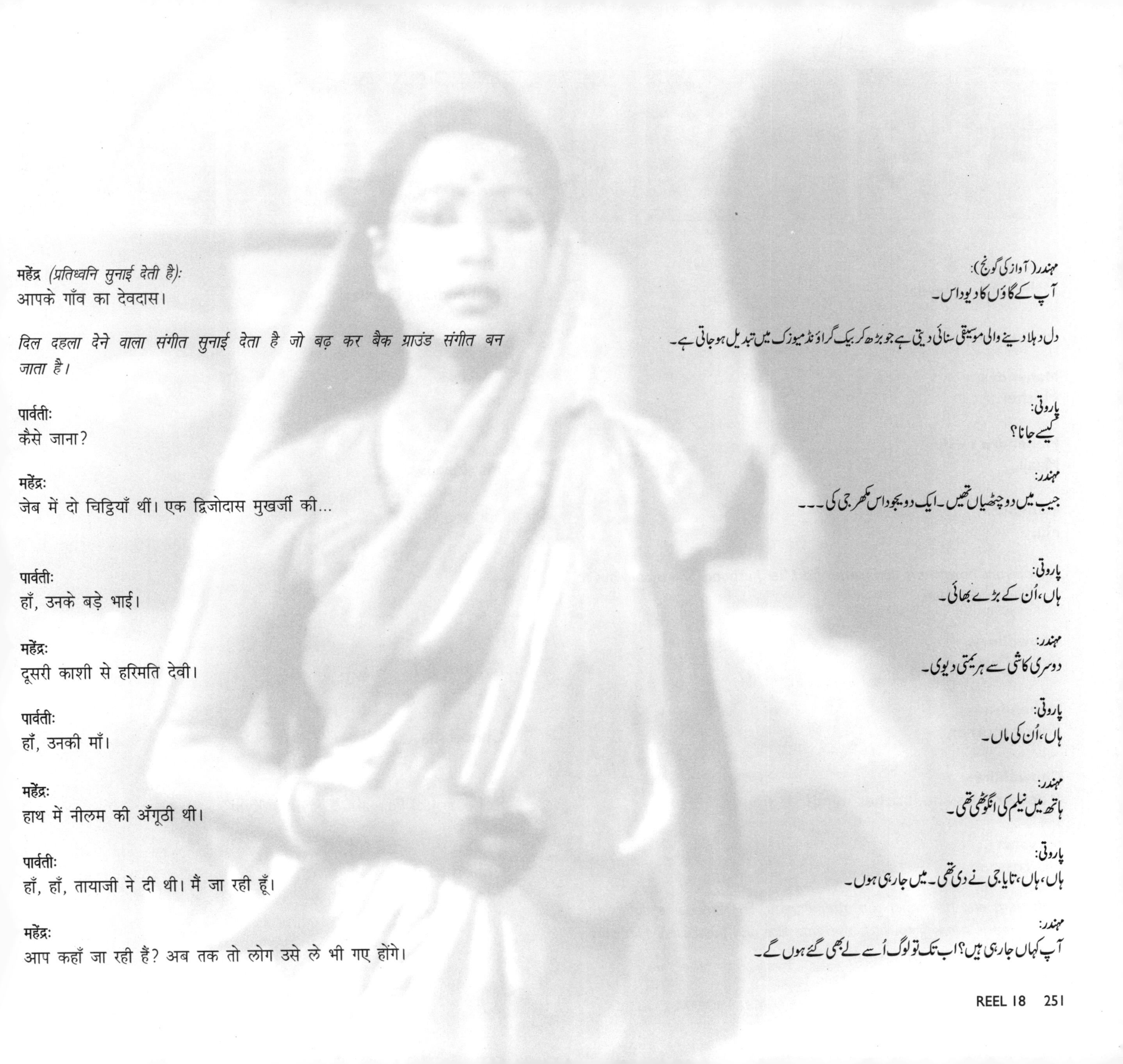

महेंद्र *(प्रतिध्वनि सुनाई देती है):*
आपके गाँव का देवदास।

दिल दहला देने वाला संगीत सुनाई देता है जो बढ़ कर बैक ग्राउंड संगीत बन जाता है।

पार्वतीः
कैसे जाना?

महेंद्रः
जेब में दो चिट्ठियाँ थीं। एक द्विजोदास मुखर्जी की...

पार्वतीः
हाँ, उनके बड़े भाई।

महेंद्रः
दूसरी काशी से हरिमति देवी।

पार्वतीः
हाँ, उनकी माँ।

महेंद्रः
हाथ में नीलम की अँगूठी थी।

पार्वतीः
हाँ, हाँ, तायाजी ने दी थी। मैं जा रही हूँ।

महेंद्रः
आप कहाँ जा रही हैं? अब तक तो लोग उसे ले भी गए होंगे।

مہندر (آواز کی گونج):
آپ کے گاؤں کا دیوداس۔

دل دہلا دینے والی موسیقی سنائی دیتی ہے جو بڑھ کر بیک گراؤنڈ میوزک میں تبدیل ہو جاتی ہے۔

پاروتی:
کیسے جانا؟

مہندر:
جیب میں دو چٹھیاں تھیں۔ ایک دویجوداس مکھرجی کی۔۔۔

پاروتی:
ہاں، اُن کے بڑے بھائی۔

مہندر:
دوسری کاشی سے ہریمتی دیوی۔

پاروتی:
ہاں، اُن کی ماں۔

مہندر:
ہاتھ میں نیلم کی انگوٹھی تھی۔

پاروتی:
ہاں، ہاں، تایا جی نے دی تھی۔ میں جا رہی ہوں۔

مہندر:
آپ کہاں جا رہی ہیں؟ اب تک تو لوگ اُسے لے بھی گئے ہوں گے۔

Parvati:
Mahendra…Devdas!

Mahendra…Devdas!

Parvati runs through the house.

Mahendra:
Mother.

Ma.

Mahendra's wife:
Maaji.

Ma. Maaji.

Mahendra:
Ma.

Ma.

Parvati runs downstairs and rushes past her husband. She is oblivious to everyone around her.

Chowdhury:
What's wrong?

Kya hua re?

Mahendra:
Young mother…

Chhoti ma.

Chowdhury:
Stop her. Has she lost her mind?

Roko, roko! Paagal ho gayi hai kya?

Servant:
Mistress…

Chhoti bahu.

Mahendra and his father run after Parvati. She has come out of the house and is running towards the gate like one possessed. Her saree trails on the ground behind her.

पार्वतीः
महेंद्र...देवदास!

पार्वती घर के गलियारों में भाग रही है।

महेंद्रः
माँ।

महेंद्र की पत्नीः
माँ। माँजी।

महेंद्रः
माँ।

अपने पति के पास से होते हुए पार्वती बाहर की ओर दौड़ती है। उसे अपने आस-पास की कोई सुध-बुध नहीं है।

चौधरीः
क्या हुआ रे?

महेंद्रः
छोटी माँ।

चौधरीः
रोको, रोको। पागल हो गई है क्या?

सेवकः
छोटी बहू।

महेंद्र और उसके पिता पार्वती के पीछे भागते हैं। किसी दीवाने की भाँति वह घर के आँगन से होती हुई बाहर फाटक की ओर भागती है। उसकी साड़ी ज़मीन पर उसके पीछे लहराती हुई चली जा रही है।

پاروتی:
مہندر۔۔۔دیوداس!

پاروتی گھر کی راہداریوں میں دوڑتی چلی جارہی ہے۔

مہندر:
ماں۔

مہندر کی بیوی:
ماں۔ ماجی۔

مہندر:
ماں۔

اپنے شوہر کے پاس سے ہوتی ہوئی پاروتی باہر کی طرف دوڑتی ہے۔ اُسے اپنے آس پاس کی کوئی خبر نہیں رہ گئی ہے۔

چودھری:
کیا ہوا رے؟

مہندر:
چھوٹی ماں۔

چودھری:
روکو، روکو۔ پاگل ہوگئی ہے کیا؟

نوکر:
چھوٹی بہو۔

مہندر اور اُس کا باپ اُس کے پیچھے لپکتے ہیں۔ کسی آسیب زدہ کی مانند وہ گھر سے آنگن میں نکل کر بیرونی دروازے کی طرف دوڑنے لگتی ہے۔ اُس کی ساڑی اُس کے پیچھے زمین پر لہراتی ہوئی چلی جارہی ہے۔

Parvati:
Devdas. — Devdas.

Mahendra:
Mother. — Ma. Ma.

Chowdhury:
Mahendra, stop her! Shut the gate! — Arey Mahendra, rok, rok, usay rok! Darwaaza bandh kar do.
(Parvati is almost at the gate)
Shut the gate! — Bandh kar do phaatak!

Just as Parvati reaches the gate, it closes on her. She tries to open it, but faints and falls to the ground. Cut to a close-up of Devdas. He has passed away.

Dissolve. Devdas's burning funeral pyre. The flames climb high into the sky and slowly fade away.

Background song. Singer: Talat Mahmood

My beloved friend, my friend. — Mitwa, mitwa, mitwa, mitwa.

A cloud gradually obscures the crescent moon. A panning shot over the dark sky. Dissolve.

A shot of the book's last page with the word "Samapt" *(The End).*

Fade out.

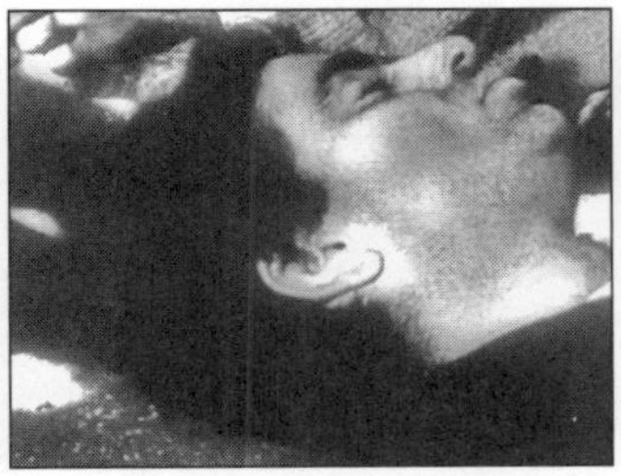
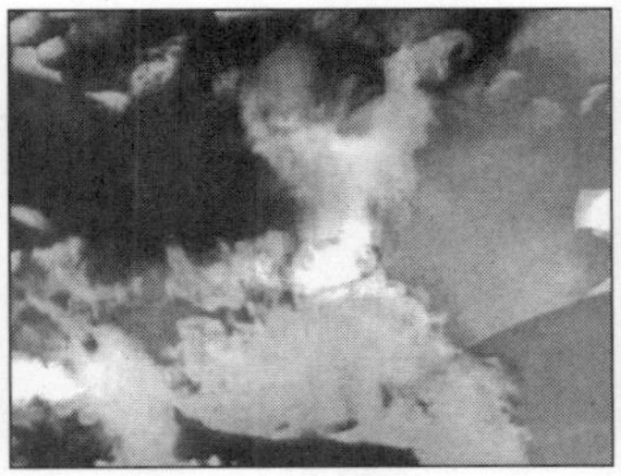

पार्वतीः
देवदास।

پاروتی:
دیوداس۔

महेंद्रः
माँ। माँ।

مہندر:
ماں۔ماں۔

चौधरीः
अरे महेंद्र, रोक, रोक, उसे रोक! दरवाज़ा बंद कर दो!
(पार्वती फाटक के निकट पहुँच चुकी है)
बंद कर दो फाटक!

چودھری:
ارے مہندر، روک، روک، اُسے روک! دروازہ بند کردو!
(پاروتی بیرونی دروازے کے بالکل قریب پہنچ چکی ہے)
بند کردو پھاٹک!

जैसे ही फाटक के निकट पहुँचती है, फाटक बंद हो जाता है। पार्वती फाटक खोलने का प्रयत्न करती है, लेकिन बेहोश होकर गिर पड़ती है। कट। देवदास का क्लोज़-अप। वह बेजान हो चुका है।

دروازے کے پاس پہنچتے پہنچتے دروازے کو بند کردیا جاتا ہے۔دروازہ کھولنے کی کوشش میں پاروتی بیہوش ہوکر زمین پر گرجاتی ہے۔کٹ۔دیوداس کا کلوزاپ۔اُس کی جان نکل چکی ہے۔

अगला दृश्य। देवदास की चिता। आग की लपटें आकाश को छूकर बादलों में गुम हो जाती हैं

اگلا منظر۔دیوداس کی جلتی ہوئی چِتا جس کے شعلے آسمان کو چھوکر مدغم ہوجاتے ہیں۔

बैक ग्राउंड गीत। स्वरः तलत महमूद

بیک گراؤنڈ گیت۔طلعت محمود

मितवा, मितवा, मितवा, मितवा।

متوا،متوا،متوا،متوا

पहली का चाँद बादलों के पीछे छिपता चला जा रहा है। काले पड़ते हुए आकाश का एक शॉट। डिज़ॉल्व।

پہلی کا چاند بادلوں کے پیچھے چھپتا چلا جارہا ہے۔تاریک پڑتے ہوئے آسمان کا شاٹ۔ڈزالو۔

पुस्तक के अंतिम पृष्ठ पर ''समाप्त'' शब्द दिखाई देता है।

کتاب کے آخری ورق پر سماپت لفظ دکھائی دیتا ہے۔

फ़ेड आउट।

فیڈآؤٹ۔

Bimal Roy remembered by his family...

With his eldest daughter, Rinki.

I am pleased to write an epilogue for the dialogue book of Bimal Roy's *Devdas*. This is the fifth title in Nasreen Munni Kabir's dialogue series. The selection of *Devdas* seems particularly challenging. Arguably, the Bimal Roy film version is an iconic, cherished celluloid classic. Sarat Chandra's novel too remains an equally iconic literary work of Indian origin.

Nasreen's inclusion of this work along with four other epics of Indian celluloid, including *Mughal-e-Azam* and *Pyaasa*, confirms the author's serious regard for the B&W period in Hindi cinema. Personally, I am in Nasreen Munni Kabir's debt. Her request to write an epilogue tempted me to read the original Sarat Chandra novel. Something I intended to do, but never got down to.

Reading the slim Bangla novella was an experience — in fact a revelation. It helped me to understand the closeness of the two — the novel and Bimal Roy's 1954/5 Hindi adaptation. It also confirmed my father's total loyalty to the spirit of Sarat Chandra's book. Filming the novel, my father visually transferred the nuanced sentiments of each character with matchless sincerity. There are almost no points of departure. The childhood chapter has been abridged retaining an essential chapter to establish Devdas and Paro's abiding affection. The only poetic license that my father took was to rewrite a scene when the two female protagonists, Paro and Chandramukhi, unknowingly cross paths. The scene is poignantly crafted. Heightened by the soulful background score, the frames radiate a gentle glow as the setting sun adds to the lyricism of this moment.

My father did not have any other passion than creating films and taking care of his family.

His world was film and family...perhaps in that order.

One must recall that my father had shot P.C. Barua's Hindi version with K.L. Saigal as Devdas. He was also engaged in Barua's camera department (1935) for the first Bengali version. This gave him twenty years to ruminate on the Sarat Chandra novel till he decided to shoot his own film. The outcome was a work of luminous, melancholic beauty — considered the most eloquent of all film versions. Rarely does a film match the written word, as does my father Bimal Roy's *Devdas*.

Sarat Chandra's "Devdas" is a death-defying saga of love and betrayal — of lovers who formed their attachment in their childhood. By the time Devdas dies, he is in his early twenties.

What I rediscovered from the original template was Paro's (Parvati) audacious courage to continue loving her childhood sweetheart even as a married woman.

In life, many women may secretly love their childhood sweethearts. But I know few women characters of that period that would openly state their love for a man other than the husband. Throughout the narrative, Parvati defies the social norms set down for her times and gender. Late one night she walks into Devdas's bedroom with the precise intention of proposing matrimony. There are several occasions when her consuming passion for the man is boldly stated. Her love is pure, distilled and unconditional. It is never blatant, nor is it slavish. Recall how fiercely she defends her parents' decision to marry her off when Devdas had already cast the dice of rejection.

In a short scene, Manorama asks the age and description of her groom. Paro obliges with a smile: "He must be 23 or 24" — she hints broadly, meaning Devdas. Manorama chides her, arguing she had heard the man Paro is marrying was elderly. The conversation between the two friends makes no secret of Paro's clarity and vision about man-woman relationship. It is a surprisingly contemporary idea of equality between the two sexes. She is a believer in women's self-assertion. Even as a married wife of a wealthy *zamindar,* Paro throws caution to wind. Unaware of flouting social conventions, or perhaps not caring, Paro seriously intends to bring Devdas to her marital home.

She convinces her stepson that this was both necessary and appropriate. The scene after Paro hears of Devdas's death at her doorstep is magnificently conceived. The slow build up to the tragic finale moves ominously like a Greek tragedy when Paro is startled from sleep, trapped by the billowing mosquito net. She imagines hearing Devdas call her. Crazed by the news of his death the next morning, she rushes to meet him like a torrential river in spate. For that master of understatement, Bimal Roy, to allow this luxurious display of uninhibited emotional outburst is a rare example of when he does *not* restrain. I believe it is inspired by the strength of Paro's character — the power of her love. She compels the director to open the floodgates of her emotion. That moment is a cinematic triumph of dizzy emotional height. It has a chilling impact on viewers, too stunned to react.

In Paro, I have met an extraordinary woman. Her intellectual clarity about love and ideal partnership are argued convincingly. Notwithstanding the fact, she may not have consummated her relationship to Devdas, Paro is well informed, as she is modern.

Chandramukhi's love on the other hand is measured by her worldliness. She too loves Devdas unconditionally. Her search for the ailing Devdas has the sanctity of a pilgrimage. Finding him, she attains nirvana. In their farewell scene, Sarat Chandra makes Devdas address Chandramukhi as *bou* — meaning wife; which is not the case in the film. But for once, Devdas is on the threshhold of commitment. Elevated to wifehood, Chandramukhi's life — unlike Paro's — is fulfilled forever. It is also a closure of sorts for Chandramukhi.

Anurag Kashyap's version, *Dev D*, takes a cue from this. In his film, Dev and Chanda reinvent themselves after a period of utter chaos. You begin to wonder if Devdas and Chandramukhi — not Paro — belonged to one another, as Anurag points out. Was this also Sarat Chandra's intention?

All his life, Devdas had been the callous escapist, contemptuous of his social obligations. Many consider him a cowardly man — he treats his beloved in a heartless fashion. His attempts to run away from himself mark him as a loner, a vagabond. If one is kind, we could see Devdas as a free spirit, unchained by domesticity or family ties — very much like a bird taking an aerial view of existence.

In conclusion, I congratulate the author's dedication. She brings time-honoured classics of Indian cinema onto the global stage. Deservedly. Her tireless work has created a small library of films we have loved and cherished. They are now accessible on paper. This is a privilege for us all, not just the Bimal Roy family — but also a privilege for lovers of cinema, students and scholars alike. Thank you, Nasreen.

Rinki Roy Bhattacharya
Mumbai, February 2012

Wearing her father's sunglasses, Yashodhara. Photograph by Bimal Roy.

Baba was an early riser. He was very fond of gardening so he spent the early hours of the morning supervising the gardener's work. His first cup of tea was with a slice of lemon, no milk or sugar. Sitting in the garden, or on our large front verandah, he would read a book or the newspaper. Ma would wake a little later and start her morning activities getting us ready for school. Baba left the house after a traditional English breakfast and was usually the first person to arrive at his Mohan Studios office. He carried a book with him when travelling to work. He was always on the lookout for a good story for his next project.

He was a quiet man and also very disciplined, both at work and in his personal life. We never knew when Baba was at home. He loved music, but when he listened to music the volume was never loud. He had some great favourites: classical music, the Lebanese singer Fairuz, and a recording of Shakespeare's *Hamlet*. Baba organised concerts at home, and singers and musicians from all over India would perform for our family and friends. I don't remember Baba ever getting angry or raising his voice. He did not approve of people raising their voices either or being disrespectful.

Ma loved people and welcomed relations and friends. Our home was full of warmth and laughter. Baba was not anti-social and yet did not like guests being around when he came back tired from work. He preferred his home to himself and his family.

One of Baba's idols was Alfred Hitchcock. He would say: "Hitchcock is a fantastic storyteller. The moment his film begins, you're right there with him." His other idol was Charlie Chaplin because Baba believed that silent films say so much, why always the need for dialogue? And so in *Devdas,* you will see many scenes that have no dialogue. For example, when we see Devdas travelling by train from city to city, and finally embarking on his last journey to see Parvati, nothing is spoken — but his whole life unfolds, the tragedy of Devdas unfolds.

Baba did not own a studio. When he made his first film in Bombay, *Do Bigha Zameen,* it was with the help of Ramnik Bhai, who was the owner of Mohan Studios and that is where he decided to have his offices and editing room. He shot most of his films at Mohan Studios, including *Devdas*. It was filmed on the studio floors. And along with Baba's art director, Sudhendhu Roy, they created rural Bengal within the studio compound and on the surrounding land.

One day my father noticed a *champa* tree in full bloom within the studio compound. He suddenly turned round to the people who were with him and said: "I have found the place for Parvati's house." So that *champa* tree became an important meeting place for Devdas and Parvati. The natural lake that Baba used in *Devdas* was near Aarey Milk Colony in Goregaon. He built the steps leading to the lake, and key moments in the film have been filmed there. Few have realised *Devdas* was not filmed in Bengal. The most important thing is that he had the eye of a cinematographer. He would find a location and create the right atmosphere there, while others might have just walked past.

I remember going to the premiere of *Devdas* at Roxy cinema in Bombay. After the film was over, people streamed out of the cinema hall. There was complete silence, and I don't think a single woman was dry eyed. The last scene of the film is so heart wrenching. I think it is very difficult to hold back your emotions when you see a film like *Devdas* — it is so well portrayed and executed.

In December 1964, he had returned home from a four-day shoot of his last film, which was going to be titled "Sahaara." This was to star Dharmendra and Sharmila Tagore. Ma was sitting next to Baba and when she touched his hand, she realised he was burning with a fever. She asked him to rest but he said: "I have a shoot tomorrow." Ma insisted that he cancel the shoot and see a doctor the next day. That was the beginning of the end. He was admitted to Breach Candy Hospital. At first the doctors thought he had double pneumonia. In January 1965, Dr. Borges, the world-famous cancer specialist, saw Baba and did a series of tests. By early March, it was confirmed that he had lung cancer. He was very weak and suffered for many months. Ma was the only person he spoke to. He just withdrew into himself.

Ma took him to London for a month's treatment. In early October 1965, a German doctor also saw Baba and said he had little chances of survival. My granduncle, uncle, and my father's brother-in-law came from Calcutta to be with us in our Bombay home. On 7 January 1966, our doctor told Ma: "Mr. Roy's condition is very critical, he should not be home. The next two or three weeks will be traumatic for you and your family." Baba passed away peacefully that same night.

I will always remember how connected Baba was to nature. He used to say that we should never go away from the purity and beauty of nature because life had a dark side, and if we stayed close to nature, it would soften the darkness of life.

There are also many silent moments in my father's films. That stillness and quietness came from his dignified presence. He was an introvert and what still strikes me when I see his films is how underplayed they are. There is a quietness and subtlety in his work. That was his character and nature.

Yashodhara Roy
Mumbai, February 2012

With daughter Aparajita. Photograph by Manobina Roy.

My father died when I was fifteen. I remember the gentle shake, the stumbling out of bed, the hour — four in the morning — the hushed whispers, the journey to his bedside to see the inert figure lying surrounded by weeping relatives, and my total bewilderment. I felt nothing. My uncle, who had roused me, said gently: "Pronam koro" (Pay your respects to your father).

As dawn broke everything changed. He had been placed in the centre of our large, nobly proportioned drawing room, whose beautiful sofas he had chosen from antique shops, and upholstered in rich Jacobean-patterned silks. The furniture had been moved to accommodate his body, lying so peacefully now, the two years of wracking cough and unbearable pain over, in one longed-for but dreaded moment. The line of people paying their respects grew steadily. I knew very few of the faces that came. I sat clutching my father's hand as I'd been instructed to, the body still warm to the touch, the troubled soul (I was given to understand) hovering overhead, unable to break free. Francis, my father's driver, arrived and stood sobbing like a child. The polite hush was suddenly broken, and the people present realised the enormity of what had happened. My sister Yashodhara, and two cousins took command, directed visitors, put out water, made tea. My brother, Joy, just 11, wandered disconsolate, confused. The house was full of relatives. In those last months we always had people staying with us. My mother looked after my father and the visitors. My sister Yashodhara spent all her time in the kitchen, producing meals for up to twenty at a time.

Many who came that day must have been important personages, but the faces were a blur for me. I guess Dilip Kumar, whom my father called Yusuf, came. He was the closest to my father in an industry where my father was always a misfit. The cancer was only the outer manifestation, I now believe, of disillusionment with an increasingly star and money driven industry in which an idealist like my father may have felt alienated.

I remember that I sat through it all. As the hands grew cold. And they came to carry him off.

When my father died someone told my mother that it was as though a banyan tree had fallen. It was no wonder that a thousand people gathered within moments, and walked in solemn silence behind the open truck that finally took my father away.

Some images never fade. As the mourners left and the house was pervaded by a deathly silence, my mother lay on her bed. In those days women did not accompany a bier. But my married sister Rinki and Yashodhara protested, wanting to go. They left, taking Joy with them, for he would do the *mukhagni* (the lighting of the pyre). Again, it was I who sat by my mother, dazed and filled with a terrible sense of dread. My mother lay, only half-conscious, murmuring incoherently.

After my father died, my mother had to struggle very hard. One day she announced that we were going on a family holiday. She needed it badly, I think. So we embarked on a journey through North Bengal and Assam — one of the happiest memories of my youth. My father never took holidays; he never had the time. Perhaps he knew that he had only ten years in Bombay to make twelve films — each one a sustained, quiet masterpiece, and now a national heritage. If he lived he would have been as bemused as we were to know that even people in remote towns knew of him — in those days before television, before film personalities became household names. It was a curiously humbling and inspiring experience.

When I was young, I found *Devdas* too sombre for my taste. I now realise that one requires a certain maturity to appreciate Devdas: to understand the protagonist's complex character one needs compassion, which youth rarely possesses. The story of Devdas has achieved an almost mythic status amongst the educated elite in India, both Bengali and non-Bengali. Myths are black and white, incapable of metamorphosis, but Dilip Kumar's Devdas has a potential to surprise. Each time I see the film I think Paro will forgive him and say: "I will." Or Devdas will say to his friend Chunni Babu: "I won't." Or he will find the courage to face his ill-tempered father and say: "I will marry Paro and no one else," thus changing the course of (Indian) film history. In my father's *Devdas*, Dilip Kumar brings out Devdas's unfailing kindness, which is so evident in his relationships with his mother and the "fallen" woman Chandramukhi.

Why did my father remake *Devdas* when he had already worked on it as a cameraman twice over at New Theatres? Devdas's story has the added dimension of the inevitability of tragedy. I think he was fascinated by the legend, and he chose Dilip Kumar, Suchitra Sen and Vyjayanthimala to embody it, for being a filmmaker of exceptional insight, he foresaw the result of this remarkable synthesis. The moment, when the radiantly beautiful now grown up Paro sees her childhood playmate by the light of the evening lamp to the sound of a conch-shell's echoing cry — first his feet, then the edge of his impeccably pleated *dhoti* and silk *kurta*, then his lovestruck face — is etched in the Indian filmgoer's collective consciousness. It is an image that is larger than life, as the archetype of Devdas is larger than life.

My father died when he was 55. Like Devdas, he died before his life was lived to fruition. His last film "Amrit ki khoj," which he could not complete, was an epic story set against the backdrop of the Kumbh mela about a man's search for meaning and spiritual fulfillment. Gulzar, who wrote the screenplay, then went on to write an apocryphal short story called *Bimalda,* it traces the terrible agony of an artist and filmmaker on a fictional train journey just like Devdas, knowing he will not be able to complete what he had begun...

Aparajita Roy Sinha
Hyderabad, February 2012

When Baba passed away, I was eleven. I remember him very clearly, but perhaps my memories would have been much more vivid were he not such an obsessed filmmaker. Baba had so little time to spend with the family. He would leave home early in the morning and return late at night. I don't remember him talking to me very much — in any case he was a man of a very few words. He left the care of the family to my mother. I don't think he was even aware which class we were in or which school we attended. He was always preoccupied by work.

I was too young to understand his films in those days and got to know his work much better when I made a documentary on him in 2007. It was through the interviews of many colleagues and actors that I learned about his extreme dedication and craftsmanship and understood better the way he conceived his films.

Among the people I interviewed was the widely respected Bengali filmmaker, Tapan Sinha, who recently passed away. He described my father as a silent and relentless worker. He told me that he could work the whole day without stopping, even under a 40° Bihar sun. Tapan Sinha also pointed out that Baba was a pioneer and was the first person to create a fog effect by mixing water with light paraffin oil.

I also learned from others about his great attention to detail. He had wanted a *leitmotif* — a sound symbol — for Sujata, who was lower-caste, and chose the call of the cuckoo to represent her — while a cawing crow was used for the orthodox Brahmin character played by Lalitha Pawar. The sound recordist had to sleep outdoors for four nights until he got the sound of a single crow. For another scene in *Sujata*, Baba had wanted a shot of a falling leaf, twirling in the air before landing on the ground. He waited for hours for a leaf to fall. The cameraman Kamal Bose got most irritated and

With son Joy. Photograph by Manobina Roy.

asked why they could not use a fan to achieve the same effect? Baba told him: "You have learned nothing as yet."

I must admit that *Devdas* is not one of my favourite films. I prefer *Madhumati* and *Sujata*. I find it deeply troubling to watch *Devdas* — it is so sad. I had a kind of mental block against it because of the subject. I kept thinking how could a man waste his entire life in pursuit of something he never attains and in the process become an alcoholic. It seemed pointless to me and I wondered why everyone made such a huge fuss about the story. But as I grew older, I began to realise that everyone has an inner Devdas. It is a story of unrequited love and we all have at least one secret and unfulfilled love. Possibly this is why people identify with the character and why there have been so many remakes because it is a story that appeals to the romantic self. Even today I get gooseflesh when I hear the *Devdas* song "Mitwa."

Devdas rises above love as we know it, and love in many forms is shown. Paro is willing to do anything for Devdas and though she marries in order to please her family, she never forgets him. When Chandramukhi first sees Devdas, she instantly falls in love with him. She gives up her livelihood and waits for him. Paro, Devdas and Chandramukhi are consumed by obsessive love and yet Baba retains such chasteness and purity in his depiction. There is also the example of love and loyalty shown by Dharamdas, Devdas's servant. His feelings too are an embodiment of love.

I think the last scene of the film is really magical and has made a deep impact on me. It is an almost mystical scene. Devdas lies dying outside the gates of Paro's house. She is in her prayer room and hears a whisper and somehow knows that Devdas is calling her. She runs to the gate in a state of abandon, her saree trailing behind her. Just as she reaches the gate, it closes on her as Devdas's body is being carried away. My father has captured this tragic moment perfectly. It has a Sufi-like mood, recreating the moment of union between the lover and the beloved — a time when all else is forgotten.

I saw other versions of *Devdas* films at the International Film Festival in Delhi. I haven't read the novel, but have been told that Baba has been extremely faithful to it; there is essentially only one place where he has strayed from the book's narrative — again for a kind of mystical meeting between Paro and Chandramukhi. Baba's version is restrained and so subdued in tone and this is its great strength. Nabendu Ghosh's adaptation of the novel to the screenplay is in resonance with Baba's lyrical touch. The dialogue by Rajinder Singh Bedi is low key and yet so effective that people still quote lines from the film.

On a technical level, I find the soundtrack of *Devdas* amazing. There is so much detailing in it. In the scenes in which Devdas travels by train aimlessly from town to town, you hear various sounds of the train, sometimes at top speed, or as it slows down to pull into a station, or when it leaves a platform. Baba was a complete perfectionist.

Despite all the global influences, Indians remain Indians and so his films will always strike a chord. I recently attended a Bimal Roy retrospective in Calcutta and many young people attended. They liked Baba's films very much because they are still relevant. Take *Do Bigha Zameen* — in the original story, the main character is driven to suicide, and even today, sadly there are farmers who still commit suicide, unable to repay loans.

My father's films always had evocative music, they were unfussy and subdued, lyrical and intensely human, emotional without ever becoming melodramatic — it is these qualities that have allowed the films to transcend time and continue to appeal to audiences of diverse cultures and nations. At least I would like to believe so.

I have known Nasreen Munni Kabir for thirty years and have always marvelled at her hard work and her zeal for the preservation of Indian film history. I thank her and Om Books International for preserving my father's heritage by the publication of this book.

Joy Bimal Roy
Mumbai, February 2012

Film Credits, as printed in the film's booklet. Year of release: 1955.

BIMAL ROY PRODUCTIONS

present

DEVDAS

Based on SARAT CHANDRA CHATTERJEE'S Immortal Classic

Dedicated to the honoured memory of

Late Shri P.C. BARUA and Late Shri K.L. SAIGAL

STARRING

DILIP KUMAR, VYJAYANTIMALA, MOTILAL & SUCHITRA SEN

with

BABY NAAZ, NAZIR HUSSAIN, KAMMO, KAMALA MUKHERJI, KAMAL, PRATIMA DEVI, ASHIM KUMAR, RAM KUMAR, BABY CHAND, KANHAIYA LAL, MURAD, IFTEKAR, MONI CHATTERJI, DULARI, NANA PALSEKAR, SHIVRAJ, SARITA DEVI, SHAKUNTALA, RUBY PAUL, BIKRAM KAPOOR, SHEOJI BHAI, JANI BHAI, GIRDHARI LAL VAID, MOHAN CHOTI, GHANSHYAM, JAGDISH RAJ, MAYA DAS

Guest Artists: PRAN & JOHNY WALKER

Produced & Directed by

BIMAL ROY

Our grateful acknowledgements are due to:

CENTRAL RAILWAYS, WESTERN RAILWAYS, AIR INDIA INTERNATIONAL & DIRECTOR CIVIL AVIATION

Credits

Screenplay	Nabendu Ghosh	Dance Direction	Hira Lal
Hindi Dialogues	Rajinder Singh Bedi	Settings	Manilal Somabhai
Music Direction	S.D. Burman	Background Sketches	Santi Das
Lyrics	Sahir Ludhianvi	Make-up	Jagat Kumar
Cinematography	Kamal Bose	Unit Managers	Chandra, Sanjiva
Associate	Montu Bose		& Peerachand
Art Direction	Sudhendu Roy	Production Secretary	Madan Bakaya
Audiography	E.M. Suratwala	Costumes	Kishen & Lakshmidas
Songs Recorded by	B.N. Sharma,	Stills	Kamat (Foto) Flash
	Mukul Bose	Extra Supplier	Dev Kumar
Editing	Hrishikesh Mukherji	Processing	Shamrao, M. Dhurendhar
Associate	Das Dhaimade		& Govindrao G. Raut

Assistants

Direction	Asit Sen, Paul Mahendra,	Music	Jaidev & Surhid Kar
	Moni Bhattacharjee,	Editing	Shridhar Misra
	Madan Gopal & Ashim Kumar		& Shankar Pradhan
Camera	Chandrakant & Chinu Shah	Make-up	Babu
Sound	B.Y. Gophan & Digamber	Production	Basant & Amrit

Produced & Processed at: Mohan Studios, Andheri

Recorded on: R.C.A. Sound System

Gramophone records are available on H.M.V.

Further Reading

Arora, Poonam, "Devdas: Indian Cinema's Emasculated Hero, Sado-Masochism and Colonialism," *Journal of South Asian Literature*, Vol. 30, nos. 1-2 (1995).

Bhattacharya, Rinki Roy, *A Man of Silence: Bimal Roy,* Indus/HarperCollins, New Delhi, 1994.

———, *The Man Who Spoke in Pictures: Bimal Roy,* Penguin Books India, New Delhi, 2009.

Chopra, Satish, "The three versions of the film Devdas," essay in the Golden Jubilee issue of the quarterly journal of Film & TV Institute of India, *Lensight,* April-June 2010.

Creekmur, Corey K., "Remembering, repeating and working through Devdas," *Indian Literature and Popular Cinema: Recasting Classics*, ed. Heidi Pauwels, Routledge, New York, 2007.

Flemming, Leslie, A., "Progressive Writer, Progressive Filmmaker: The Films of R.S. Bedi, Annual of Urdu Studies, Vol. 5, p. 8, University of Chicago, 1985.
Weblink: http:/dsal.uchicago.edu/books/annualofurdustudies

Guha, Sreejata, "Introduction" in the English translation of *Devdas* by Saratchandra Chattopadhyay, Penguin Books India, New Delhi, 2002.

Nair, P.K., "The Devdas Syndrome in Indian Cinema," *Cinemaya* 56/57, Autumn-Winter, 2002.

Nandy, Ashis, "Invitation to an Antique Death: The Journey of Pramathesh Barua as the Origin of the Terribly Effeminate, Maudlin, Self-Destructive Heroes of Indian Cinema," in *Pleasure and the Nation: The History, Politics, and Consumption of Public Culture in India*, eds. Rachel Dwyer and Christopher Pinney, Oxford University Press, New Delhi, 2001.

Naravane, V.S., translator, abridged version, included in Sarat Chandra Chatterji, *Devdas and Other Stories*, New Delhi, Roli Books, 1996.

Singhal, Rahul, edited and compiled, *Devdas: The Eternal Saga of Love,* Pentagon Paperbacks, New Delhi, 2002.